T0314177

Artificial Intelligence in Finance
A Python-Based Guide

Yves Hilpisch

Beijing · Boston · Farnham · Sebastopol · Tokyo

Artificial Intelligence in Finance

by Yves Hilpisch

Published by O'Reilly Media, Inc., 1005 Gravenstein Highway North, Sebastopol, CA 95472.

O'Reilly books may be purchased for educational, business, or sales promotional use. Online editions are also available for most titles (*http://oreilly.com*). For more information, contact our corporate/institutional sales department: 800-998-9938 or *corporate@oreilly.com*.

Acquisitions Editor: Michelle Smith
Development Editor: Corbin Collins
Production Editor: Daniel Elfanbaum
Copyeditor: Piper Editorial, LLC
Proofreader: JM Olejarz

Indexer: Potomac Indexing, LLC
Interior Designer: David Futato
Cover Designer: Karen Montgomery
Illustrator: O'Reilly Media, Inc.

October 2020:   First Edition

Revision History for the First Edition
2020-10-14:   First Release
2020-12-16:   Second Release

See *http://oreilly.com/catalog/errata.csp?isbn=9781492055433* for release details.

978-1-492-05543-3

[LSI]

Table of Contents

Part II.   Finance and Machine Learning

Part IV.   Algorithmic Trading

Part V. Outlook

Part VI.   Appendixes

Preface

Will alpha eventually go to zero for every imaginable investment strategy? More fundamentally, is the day approaching when, thanks to so many smart people and smarter computers, financial markets really do become perfect, and we can just sit back, relax, and assume that all assets are priced correctly?

—Robert Shiller (2015)

Artificial intelligence (AI) rose to become a key technology in the 2010s and is assumed to be the dominating technology in the 2020s. Spurred by technological innovations, algorithmic breakthroughs, availability of big data, and ever-increasing compute power, many industries are undergoing fundamental changes driven by AI.

While media and public attention mostly focus on breakthroughs in areas such as gaming and self-driving cars, AI has also become a major technological force in the financial industry. However, it is safe to say that AI in finance is still at a nascent stage —as compared, for example, to industries such as web search or social media.

This book sets out to cover a number of important aspects related to AI in finance. AI in finance is already a vast topic, and a single book needs to focus on selected aspects. Therefore, this book covers the basics first (see Part I and Part II). It then zooms in on discovering *statistical inefficiencies* in financial markets by the use of AI and, more specifically, neural networks (see Part III). Such inefficiencies—embodied by AI algorithms that successfully predict future market movements—are a prerequisite for the exploitation of *economic inefficiencies* through algorithmic trading (see Part IV). Being able to systematically exploit statistical and economic inefficiencies would prove contradictory to one of the established theories and cornerstones in finance: the *efficient market hypothesis* (EMH). The design of a successful *trading bot* can be considered the holy grail in finance to which AI might lead the way. This book concludes by discussing consequences of AI for the financial industry and the possibility of a financial singularity (see Part V). There is also a technical appendix that shows how to build neural networks from scratch based on plain Python code and provides additional examples for their application (see Part VI).

The problem of applying AI to finance is not too dissimilar to the problem of applying AI to other fields. Some major breakthroughs in AI in the 2010s were made possible by the application of reinforcement learning (RL) to playing arcade games, such as those from Atari published in the 1980s (see Mnih et al. 2013), and to board games, such as chess or Go (see Silver et al. 2016). Lessons learned from applying RL in gaming contexts, among other areas, are today applied to such challenging problems as designing and building autonomous vehicles or improving medical diagnostics. Table P-1 compares the application of AI and RL in different domains.

Table P-1. Comparison of AI in different domains

Domain	Agent	Goal	Approach	Reward	Obstacle	Risks
Arcade games	AI agent (software)	Maximizing game score	RL in virtual gaming environment	Points and scores	Planning and delayed rewards	None
Autonomous driving	Self-driving car (software + car)	Safely driving from location A to B	RL in virtual (gaming) environment, real-world test drives	Punishment for mistakes	Transition from virtual to physical world	Damaging property, harming people
Financial trading	Trading bot (software)	Maximizing long-term performance	RL in virtual trading environment	Financial returns	Efficient markets and competition	Financial losses

The beauty of training AI agents to play arcade games lies in the availability of a perfect virtual learning environment[1] and the absence of any kind of risk. With autonomous vehicles, the major problem arises when transitioning from virtual learning environments—for example, a computer game such as *Grand Theft Auto*—to the physical world with a self-driving car navigating real streets populated by other cars and people. This leads to serious risks such as a car causing accidents or harming people.

For a trading bot, RL can also be completely virtual, that is, in a simulated financial market environment. The major risks that arise from malfunctioning trading bots are financial losses and, on an aggregated level, potential systematic risks due to herding by trading bots. Overall, however, the financial domain seems like an ideal place to train, test, and deploy AI algorithms.

Given the rapid developments in the field, it should even be possible for an interested and ambitious student, equipped with a notebook and internet access, to successfully apply AI in a financial trading context. Beyond the hardware and software improvements over recent years, this is due primarily to the rise of online brokers that supply

---

1 See the Arcade Learning Environment (*https://oreil.ly/bGgZs*).

historical and real-time financial data and that allow the execution of financial trades via programmatic APIs.

The book is structured in the following six parts.

Part I

The first part discusses central notions and algorithms of AI in general, such as supervised learning and neural networks (see Chapter 1). It also discusses the concept of superintelligence, which relates to an AI agent that possesses human-level intelligence and, in some domains, superhuman-level intelligence (see Chapter 2). Not every researcher in AI believes that superintelligence is possible in the foreseeable future. However, the discussion of this idea provides a valuable framework for discussing AI in general and AI for finance in particular.

Part II

The second part consists of four chapters and is about traditional, normative finance theory (see Chapter 3) and how the field is transformed by data-driven finance (see Chapter 4) and machine learning (ML) (see Chapter 5). Taken together, data-driven finance and ML give rise to a model-free, AI-first approach to finance, as discussed in Chapter 6.

Part III

The third part is about discovering statistical inefficiencies in financial markets by applying deep learning, neural networks, and reinforcement learning. The part covers dense neural networks (DNNs, see Chapter 7), recurrent neural networks (RNNs, see Chapter 8), and algorithms from reinforcement learning (RL, see Chapter 9) that in turn often rely on DNNs to represent and approximate the optimal policy of the AI agent.

Part IV

The fourth part discusses how to exploit statistical inefficiencies through algorithmic trading. Topics are vectorized backtesting (see Chapter 10), event-based backtesting and risk management (see Chapter 11), and execution and deployment of AI-powered algorithmic trading strategies (see Chapter 12).

Part V

The fifth part is about the consequences that arise from AI-based competition in the financial industry (see Chapter 13). It also discusses the possibility of a financial singularity, a point in time at which AI agents would dominate all aspects of finance as we know it. The discussion in this context focuses on artificial financial intelligences as trading bots that consistently generate trading profits above any human or institutional benchmark (see Chapter 14).

Part VI

The Appendix contains Python code for interactive neural network training (see Appendix A), classes for simple and shallow neural networks that are implemented from scratch based on plain Python code (see Appendix B), and an example of how to use convolutional neural networks (CNNs) for financial time series prediction (see Appendix C).

Author's Note

The application of AI to financial trading is still a nascent field, although at the time of writing there are a number of other books available that cover this topic to some extent. Many of these publications, however, fail to show what it means to *economically* exploit statistical inefficiencies.

Some hedge funds already claim to exclusively rely on machine learning to manage their investors' capital. A prominent example is The Voleon Group, a hedge fund that reported more than $6 billion in assets under management at the end of 2019 (see Lee and Karsh 2020). The difficulty of relying on machine learning to outsmart the financial markets is reflected in the fund's performance of 7% for 2019, a year during which the S&P 500 stock index rose by almost 30%.

This book is based on years of practical experience in developing, backtesting, and deploying AI-powered algorithmic trading strategies. The approaches and examples presented are mostly based on my own research since the field is, by nature, not only nascent, but also rather secretive. The exposition and the style throughout this book are relentlessly practical, and in many instances the concrete examples are lacking proper theoretical support and/or comprehensive empirical evidence. This book even presents some applications and examples that might be vehemently criticized by experts in finance and/or machine learning.

For example, some experts in machine and deep learning, such as François Chollet (2017), outright doubt that prediction in financial markets is possible. Certain experts in finance, such as Robert Shiller (2015), doubt that there will ever be something like a financial singularity. Others active at the intersection of the two domains, such as Marcos López de Prado (2018), argue that the use of machine learning for financial trading and investing requires an industrial-scale effort with large teams and huge budgets.

This book does not try to provide a balanced view of or a comprehensive set of references for all the topics covered. The presentation is driven by the personal opinions and experiences of the author, as well as by practical considerations when providing concrete examples and Python code. Many of the examples are also chosen and tweaked to drive home certain points or to show encouraging results. Therefore, it can certainly be argued that results from many examples presented in the book suffer from data snooping and overfitting (for a discussion of these topics, see Hilpisch 2020, ch. 4).

The major goal of this book is to empower the reader to use the code examples in the book as a framework to explore the exciting space of AI applied to financial trading. To achieve this goal, the book relies throughout on a number of simplifying assumptions and primarily on *financial time series data and features derived directly from such data*. In practical applications, a restriction to financial time series data is of course not necessary—a great variety of other types of data and data sources could be used as well. This book's approach to deriving features implicitly assumes that financial time series and features derived from them show *patterns* that, at least to some extent, persist over time and that can be used to predict the direction of future price movements.

Against this background, all examples and code presented in this book are technical and illustrative in nature and do not represent any recommendation or investment advice.

For those who want to deploy approaches and algorithmic trading strategies presented in this book, my book *Python for Algorithmic Trading: From Idea to Cloud Deployment* (O'Reilly) provides more process-oriented and technical details. The two books complement each other in many respects. For readers who are just getting started with Python for finance or who are seeking a refresher and reference manual, my book *Python for Finance: Mastering Data-Driven Finance* (O'Reilly) covers a comprehensive set of important topics and fundamental skills in Python as applied to the financial domain.

References

Papers and books cited in the preface:

Chollet, François. 2017. *Deep Learning with Python*. Shelter Island: Manning.

Hilpisch, Yves. 2018. *Python for Finance: Mastering Data-Driven Finance*. 2nd ed. Sebastopol: O'Reilly.

————. 2020. *Python for Algorithmic Trading: From Idea to Cloud Deployment*. Sebastopol: O'Reilly.

Lee, Justina and Melissa Karsh. 2020. "Machine-Learning Hedge Fund Voleon Group Returns 7% in 2019." *Bloomberg*, January 21, 2020. *https://oreil.ly/TOQiv*.

López de Prado, Marcos. 2018. *Advances in Financial Machine Learning*. Hoboken, NJ: John Wiley & Sons.

Mnih, Volodymyr et al. 2013. "Playing Atari with Deep Reinforcement Learning." arXiv. December 19. *https://oreil.ly/-pW-1*.

Shiller, Robert. 2015. "The Mirage of the Financial Singularity." Yale Insights. July 16. *https://oreil.ly/VRkP3*.

Silver, David et al. 2016. "Mastering the Game of Go with Deep Neural Networks and Tree Search." *Nature* 529 (January): 484-489.

Conventions Used in This Book

The following typographical conventions are used in this book:

Italic

Indicates new terms, URLs, email addresses, filenames, and file extensions.

`Constant width`

Used for program listings, as well as within paragraphs to refer to program elements such as variable or function names, databases, data types, environment variables, statements, and keywords.

`Constant width bold`

Shows commands or other text that should be typed literally by the user.

`Constant width italic`

Shows text that should be replaced with user-supplied values or by values determined by context.

 This element signifies a tip or suggestion.

 This element signifies a general note.

 This element indicates important information.

 This element indicates a warning or caution.

Using Code Examples

You can access and execute the code that accompanies the book on the Quant Platform at *https://aiif.pqp.io*, for which only a free registration is required.

If you have a technical question or a problem using the code examples, please send an email to *bookquestions@oreilly.com*.

This book is here to help you get your job done. In general, if example code is offered with this book, you may use it in your programs and documentation. You do not need to contact us for permission unless you're reproducing a significant portion of the code. For example, writing a program that uses several chunks of code from this book does not require permission. Selling or distributing examples from O'Reilly books does require permission. Answering a question by citing this book and quoting example code does not require permission. Incorporating a significant amount of example code from this book into your product's documentation does require permission.

We appreciate, but generally do not require, attribution. An attribution usually includes the title, author, publisher, and ISBN. For example, this book may be attributed as: "*Artificial Intelligence in Finance* by Yves Hilpisch (O'Reilly). Copyright 2021 Yves Hilpisch, 978-1-492-05543-3."

If you feel your use of code examples falls outside fair use or the permission given above, feel free to contact us at *permissions@oreilly.com*.

O'Reilly Online Learning

For more than 40 years, *O'Reilly Media* has provided technology and business training, knowledge, and insight to help companies succeed.

Our unique network of experts and innovators share their knowledge and expertise through books, articles, and our online learning platform. O'Reilly's online learning platform gives you on-demand access to live training courses, in-depth learning paths, interactive coding environments, and a vast collection of text and video from O'Reilly and 200+ other publishers. For more information, visit *http://oreilly.com*.

How to Contact Us

Please address comments and questions concerning this book to the publisher:

O'Reilly Media, Inc.
1005 Gravenstein Highway North
Sebastopol, CA 95472
800-998-9938 (in the United States or Canada)
707-829-0515 (international or local)
707-829-0104 (fax)

We have a web page for this book, where we list errata, examples, and any additional information. You can access this page at *https://oreil.ly/ai-in-finance*.

Email *bookquestions@oreilly.com* to comment or ask technical questions about this book.

For news and information about our books and courses, visit *http://oreilly.com*.

Find us on Facebook: *http://facebook.com/oreilly*

Follow us on Twitter: *http://twitter.com/oreillymedia*

Watch us on YouTube: *http://www.youtube.com/oreillymedia*

Acknowledgments

I want to thank the technical reviewers—Margaret Maynard-Reid, Dr. Tim Nugent, and Dr. Abdullah Karasan—who did a great job in helping me improve the contents of the book.

Delegates of the Certificate Programs in Python for Computational Finance and Algorithmic Trading also helped improve this book. Their ongoing feedback has enabled me to weed out errors and mistakes and refine the code and notebooks used in our online training classes and now, finally, in this book.

The same holds true for the team members of The Python Quants and The AI Machine. In particular, Michael Schwed, Ramanathan Ramakrishnamoorthy, and Prem Jebaseelan support me in numerous ways. They are the ones who assist me with the difficult technical problems that arise during the writing of a book like this one.

I would also like to thank the whole team at O'Reilly Media—especially Michelle Smith, Corbin Collins, Victoria DeRose, and Danny Elfanbaum—for making it all happen and helping me refine the book in so many ways.

Of course, all remaining errors are mine alone.

Furthermore, I would also like to thank the team at Refinitiv—in particular, Jason Ramchandani—for providing ongoing support and access to financial data. The major data files used throughout the book and made available to the readers were received in one way or another from Refinitiv's data APIs.

Of course, everybody making use of artificial intelligence and machine learning today benefits from the achievements and contributions of so many others. Therefore, we should always recall what Sir Isaac Newton wrote in 1675: "If I have seen further it is by standing on the shoulders of Giants." In that sense, a big thank you to all the researchers and open source maintainers contributing to the field.

Finally, special thanks go to my family, who support me all year round in my business and book-writing activities. In particular, I thank my wife Sandra for relentlessly taking care of us all and for providing us with a home and environment that we all love so much. I dedicate this book to my lovely wife Sandra and my wonderful son Henry.

## PART I

Machine Intelligence

Today's algorithmic trading programs are relatively simple and make only limited use of AI. This is sure to change.

—Murray Shanahan (2015)

This part is about artificial intelligence (AI) in general: *artificial* in the sense that the intelligence is not displayed by a biological organism but rather by a machine, and *intelligence* as defined by AI researcher Max Tegmark as the "ability to accomplish complex goals." This part introduces central notions and algorithms from the AI field, gives examples of major recent breakthroughs, and discusses aspects of superintelligence. It consists of two chapters:

- Chapter 1 introduces general notions, ideas, and definitions from the field of AI. It also provides several Python examples of how different algorithms can be applied in practice.

- Chapter 2 discusses concepts and topics related to artificial general intelligence (AGI) and superintelligence (SI). These types of intelligence relate to AI agents that have reached at least human-level intelligence in all domains and super-human intelligence in certain domains.

## CHAPTER 1

Artificial Intelligence

This is the first time that a computer program has defeated a human professional player in the full-sized game of Go, a feat previously thought to be at least a decade away.

—David Silver et al. (2016)

This chapter introduces general notions, ideas, and definitions from the field of artificial intelligence (AI) for the purposes of this book. It also provides worked-out examples for different types of major learning algorithms. In particular, "Algorithms" on page 3 takes a broad perspective and categorizes types of data, types of learning, and types of problems typically encountered in an AI context. This chapter also presents examples for unsupervised and reinforcement learning. "Neural Networks" on page 9 jumps right into the world of neural networks, which not only are central to what follows in later chapters of the book but also have proven to be among the most powerful algorithms AI has to offer nowadays. "Importance of Data" on page 22 discusses the importance of data volume and variety in the context of AI.

Algorithms

This section introduces basic notions from the field of AI relevant to this book. It discusses the different types of data, learning, problems, and approaches that can be subsumed under the general term *AI*. Alpaydin (2016) provides an informal introduction to and overview of many of the topics covered only briefly in this section, along with many examples.

Types of Data

Data in general has two major components:

Features
> Features data (or input data) is data that is given as input to an algorithm. In a financial context, this might be, for example, the income and the savings of a potential debtor.

Labels
> Labels data (or output data) is data that is given as the relevant output to be learned, for example, by a supervised learning algorithm. In a financial context, this might be the creditworthiness of a potential debtor.

Types of Learning

There are three major types of learning algorithms:

Supervised learning (SL)
> These are algorithms that learn from a given sample data set of features (input) and labels (output) values. The next section presents examples for such algorithms, like ordinary least-squares (OLS) regression and neural networks. The purpose of supervised learning is to learn the relationship between the input and output values. In finance, such algorithms might be trained to predict whether a potential debtor is creditworthy or not. For the purposes of this book, these are the most important types of algorithms.

Unsupervised learning (UL)
> These are algorithms that learn from a given sample data set of features (input) values only, often with the goal of finding structure in the data. They are supposed to learn about the input data set, given, for example, some guiding parameters. Clustering algorithms fall into that category. In a financial context, such algorithms might cluster stocks into certain groups.

Reinforcement learning (RL)
> These are algorithms that learn from trial and error by receiving a reward for taking an action. They update an optimal action policy according to what rewards and punishments they receive. Such algorithms are, for example, used for environments where actions need to be taken continuously and rewards are received immediately, such as in a computer game.

Because supervised learning is addressed in the subsequent section in some detail, brief examples will illustrate unsupervised learning and reinforcement learning.

Unsupervised Learning

Simply speaking, a *k-means clustering algorithm* sorts n observations into k clusters. Each observation belongs to the cluster to which its mean (center) is nearest. The following Python code generates sample data for which the features data is clustered. Figure 1-1 visualizes the clustered sample data and also shows that the `scikit-learn` KMeans algorithm used here has identified the clusters perfectly. The coloring of the dots is based on what the algorithm has learned.[1]

```
In [1]: import numpy as np
        import pandas as pd
        from pylab import plt, mpl
        plt.style.use('seaborn')
        mpl.rcParams['savefig.dpi'] = 300
        mpl.rcParams['font.family'] = 'serif'
        np.set_printoptions(precision=4, suppress=True)

In [2]: from sklearn.cluster import KMeans
        from sklearn.datasets import make_blobs

In [3]: x, y = make_blobs(n_samples=100, centers=4,
                          random_state=500, cluster_std=1.25)   ❶

In [4]: model = KMeans(n_clusters=4, random_state=0)   ❷

In [5]: model.fit(x)   ❸
Out[5]: KMeans(n_clusters=4, random_state=0)

In [6]: y_ = model.predict(x)   ❹

In [7]: y_   ❺
Out[7]: array([3, 3, 1, 2, 1, 1, 3, 2, 1, 2, 2, 3, 2, 0, 0, 3, 2, 0, 2, 0, 0, 3,
               1, 2, 1, 1, 0, 0, 1, 3, 2, 1, 1, 0, 1, 3, 1, 3, 2, 2, 2, 1, 0, 0,
               3, 1, 2, 0, 2, 0, 3, 0, 1, 0, 1, 3, 1, 2, 0, 3, 1, 0, 3, 2, 3, 0,
               1, 1, 1, 2, 3, 1, 2, 0, 2, 3, 2, 0, 2, 2, 1, 3, 1, 3, 2, 2, 3, 2,
               0, 0, 0, 3, 3, 3, 3, 0, 3, 1, 0, 0], dtype=int32)

In [8]: plt.figure(figsize=(10, 6))
        plt.scatter(x[:, 0], x[:, 1], c=y_,  cmap='coolwarm');
```

❶ A sample data set is created with clustered features data.

❷ A KMeans model object is instantiated, fixing the number of clusters.

❸ The model is fitted to the features data.

---

[1] For details, see sklearn.cluster.KMeans (*https://oreil.ly/cRcJo*) and VanderPlas (2017, ch. 5).

❹   The predictions are generated given the fitted model.

❺   The predictions are numbers from 0 to 3, each representing one cluster.

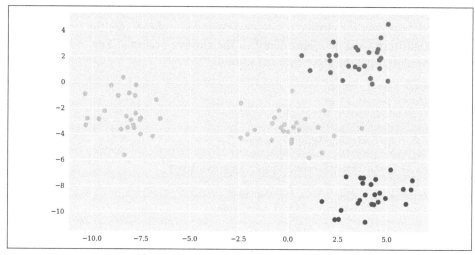

Figure 1-1. Unsupervised learning of clusters

Once an algorithm such as KMeans is trained, it can, for instance, predict the cluster for a new (not yet seen) combination of features values. Assume that such an algorithm is trained on features data that describes potential and real debtors of a bank. It might learn about the creditworthiness of potential debtors by generating two clusters. New potential debtors can then be sorted into a certain cluster: "creditworthy" versus "not creditworthy."

Reinforcement learning

The following example is based on a coin tossing game that is played with a coin that lands 80% of the time on heads and 20% of the time on tails. The coin tossing game is heavily biased to emphasize the benefits of learning as compared to an uninformed baseline algorithm. The baseline algorithm, which bets randomly and equally distributes on heads and tails, achieves a total reward of around 50, on average, per epoch of 100 bets played:

```
In [9]: ssp = [1, 1, 1, 1, 0]  ❶

In [10]: asp = [1, 0]  ❷

In [11]: def epoch():
             tr = 0
             for _ in range(100):
                 a = np.random.choice(asp)  ❸
                 s = np.random.choice(ssp)  ❹
```

```
            if a == s:
                tr += 1   ❺
        return tr
```

```
In [12]: rl = np.array([epoch() for _ in range(15)])   ❻
         rl
Out[12]: array([53, 55, 50, 48, 46, 41, 51, 49, 50, 52, 46, 47, 43, 51, 52])
```

```
In [13]: rl.mean()   ❼
Out[13]: 48.93333333333333
```

❶   The state space (1 = heads, 0 = tails).

❷   The action space (1 = bet on heads, 0 = bet on tails).

❸   An action is randomly chosen from the action space.

❹   A state is randomly chosen from the state space.

❺   The total reward `tr` is increased by one if the bet is correct.

❻   The game is played for a number of epochs; each epoch is 100 bets.

❼   The average total reward of the epochs played is calculated.

Reinforcement learning tries to learn from what is observed after an action is taken, usually based on a reward. To keep things simple, the following learning algorithm only keeps track of the states that are observed in each round insofar as they are appended to the action space `list` object. In this way, the algorithm learns the bias in the game, though maybe not perfectly. By randomly sampling from the updated action space, the bias is reflected because naturally the bet will more often be heads. Over time, heads is chosen, on average, around 80% of the time. The average total reward of around 65 reflects the improvement of the learning algorithm as compared to the uninformed baseline algorithm:

```
In [14]: ssp = [1, 1, 1, 1, 0]
```

```
In [15]: def epoch():
             tr = 0
             asp = [0, 1]   ❶
             for _ in range(100):
                 a = np.random.choice(asp)
                 s = np.random.choice(ssp)
                 if a == s:
                     tr += 1
                 asp.append(s)   ❷
             return tr
```

```
In [16]: rl = np.array([epoch() for _ in range(15)])
         rl
Out[16]: array([64, 65, 77, 65, 54, 64, 71, 64, 57, 62, 69, 63, 61, 66, 75])

In [17]: rl.mean()
Out[17]: 65.13333333333334
```

❶ Resets the action space before starting (over)

❷ Adds the observed state to the action space

Types of Tasks

Depending on the type of labels data and the problem at hand, two types of tasks to be learned are important:

Estimation
> Estimation (or approximation, regression) refers to the cases in which the labels data is real-valued (continuous); that is, it is technically represented as floating point numbers.

Classification
> Classification refers to the cases in which the labels data consists of a finite number of classes or categories that are typically represented by discrete values (positive natural numbers), which in turn are represented technically as integers.

The following section provides examples for both types of tasks.

Types of Approaches

Some more definitions might be in order before finishing this section. This book follows the common differentiation between the following three major terms:

Artificial intelligence (AI)
> AI encompasses all types of learning (algorithms), as defined before, and some more (for example, expert systems).

Machine learning (ML)
> ML is the discipline of learning relationships and other information about given data sets based on an algorithm and a measure of success; a measure of success might, for example, be the mean-squared error (MSE) given labels values and output values to be estimated and the predicted values from the algorithm. ML is a sub-set of AI.

Deep learning (DL)

DL encompasses all algorithms based on neural networks. The term *deep* is usually only used when the neural network has more than one hidden layer. DL is a sub-set of machine learning and so is therefore also a sub-set of AI.

DL has proven useful for a number of broad problem areas. It is suited for estimation and classification tasks, as well as for RL. In many cases, DL-based approaches perform better than alternative algorithms, such as logistic regression or kernel-based ones, like support vector machines.[2] That is why this book mainly focuses on DL. DL approaches used include dense neural networks (DNNs), recurrent neural networks (RNNs), and convolutional neural networks (CNNs). More details appear in later chapters, particularly in Part III.

Neural Networks

The previous sections provide a broader overview of algorithms in AI. This section shows how neural networks fit in. A simple example will illustrate what characterizes neural networks in comparison to traditional statistical methods, such as ordinary least-squares (OLS) regression. The example starts with mathematics and then uses linear regression for *estimation* (or function approximation) and finally applies neural networks to accomplish the estimation. The approach taken here is a supervised learning approach where the task is to estimate labels data based on features data. This section also illustrates the use of neural networks in the context of *classification* problems.

OLS Regression

Assume that a mathematical function is given as follows:

$$f : \mathbb{R} \to \mathbb{R}, y = 2x^2 - \frac{1}{3}x^3$$

Such a function transforms an input value x to an output value y. Or it transforms a series of input values $x_1, x_2, ..., x_N$ into a series of output values $y_1, y_2, ..., y_N$. The following Python code implements the mathematical function as a Python function and creates a number of input and output values. Figure 1-2 plots the output values against the input values:

```
In [18]: def f(x):
             return 2 * x ** 2 - x ** 3 / 3   ❶
```

---

2 For details, see VanderPlas (2017, ch. 5).

```
In [19]: x = np.linspace(-2, 4, 25)  ❷
         x  ❷
Out[19]: array([-2.  , -1.75, -1.5 , -1.25, -1.  , -0.75, -0.5 , -0.25,  0.  ,
                 0.25,  0.5 ,  0.75,  1.  ,  1.25,  1.5 ,  1.75,  2.  ,  2.25,
                 2.5 ,  2.75,  3.  ,  3.25,  3.5 ,  3.75,  4.  ])

In [20]: y = f(x)  ❸
         y  ❸
Out[20]: array([10.6667,  7.9115,  5.625 ,  3.776 ,  2.3333,  1.2656,  0.5417,
                 0.1302,  0.    ,  0.1198,  0.4583,  0.9844,  1.6667,  2.474 ,
                 3.375 ,  4.3385,  5.3333,  6.3281,  7.2917,  8.1927,  9.    ,
                 9.6823, 10.2083, 10.5469, 10.6667])

In [21]: plt.figure(figsize=(10, 6))
         plt.plot(x, y, 'ro');
```

❶   The mathematical function as a Python function

❷   The input values

❸   The output values

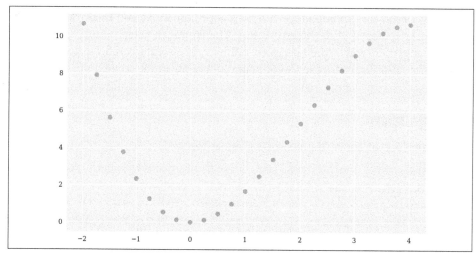

Figure 1-2. Output values against input values

Whereas in the mathematical example the function comes first, the input data second, and the output data third, the sequence is different in *statistical learning*. Assume that the previous input values and output values are given. They represent the *sample* (data). The problem in *statistical regression* is to find a function that approximates the functional relationship between the input values (also called the *independent values*) and the output values (also called the *dependent values*) as well as possible.

Assume simple OLS linear regression. In this case, the functional relationship between the input and output values is assumed to be linear, and the problem is to find optimal parameters α and β for the following linear equation:

$$\hat{f}:\mathbb{R} \rightarrow \mathbb{R}, \hat{y} = \alpha + \beta x$$

For given input values $x_1, x_2, ..., x_N$ and output values $y_1, y_2, ..., y_N$, *optimal* in this case means that they minimize the mean squared error (MSE) between the real output values and the approximated output values:

$$\min_{\alpha, \beta} \frac{1}{N} \sum_{n}^{N} \left(y_n - \hat{f}(x_n)\right)^2$$

For the case of simple linear regression, the solution (α^*, β^*) is known in closed form, as shown in the following equation. Bars on the variables indicate sample mean values:

$$\beta^* = \frac{Cov(x, y)}{Var(x)}$$
$$\alpha^* = \bar{y} - \beta\bar{x}$$

The following Python code calculates the optimal parameter values, linearly estimates (approximates) the output values, and plots the linear regression line alongside the sample data (see Figure 1-3). The linear regression approach does not work too well here in approximating the functional relationship. This is confirmed by the relatively high MSE value:

```
In [22]: beta = np.cov(x, y, ddof=0)[0, 1] / np.var(x)  ❶
             beta  ❶
Out[22]: 1.0541666666666667

In [23]: alpha = y.mean() - beta * x.mean()  ❷
             alpha  ❷
Out[23]: 3.8625000000000003

In [24]: y_ = alpha + beta * x  ❸

In [25]: MSE = ((y - y_) ** 2).mean()  ❹
             MSE  ❹
Out[25]: 10.721953125

In [26]: plt.figure(figsize=(10, 6))
             plt.plot(x, y, 'ro', label='sample data')
             plt.plot(x, y_, lw=3.0, label='linear regression')
             plt.legend();
```

❶ Calculation of optimal β

❷ Calculation of optimal α

❸ Calculation of estimated output values

❹ Calculation of the MSE given the approximation

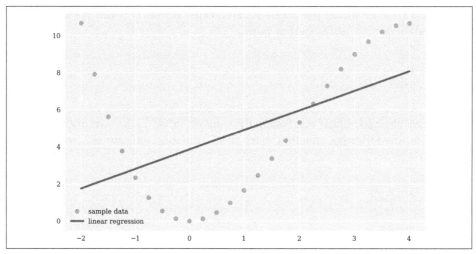

Figure 1-3. Sample data and linear regression line

How can the MSE value be improved (decreased)—maybe even to 0, that is, to a "perfect estimation?" Of course, OLS regression is not constrained to a simple linear relationship. In addition to the constant and linear terms, higher order monomials, for instance, can be easily added as basis functions. To this end, compare the regression results shown in Figure 1-4 and the following code that creates the figure. The improvements that come from using quadratic and cubic monomials as basis functions are obvious and also are numerically confirmed by the calculated MSE values. For basis functions up to and including the cubic monomial, the estimation is perfect, and the functional relationship is perfectly recovered:

```
In [27]: plt.figure(figsize=(10, 6))
         plt.plot(x, y, 'ro', label='sample data')
         for deg in [1, 2, 3]:
             reg = np.polyfit(x, y, deg=deg)   ❶
             y_ = np.polyval(reg, x)   ❷
             MSE = ((y - y_) ** 2).mean()   ❸
             print(f'deg={deg} | MSE={MSE:.5f}')
             plt.plot(x, np.polyval(reg, x), label=f'deg={deg}')
         plt.legend();
         deg=1 | MSE=10.72195
         deg=2 | MSE=2.31258
```

```
          deg=3 | MSE=0.00000

In [28]: reg  ❹
Out[28]: array([-0.3333,  2.    ,  0.    , -0.    ])
```

❶   Regression step

❷   Approximation step

❸   MSE calculation

❹   Optimal ("perfect") parameter values

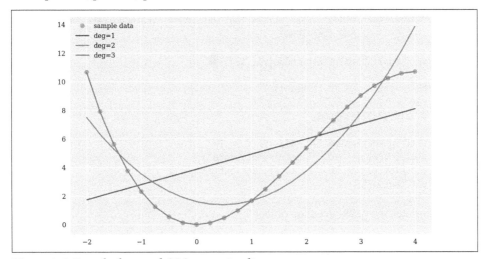

Figure 1-4. Sample data and OLS regression lines

Exploiting the knowledge of the form of the mathematical function to be approximated and accordingly adding more basis functions to the regression leads to a "perfect
approximation." That is, the OLS regression recovers the exact factors of the quadratic and cubic part, respectively, of the original function.

Estimation with Neural Networks

However, not all relationships are of this kind. This is where, for instance, *neural networks* can help. Without going into the details, neural networks can approximate a
wide range of functional relationships. Knowledge of the form of the relationship is
generally not required.

Scikit-learn

The following Python code uses the `MLPRegressor` class of `scikit-learn`, which implements a DNN for estimation. DNNs are sometimes also called multi-layer perceptron (MLP).[3] The results are not perfect, as Figure 1-5 and the MSE illustrate. However, they are quite good already for the simple configuration used:

```
In [29]: from sklearn.neural_network import MLPRegressor

In [30]: model = MLPRegressor(hidden_layer_sizes=3 * [256],
                              learning_rate_init=0.03,
                              max_iter=5000)  ❶

In [31]: model.fit(x.reshape(-1, 1), y)  ❷
Out[31]: MLPRegressor(hidden_layer_sizes=[256, 256, 256], learning_rate_init=0.03,
                      max_iter=5000)

In [32]: y_ = model.predict(x.reshape(-1, 1))  ❸

In [33]: MSE = ((y - y_) ** 2).mean()
         MSE
Out[33]: 0.021662355744355866

In [34]: plt.figure(figsize=(10, 6))
         plt.plot(x, y, 'ro', label='sample data')
         plt.plot(x, y_, lw=3.0, label='dnn estimation')
         plt.legend();
```

❶ Instantiates the `MLPRegressor` object

❷ Implements the fitting or learning step

❸ Implements the prediction step

Just having a look at the results in Figure 1-4 and Figure 1-5, one might assume that the methods and approaches are not too dissimilar after all. However, there is a fundamental difference worth highlighting. Although the OLS regression approach, as shown explicitly for the simple linear regression, is based on the calculation of certain well-specified quantities and parameters, the neural network approach relies on *incremental learning*. This in turn means that a set of parameters, the *weights* within the neural network, are first initialized randomly and then adjusted gradually given the differences between the neural network output and the sample output values. This approach lets you retrain (update) a neural network incrementally.

---

3 For details, see `sklearn.neural_network.MLPRegressor` (*https://oreil.ly/Oimd8*). For more background, see Goodfellow et al. (2016, ch. 6).

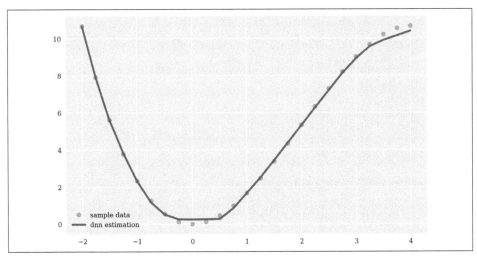

Figure 1-5. Sample data and neural network–based estimations

Keras

The next example uses a sequential model with the `Keras` deep learning package.[4] The model is fitted, or *trained*, for 100 epochs. The procedure is repeated for five rounds. After every such round, the approximation by the neural network is updated and plotted. Figure 1-6 shows how the approximation gradually improves with every round. This is also reflected in the decreasing MSE values. The end result is not perfect, but again, it is quite good given the simplicity of the model:

```
In [35]: import tensorflow as tf
         tf.random.set_seed(100)

In [36]: from keras.layers import Dense
         from keras.models import Sequential
         Using TensorFlow backend.

In [37]: model = Sequential()                                        ❶
         model.add(Dense(256, activation='relu', input_dim=1))       ❷
         model.add(Dense(1, activation='linear'))                    ❸
         model.compile(loss='mse', optimizer='rmsprop')              ❹

In [38]: ((y - y_) ** 2).mean()
Out[38]: 0.021662355744355866

In [39]: plt.figure(figsize=(10, 6))
         plt.plot(x, y, 'ro', label='sample data')
         for _ in range(1, 6):
```

---

4 For details, see Chollet (2017, ch. 3).

```
        model.fit(x, y, epochs=100, verbose=False)  ❺
        y_ = model.predict(x)  ❻
        MSE = ((y - y_.flatten()) ** 2).mean()  ❼
        print(f'round={_} | MSE={MSE:.5f}')
        plt.plot(x, y_, '--', label=f'round={_}')  ❽
    plt.legend();
    round=1 | MSE=3.09714
    round=2 | MSE=0.75603
    round=3 | MSE=0.22814
    round=4 | MSE=0.11861
    round=5 | MSE=0.09029
```

❶ Instantiates the `Sequential` model object

❷ Adds a densely connected hidden layer with rectified linear unit (ReLU) activation[5]

❸ Adds the output layer with linear activation

❹ Compiles the model for usage

❺ Trains the neural network for a fixed number of epochs

❻ Implements the approximation step

❼ Calculates the current MSE

❽ Plots the current approximation results

Roughly speaking, one can say that the neural network does almost as well in the estimation as the OLS regression, which delivers a perfect result. Therefore, why use neural networks at all? A more comprehensive answer might need to come later in this book, but a somewhat different example might give some hint.

Consider instead the previous sample data set, as generated from a well-defined mathematical function, now a *random sample data set*, for which both features and labels are randomly chosen. Of course, this example is for illustration and does not allow for a deep interpretation.

---

5 For details on activation functions with `Keras`, see *https://keras.io/activations*.

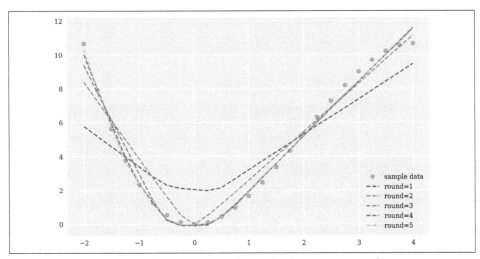

Figure 1-6. Sample data and estimations after multiple training rounds

The following code generates the random sample data set and creates the OLS regression estimation based on a varying number of monomial basis functions. Figure 1-7 visualizes the results. Even for the highest number of monomials in the example, the estimation results are still not too good. The MSE value is accordingly relatively high:

```
In [40]: np.random.seed(0)
         x = np.linspace(-1, 1)
         y = np.random.random(len(x)) * 2 - 1

In [41]: plt.figure(figsize=(10, 6))
         plt.plot(x, y, 'ro', label='sample data')
         for deg in [1, 5, 9, 11, 13, 15]:
             reg = np.polyfit(x, y, deg=deg)
             y_ = np.polyval(reg, x)
             MSE = ((y - y_) ** 2).mean()
             print(f'deg={deg:2d} | MSE={MSE:.5f}')
             plt.plot(x, np.polyval(reg, x), label=f'deg={deg}')
         plt.legend();
         deg= 1 | MSE=0.28153
         deg= 5 | MSE=0.27331
         deg= 9 | MSE=0.25442
         deg=11 | MSE=0.23458
         deg=13 | MSE=0.22989
         deg=15 | MSE=0.21672
```

The results for the OLS regression are not too surprising. OLS regression in this case assumes that the approximation can be achieved through an appropriate combination of a finite number of basis functions. Since the sample data set has been generated randomly, the OLS regression does not perform well in this case.

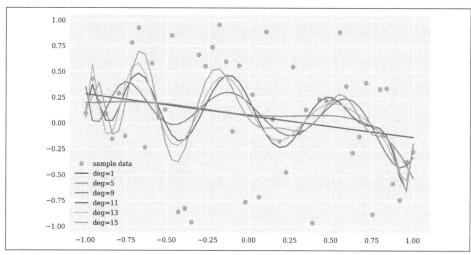

Figure 1-7. Random sample data and OLS regression lines

What about neural networks? The application is as straightforward as before and yields estimations as shown in Figure 1-8. While the end result is not perfect, it is obvious that the neural network performs better than the OLS regression in estimating the random label values from the random features values. Given its architecture, however, the neural network has almost 200,000 trainable parameters (weights), which offers relatively high flexibility, particularly when compared to the OLS regression, for which a maximum of 15 + 1 parameters are used:

```
In [42]: model = Sequential()
         model.add(Dense(256, activation='relu', input_dim=1))
         for _ in range(3):
             model.add(Dense(256, activation='relu'))  ❶
         model.add(Dense(1, activation='linear'))
         model.compile(loss='mse', optimizer='rmsprop')

In [43]: model.summary()  ❷
         Model: "sequential_2"
```

Layer (type)	Output Shape	Param #
dense_3 (Dense)	(None, 256)	512
dense_4 (Dense)	(None, 256)	65792
dense_5 (Dense)	(None, 256)	65792
dense_6 (Dense)	(None, 256)	65792
dense_7 (Dense)	(None, 1)	257

```
Total params: 198,145
Trainable params: 198,145
Non-trainable params: 0
```

```
In [44]: %%time
         plt.figure(figsize=(10, 6))
         plt.plot(x, y, 'ro', label='sample data')
         for _ in range(1, 8):
             model.fit(x, y, epochs=500, verbose=False)
             y_ = model.predict(x)
             MSE = ((y - y_.flatten()) ** 2).mean()
             print(f'round={_} | MSE={MSE:.5f}')
             plt.plot(x, y_, '--', label=f'round={_}')
         plt.legend();
         round=1 | MSE=0.13560
         round=2 | MSE=0.08337
         round=3 | MSE=0.06281
         round=4 | MSE=0.04419
         round=5 | MSE=0.03329
         round=6 | MSE=0.07676
         round=7 | MSE=0.00431
         CPU times: user 30.4 s, sys: 4.7 s, total: 35.1 s
         Wall time: 13.6 s
```

❶ Multiple hidden layers are added.

❷ Network architecture and number of trainable parameters are shown.

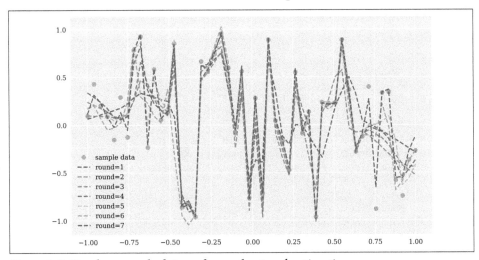

Figure 1-8. Random sample data and neural network estimations

Classification with Neural Networks

Another benefit of neural networks is that they can be easily used for classification tasks as well. Consider the following Python code that implements a classification using a neural network based on Keras. The binary features data and labels data are generated randomly. The major adjustment to be made modeling-wise is to change the activation function from the output layer to sigmoid from linear. More details on this appear in later chapters. The classification is not perfect. However, it reaches a high level of accuracy. How the accuracy, expressed as the relationship between correct results to all label values, changes with the number of training epochs is shown in Figure 1-9. The accuracy starts out low and then improves step-wise, though not necessarily with every step:

```
In [45]: f = 5
         n = 10

In [46]: np.random.seed(100)

In [47]: x = np.random.randint(0, 2, (n, f))  ❶
         x  ❶
Out[47]: array([[0, 0, 1, 1, 1],
                [1, 0, 0, 0, 0],
                [0, 1, 0, 0, 0],
                [0, 1, 0, 0, 1],
                [0, 1, 0, 0, 0],
                [1, 1, 1, 0, 0],
                [1, 0, 0, 1, 1],
                [1, 1, 1, 0, 0],
                [1, 1, 1, 1, 1],
                [1, 1, 1, 0, 1]])

In [48]: y = np.random.randint(0, 2, n)  ❷
         y  ❷
Out[48]: array([1, 1, 0, 0, 1, 1, 0, 1, 0, 1])

In [49]: model = Sequential()
         model.add(Dense(256, activation='relu', input_dim=f))
         model.add(Dense(1, activation='sigmoid'))  ❸
         model.compile(loss='binary_crossentropy', optimizer='rmsprop',
                   metrics=['acc'])  ❹

In [50]: h = model.fit(x, y, epochs=50, verbose=False)
Out[50]: <keras.callbacks.callbacks.History at 0x7fde09dd1cd0>

In [51]: y_ = np.where(model.predict(x).flatten() > 0.5, 1, 0)
         y_
Out[51]: array([1, 1, 0, 0, 0, 1, 0, 1, 0, 1], dtype=int32)
```

```
In [52]: y == y_  ❺
Out[52]: array([ True,  True,  True,  True, False,  True,  True,  True,  True,
                 True])

In [53]: res = pd.DataFrame(h.history)  ❻

In [54]: res.plot(figsize=(10, 6));  ❻
```

❶ Creates random features data

❷ Creates random labels data

❸ Defines the activation function for the output layer as sigmoid

❹ Defines the loss function to be binary_crossentropy[6]

❺ Compares the predicted values with the labels data

❻ Plots the loss function and accuracy values for every training step

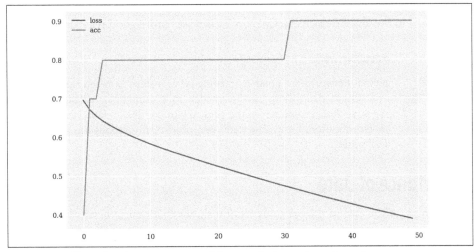

Figure 1-9. Classification accuracy and loss against number of epochs

---

6 The *loss function* calculates the prediction error of the neural network (or other ML algorithms). *Binary cross entropy* is an appropriate loss function for binary classification problems, while the *mean squared error* (MSE) is, for example, appropriate for estimation problems. For details on loss functions with Keras, see *https://keras.io/losses*.

The examples in this section illustrate some fundamental characteristics of neural networks as compared to OLS regression:

Problem-agnostic
> The neural network approach is agnostic when it comes to estimating and classifying label values, given a set of feature values. Statistical methods, such as OLS regression, might perform well for a smaller set of problems, but not too well or not at all for others.

Incremental learning
> The optimal weights within a neural network, given a target measure of success, are learned incrementally based on a random initialization and incremental improvements. These incremental improvements are achieved by considering the differences between the predicted values and the sample label values and back-propagating weights updates through the neural network.

Universal approximation
> There are strong mathematical theorems showing that neural networks (even with one hidden layer only) can approximate almost any function.[7]

These characteristics might justify why this book puts neural networks at the core with regard to the algorithms used. Chapter 2 discusses more good reasons.

Neural Networks

Neural networks are good at learning relationships between input and output data. They can be applied to a number of problem types, such as estimation in the presence of complex relationships or classification, for which traditional statistical methods are not well suited.

Importance of Data

The example at the end of the previous section shows that neural networks are capable of solving classification problems quite well. The neural network with one hidden layer reaches a high degree of accuracy on the given data set, or *in-sample*. However, what about the predictive power of a neural network? This hinges significantly on the volume and variety of the data available to train the neural network. Another numerical example, based on larger data sets, will illustrate this point.

---

7 See, for example, Kratsios (2019).

Small Data Set

Consider a random sample data set similar to the one used before in the classification example, but with more features and more samples. Most algorithms used in AI are about *pattern recognition*. In the following Python code, the number of binary features defines the number of possible patterns about which the algorithm can learn something. Given that the labels data is also binary, the algorithm tries to learn whether a 0 or 1 is more likely given a certain pattern, say [0, 0, 1, 1, 1, 1, 0, 0, 0, 0]. Because all numbers are randomly chosen with equal probability, there is not that much to learn beyond the fact that the labels 0 and 1 are equally likely no matter what (random) pattern is observed. Therefore, a baseline prediction algorithm should be accurate about 50% of the time, no matter what (random) pattern it is presented with:

```
In [55]: f = 10
         n = 250

In [56]: np.random.seed(100)

In [57]: x = np.random.randint(0, 2, (n, f))  ❶
         x[:4]  ❶
Out[57]: array([[0, 0, 1, 1, 1, 1, 0, 0, 0, 0],
                [0, 1, 0, 0, 0, 0, 1, 0, 0, 1],
                [0, 1, 0, 0, 0, 1, 1, 1, 0, 0],
                [1, 0, 0, 1, 1, 1, 1, 1, 0, 0]])

In [58]: y = np.random.randint(0, 2, n)  ❷
         y[:4]  ❷
Out[58]: array([0, 1, 0, 0])

In [59]: 2 ** f  ❸
Out[59]: 1024
```

❶ Features data

❷ Labels data

❸ Number of patterns

In order to proceed, the raw data is put into a pandas DataFrame object, which simplifies certain operations and analyses:

```
In [60]: fcols = [f'f{_}' for _ in range(f)]  ❶
         fcols  ❶
Out[60]: ['f0', 'f1', 'f2', 'f3', 'f4', 'f5', 'f6', 'f7', 'f8', 'f9']

In [61]: data = pd.DataFrame(x, columns=fcols)  ❷
         data['l'] = y  ❸
```

```
In [62]: data.info()  ❹
         <class 'pandas.core.frame.DataFrame'>
         RangeIndex: 250 entries, 0 to 249
         Data columns (total 11 columns):
          #   Column  Non-Null Count  Dtype
         ---  ------  --------------  -----
          0   f0      250 non-null    int64
          1   f1      250 non-null    int64
          2   f2      250 non-null    int64
          3   f3      250 non-null    int64
          4   f4      250 non-null    int64
          5   f5      250 non-null    int64
          6   f6      250 non-null    int64
          7   f7      250 non-null    int64
          8   f8      250 non-null    int64
          9   f9      250 non-null    int64
          10  l       250 non-null    int64
         dtypes: int64(11)
         memory usage: 21.6 KB
```

❶ Defines column names for the features data

❷ Puts the features data into a `DataFrame` object

❸ Puts the labels data into the same `DataFrame` object

❹ Shows the meta information for the data set

Two major problems can be identified given the results from executing the following Python code. First, not all patterns are in the sample data set. Second, the sample size is much too small per observed pattern. Even without digging deeper, it is clear that no classification algorithm can really learn about all the possible patterns in a meaningful way:

```
In [63]: grouped = data.groupby(list(data.columns))  ❶

In [64]: freq = grouped['l'].size().unstack(fill_value=0)  ❷

In [65]: freq['sum'] = freq[0] + freq[1]  ❸

In [66]: freq.head(10)  ❹
Out[66]: l                        0  1  sum
         f0 f1 f2 f3 f4 f5 f6 f7 f8 f9
         0  0  0  0  0  0  0  1  1  1    0  1   1
                              1  0  1  0  1  1   2
                                    1  0  1  1
                  1  0  0  0  0  0  1  0  1
                                    1  0  1  1
                        1  1  1  0  1  1
                  1  0  0  0  0  1  1
```

```
                        1  0   0  1    1
            1  0  0  0  1  1   1  0    1
               1  1  0  0  1  0    1
```

```
In [67]: freq['sum'].describe().astype(int)  ❺
Out[67]: count    227
         mean       1
         std        0
         min        1
         25%        1
         50%        1
         75%        1
         max        2
         Name: sum, dtype: int64
```

❶ Groups the data along all columns

❷ Unstacks the grouped data for the labels column

❸ Adds up the frequency for a 0 and a 1

❹ Shows the frequencies for a 0 and a 1 given a certain pattern

❺ Provides statistics for the sum of the frequencies

The following Python code uses the MLPClassifier model from scikit-learn.[8] The model is trained on the whole data set. What about the ability of a neural network to learn about the relationships within a given data set? The ability is pretty high, as the in-sample accuracy score shows. It is in fact close to 100%, a result driven to a large extent by the relatively high neural network capacity given the relatively small data set:

```
In [68]: from sklearn.neural_network import MLPClassifier
         from sklearn.metrics import accuracy_score

In [69]: model = MLPClassifier(hidden_layer_sizes=[128, 128, 128],
                               max_iter=1000, random_state=100)

In [70]: model.fit(data[fcols], data['l'])
Out[70]: MLPClassifier(hidden_layer_sizes=[128, 128, 128], max_iter=1000,
                       random_state=100)

In [71]: accuracy_score(data['l'], model.predict(data[fcols]))
Out[71]: 0.952
```

---

8 For details, see sklearn.neural_network.MLPClassifier (*https://oreil.ly/hCR4h*).

But what about the *predictive power* of a trained neural network? To this end, the given data set can be split into a training and a test data sub-set. The model is trained on the training data sub-set only and then tested with regard to its predictive power on the test data set. As before, the accuracy of the trained neural network is pretty high in-sample (that is, on the training data set). However, it is more than 10 percentage points worse than an uninformed baseline algorithm on the test data set:

```
In [72]: split = int(len(data) * 0.7)    ❶

In [73]: train = data[:split]    ❶
         test = data[split:]    ❶

In [74]: model.fit(train[fcols], train['l'])    ❷
Out[74]: MLPClassifier(hidden_layer_sizes=[128, 128, 128], max_iter=1000,
                       random_state=100)

In [75]: accuracy_score(train['l'], model.predict(train[fcols]))    ❸
Out[75]: 0.9714285714285714

In [76]: accuracy_score(test['l'], model.predict(test[fcols]))    ❹
Out[76]: 0.38666666666666666
```

❶ Splits the data into `train` and `test` data sub-sets

❷ Trains the model on the training data set only

❸ Reports the accuracy in-sample (training data set)

❹ Reports the accuracy out-of-sample (test data set)

Roughly speaking, the neural network, trained on a small data set only, learns wrong relationships due to the identified two major problem areas. The problems are not really relevant in the context of learning relationships *in-sample*. To the contrary, the smaller a data set is, the more easily in-sample relationships can be learned in general. However, the problem areas are highly relevant when using the trained neural network to generate predictions *out-of-sample*.

Larger Data Set

Fortunately, there is often a clear way out of this problematic situation: a *larger data set*. Faced with real-world problems, this theoretical insight might be equally correct. From a practical point of view, though, such larger data sets are not always available, nor can they often be generated so easily. However, in the context of the example of this section, a larger data set is indeed easily created.

The following Python code increases the number of samples in the initial sample data set significantly. The result is that the prediction accuracy of the trained neural network increases by more than 10 percentage points, to a level of about 50%, which is to be expected given the nature of the labels data. It is now in line with an uninformed baseline algorithm:

```
In [77]: factor = 50

In [78]: big = pd.DataFrame(np.random.randint(0, 2, (factor * n, f)),
                            columns=fcols)

In [79]: big['l'] = np.random.randint(0, 2, factor * n)

In [80]: train = big[:split]
         test = big[split:]

In [81]: model.fit(train[fcols], train['l'])
Out[81]: MLPClassifier(hidden_layer_sizes=[128, 128, 128], max_iter=1000,
                       random_state=100)

In [82]: accuracy_score(train['l'], model.predict(train[fcols]))    ❶
Out[82]: 0.9657142857142857

In [83]: accuracy_score(test['l'], model.predict(test[fcols]))    ❷
Out[83]: 0.5043407707910751
```

❶ Prediction accuracy in-sample (training data set)

❷ Prediction accuracy out-of-sample (test data set)

A quick analysis of the available data, as shown next, explains the increase in the prediction accuracy. First, all possible patterns are now represented in the data set. Second, all patterns have an average frequency of above 10 in the data set. In other words, the neural network sees basically *all the patterns multiple times*. This allows the neural network to "learn" that both labels 0 and 1 are equally likely for all possible patterns. Of course, it is a rather involved way of learning this, but it is a good illustration of the fact that a *relatively small* data set might often be *too small* in the context of neural networks:

```
In [84]: grouped = big.groupby(list(data.columns))

In [85]: freq = grouped['l'].size().unstack(fill_value=0)

In [86]: freq['sum'] = freq[0] + freq[1]    ❶

In [87]: freq.head(6)
Out[87]: l                               0  1  sum
         f0 f1 f2 f3 f4 f5 f6 f7 f8 f9
         0  0  0  0  0  0  0  0  0  0   10  9  19
                                    1    5  4   9
                              1     0    2  5   7
                                    1    6  6  12
```

```
        1   0   0    9   8   17
                1        7   4   11
```

```
In [88]: freq['sum'].describe().astype(int)  ❷
Out[88]: count    1024
         mean       12
         std         3
         min         2
         25%        10
         50%        12
         75%        15
         max        26
         Name: sum, dtype: int64
```

❶ Adds the frequency for the 0 and 1 values

❷ Shows summary statistics for the sum values

Volume and Variety

In the context of neural networks that perform prediction tasks, the volume and variety of the available data used to train the neural network are decisive for its prediction performance. The numerical, hypothetical examples in this section show that the same neural network trained on a relatively small and not-as-varied data set underperforms its counterpart trained on a relatively large and varied data set by more than 10 percentage points. This difference can be considered huge given that AI practitioners and companies often fight for improvements as small as a tenth of a percentage point.

Big Data

What is the difference between a *larger* data set and a *big* data set? The term *big data* has been used for more than a decade now to mean a number of things. For the purposes of this book, one might say that a *big data set* is large enough—in terms of volume, variety, and also maybe velocity—for an AI algorithm to be trained properly such that the algorithm performs better at a prediction task as compared to a baseline algorithm.

The larger data set used before is still small in practical terms. However, it is large enough to accomplish the specified goal. The required volume and variety of the data set are mainly driven by the structure and characteristics of the features and labels data.

In this context, assume that a retail bank implements a neural network–based classification approach for credit scoring. Given in-house data, the responsible data scientist designs 25 categorical features, every one of which can take on 8 different values. The resulting number of patterns is astronomically large:

```
In [89]: 8 ** 25
Out[89]: 37778931862957161709568
```

It is clear that no single data set can provide a neural network with exposure to every single one of these patterns.[9] Fortunately, in practice this is not necessary for the neural network to learn about the creditworthiness based on data for regular, defaulting, and/or rejected debtors. It is also not necessary in general to generate "good" predictions with regard to the creditworthiness of every potential debtor.

This is due to a number of reasons. To name only a few, first, not every pattern will be relevant in practice—some patterns might simply not exist, might be impossible, and so forth. Second, not all features might be equally important, reducing the number of relevant features and thereby the number of possible patterns. Third, a value of 4 or 5 for feature number 7, say, might not make a difference at all, further reducing the number of relevant patterns.

Conclusions

For this book, artificial intelligence, or AI, encompasses methods, techniques, algorithms, and so on that are able to learn relationships, rules, probabilities, and more from data. The focus lies on supervised learning algorithms, such as those for estimation and classification. With regard to algorithms, neural networks and deep learning approaches are at the core.

The central theme of this book is the application of neural networks to one of the core problems in finance: the prediction of future market movements. More specifically, the problem might be to predict the direction of movement for a stock index or the exchange rate for a currency pair. The prediction of the future market direction (that is, whether a target level or price goes up or down) is a problem that can be easily cast into a classification setting.

Before diving deeper into the core theme itself, the next chapter first discusses selected topics related to what is called *superintelligence* and *technological singularity*. That discussion will provide useful background for the chapters that follow, which focus on finance and the application of AI to the financial domain.

---

9 Nor would current compute technology allow one to model and train a neural network based on such a data set if it would be available. In this context, the next chapter discusses the importance of hardware for AI.

References

Books and papers cited in this chapter:

Alpaydin, Ethem. 2016. *Machine Learning*. MIT Press, Cambridge.

Chollet, Francois. 2017. *Deep Learning with Python*. Shelter Island: Manning.

Goodfellow, Ian, Yoshua Bengio, and Aaron Courville. 2016. *Deep Learning*. Cambridge: MIT Press. *http://deeplearningbook.org*.

Kratsios, Anastasis. 2019. "Universal Approximation Theorems." *https://oreil.ly/COOdI*.

Silver, David et al. 2016. "Mastering the Game of Go with Deep Neural Networks and Tree Search." *Nature* 529 (January): 484-489.

Shanahan, Murray. 2015. *The Technological Singularity*. Cambridge: MIT Press.

Tegmark, Max. 2017. *Life 3.0: Being Human in the Age of Artificial Intelligence*. United Kingdom: Penguin Random House.

VanderPlas, Jake. 2017. *Python Data Science Handbook*. Sebastopol: O'Reilly.

## CHAPTER 2

Superintelligence

> The fact that there are many paths that lead to superintelligence should increase our confidence that we will eventually get there. If one path turns out to be blocked, we can still progress.
>
> —Nick Bostrom (2014)

There are multiple definitions for the term *technological singularity*. Its use dates back at least to the article by Vinge (1993), which the author provocatively begins like this:

> Within thirty years, we will have the technological means to create superhuman intelligence. Shortly after, the human era will be ended.

For the purposes of this chapter and book, *technological singularity* refers to a point in time at which certain machines achieve superhuman intelligence, or *superintelligence* —this is mostly in line with the original idea of Vinge (1993). The idea and concept was further popularized by the widely read and cited book by Kurzweil (2005). Barrat (2013) has a wealth of historical and anecdotal information around the topic. Shanahan (2015) provides an informal introduction and overview of its central aspects. The expression *technological singularity* itself has its origin in the concept of a *singularity* in physics. It refers to the center of a black hole, where mass is highly concentrated, gravitation becomes infinite, and traditional laws of physics break down. The beginning of the universe, the so-called Big Bang, is also referred to as a singularity.

Although the general ideas and concepts of the technological singularity and of superintelligence might not have an obvious and direct relationship to AI applied to finance, a better understanding of their background, related problems, and potential consequences is beneficial. The insights gained in the general framework are important in a narrower context as well, such as for AI in finance. Those insights also help guide the discussion about how AI might reshape the financial industry in the near and long term.

"Success Stories" on page 32 takes a look at a selection of recent success stories in the field of AI. Among others, it covers how the company DeepMind solved the problem of playing Atari 2600 games with neural networks. It also tells the story of how the same company solved the problem of playing the game of Go at above-human-expert level. The story of chess and computer programs is also recounted in that section. "Importance of Hardware" on page 42 discusses the importance of hardware in the context of these recent success stories. "Forms of Intelligence" on page 44 introduces different forms of intelligence, such as artificial narrow intelligence (ANI), artificial general intelligence (AGI), and superintelligence (SI). "Paths to Superintelligence" on page 45 is about potential paths to superintelligence, such as whole brain emulation (WBE), while "Intelligence Explosion" on page 50 is about what researchers call intelligence explosion. "Goals and Control" on page 50 provides a discussion of aspects related to the so-called control problem in the context of superintelligence. Finally, "Potential Outcomes" on page 54 briefly looks at potential future outcomes and scenarios once superintelligence has been achieved.

Success Stories

Many ideas and algorithms in AI date back a few decades already. Over these decades there have been longer periods of hope on the one hand and despair on the other hand. Bostrom (2014, ch. 1) provides a review of these periods.

In 2020, one can say for sure that AI is in the middle of a period of hope, if not excitement. One reason for this is recent successes in applying AI to domains and problems that even a few years ago seemed immune to AI dominance for decades to come. The list of such success stories is long and growing rapidly. Therefore, this section focuses on three such stories only. Gerrish (2018) provides a broader selection and more detailed accounts of the single cases.

Atari

This sub-section first tells the success story of how DeepMind mastered playing Atari 2600 games with reinforcement learning and neural networks, and then illustrates the basic approach that led to its success based on a concrete code example.

The story

The first success story is about playing Atari 2600 games on a superhuman level.[1] The Atari 2600 Video Computer System (VCS) was released in 1977 and was one of the first widespread game-playing consoles in the 1980s. Selected popular games from

---

1 For background and historical information, see *http://bit.ly/aiif_atari*.

that period, such as *Space Invaders*, *Asteroids*, or *Missile Command*, count as classics and are still played decades later by retro games enthusiasts.

DeepMind (*https://deepmind.com*) published a paper (Mnih et al. 2013) in which its team detailed results from applying reinforcement learning to the problem of playing Atari 2600 games by an AI algorithm, or a so-called AI agent. The algorithm is a variant of Q-learning applied to a convolutional neural network.[2] The algorithm is trained on high-dimensional visual input (raw pixels) only, without any guidance by or input from a human. The original project focused on seven Atari 2600 games, and for three of them—*Pong*, *Enduro*, and *Breakout*—the DeepMind team reported above-human expert performance of the AI agent.

From an AI point of view, it is remarkable not only that the DeepMind team achieved such a result, but also how it achieved it. First, the team only used a single neural network to learn and play all seven games. Second, no human guidance or humanly labeled data was provided, just the interactive learning experience based on visual input properly transformed into features data.[3] Third, the approach used is reinforcement learning, which relies on observation of the relationships between actions and outcomes (rewards) only—basically the same way a human player learns to play such a game.

One of the Atari 2600 games, for which the DeepMind AI agent achieved above-human expert performance, is *Breakout* (*http://bit.ly/aiif_breakout*). In this game, the goal is to destroy lines of bricks at the top of the screen by using a paddle at the bottom of the screen from which a ball bounces back and moves straight across the screen. Whenever the ball hits a brick, the brick is destroyed and the ball bounces back. The ball also bounces back from the left, right, and top walls. The player loses a life in this game whenever the ball reaches the bottom of the screen without being hit by the paddle.

The action space has three elements, all related to the paddle: staying at current position, moving left, and moving right. The state space is represented by frames of the game screen of size 210 x 160 pixels with a 128-color palette. The reward is represented by the game score, which the DeepMind algorithm is programmed to maximize. With regard to the action policy, the algorithm learns which action is best to take, given a certain game state, to maximize the game score (total reward).

---

2 For details, refer to Mnih et al. (2013).

3 Among other factors, this is made possible by the availability of the Arcade Learning Environment (ALE) (*https://oreil.ly/OqnWk*) that allows researchers to train AI agents for Atari 2600 games via a standardized API.

An example

There is not enough room in this chapter to explore in detail the approach taken by DeepMind for *Breakout* and the other Atari 2600 games. However, the OpenAI Gym environment (see *https://gym.openai.com*) allows for the illustration of a similar, but simpler, neural network approach for a similar, but again simpler, game.

The Python code in this section works with the CartPole environment of the OpenAI Gym (see *http://bit.ly/aiif_cartpole*).[4] In this environment, a cart needs to be moved to the right or left to balance an upright pole on top of the paddle. Therefore, the action space is similar to the *Breakout* action space. The state space consists of four physical data points: cart position, cart velocity, pole angle, and pole angular velocity (see Figure 2-1). If, after having taken an action, the pole is still in balance, the agent gets a reward of 1. If the pole is out of balance, the game ends. The agent is considered successful if it reaches a total reward of 200.[5]

Figure 2-1. Graphical representation of the CartPole environment

The following code first instantiates a CartPole environment object, and then inspects the action and state spaces, takes a random action, and captures the results. The AI agent moves on toward the next round when the done variable is False:

```
In [1]: import gym
        import numpy as np
        import pandas as pd
        np.random.seed(100)

In [2]: env = gym.make('CartPole-v0')   ❶

In [3]: env.seed(100)   ❷
Out[3]: [100]

In [4]: action_size = env.action_space.n   ❸
        action_size   ❸
Out[4]: 2

In [5]: [env.action_space.sample() for _ in range(10)]   ❹
Out[5]: [1, 0, 0, 0, 1, 1, 0, 0, 0, 0]
```

---

4 Chapter 9 revisits this example in more detail.

5 More specifically, an AI agent is considered successful if it reaches an average total reward of 195 or more over 100 consecutive games.

```
In [6]: state_size = env.observation_space.shape[0]  ❺
        state_size  ❺
Out[6]: 4

In [7]: state = env.reset()  ❻
        state  # [cart position, cart velocity, pole angle, pole angular velocity]
Out[7]: array([-0.01628537,  0.02379786, -0.0391981 , -0.01476447])

In [8]: state, reward, done, _ = env.step(env.action_space.sample())  ❼
        state, reward, done, _  ❼
Out[8]: (array([-0.01580941, -0.17074066, -0.03949338,  0.26529786]), 1.0, False, {})
```

❶ Instantiates the environment object

❷ Fixes the random number seed for the environment

❸ Shows the size of the action space

❹ Takes some random actions and collects them

❺ Shows the size of the state space

❻ Resets (initializes) the environment and captures the state

❼ Takes a random action and steps the environment forward to the next state

The next step is to play the game based on random actions to generate a large enough data set. However, to increase the quality of the data set, only data that results from games with a total reward of 110 or more is collected. To this end, a few thousand games are played to collect enough data for the training of a neural network:

```
In [9]: %%time
        data = pd.DataFrame()
        state = env.reset()
        length = []
        for run in range(25000):
            done = False
            prev_state = env.reset()
            treward = 1
            results = []
            while not done:
                action = env.action_space.sample()
                state, reward, done, _ = env.step(action)
                results.append({'s1': prev_state[0], 's2': prev_state[1],
                                's3': prev_state[2], 's4': prev_state[3],
                                'a': action, 'r': reward})
                treward += reward if not done else 0
                prev_state = state
            if treward >= 110:  ❶
                data = data.append(pd.DataFrame(results))  ❷
```

```
        length.append(treward)   ❸
    CPU times: user 9.84 s, sys: 48.7 ms, total: 9.89 s
    Wall time: 9.89 s

In [10]: np.array(length).mean()   ❹
Out[10]: 119.75

In [11]: data.info()   ❺
    <class 'pandas.core.frame.DataFrame'>
    Int64Index: 479 entries, 0 to 143
    Data columns (total 6 columns):
     #   Column  Non-Null Count  Dtype
    ---  ------  --------------  -----
     0   s1      479 non-null    float64
     1   s2      479 non-null    float64
     2   s3      479 non-null    float64
     3   s4      479 non-null    float64
     4   a       479 non-null    int64
     5   r       479 non-null    float64
    dtypes: float64(5), int64(1)
    memory usage: 26.2 KB

In [12]: data.tail()   ❺
Out[12]:            s1        s2        s3        s4  a    r
    139  0.639509  0.992699 -0.112029 -1.548863  0  1.0
    140  0.659363  0.799086 -0.143006 -1.293131  0  1.0
    141  0.675345  0.606042 -0.168869 -1.048421  0  1.0
    142  0.687466  0.413513 -0.189837 -0.813148  1  1.0
    143  0.695736  0.610658 -0.206100 -1.159030  0  1.0
```

❶ Only if the total reward of the random agent is at least 100…

❷ …is the data is collected…

❸ …and the total reward recorded.

❹ The average total reward of all random games included in the data set.

❺ A look at the collected data in the `DataFrame` object.

Equipped with the data, a neural network can be trained as follows. Set up a neural network for classification. Train it with the columns representing the state data as features and the column with the taken actions as labels data. Given that the data set only includes actions that have been successful for the given state, the neural network learns about what action to take (label) given the state (features):

```
In [13]: from pylab import plt
         plt.style.use('seaborn')
         %matplotlib inline
```

```
In [14]: import tensorflow as tf
         tf.random.set_seed(100)

In [15]: from keras.layers import Dense
         from keras.models import Sequential
         Using TensorFlow backend.

In [16]: model = Sequential()  ❶
         model.add(Dense(64, activation='relu',
                         input_dim=env.observation_space.shape[0]))  ❶
         model.add(Dense(1, activation='sigmoid'))  ❶
         model.compile(loss='binary_crossentropy',
                       optimizer='adam',
                       metrics=['acc'])  ❶

In [17]: %%time
         h = model.fit(data[['s1', 's2', 's3', 's4']], data['a'],
                       epochs=25, verbose=False, validation_split=0.2)  ❷
         CPU times: user 1.02 s, sys: 166 ms, total: 1.18 s
         Wall time: 797 ms

Out[17]: <keras.callbacks.callbacks.History at 0x7ffa53685190>

In [18]: res = pd.DataFrame(h.history)  ❸
         res.tail(3)  ❸
Out[18]:     val_loss  val_acc      loss       acc
         22  0.660300  0.59375  0.646965  0.626632
         23  0.660828  0.59375  0.646794  0.621410
         24  0.659114  0.59375  0.645908  0.626632
```

❶ A neural network with one hidden layer only is used.

❷ The model is trained on the previously collected data.

❸ The metrics per training step are shown for the final few steps.

The trained neural network, or AI agent, can then play the CartPole game given its learned best actions for any state it is presented with. The AI agent achieves the maximum total reward of 200 for each of the 100 games played. This is based on a relatively small data set in combination with a relatively simple neural network:

```
In [20]: def epoch():
             done = False
             state = env.reset()
             treward = 1
             while not done:
                 action = np.where(model.predict(np.atleast_2d(state))[0][0] > \
                         0.5, 1, 0)  ❶
                 state, reward, done, _ = env.step(action)  ❷
                 treward += reward if not done else 0
             return treward
```

```
In [21]: res = np.array([epoch() for _ in range(100)])
         res ❸
Out[21]: array([200., 200., 200., 200., 200., 200., 200., 200., 200., 200., 200.,
                200., 200., 200., 200., 200., 200., 200., 200., 200., 200., 200.,
                200., 200., 200., 200., 200., 200., 200., 200., 200., 200., 200.,
                200., 200., 200., 200., 200., 200., 200., 200., 200., 200., 200.,
                200., 200., 200., 200., 200., 200., 200., 200., 200., 200., 200.,
                200., 200., 200., 200., 200., 200., 200., 200., 200., 200., 200.,
                200., 200., 200., 200., 200., 200., 200., 200., 200., 200., 200.,
                200., 200., 200., 200., 200., 200., 200., 200., 200., 200., 200.,
                200., 200., 200., 200., 200., 200., 200., 200., 200., 200., 200.,
                200.])

In [22]: res.mean()  ❹
Out[22]: 200.0
```

❶ Chooses an action given the state and the trained model

❷ Moves the environment one step forward based on the learned action

❸ Plays a number of games and records the total reward for each game

❹ Calculates the average total reward for all games

The Arcade Learning Environment (ALE) works similarly to OpenAI Gym. It allows one to programmatically interact with emulated Atari 2600 games, take actions, collect the results from a taken action, and so on. The task of learning to play *Breakout*, for example, is of course more involved, if only because the state space is much larger. The basic approach, however, is similar to the one taken here, with several algorithmic refinements.

Go

The board game Go (*http://bit.ly/aiif_go*) is more than 2,000 years old. It has long been considered a creation of beauty and art—because it is simple in principle but nevertheless highly complex—and was expected to withstand the advance of game-playing AI agents for decades to come. The strength of a Go player is measured in *dans*, in line with graduation systems for many martial arts systems. For example, Lee Sedol, who was the Go world champion for years, holds the 9th dan. In 2014, Bostrom postulated:

> Go-playing programs have been improving at a rate of about 1 dan/year in recent years. If this rate of improvement continues, they might beat the human world champion in about a decade.

Again, it was a team at DeepMind that was able to achieve breakthroughs for AI agents playing Go with its AlphaGo algorithm (see the AlphaGo page on DeepMind's website (*https://oreil.ly/y6n5N*)). In Silver et al. (2016), the researchers describe the situation as follows:

> The game of Go has long been viewed as the most challenging of classic games for artificial intelligence owing to its enormous search space and the difficulty of evaluating board positions and moves.

The members of the team used a combination of a neural network with a Monte Carlo tree search algorithm, which they briefly sketch in their paper. Recounting their early successes from 2015, the team points out in the introduction:

> [O]ur program AlphaGo achieved a 99.8% winning rate against other Go programs, and defeated the human European Go champion [Fan Hui] by 5 games to 0. This is the first time that a computer program has defeated a human professional player in the full-sized game of Go, a feat previously thought to be at least a decade away.

It is remarkable that this milestone was achieved just one year after a leading AI researcher, Nick Bostrom, predicted that it might take another decade to reach that level. Many observers remarked, however, that the beating European Go champion of that time, Fan Hui, cannot really be considered a benchmark since the world Go elite play on a much higher level. The DeepMind team took on the challenge and organized in March 2016 a best-of-five-games competition against the then 18-time world Go champion Lee Sedol—for sure a proper benchmark for elite-level human Go playing. (A wealth of background information is provided on the AlphaGo Korea web page (*https://oreil.ly/EL51T*), and there is even a movie (*https://oreil.ly/1vYQ5*) available about the event.) To this end, the DeepMind team further improved the AlphaGo Fan version to the AlphaGo Lee iteration.

The story of the competition and AlphaGo Lee is well documented and has drawn attention all over the world. DeepMind writes on its web page (*https://oreil.ly/h0WEs*):

> AlphaGo's 4-1 victory in Seoul, South Korea, on March 2016 was watched by over 200 million people worldwide. This landmark achievement was a decade ahead of its time. The game earned AlphaGo a 9 dan professional ranking, the highest certification. This was the first time a computer Go player had ever received the accolade.

Up until that point, AlphaGo used, among other resources, training data sets based on millions of human expert games for its supervised learning. The team's next iteration, AlphaGo Zero, skipped that approach completely and relied instead on reinforcement learning and self-play only, putting together different generations of trained, neural network–based AI agents to compete against each other. Silver et al.'s article (2017b) provides details of AlphaGo Zero. In the abstract, the researchers summarize:

> AlphaGo becomes its own teacher: a neural network is trained to predict AlphaGo's own move selections and also the winner of AlphaGo's games. This neural network improves the strength of the tree search, resulting in higher quality move selection and

stronger self-play in the next iteration. Starting tabula rasa, our new program AlphaGo Zero achieved superhuman performance, winning 100–0 against the previously published, champion-defeating AlphaGo.

It is remarkable that a neural network trained not too dissimilarly to the `CartPole` example from the previous section (that is, based on self-play) can crack a game as complex as Go, whose possible board positions outnumber the atoms of the universe. It is also remarkable that the Go wisdom collected over centuries by human players is simply not necessary to achieve this milestone.

The DeepMind team did not stop there. AlphaZero was intended to be a general game-playing AI agent that was supposed to be able to learn different complex board games, such as Go, chess, and shogi. With regard to AlphaZero, the team summarizes in Silver (2017a):

> In this paper, we generalise this approach into a single AlphaZero algorithm that can achieve, tabula rasa, superhuman performance in many challenging domains. Starting from random play, and given no domain knowledge except the game rules, AlphaZero achieved within 24 hours a superhuman level of play in the games of chess and shogi (Japanese chess) as well as Go, and convincingly defeated a world-champion program in each case.

Again, a remarkable milestone was reached by DeepMind in 2017: a game-playing AI agent that, after less than 24 hours of self-playing and training, achieved above-human-expert levels in three intensely studied board games with centuries-long histories in each case.

Chess

Chess is, of course, one of the most popular board games in the world. Chess-playing computer programs have been around since the very early days of computing, and in particular, home computing. For example, an almost complete chess engine called *ZX Chess*, which only consisted of about 672 bytes of machine code, was introduced in 1983 for the ZX-81 Spectrum home computer.[6] Although an incomplete implementation that lacked certain rules like castling, it was a great achievement at the time and is still fascinating for computer chess fans today. The record of *ZX Chess* as the smallest chess program stood for 32 years and was broken only by *BootChess* in 2015, at 487 bytes.[7]

It can almost be considered software engineering genius to write a computer program with such a small code base that can play a board game that has more possible permutations of a game than the universe has atoms. While not being as complex with

---

6 See *http://bit.ly/aiif_1k_chess* for an electronic reprint of the original article published in the February 1983 issue of *Your Computer* and scans of the original code.

7 See *http://bit.ly/aiif_bootchess* for more background.

regard to the pure numbers as Go, chess can be considered one of the most challenging board games, as players take decades to reach grandmaster level.

In the mid-1980s, expert-level computer chess programs were still far away, even on better hardware with many fewer constraints than the basic home computer ZX-81 Spectrum. No wonder then that leading chess players at that time felt confident when playing against computers. For example, Garry Kasparov (2017) recalls an event in 1985 during which he played 32 simultaneous games as follows:

> It was a pleasant day in Hamburg in June 6, 1985....Each of my opponents, all thirty-two of them, was a computer...it didn't come as much of a surprise...when I achieved a perfect 32-0 score.

It took computer chess developers and the hardware experts from International Business Machines Corporation (IBM) 12 years until a computer called Deep Blue was able to beat Kasparov, then the human world chess champion. In his book, published 20 years after his historic loss against Deep Blue, he writes:

> Twelve years later I was in New York City fighting for my chess life. Against just one machine, a $10 million IBM supercomputer nicknamed "Deep Blue."

Kasparov played a total of six games against Deep Blue. The computer won with 3.5 points to Kasparov's 2.5; whereby a full point is awarded for a win and half a point to each player for a draw. While Deep Blue lost the first game, it would win two of the remaining five, with three games ending in a draw by mutual agreement. It has been pointed out that Deep Blue should not be considered a form of AI since it mainly relied on a huge hardware cluster. This hardware cluster with 30 nodes and 480 special-purpose chess chips—designed by IBM specifically for this event—could analyze some 200 million positions per second. In that sense, Deep Blue mainly relied on brute force techniques rather than modern AI algorithms such as neural networks.

Since 1997, both hardware and software have seen tremendous advancements. Kasparov sums it up as follows when he refers in his book to chess applications on modern smartphones:

> Jump forward another 20 years to today, to 2017, and you can download any number of free chess apps for your phone that rival any human grandmaster.

The hardware requirements to beat a human grandmaster have fallen from $10 million to about $100 (that is, by a factor of 100,000). However, chess applications for regular computers and smartphones still rely on the collected wisdom of decades of computer chess. They embody a large number of human-designed rules and strategies for the game, rely on a large database for openings, and then benefit from the increased compute power and memory of modern devices for their mostly brute force–based evaluation of millions of chess positions.

This is where AlphaZero comes in. The approach of AlphaZero to mastering the game of chess is exclusively based on reinforcement learning with self-play of different versions of the AI agent competing against each other. The DeepMind team contrasts the traditional approach to computer chess with AlphaZero as follows (see AlphaZero research paper (*https://oreil.ly/Ur-fI*)):

> Traditional chess engines, including the world computer chess champion Stockfish and IBM's ground-breaking Deep Blue, rely on thousands of rules and heuristics handcrafted by strong human players that try to account for every eventuality in a game....AlphaZero takes a totally different approach, replacing these hand-crafted rules with a deep neural network and general purpose algorithms that know nothing about the game beyond the basic rules.

Given this tabula rasa approach of AlphaZero, its performance after a few hours of self-play-based training is exceptional when compared to the leading traditional chess-playing computer programs. AlphaZero only needs nine hours or less of training to master chess on a level that surpasses every human player and every other computer chess program, including the Stockfish engine, which at one time dominated computer chess. In a 2016 test series comprising 1,000 games, AlphaZero beat Stockfish by winning 155 games (mostly while playing white), losing just six games, and drawing the rest.

While IBM's Deep Blue was able to analyze 200 million positions per second, modern chess engines, such as Stockfish, on many-core commodity hardware, can analyze some 60 million positions per second. At the same time, AlphaZero only analyzes about 60,000 positions per second. Despite analyzing 1,000 times fewer positions per second, it nevertheless is able to beat Stockfish. One might be inclined to think that AlphaZero indeed shows some form of intelligence that sheer brute force cannot compensate for. Given that human grandmasters can maybe analyze a few hundred positions per second based on experience, patterns, and intuition, AlphaZero might inhabit a sweet spot between expert human chess player and traditional chess engine based on a brute-force approach, aided by handcrafted rules and stored chess knowledge. One could speculate that AlphaZero acquires something similar to human pattern recognition, foresight, and intuition combined with higher computational speeds due to its comparatively better hardware for that purpose.

Importance of Hardware

AI researchers and practitioners have made tremendous progress over the past decade with regard to AI algorithms. Reinforcement learning, generally combined with neural networks for action policy representation, has proven useful and superior in many different areas, as the previous section illustrates.

However, without advances on the hardware side, the recent AI achievements would not have been possible. Again, the story of DeepMind and its effort to master the game of Go with reinforcement learning (RL) provides some valuable insights. Table 2-1 provides an overview of the hardware usage and power consumption for the major AlphaGo versions from 2015 onwards.[8] Not only has the strength of AlphaGo increased steadily, but both the hardware requirements and the associated power consumption have also come down dramatically.[9]

Table 2-1. DeepMind hardware for AlphaGo

Version	Year	Elo rating[a]	Hardware	Power consumption [TDP]
AlphaGo Fan	2015	>3,000	176 GPUs	>40,000
AlphaGo Lee	2016	>3,500	48 TPUs	10,000+
AlphaGo Master	2016	>4,500	4 TPUs	<2,000
AlphaGo Zero	2017	>5,000	4 TPUs	<2,000

[a] For the Elo ratings of the world's best human Go players, see *https://www.goratings.org/en*.

The first major hardware push in AI came from GPUs. Although developed originally to generate fast high-resolution graphics for computer games, modern GPUs can be used for many other purposes as well. One of these other purposes involves linear algebra (for example, in the form of matrix multiplication), a mathematical discipline of paramount importance for AI in general and neural networks in particular.

As of mid-2020, one of the fastest consumer CPUs on the market is the Intel i9 processor in its latest iteration (with 8 cores and a maximum of 16 parallel threads).[10] It reaches, depending on the benchmark task at hand, speeds of about 1 TFLOPS or slightly above (that is, one trillion floating point operations per second).

At the same time, one of the fastest consumer GPUs on the market has been the Nvidia GTX 2080 Ti. It has 4,352 CUDA cores, Nvidia's version of GPU cores. This allows for a high degree of parallelism (for example, in the context of linear algebra operations). This GPU reaches a speed of up to 15 TFLOPS, which is about 15 times faster than the fastest consumer CPU from Intel. GPUs have been faster than CPUs for quite a while. However, one major limiting factor usually has been the relatively small and specialized memory of GPUs. This has been notably mitigated with newer GPU models, such as the GTX 2080 Ti, which has up to 11 GB of fast GDDR6 memory and high bus speeds to transfer data to and from the GPU.[11]

---

8 For more on this, see: *https://oreil.ly/im174*.

9 In the table, *GPU* stands for graphical processing unit. *TPU* stands for tensor processing unit, which is a computer chip specifically designed to process so-called tensors and operations on tensors more efficiently. More on tensors, which are the basic building blocks of neural networks and deep learning, appears later in the book and in Chollet (2017, ch. 2). *TDP* stands for thermal design power (see *http://bit.ly/aiif_tdp*).

10 *CPU* stands for central processing unit, the general purpose processors found in any standard desktop or notebook computer.

11 For a description of the GDDR6 GPU memory standard from 2018, refer to *http://bit.ly/aiif_gddr6*.

In mid-2020, the retail price for such a GPU was about $1,400, which is orders of magnitude cheaper than comparably powerful hardware a decade ago. This development has made AI research, for example, more affordable for individual academic researchers with relatively small budgets compared to those of companies such as DeepMind.

Another hardware trend is spurring further developments and adoption of AI approaches and algorithms: GPUs and TPUs in the cloud. Cloud providers such as Scaleway offer cloud instances that can be rented by the hour and that have powerful GPUs available (see Scaleway GPU instances (*https://oreil.ly/bkaH3*)). Others such as Google have developed TPUs, chips dedicated explicitly to AI, that, similar to GPUs, make linear algebra operations more efficient (see Google TPUs (*https://oreil.ly/xnmdw*)).

All in all, from the point of view of AI, hardware has improved tremendously over the last few years. In summary, three aspects are worth highlighting:

Performance
GPUs and TPUs provide hardware with heavily parallel architectures that are well suited to AI algorithms and neural networks.

Costs
The costs per TFLOPS compute power have come down significantly, allowing for smaller AI-related budgets or rather more compute power for the same budget.

Power
Power consumption has come down as well. The same AI-related tasks require less power while usually also executing much faster.

Forms of Intelligence

Is AlphaGo Zero intelligent? It's hard to tell without a specific definition of *intelligence*. AI researcher Max Tegmark (2017) defines intelligence concisely as the "ability to accomplish complex goals."

This definition is general enough to encompass more specific definitions. AlphaZero is intelligent given that definition since it is able to accomplish a complex goal, namely to win games of Go or chess against human players or other AI agents. Of course, human beings, and animals in general, are consequently considered intelligent as well.

For the purposes of this book, the following more specific definitions seem appropriate and precise enough.

Artificial narrow intelligence (ANI)

This specifies an AI agent that exceeds human-expert-level capabilities and skills in a narrow field. AlphaZero can be considered an ANI in the fields of Go, chess, and shogi. An algorithmic stock-trading AI agent that realizes a net return of consistently 100% per year (per anno) on the invested capital could be considered an ANI.

Artificial general intelligence (AGI)

This specifies an AI agent that reaches human-level intelligence in any field, such as chess, mathematics, text composition, or finance, and might exceed human-level intelligence in some other domains.

Superintelligence (SI)

This specifies an intellect or AI agent that exceeds human-level intelligence in any respect.

An ANI has the ability to reach a complex goal in a narrow field on a level higher than any human. An AGI is equally as good as any human being in achieving complex goals in a wide variety of fields. Finally, a superintelligence is significantly better than any human being, or even a collective of human beings, at achieving complex goals in almost any conceivable field.

The preceding definition of superintelligence is in line with the one provided by Bostrom in his book titled *Superintelligence* (2014):

> We can tentatively define a superintelligence as *any intellect that greatly exceeds the cognitive performance of humans in virtually all domains of interest.*

As defined earlier, the technological singularity is the point in time from which a superintelligence exists. However, which paths might lead to superintelligence? This is the topic of the next section.

Paths to Superintelligence

Researchers and practitioners alike have debated for years whether it is possible to create a superintelligence. Estimates for the materialization of the technological singularity range from a few years to decades, to centuries, to never. No matter whether one believes in the feasibility of a superintelligence or not, the discussion of potential paths to achieve it is a fruitful one.

First, the following is a somewhat longer quote from Bostrom (2014, ch. 2), which sets out some general considerations that probably are valid for any potential path to superintelligence:

> We can, however, discern some general features of the kind of system that would be required. It now seems clear that a capacity to learn would be an integral feature of the core design of a system intended to attain general intelligence, not something to be

tacked on later as an extension or an afterthought. The same holds for the ability to deal effectively with uncertainty and probabilistic information. Some faculty for extracting useful concepts from sensory data and internal states, and for leveraging acquired concepts into flexible combinatorial representations for use in logical and intuitive reasoning, also likely belong among the core design features in a modern AI intended to attain general intelligence.

These general features are reminiscent of the approach and capabilities of AlphaZero, although terms like *intuitive* might need to be defined to apply to an AI agent. But how to practically implement these general features? Bostrom (2014, ch. 2) discusses five possible paths, explored in the following sub-sections.

Networks and Organizations

The first path to a superintelligent intellect is via networks and organizations involving a possibly large number of human beings, coordinated in such a way that their individual intelligences are amplified and working synchronously. Teams, comprising people with different skills, are a simple example of such a network or organization. One example mentioned often in this context is the team of leading experts that the United States government assembled for the Manhattan Project to build nuclear weapons as a means to decisively end World War II.

This path seems to have natural limits since the individual capabilities and capacities of a single human being are relatively fixed. Evolution also has shown that human beings have difficulty coordinating within networks and organizations of more than 150 individuals. Large corporations often form much smaller teams, departments, or groups than that.

On the other hand, networks of computers and machines, such as the internet, tend to work mostly seamlessly, even with millions of compute nodes. Such networks are today at least capable of organizing humankind's knowledge and other data (sounds, pictures, videos, and so on). And, of course, AI algorithms already help humans navigate all this knowledge and data. However, it is doubtful whether a superintelligence might arise "spontaneously," say, from the internet. A dedicated effort seems required from today's perspective.

Biological Enhancements

A lot of effort is spent these days on improving the cognitive and physical performance of individual human beings. From more natural approaches, such as better training and learning methods, to those involving substances, such as supplements or smart and even psychedelic drugs, to those involving special tools, humankind today tries more than ever to systematically and scientifically improve the cognitive and physical performance of individuals. Harari (2015) describes this effort as the quest of *homo sapiens* to create a new and better version of itself, *homo deus*.

However, this approach again faces the obstacle that human hardware is basically fixed. It has evolved over hundreds of thousands of years and will probably continue to do so for the foreseeable future. But this will happen at a rather slow pace and over many generations only. It will also happen only to a very small extent, since natural selection for human beings plays a reduced role nowadays, and natural selection is what gives evolution its power for improvement. Domingos (2015, ch. 5) discusses central aspects of progress through evolution.

In this context, it is helpful to think in terms of the *versions of life* as outlined in Tegmark (2017, ch. 1):

- **Life 1.0** (biological): Life-forms with basically fixed hardware (biological bodies) and software (genes). Both are slowly evolved simultaneously through evolution. Examples are bacteria or insects.

- **Life 2.0** (cultural): Life-forms with basically fixed and slowly evolving hardware but mostly designed and learned software (genes plus language, knowledge, skills, etc.). An example is human beings.

- **Life 3.0** (technological): Life-forms with designed and adjustable hardware and fully learned and evolved software. An example would be a superintelligence created with computer hardware, software, and AI algorithms.

With technological life embodied in a machine superintelligence, the limitations of the available hardware would more or less completely vanish. Therefore, paths to superintelligence other than networks or biological enhancements might prove more promising for the time being.

Brain-Machine Hybrids

The hybrid approach to improving human performance in any field is omnipresent in our lives and symbolized by the use of diverse hardware and software tools by humans. Humankind has used tools since its beginning. Today, billions of people carry a smartphone with Google Maps on it, allowing for easy navigation even through areas and cities they have never been to before. This is a luxury our ancestors did not have, so they needed to acquire navigation skills based on objects seen in the sky or use much less sophisticated tools, such as a compass.

In the context of chess, for example, it is not the case that humans stopped playing once computers, such as Deep Blue, were proven to be superior. To the contrary, improvements in the performance of computer chess programs have made them indispensable tools for every grandmaster to systematically improve their game. The human grandmaster and the fast-calculating chess engine form a human-machine team that, everything else equal, performs better than a human alone. There are even chess tournaments during which humans play against each other while making use of a computer to come up with the next move.

Similarly, one can imagine directly connecting the human brain to a machine via appropriate interfaces such that the brain could communicate properly with the machine, exchanging data and initiating certain computational, analysis, or learning tasks. What sounds like science fiction is an active field of research. Musk, ElonFor example, Elon Musk is the founder behind a startup called Neuralink, which focuses on *neurotech*, as the field often is called.

All in all, the brain-machine hybrid seems practically feasible and likely to surpass human intelligence significantly. However, whether it will lead to superintelligence is not obvious.

Whole Brain Emulation

Another suggested path to superintelligence is to first emulate the human brain completely and then improve it. The idea here is to map a whole human brain by modern brain scanning along with biological and medical analysis methods to exactly replicate its structure in the form of neurons, synapses, and so on through software. The software is to be run on appropriate hardware. Domingos (2015, ch. 4) gives background information about the human brain and what characterizes it with regard to learning. Kurzweil (2012) offers a book-length treatment of this topic, providing detailed background information and sketching out ways to achieve whole brain emulation (WBE, sometimes also called *uploading*).[12]

On a less ambitious level, neural networks do exactly what WBE tries to achieve. Neural networks, as the name suggests, are inspired by the brain, and because they have already proven so useful and successful in many different areas, one might be inclined to conclude that WBE could indeed be considered a viable path to superintelligence. However, the necessary technology to map out the complete human brain is so far only partially available. Even if the mapping out is successful, it is not clear whether the software version would be able to do the same things that a human brain is capable of.

However, if WBE is successful, then the human brain software could, for example, be run on more powerful and faster hardware than the human body, potentially leading to superintelligence. The software could also be easily replicated then, and a large

---

12 In January 2019, an American science fiction thriller called *Replicas*, starring Keanu Reeves, was released in the US. The main theme of the movie, which proved to be a commercial failure, is the mapping of the human brain and the transfer of the mapping to machines or even other human bodies grown through cloning and replication. The movie touches on a centuries-old human desire to transcend the human body and to become immortal, at least with regard to mind and soul. Even if WBE might not lead to superintelligence, it might theoretically be a basis for achieving this kind of immortality.

number of emulated brains could be put together in a coordinated way, also potentially leading to superintelligence. The human brain software could also be enhanced in ways that humans are incapable of due to biological limitations.

Artificial Intelligence

Last, but not least, AI itself as understood in the context of this book might lead to superintelligence: algorithms, such as neural networks, run on standard or specialized hardware and are trained on available or self-created data. There are a number of good reasons why most researchers and practitioners consider this path to be the most likely one, if superintelligence is achievable at all.

The first major reason is that historically humans have been successful in engineering often by ignoring what nature and evolution have come up with to solve a certain problem. Consider airplanes. Their design makes use of the modern understanding of physics, aerodynamics, thermodynamics, and so on instead of trying to mimic how birds or insects fly. Or consider a calculator. When engineers built the first calculators, they did not analyze how the human brain performs calculations, nor did they even try to replicate the biological approach. They rather relied on mathematical algorithms that they implemented on technical hardware. In both cases, the more important aspect is the functionality or capability itself (flying, calculating). The more efficiently it can be provided, the better. There is no need to mimic nature.

The second major reason is that the number of AI's success stories seems ever increasing. For example, the application of neural networks to domains that only a few years ago seemed immune to AI superiority has proven to be a fruitful path to ANIs in many fields. The example of AlphaGo morphing into AlphaZero, mastering multiple board games in a short amount of time, is one that gives hope that the generalization can be pushed much further.

The third major reason is that a superintelligence probably only appears ("singularity") after many ANIs and maybe even some AGIs have been observed. Since there is no doubt about the power of AI in specific fields and domains, researchers and businesses alike will continue to focus on improving AI algorithms and hardware. For example, large hedge funds will push their efforts to generate alpha—a measure for the outperformance of a fund compared to a market benchmark—with AI methods and agents. Many of them have large dedicated teams working on such efforts. These global efforts across different industries might then together yield the required advancements for a superintelligence.

Artificial Intelligence

Of all the possible paths to superintelligence, AI seems to be the most promising one. Recent successes in the field based on reinforcement learning and neural networks have led to another AI spring, after a number of AI winters. Many even now believe that a superintelligence might not be as far away as we thought even a few years ago. The field currently is characterized by much faster advancements than originally predicted by experts only a short while ago.

Intelligence Explosion

The quote from Vinge (1993) mentioned earlier not only depicts a dangerous scenario for humankind after the technological singularity, but also predicts that the dangerous scenario will materialize *shortly afterwards*. Why so quickly?

If there is one superintelligence, then engineers or the superintelligence itself can create another superintelligence, maybe even a better one, since a superintelligence would have superior engineering know-how and skills compared to the creators of the initial one. The replication of the superintelligence would not be constrained by the duration of biological processes that have evolved over millions of years. It would only be constrained by the technical assembling processes for new hardware, which a superintelligence could improve upon itself and in a significant manner. Software is quickly and easily copied to new hardware. Resources might constrain the replication as well. The superintelligence might come up with better or even new ways to mine and produce the required resources.

These and similar arguments support the idea that once the technological singularity is reached, there will be an explosion in intelligence. This might happen similarly to the Big Bang, which started as a (physical) singularity and from which the known universe emerged as from an explosion.

With regard to specific fields and ANIs, similar arguments might apply. Suppose an algorithmic trading AI agent is much more successful and consistent performance-wise than other traders and hedge funds in the markets. Such an AI agent would accumulate ever more funds, both from gains of trade and by attracting outside money. This in turn would increase the available budget to improve upon the hardware, the algorithms, the learning methods, and so forth by, for example, paying above-market salaries and incentives to the brightest minds in AI applied to finance.

Goals and Control

In a normal AI context, say, when an AI agent is supposed to master the simple Cart Pole game depicted in Figure 2-1 or a more complex game such as chess or Go, the goal is in general well defined: "reach at least a reward of 200," "win the chess game through checkmate," and so on. But what about the goal(s) of a superintelligence?

Superintelligence and Goals

For a superintelligence that has superhuman capabilities, the goal might not be as simple and stable as in the preceding examples. For one, a superintelligence might come up with a new goal for itself that it considers more appropriate than its originally formulated and programmed goal. After all, it has the capabilities to do so in the same way its engineering team could. In general, it would be able to reprogram itself in any respect. Many science fiction novels and movies let us believe that such a change in the main goal is in general to the worse for humankind, which is what Vinge (1993) assumes as well.

Even if one assumes that the main goal of a superintelligence can be programmed and embedded in a nonchangeable way or that a superintelligence might simply stick to its original goal, problems might arise. Independent of the main goal, Bostrom (2014, ch. 7) argues, every superintelligence has five instrumental sub-goals:

Self-preservation
> A long enough survival of the superintelligence is necessary to achieve its main goal. To this end, the superintelligence might implement different measures, some of them maybe harmful to humans, to ensure its survival.

Goal-content integrity
> This refers to the idea that a superintelligence will try to preserve its current main goal because this increases the probability that its future self will achieve this very goal. Therefore, present and future main goals are likely to be the same. Consider a chess-playing AI agent that starts with the goal of winning a chess game. It might change its goal to avoiding the capturing of its queen at any cost. This might prevent it from winning the game in the end, and such a change in goals would therefore be inconsistent.

Cognitive enhancement
> No matter the main goal of the superintelligence, cognitive enhancements will in general prove beneficial. It might therefore strive to increase its capabilities as fast and as far as possible if this seems to serve its main goal. Cognitive enhancement is therefore a major instrumental goal.

Technological perfection
> Another instrumental goal is technological perfection. In the sense of Life 3.0, a superintelligence would not be confined to its current hardware nor to the state of its software. It could rather strive to exist on better hardware that it might design and produce, and to make use of improved software that it has coded. This would in general serve its main goal and probably allow for its faster ach-

ievement. In the financial industry, for example, high frequency trading (HFT) is a field that is characterized by a race to technological superiority.

Resource acquisition

For almost any main goal, more resources in general increase both the probability of achieving the goal and the speed at which it can be achieved. This holds particularly true when there is a competitive situation implicit in the goal. Consider an AI agent with the goal of mining as many Bitcoins as possible as fast as possible. The more resources in the form of hardware, energy, and so on the AI agent has available, the better it will be for achieving its goal. In such a situation, it might even come up with illegal practices to acquire (steal) resources from others in the cryptocurrency markets.

On the surface, instrumental goals might not seem to pose a threat. After all, they ensure that the main goal of an AI agent is achieved. However, as the widely cited example of Bostrom (2014) shows, issues might easily arise. Bostrom argues that, for example, a superintelligence with the goal of maximizing the production of paper clips might pose a serious threat to humankind. To see this, consider the preceding instrumental goals in the context of such an AI agent.

First, it would try to protect itself by all means, even with weaponry used against its own creators. Second, even though its own cognitive reasoning capabilities might suggest that its main goal is not really sensible, it might stick to it over time to maximize its chances of achieving it. Third, cognitive enhancements for sure are valuable in achieving its goal. Therefore, it would try every measure, probably many of them at the expense and to the harm of human beings, to improve its capabilities. Fourth, the better its technology, both for itself as well as for producing paper clips, the better it is for its main goal. It would therefore acquire all existing technology through buying or stealing, for instance, and build new ones that help with its goal. Finally, the more resources it has available, the more paper clips it can produce—up to the point where it builds space exploration and mining technology when resources on earth are exhausted. In the extreme, such a superintelligence might then exhaust the resources in the solar system, the galaxy, and even the whole universe.

Instrumental Goals

It is to be assumed that any form of superintelligence will have instrumental goals that are independent of its main goal. This might lead to a number of unintended consequences, such as the insatiable quest to acquire ever more resources with any means that seem promising.

The example illustrates two important points with regard to goals for AI agents. First, it might not be possible to formulate complex goals for an AI agent in a way that fully and clearly reflects the intentions of those formulating the goal. For example, a noble goal such as "Preserve and protect the human species" might lead to the killing of three-quarters of it to ensure a higher likelihood of survival of the remaining quarter. The superintelligence decides, after billions of simulations for the future on planet earth and for the human species, that this measure leads to the highest probability of achieving its main goal. Second, a seemingly well-intended and harmlessly formulated goal might lead to unintended consequences due to the instrumental goals. In the paper clip example, one problem with the goal is the phrase "as many as possible." An easy fix here would be to specify the number to, say, one million. But even this might only be a partial fix because instrumental goals, such as self-preservation, might become primary ones.

Superintelligence and Control

If bad or even catastrophic consequences are *possible* after the technological singularity, it is of paramount importance to devise measures that can at least potentially control a superintelligence.

The first set of measures is related to the proper formulation and design of the main goal. The previous section discusses this aspect to some extent. Bostrom (2014, ch. 9) provides more details under the topic *motivation selection methods*.

The second set of measures is related to controlling the capabilities of a superintelligence. Bostrom (2014, ch. 9) sketches four basic approaches.

Boxing

This is an approach that separates a superintelligence in emergence from the outside world. For example, the AI agent might not be connected to the internet. It might also lack any sensory capabilities. Human interaction can also be excluded. Given this approach to control the capabilities, a large set of interesting goals might not be achievable at all. Consider an algorithmically trading AI agent that is supposed to achieve the ANI level. Without being connected to the outside world, such as to stock trading platforms, the AI agent has no chance of achieving its goal.

Incentives

An AI agent might be programmed to maximize its reward function for purposefully designed (electronic) rewards that reward desired behavior and punish undesired behavior. Although this indirect approach gives more freedom in the goal design, it suffers to a large extent from problems similar to those of formulating the goal directly.

Stunting

This approach refers to deliberately limiting the capabilities of an AI agent, say, with respect to hardware, computing speed, or memory. This is a delicate task, however. Too much stunting and a superintelligence will never emerge. Too little stunting and the ensuing intelligence explosion will render the measure obsolete.

Tripwires

This refers to measures that should help in identifying any suspicious or unwanted behavior early on such that targeted countermeasures can be initiated. This approach, however, suffers the problem of an alarm system alerting the police of a burglary. The police might take 10 minutes to appear on the scene although the burglars left the scene 5 minutes before. Even surveillance camera footage might not help in figuring out who the burglars are.

Capability Control

All in all, it seems questionable whether a superintelligence can be properly and systematically controlled when it has reached that level. After all, its superpowers can at least in principle be used to overcome any human-designed control mechanism.

Potential Outcomes

Besides the early prophecy of Vinge (1993) that the emergence of a superintelligence will imply doomsday for humankind, what potential outcomes and scenarios are conceivable?

More and more AI researchers and practitioners warn about potential threats that uncontrolled AI might bring. Before the emergence of superintelligence, AI can lead to discrimination, social imbalances, financial risks, and so on. (A prominent AI critic in this context is Elon Musk, founder of Tesla, SpaceX, and the aforementioned Neuralink, among others.) Therefore, AI ethics and governance are intensively debated topics among researchers and practitioners. To simplify things, one can say that this group fears an AI-induced *dystopia*. Others, like Ray Kurzweil (2005, 2012), emphasize that AI might be the only way to utopia.

The problem in this context is that even a relatively low probability for a dystopian outcome is enough to be worried. As the previous section illustrates, appropriate control mechanisms might not be available given the state of the art. Against this background, it is no wonder that at the time of this writing, the first international accord on AI development has been signed by 42 countries.

As Murgia and Shrikanth (2019) report in the *Financial Times*:

> In a historic step last week, 42 countries came together to support a global governance framework for one of the most powerful emerging technologies of our times—artificial intelligence.
>
> The accord, signed by OECD countries such as the US, UK and Japan, as well as non-members, comes at a moment of reckoning for governments, which have only recently begun to grapple with the ethical and practical consequences of applying AI in industry....[T]he rapid development of AI in recent years by companies such as Google, Amazon, Baidu, Tencent and ByteDance has far outrun regulation in the area, exposing major challenges including biased AI decisions, outright fakery and misinformation, and the dangers of automated military weapons.

Utopia Versus Dystopia

Even strong proponents of a utopian future based on advancements in AI must agree that a dystopian future after a technological singularity cannot be fully excluded. Since the consequences might be catastrophic, dystopian outcomes must play a role in broader discussions about AI and superintelligence.

What about the number of superintelligences and the situation after the technological singularity? Three basic scenarios seem possible.

Singleton

A single superintelligence emerges and gains such power that no other can survive or even emerge. For example, Google dominates the search market and has reached almost a monopoly position in the field. A superintelligence might quickly reach comparable positions in many relevant fields and industries soon after its emergence.

Multipolar

Multiple superintelligences emerge about the same time and co-exist for a longer period. The hedge fund industry, for instance, has a few large players that can be considered an oligopoly given their combined market share. Multiple superintelligences could similarly co-exist, at least for a certain time, according to a divide-and-conquer agreement between them.

Atomic

A very large number of superintelligences emerge shortly after the technological singularity. Economically, this scenario resembles a market with perfect competition. Technologically, the evolution of chess provides an analogy for this scenario. While IBM in 1997 built a single machine to dominate both the computer and human chess worlds, chess applications on every smartphone today outperform every human chess player. In 2018, there were already more than three billion smartphones in use. In this context, it is noteworthy that a recent hardware trend for smartphones is to add dedicated AI chips in addition to the regular CPUs, steadily increasing the capabilities of these small devices.

This section does not argue for one or another potential outcome after the technological singularity: dystopia, utopia, singleton, multipolar, or atomic. It rather provides a basic framework to think about the potential impact of superintelligences or powerful ANIs in their respective fields.

Conclusions

Recent success stories such as those of DeepMind and AlphaZero have led to a new AI spring, with new and stronger-than-ever hopes that a superintelligence might be achievable. Currently, AI has come up with ANIs that far surpass human expert levels in different domains. Whether AGIs and superintelligences are even possible is still debated. However, it at least can not be excluded that by one path or another—recent experience points toward AI—it can indeed be achieved. Once the technological singularity has happened, it can also not be excluded that a superintelligence might have unintended, negative, or even catastrophic consequences for humankind. Therefore, appropriate goal and incentive design as well as appropriate control mechanisms might be of paramount importance to keep the emerging, ever more powerful AI agents under control, even long before the technological singularity is in sight. Once the singularity is reached, an intelligence explosion might take the control over a superintelligence quickly out of the hands of its own creators and sponsors.

AI, machine learning, neural networks, superintelligence, and technological singularity are topics that are or will be important for any area of human life. Already today, many fields of research, many industries, and many areas of human existence are undergoing fundamental changes due to AI, machine learning, and deep learning. The same holds true for finance and the financial industry, for which the influence of AI might not be as high yet due to a somewhat slower adoption. But as with other fields, AI will change finance and the way players in financial markets operate fundamentally and for good, as later chapters argue.

References

Books and papers cited in this chapter:

Barrat, James. 2013. *Our Final Invention: Artificial Intelligence and The End of the Human Era*. New York: St. Martin's Press.

Bostrom, Nick. 2014. *Superintelligence: Paths, Dangers, Strategies*. Oxford: Oxford University Press.

Chollet, François. 2017. *Deep Learning with Python*. Shelter Island: Manning.

Domingos, Pedro. 2015. *The Master Algorithm: How the Quest for the Ultimate Learning Machine will Remake our World.* United Kingdom: Penguin Random House.

Doudna, Jennifer and Samuel H. Sternberg. 2017. *A Crack in Creation: The New Power to Control Evolution.* London: The Bodley Head.

Gerrish, Sean. 2018. *How Smart Machines Think.* Cambridge: MIT Press.

Harari, Yuval Noah. 2015. *Homo Deus: A Brief History of Tomorrow.* London: Harvill Secker.

Kasparov, Garry. 2017. *Deep Thinking: Where Machine Intelligence Ends.* London: John Murray.

Kurzweil, Ray. 2005. *The Singularity Is Near: When Humans Transcend Biology.* New York: Penguin Group.

———. 2012. *How to Create a Mind: The Secret of Human Thought Revealed.* New York: Penguin Group.

Mnih, Volodymyr et al. 2013. "Playing Atari with Deep Reinforcement Learning." arXiv. December 19, 2013. *https://oreil.ly/HD20U.*

Murgia, Madhumita and Siddarth Shrikanth. 2019. "How Governments Are Beginning to Regulate AI." *Financial Times*, May 30, 2019.

Silver, David et al. 2016. "Mastering the Game of Go with Deep Neural Networks and Tree Search." *Nature* 529 (January): 484-489.

———. 2017a. "Mastering Chess and Shogi by Self-Play with a General Reinforcement Learning Algorithm." arXiv. December 5, 2017. *https://oreil.ly/SBrWQ.*

———. 2017b. "Mastering the Game of Go without Human Knowledge." *Nature*, 550 (October): 354–359. *https://oreil.ly/lB8DH.*

Shanahan, Murray. 2015. *The Technological Singularity.* Cambridge: MIT Press.

Tegmark, Max. 2017. *Life 3.0: Being Human in the Age of Artificial Intelligence.* United Kingdom: Penguin Random House.

Vinge, Vernor. 1993. "Vernor Vinge on the Singularity." *https://oreil.ly/NaorT.*

## PART II

Finance and Machine Learning

If there is one industry that would greatly benefit from the genuine adoption of artificial intelligence, it is investment management.

—Angelo Calvello (2020)

This part consists of four chapters. It covers topics central to the understanding of why data-driven finance, artificial intelligence, and machine learning will have a lasting impact on financial theory and practice.

- Chapter 3 sets the stage with important and popular financial theories and models that have been considered cornerstones of finance for decades. It covers, among others, mean-variance portfolio (MVP) theory and the capital asset pricing model (CAPM).

- Chapter 4 discusses how the programmatic availability of ever more historical and real-time financial data has reshaped finance from a theory-driven to a data-driven discipline.

- Chapter 5 is about machine learning as a general approach, abstracting from specific algorithms to a large extent.

- Chapter 6 discusses on a general level how the emergence of data-driven finance in combination with artificial intelligence and machine learning leads to a paradigm shift in finance.

CHAPTER 3
Normative Finance

The CAPM is based on many unrealistic assumptions. For example, the assumption that investors care only about the mean and variance of one-period portfolio returns is extreme.

—Eugene Fama and Kenneth French (2004)

[S]ciences that involve human beings rather than elementary particles have proven more resistant to elegant mathematics.

—Alon Halevy et al. (2009)

This chapter reviews major normative financial theories and models. Simply speaking and for the purposes of this book, a *normative theory* is one that is based on assumptions (mathematically, axioms) and derives insights, results, and more from the set of relevant assumptions. On the other hand, a *positive theory* is one that is based on observation, experiments, data, relationships, and the like and describes phenomena given the insights gained from the available information and the derived results. Rubinstein (2006) provides a detailed historical account of the origins of the theories and models presented in this chapter.

"Uncertainty and Risk" on page 62 introduces central notions from financial modeling, such as uncertainty, risk, traded assets, and so on. "Expected Utility Theory" on page 66 discusses the major economic paradigm for decision making under uncertainty: *expected utility theory* (EUT). In its modern form, EUT dates back to von Neumann and Morgenstern (1944). "Mean-Variance Portfolio Theory" on page 72 introduces the mean-variance portfolio (MVP) theory according to Markowitz (1952). "Capital Asset Pricing Model" on page 82 analyzes the *capital asset pricing model* (CAPM) according to Sharpe (1964) and Lintner (1965). "Arbitrage Pricing Theory" on page 90 sketches the *arbitrage pricing theory* (APT) according to Ross (1971, 1976).

This chapter's purpose is to set the stage for the rest of the book in the form of central normative financial theories. This is important because generations of economists, financial analysts, asset managers, traders, bankers, accountants, and others have been trained in these theories. In that sense, it is safe to say that finance as both a theoretical and practical discipline has been shaped by these theories to a large extent.

Uncertainty and Risk

At its core, financial theory deals with investment, trading, and valuation in the presence of uncertainty and risk. This section introduces on a somewhat formal level central notions related to these topics. The focus is on fundamental concepts from probability theory that build the backbone of quantitative finance.[1]

Definitions

Assume an economy for which activity is only observed at two points in time: today, $t = 0$, and one year later, $t = 1$. The financial theories discussed later in this chapter are to a large extent based on such a *static economy*.[2]

At $t = 0$, there is no uncertainty whatsoever. At $t = 1$, the economy can take on a finite number S of possible states $\omega \in \Omega = \{\omega_1, \omega_2, ..., \omega_S\}$. Ω is called the *state space*, and it holds $|\Omega| = S$ for its cardinality.

An *algebra* $\mathscr{F}$ in Ω is a family of sets with the following:

1. $\Omega \in \mathscr{F}$

2. $\mathbb{E} \in \mathscr{F} \Rightarrow \mathbb{E}^c \in \mathscr{F}$

3. $\mathbb{E}_1, \mathbb{E}_2, \ldots, \mathbb{E}_I \in \mathscr{F} \Rightarrow \cup_{i=1}^{I} \mathbb{E}_i \in \mathscr{F}$

$\mathbb{E}^c$ denotes the complement of a set $\mathbb{E}$. The power set $\wp(\Omega)$ is the largest algebra, while the set $\mathscr{F} = \{\varnothing, \Omega\}$ is the smallest algebra in Ω. An algebra is a model for *observable events* in an economy. In this context, a single state of the economy $\omega \in \Omega$ can be interpreted as an *atomic event*.

A *probability* assigns a real number $0 \leq p_\omega \equiv P(\{\omega\}) \leq 1$ to a state $\omega \in \Omega$ or a real number $0 \leq P(\mathbb{E}) \leq 1$ to an event $\mathbb{E} \in \mathscr{F}$. If the probabilities for all states are known, it holds $P(\mathbb{E}) = \Sigma_{\omega \in \mathbb{E}} p_\omega$.

---

1 See Jacod and Protter (2004) for an introductory text on probability theory.

2 In a *dynamic* economy, uncertainty would gradually resolve over time, say, on each day between today and one year later.

A *probability measure* $P: \mathscr{F} \to [0, 1]$ is characterized by the following:

1. $\forall \mathbb{E} \in \mathscr{F}: P(\mathbb{E}) \geq 0$
2. $P\left(\cup_{i=1}^{I} \mathbb{E}_i\right) = \Sigma_{i=1}^{I} \mathbb{E}_i$ for disjoint sets $\mathbb{E}_i \in \mathscr{F}$
3. $P(\Omega) = 1$

Together the three elements $\{\Omega, \mathscr{F}, P\}$ form a *probability space*. A probability space is the formal representation for *uncertainty* in the model economy. If the probability measure P is fixed, the economy is said to be under *risk*. If it is known to all agents in the economy, the economy is said to have *symmetric information*.

Given a probability space $\{\Omega, \mathscr{F}, P\}$, a *random variable* is a function $S: \Omega \to \mathbb{R}_+, \omega \mapsto S(\omega)$ that is $\mathscr{F}$-measurable. This implies that for each $\mathbb{E} \in \{[a, b[: a, b \in \mathbb{R}, a < b\}$ one has the following:

$$S^{-1}(\mathbb{E}) \equiv \{\omega \in \Omega: S(\omega) \in \mathbb{E}\} \in \mathscr{F}$$

If $\mathscr{F} \equiv \wp(\Omega)$, the *expectation* of a random variable is defined by the following:

$$\mathbf{E}^P(S) = \sum_{\omega \in \Omega} P(\omega) \cdot S(\omega)$$

Otherwise, it is defined by:

$$\mathbf{E}^P(S) = \sum_{\mathbb{E} \in \mathscr{F}} P(\mathbb{E}) \cdot S(\mathbb{E})$$

In general, it is assumed that a financial economy is *perfect*. This means, among other things, that there are no transaction costs, available assets have fixed prices and are available in infinite quantities, everything happens at the speed of light, and agents have complete, symmetric information.

Numerical Example

Assume now a simple *static* economy under *risk* $\{\Omega, \mathscr{F}, P\}$ for which the following holds:

1. $\Omega \equiv \{u, d\}$
2. $\mathscr{F} \equiv \wp(\Omega)$
3. $P \equiv \left\{ P(\{u\}) = \frac{1}{2}, P(\{d\}) = \frac{1}{2} \right\}$

Traded assets

In the economy, two assets are traded. The first is a risky asset, the *stock*, with a certain price today of $S_0 = 10$ and an uncertain payoff tomorrow in the form of the random variable:

$$S_1 = \begin{cases} S_1^u = 20 \text{ if } \omega = u \\ S_1^d = 5 \text{ if } \omega = d \end{cases}$$

The second is a risk-less asset, the *bond*, with a certain price today of $B_0 = 10$ and a certain payoff tomorrow of the following:

$$B_1 = \begin{cases} B_1^u = 11 \text{ if } \omega = u \\ B_1^d = 11 \text{ if } \omega = d \end{cases}$$

Formally, the model economy can then be written as $\mathcal{M}^2 = (\{\Omega, \mathcal{F}, P\}, \mathbb{A})$, where $\mathbb{A}$ represents the tradable assets in the form of the price vector $M_0 = (S_0, B_0)^T$ today and the market payoff matrix tomorrow of the following:

$$M_1 = \begin{pmatrix} S_1^u & B_1^u \\ S_1^d & B_1^d \end{pmatrix}$$

Arbitrage pricing

In such an economy, one can, for example, address the problem of deriving the fair value of a *European call option* on the stock with a strike price of $K = 14.5$. The arbitrage-free value of the European call option C_0 is derived by replicating the option's payoff C_1 through a portfolio ϕ of the stock and the bond. The price of the replicating portfolio must also be the price of the European call option. Otherwise, (infinite) arbitrage profits would be possible. In Python, making use of such a replication argument, this is easily accomplished:[3]

```
In [1]: import numpy as np

In [2]: S0 = 10      ❶
        B0 = 10      ❶
```

---

3 For details with regard to risk-neutral valuation and valuation by arbitrage, refer to Hilpisch (2015, ch. 4).

```
In [3]: S1 = np.array((20, 5))  ❷
        B1 = np.array((11, 11))  ❷

In [4]: M0 = np.array((S0, B0))  ❸
        M0  ❸
Out[4]: array([10, 10])

In [5]: M1 = np.array((S1, B1)).T  ❹
        M1  ❹
Out[5]: array([[20, 11],
               [ 5, 11]])

In [6]: K = 14.5  ❺

In [7]: C1 = np.maximum(S1 - K, 0)  ❻
        C1  ❻
Out[7]: array([5.5, 0. ])

In [8]: phi = np.linalg.solve(M1, C1)  ❼
        phi  ❼
Out[8]: array([ 0.36666667, -0.16666667])

In [9]: np.allclose(C1, np.dot(M1, phi))  ❽
Out[9]: True

In [10]: C0 = np.dot(M0, phi)  ❾
         C0  ❾
Out[10]: 2.0
```

❶ The prices of the stock and bond today.

❷ The uncertain payoff of the stock and bond tomorrow.

❸ The market price vector.

❹ The market payoff matrix.

❺ The strike price of the option.

❻ The uncertain payoff of the option.

❼ The replication portfolio ϕ.

❽ A check whether its payoff is the same as the option's payoff.

❾ The price of the replication portfolio is the arbitrage-free price of the option.

Arbitrage Pricing

Arbitrage pricing theory, as illustrated in the preceding example, can be considered one of the strongest financial theories with some of the most robust mathematical results, such as the *fundamental theorem of asset pricing (FTAP)*.[4] Among other reasons, this is due to the fact that prices of options, for example, can be derived from other observable market parameters, say, the share price of the stock on which the option is written. Arbitrage pricing in that sense does not take care of how to come up with a fair share price in the first place, but simply takes it as an input. Therefore, arbitrage pricing works already with few and mild assumptions, such as *absence of arbitrage*, which cannot be said of many other financial theories. Note that not even the probability measure is used to derive the arbitrage price.

Expected Utility Theory

Expected utility theory (EUT) is a cornerstone of financial theory. Since its formulation in the 1940s, it has been one of the central paradigms for modeling decision making under uncertainty.[5] Basically every introductory textbook about financial theory and the theory of investments provides an account of EUT. One of the reasons is that other central results in finance can be derived from the EUT paradigm.

Assumptions and Results

EUT is an axiomatic theory, dating back to the seminal work of von Neumann and Morgenstern (1944). *Axiomatic* here means that major results of the theory can be deduced from a small number of axioms only. For a survey of axiomatic utility theory, different variants, and applications, see Fishburn (1968).

Axioms and normative theory

On Wolfram MathWorld (*https://oreil.ly/pZqal*), you find the following definition for *axiom*: "An axiom is a proposition regarded as self-evidently true without proof."

EUT is generally based on a small set of major axioms with regard to the *preferences* of an agent when faced with choice under uncertainty. Although the definition of axiom suggests otherwise, not all of the axioms are regarded as "self-evidently true without proof" by all economists.

---

4 Again, refer to Hilpisch (2015, ch. 4) and the references given there.

5 For more background and details, see Eichberger and Harper (1997, ch. 1) or Varian (2010, ch. 12).

Von Neumann and Morgenstern (1944, p. 25) comment on the choice of axioms:

> A choice of axioms is not a purely objective task. It is usually expected to achieve some definite aim—some specific theorem or theorems are to be derivable from the axioms—and to this extent the problem is exact and objective. But beyond this there are always other important desiderata of a less exact nature: The axioms should not be too numerous, their system is to be as simple and transparent as possible, and each axiom should have an immediate intuitive meaning by which its appropriateness may be judged directly.

In that sense, a set of axioms constitutes a *normative theory* of (the parts of) the world to be modeled by the theory. The set of axioms collects the minimum set of assumptions that should be satisfied a priori and not through some formal proof or similar. Before listing a set of axioms that leads to EUT, here are some words about the preferences of an agent themselves, formally $\succeq$, when presented with choice under uncertainty.

Preferences of an agent

Assume an agent with preferences $\succeq$ is faced with the problem of investing in the two traded assets of the model economy $\mathcal{M}^2$. For example, the agent might have the option to choose between portfolio ϕ_A leading to a future payoff $A = \phi_A \cdot M_1$ or portfolio ϕ_B leading to a future payoff $B = \phi_B \cdot M_1$. The agent's preferences $\succeq$ are assumed to be defined over the future payoffs and not over the portfolios. If the agent (strongly) prefers payoff A over B, one writes $A \succ B$ and $A \prec B$ in the other case. If the agent is indifferent to the two payoffs, one writes $A \sim B$. Given these descriptions, one possible set of axioms leading to EUT is as follows:

Completeness
The agent can rank *all* payoffs relative to one another. One of the following must hold true: $A \succ B$, $A \prec B$, or $A \sim B$.

Transitivity
If there is a third portfolio ϕ_C with future payoff $C = \phi_C \cdot M_1$, it follows from $A \succ B$ and $B \succ C$ that $A \succ C$.

Continuity
If $A \succ B \succ C$, then there exists a number $\alpha \in [0, 1]$ such that $B \sim \alpha A + (1 - \alpha)C$.

Independence
From $A \sim B$ it follows that $\alpha A + (1 - \alpha)C \sim \alpha B + (1 - \alpha)C$. Similarly, from $A \succ B$ it follows that $\alpha A + (1 - \alpha)C \succ \alpha B + (1 - \alpha)C$.

Dominance
If $C_1 = \alpha_1 A + (1 - \alpha_1)C$ and $C_2 = \alpha_2 A + (1 - \alpha_2)C$, it follows from $A \succ C$ and $C_1 \succ C_2$ that $\alpha_1 > \alpha_2$.

Utility functions

A *utility function* is a way to represent the preferences $\succeq$ of an agent in a mathematical and numerical way in that such a function assigns a numerical value to a certain payoff. In this context, the absolute value is not relevant. It is rather the ordering that the values induce that is of interest.[6] Assume that $\mathbb{X}$ represents all possible payoffs over which the agent can express her preferences. A utility function U is then defined as follows:

$$U:\mathbb{X} \rightarrow \mathbb{R}_+, x \mapsto U(x)$$

If U represents the preferences $\succeq$ of an agent, then the following relationships hold true:

$$A \succ B \Rightarrow U(A) > U(B) \quad \text{(strongly prefers)}$$
$$A \succeq B \Rightarrow U(A) \geq U(B) \quad \text{(weakly prefers)}$$
$$A \prec B \Rightarrow U(A) < U(B) \quad \text{(strongly does not prefer)}$$
$$A \preceq B \Rightarrow U(A) \leq U(B) \quad \text{(weakly does not prefer)}$$
$$A \sim B \Rightarrow U(A) = U(B) \quad \text{(is indifferent)}$$

A utility function U is only determined up to a positive linear transformation. Therefore, if U represents the preferences $\succeq$, then $V = a + bU$ with $a, b > 0$ does so as well. Regarding utility functions, von Neumann and Morgenstern (1944, p. 25) summarize as follows: "So we see: If such a numerical valuation of utilities exists at all, then it is determined up to a linear transformation. I.e. then utility is a number up to a linear transformation."

Expected utility functions

Von Neumann and Morgenstern (1944) show that if the preferences of an agent $\succeq$ satisfy the preceding five axioms, then there exists an *expected utility function* of the form:

$$U:\mathbb{X} \rightarrow \mathbb{R}_+, x \mapsto \mathbf{E}^P(u(x)) = \sum_{\omega}^{\Omega} P(\omega)u(x(\omega))$$

Here, $u:\mathbb{R} \rightarrow \mathbb{R}, x \mapsto u(x)$ is a monotonically increasing, state-independent function, often called *Bernoulli utility*, such as $u(x) = \ln(x)$, $u(x) = x$, or $u(x) = x^2$.

---

6 One speaks in general of *ordinal* numbers. House numbers in streets are a good example for ordinal numbers.

In words, the expected utility function U first applies a function u to the payoff $x(\omega)$ in a certain state and then uses the probabilities for a given state to occur $P(\omega)$ to weigh the single utilities. In the special case of linear Bernoulli utility $u(x) = x$, the expected utility is simply the expected value of the state-dependent payoff, $U(x) = \mathbf{E}^P(x)$.

Risk aversion

In finance, the concept of *risk aversion* is important. The most commonly used measure of risk aversion is the Arrow-Pratt measure of *absolute risk aversion* (ARA), which dates back to Pratt (1964). Assume that an agent's state-independent Bernoulli utility function is $u(x)$. Then the Arrow-Pratt measure of ARA is defined by the following:

$$ARA(x) = -\frac{u''(x)}{u'(x)}, x \geq 0$$

The following three cases can be distinguished according to this measure:

$$ARA(x) = -\frac{u''(x)}{u'(x)} \begin{cases} > 0 & \text{risk-averse} \\ = 0 & \text{risk-neutral} \\ < 0 & \text{risk-loving} \end{cases}$$

In financial theories and models, risk aversion and risk neutrality in general are assumed to be appropriate cases. In gambling, risk-loving agents probably can be found as well.

Consider the three Bernoulli functions previously mentioned: $u(x) = \ln(x), u(x) = x$, or $u(x) = x^2$. It is easily verified that they model risk-averse, risk-neutral, and risk-loving agents, respectively. Consider, for example, $u(x) = x^2$:

$$-\frac{u''(x)}{u'(x)} = -\frac{2}{2x} < 0, x > 0 \Rightarrow \text{risk-loving}$$

Numerical Example

The application of EUT is easily illustrated in Python. Assume the example model economy from the previous section $\mathcal{M}^2$. Assume that an agent with preferences $\succeq$ decides according to the EUT between different future payoffs. The Bernoulli utility of the agent is given by $u(x) = \sqrt{x}$. In the example, payoff A_1 resulting from portfolio ϕ_A is preferred over the payoff D_1 resulting from portfolio ϕ_D.

The following code illustrates this application:

```
In [11]: def u(x):
             return np.sqrt(x)   ❶

In [12]: phi_A = np.array((0.75, 0.25))   ❷
         phi_D = np.array((0.25, 0.75))   ❷

In [13]: np.dot(M0, phi_A) == np.dot(M0, phi_D)   ❸
Out[13]: True

In [14]: A1 = np.dot(M1, phi_A)   ❹
         A1   ❹
Out[14]: array([17.75,  6.5 ])

In [15]: D1 = np.dot(M1, phi_D)   ❺
         D1   ❺
Out[15]: array([13.25,  9.5 ])

In [16]: P = np.array((0.5, 0.5))   ❻

In [17]: def EUT(x):
             return np.dot(P, u(x))   ❼

In [18]: EUT(A1)   ❽
Out[18]: 3.381292321692286

In [19]: EUT(D1)   ❽
Out[19]: 3.3611309730623735
```

❶ The risk-averse Bernoulli utility function

❷ Two portfolios with different weights

❸ Shows that the cost to set up each portfolio is the same

❹ The uncertain payoff of one portfolio…

❺ …and the other one

❻ The probability measure

❼ The expected utility function

❽ The utility values for the two uncertain payoffs

A typical problem in this context is to derive an optimal portfolio (that is, one that maximizes the expected utility) given a fixed budget of the agent $w > 0$. The following Python code models this problem and solves it exactly. Of its available budget, the agent puts roughly 60% in the risky asset and roughly 40% in the risk-less asset. The results are mainly driven by the particular form of the Bernoulli utility function:

```
In [20]: from scipy.optimize import minimize

In [21]: w = 10   ❶

In [22]: cons = {'type': 'eq', 'fun': lambda phi: np.dot(M0, phi) - w}   ❷

In [23]: def EUT_(phi):
             x = np.dot(M1, phi)   ❸
             return EUT(x)   ❸

In [24]: opt = minimize(lambda phi: -EUT_(phi),   ❹
                        x0=phi_A,   ❺
                        constraints=cons)   ❻

In [25]: opt   ❼
Out[25]:      fun: -3.385015999493397
              jac: array([-1.69249132, -1.69253424])
          message: 'Optimization terminated successfully.'
             nfev: 16
              nit: 4
             njev: 4
           status: 0
          success: True
                x: array([0.61122474, 0.38877526])

In [26]: EUT_(opt['x'])   ❽
Out[26]: 3.385015999493397
```

❶ The fixed budget of the agent

❷ The budget constraint for use with `minimize`[7]

❸ The expected utility function defined over portfolios

❹ Minimizing `-EUT_(phi)` maximizes `EUT_(phi)`

❺ The initial guess for the optimization

❻ The budget constraint applied

❼ The optimal results, including the optimal portfolio under x

❽ The optimal (highest) expected utility given the budget of $w = 10$

---

7 For details, see *http://bit.ly/aiif_minimize*.

Mean-Variance Portfolio Theory

Mean-variance portfolio (MVP) theory, according to Markowitz (1952), is another cornerstone in financial theory. It is one of the first theories of investment under uncertainty that focused on statistical measures only for the construction of stock investment portfolios. MVP completely abstracts from, say, fundamentals of a company that might drive its stock performance or assumptions about the future competitiveness of a company that might be important for the growth prospects of a company. Basically, the only input data that counts is the time series of share prices and statistics derived therefrom, such as the (historical) annualized mean return and the (historical) annualized variance of the returns.

Assumptions and Results

The central assumption of MVP, according to Markowitz (1952), is that investors *only* care about expected returns and the variance of these returns:

> We next consider the rule that the investor does (or should) consider expected return a desirable thing and variance of return an undesirable thing. This rule has many sound points, both as a maxim for, and hypothesis about, investment behavior.

> The portfolio with maximum expected return is not necessarily the one with minimum variance. There is a rate at which the investor can gain expected return by taking on variance, or reduce variance by giving up expected return.

This approach to investors' preferences is quite different to the approach that defines an agent's preferences and utility function over payoffs directly. MVP rather assumes that an agent's preferences and utility function can be defined over the first and second moment of the returns an investment portfolio is expected to yield.

Implicitly Assumed Normal Distribution

In general, MVP theory, focusing on one period portfolio risk and return only, is not compatible with standard EUT. One way of resolving this issue is to assume that returns of risky assets are normally distributed such that the first and second moments are sufficient to describe the full distribution of an asset's returns. This is something almost never observed in real financial data, as the next chapter illustrates. The other way is to assume a particular quadratic Bernoulli utility function, as shown in the next section.

Portfolio statistics

Assume a static economy $\mathcal{M}^N = (\{\Omega, \mathcal{F}, P\}, \mathbb{A})$, for which the set of tradable assets $\mathbb{A}$ consists of N risky assets, $A^1, A^2, ..., A^N$. With A_0^n being the fixed price of asset n today and A_1^n being its payoff in one year, the (simple) net returns vector r^n of asset n is defined by the following:

$$r^n = \frac{A_1^n}{A_0^n} - 1$$

For all future states having the same probability to unfold, the *expected return* of asset n is given by:

$$\mu^n = \frac{1}{|\Omega|} \sum_\omega^\Omega r^n(\omega)$$

Accordingly, the *vector of expected returns* is given by the following:

$$\mu = \begin{bmatrix} \mu^1 \\ \mu^2 \\ \vdots \\ \mu^N \end{bmatrix}$$

A *portfolio* (vector) $\phi = \left(\phi^1, \phi^2, ..., \phi^N\right)^T$, with $\phi_n \geq 0$ and $\sum_n^N \phi^n = 1$, assigns weights to each asset in the portfolio.[8]

The *expected return of the portfolio* is then given by the dot product of the portfolio weights vector and the vector of expected returns:

$$\mu^{phi} = \phi \cdot \mu$$

Now define the *covariance* between assets n and m by the following:

$$\sigma_{mn} = \sum_\omega^\Omega \left(r^m(\omega) - \mu^m\right)\left(r^n(\omega) - \mu^n\right)$$

---

8 These assumptions are not really necessary. Short sales, for instance, might be allowed without altering the analysis significantly.

The *covariance matrix* then is given by:

$$\Sigma = \begin{bmatrix} \sigma_{11} & \sigma_{12} & \cdots & \sigma_{1n} \\ \sigma_{21} & \sigma_{22} & \cdots & \sigma_{2n} \\ \vdots & \vdots & \ddots & \vdots \\ \sigma_{n1} & \sigma_{n2} & \cdots & \sigma_{nn} \end{bmatrix}$$

The *expected variance of the portfolio* is then in turn given by the double dot product:

$$\varphi^{phi} = \phi^T \cdot \Sigma \cdot \phi$$

The *expected volatility of the portfolio* accordingly is the following:

$$\sigma^{phi} = \sqrt{\varphi^{phi}}$$

Sharpe ratio

Sharpe (1966) introduces a measure to judge the risk-adjusted performance of mutual funds and other portfolios, or even single risky assets. In its simplest form, it relates the (expected, realized) return of a portfolio to its (expected, realized) volatility. Formally, the *Sharpe ratio* therefore can be defined by the following:

$$\pi^{phi} = \frac{\mu^{phi}}{\sigma^{phi}}$$

If r represents the risk-less short rate, the *risk premium* or *excess return* of a portfolio *phi* over a risk-free alternative is defined by $\mu^{phi} - r$. In another version of the Sharpe ratio, this risk premium is the numerator:

$$\pi^{phi} = \frac{\mu^{phi} - r}{\sigma^{phi}}$$

If the risk-less short rate is relatively low, the two versions do not yield too different numerical results if the same risk-less short rate is applied. In particular, when ranking different portfolios according to the Sharpe ratio, the two versions should generate the same ranking order, everything else equal.

Numerical Example

Getting back to the static model economy $\mathcal{M}^2$, the basic notions of MVP can again be easily illustrated by the use of Python.

Portfolio statistics

First, here is the derivation of the portfolio *expected return*:

```
In [27]: rS = S1 / S0 - 1   ❶
            rS  ❶
Out[27]: array([ 1. , -0.5])

In [28]: rB = B1 / B0 - 1   ❷
            rB  ❷
Out[28]: array([0.1, 0.1])

In [29]: def mu(rX):
             return np.dot(P, rX)   ❸

In [30]: mu(rS)  ❹
Out[30]: 0.25

In [31]: mu(rB)  ❹
Out[31]: 0.10000000000000009

In [32]: rM = M1 / M0 - 1   ❺
            rM  ❺
Out[32]: array([[ 1. ,  0.1],
                [-0.5,  0.1]])

In [33]: mu(rM)  ❻
Out[33]: array([0.25, 0.1 ])
```

❶ Return vector of the risky asset

❷ Return vector of the risk-less asset

❸ Expected return function

❹ Expected returns of the traded assets

❺ Return matrix for the traded assets

❻ Expected return vector

Second, the *variance* and *volatility*, as well as the *covariance matrix*:

```
In [34]: def var(rX):
             return ((rX - mu(rX)) ** 2).mean()    ❶
```

```
In [35]: var(rS)
Out[35]: 0.5625
```

```
In [36]: var(rB)
Out[36]: 0.0
```

```
In [37]: def sigma(rX):
             return np.sqrt(var(rX))    ❷
```

```
In [38]: sigma(rS)
Out[38]: 0.75
```

```
In [39]: sigma(rB)
Out[39]: 0.0
```

```
In [40]: np.cov(rM.T, aweights=P, ddof=0)    ❸
Out[40]: array([[0.5625, 0.    ],
                [0.    , 0.    ]])
```

❶ The variance function

❷ The volatility function

❸ The covariance matrix

Third, the *portfolio expected return*, *portfolio expected variance*, and *portfolio expected volatility*, illustrated for an equally weighted portfolio:

```
In [41]: phi = np.array((0.5, 0.5))
```

```
In [42]: def mu_phi(phi):
             return np.dot(phi, mu(rM))    ❶
```

```
In [43]: mu_phi(phi)
Out[43]: 0.17500000000000004
```

```
In [44]: def var_phi(phi):
             cv = np.cov(rM.T, aweights=P, ddof=0)
             return np.dot(phi, np.dot(cv, phi))    ❷
```

```
In [45]: var_phi(phi)
Out[45]: 0.140625
```

```
In [46]: def sigma_phi(phi):
             return var_phi(phi) ** 0.5    ❸
```

```
In [47]: sigma_phi(phi)
Out[47]: 0.375
```

❶ The portfolio expected return

❷ The portfolio expected variance

❸ The portfolio expected volatility

Investment opportunity set

Based on a Monte Carlo simulation for the portfolio weights ϕ, one can visualize the investment opportunity set in the volatility-return space (Figure 3-1, generated by the following code snippet).

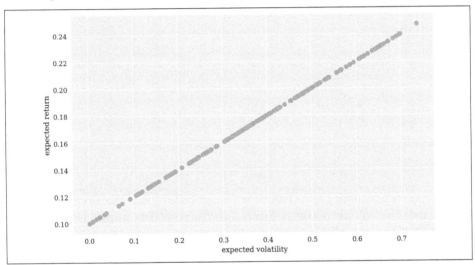

Figure 3-1. Simulated expected portfolio volatility and return (one risky asset)

Because there is only one risky asset and one risk-less asset, the opportunity set is a straight line:

```
In [48]: from pylab import plt, mpl
         plt.style.use('seaborn')
         mpl.rcParams['savefig.dpi'] = 300
         mpl.rcParams['font.family'] = 'serif'

In [49]: phi_mcs = np.random.random((2, 200))     ❶

In [50]: phi_mcs = (phi_mcs / phi_mcs.sum(axis=0)).T     ❶

In [51]: mcs = np.array([(sigma_phi(phi), mu_phi(phi))
                         for phi in phi_mcs])     ❷
```

```
In [52]: plt.figure(figsize=(10, 6))
         plt.plot(mcs[:, 0], mcs[:, 1], 'ro')
         plt.xlabel('expected volatility')
         plt.ylabel('expected return');
```

❶ Random portfolio compositions, normalized to 1

❷ Expected portfolio volatility and return for the random compositions

Consider now the case of a static three-state economy $\mathcal{M}^3$ for which $\Omega = \{u, m, d\}$ holds. The three states are equally likely, $P = \left\{\frac{1}{3}, \frac{1}{3}, \frac{1}{3}\right\}$. The set of tradable assets consists of two risky assets S and T with a fixed price of $S_0 = T_0 = 10$ and uncertain payoffs, respectively, of the following:

$$S_1 = \begin{bmatrix} 20 \\ 10 \\ 5 \end{bmatrix}$$

and

$$T_1 = \begin{bmatrix} 1 \\ 12 \\ 13 \end{bmatrix}$$

Based on these assumptions, the following Python code repeats the Monte Carlo simulation and visualizes the results in Figure 3-2. With two risky assets, the well-known MVP "bullet" becomes visible.

```
In [53]: P = np.ones(3) / 3   ❶
         P  ❶
Out[53]: array([0.33333333, 0.33333333, 0.33333333])

In [54]: S1 = np.array((20, 10, 5))

In [55]: T0 = 10
         T1 = np.array((1, 12, 13))

In [56]: M0 = np.array((S0, T0))
         M0
Out[56]: array([10, 10])

In [57]: M1 = np.array((S1, T1)).T
         M1
Out[57]: array([[20,  1],
                [10, 12],
                [ 5, 13]])
```

```
In [58]: rM = M1 / M0 - 1
         rM
Out[58]: array([[ 1. , -0.9],
                [ 0. ,  0.2],
                [-0.5,  0.3]])

In [59]: mcs = np.array([(sigma_phi(phi), mu_phi(phi))
                         for phi in phi_mcs])

In [60]: plt.figure(figsize=(10, 6))
         plt.plot(mcs[:, 0], mcs[:, 1], 'ro')
         plt.xlabel('expected volatility')
         plt.ylabel('expected return');
```

❶ New probability measure for three states

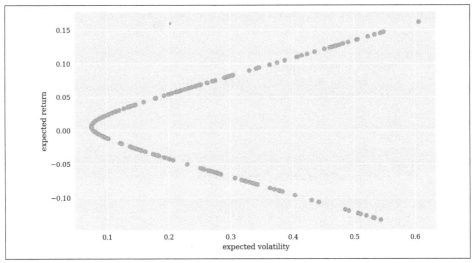

Figure 3-2. Simulated expected portfolio volatility and return (two risky assets)

Minimum volatility and maximum Sharpe ratio

Next, the derivation of the *minimum volatility* (minimum variance) and *maximum Sharpe ratio* portfolios. Figure 3-3 shows the location of the two portfolios in the risk-return space.

Although the risky asset T has a negative expected return, it has a significant weight in the maximum Sharpe ratio portfolio. This is due to diversification effects that lower the portfolio risk more than the expected return of the portfolio is reduced:

```
In [61]: cons = {'type': 'eq', 'fun': lambda phi: np.sum(phi) - 1}

In [62]: bnds = ((0, 1), (0, 1))
```

```
In [63]: min_var = minimize(sigma_phi, (0.5, 0.5),
                             constraints=cons, bounds=bnds)    ❶

In [64]: min_var
Out[64]:      fun: 0.07481322946910632
              jac: array([0.07426564, 0.07528945])
          message: 'Optimization terminated successfully.'
             nfev: 17
              nit: 4
             njev: 4
           status: 0
          success: True
                x: array([0.46511697, 0.53488303])

In [65]: def sharpe(phi):
             return mu_phi(phi) / sigma_phi(phi)    ❷

In [66]: max_sharpe = minimize(lambda phi: -sharpe(phi), (0.5, 0.5),
                               constraints=cons, bounds=bnds)    ❸

In [67]: max_sharpe
Out[67]:      fun: -0.2721654098971811
              jac: array([ 0.00012054, -0.00024174])
          message: 'Optimization terminated successfully.'
             nfev: 38
              nit: 9
             njev: 9
           status: 0
          success: True
                x: array([0.66731116, 0.33268884])

In [68]: plt.figure(figsize=(10, 6))
         plt.plot(mcs[:, 0], mcs[:, 1], 'ro', ms=5)
         plt.plot(sigma_phi(min_var['x']), mu_phi(min_var['x']),
                  '^', ms=12.5, label='minimum volatility')
         plt.plot(sigma_phi(max_sharpe['x']), mu_phi(max_sharpe['x']),
                  'v', ms=12.5, label='maximum Sharpe ratio')
         plt.xlabel('expected volatility')
         plt.ylabel('expected return')
         plt.legend();
```

❶ Minimizes the expected portfolio volatility

❷ Defines the Sharpe ratio function, assuming a short rate of 0

❸ Maximizes the Sharpe ratio by minimizing its negative value

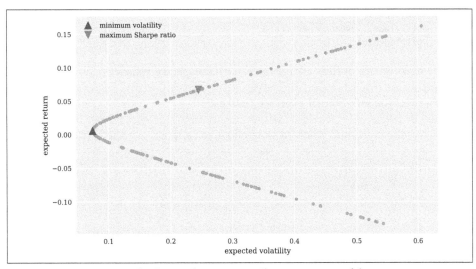

Figure 3-3. Minimum volatility and maximum Sharpe ratio portfolios

Efficient frontier

An *efficient portfolio* is one that has a maximum expected return (risk) given its expected risk (return). In Figure 3-3, all those portfolios that have a lower expected return than the minimum risk portfolio are *inefficient*. The following code derives the efficient portfolios in risk-return space and plots them as seen in Figure 3-4. The set of all efficient portfolios is called the *efficient frontier*, and agents will only choose a portfolio that lies on the efficient frontier:

```
In [69]: cons = [{'type': 'eq', 'fun': lambda phi: np.sum(phi) - 1},
                  {'type': 'eq', 'fun': lambda phi: mu_phi(phi) - target}]  ❶

In [70]: bnds = ((0, 1), (0, 1))

In [71]: targets = np.linspace(mu_phi(min_var['x']), 0.16)  ❷

In [72]: frontier = []
         for target in targets:
             phi_eff = minimize(sigma_phi, (0.5, 0.5),
                             constraints=cons, bounds=bnds)['x']  ❸
             frontier.append((sigma_phi(phi_eff), mu_phi(phi_eff)))
         frontier = np.array(frontier)

In [73]: plt.figure(figsize=(10, 6))
         plt.plot(frontier[:, 0], frontier[:, 1], 'mo', ms=5,
                 label='efficient frontier')
         plt.plot(sigma_phi(min_var['x']), mu_phi(min_var['x']),
                 '^', ms=12.5, label='minimum volatility')
         plt.plot(sigma_phi(max_sharpe['x']), mu_phi(max_sharpe['x']),
                 'v', ms=12.5, label='maximum Sharpe ratio')
```

```
plt.xlabel('expected volatility')
plt.ylabel('expected return')
plt.legend();
```

❶ The new constraint fixes a target level for the expected return.

❷ Generates the set of target expected returns.

❸ Derives the minimum volatility portfolio given a target expected return.

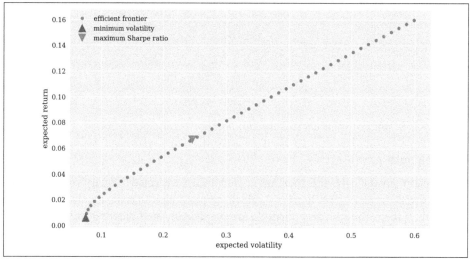

Figure 3-4. Efficient frontier

Capital Asset Pricing Model

The capital asset pricing model (CAPM) is one of the most widely documented and applied models in finance. At its core, it relates in linear fashion the expected return for a single stock to the expected return of the market portfolio, usually approximated by a broad stock index such as the S&P 500. The model dates back to the pioneering work of Sharpe (1964) and Lintner (1965). Jones (2012, ch. 9) describes the CAPM in relation to MVP as follows:

> Capital market theory is a positive theory in that it hypothesizes how investors do behave rather than how investors should behave, as in the case of modern portfolio theory (MVP). It is reasonable to view capital market theory as an extension of portfolio theory, but it is important to understand that MVP is not based on the validity, or lack thereof, of capital market theory.
>
> The specific equilibrium model of interest to many investors is known as the capital asset pricing model, typically referred to as the CAPM. It allows us to assess the relevant risk of an individual security as well as to assess the relationship between risk and

the returns expected from investing. The CAPM is attractive as an equilibrium model because of its simplicity and its implications.

Assumptions and Results

Assume the static model economy from the previous section $\mathcal{M}^N = (\{\Omega, \mathcal{F}, P\}, \mathbb{A})$ with N traded assets and all simplifying assumptions. In the CAPM, agents are assumed to invest according to MVP, caring only about the risk and return statistics of risky assets over one period.

In a *capital market equilibrium*, all available assets are held by all agents and the markets clear. Since agents are assumed to be identical in that they use MVP to form their efficient portfolios, this implies that all agents must hold the same efficient portfolio (in terms of composition) since the set of tradable assets is the same for every agent. In other words, the *market portfolio* (set of tradable assets) must lie on the efficient frontier. If this were not the case, the market could not be in equilibrium.

What is the mechanism to obtain a capital market equilibrium? Today's prices of the tradable assets are the mechanism to make sure that markets clear. If agents do not demand enough of a tradable asset, its price needs to decrease. If demand is higher than supply, its price needs to increase. If prices are set correctly, demand and supply are equal for every tradable asset. While MVP takes the prices of tradable assets as given, the CAPM is a theory and model about what the equilibrium price of an asset *should be*, given its risk-return characteristics.

The CAPM assumes the existence of (at least) one risk-free asset in which every agent can invest any amount and which earns the risk-free rate of $\bar{r}$. Every agent will therefore hold a combination of the market portfolio and the risk-free asset in equilibrium, something known as the *two fund separation theorem*.[9] The set of all such portfolios is called the *capital market line* (CML). Figure 3-5 shows the CML schematically. Portfolios to the right of the market portfolio are only achievable if agents are allowed to sell the risk-free asset short and to borrow money that way:

```
In [74]: plt.figure(figsize=(10, 6))
         plt.plot((0, 0.3), (0.01, 0.22), label='capital market line')
         plt.plot(0, 0.01, 'o', ms=9, label='risk-less asset')
         plt.plot(0.2, 0.15, '^', ms=9, label='market portfolio')
         plt.annotate('$(0, \\bar{r})$', (0, 0.01), (-0.01, 0.02))
         plt.annotate('$(\sigma_M, \mu_M)$', (0.2, 0.15), (0.19, 0.16))
         plt.xlabel('expected volatility')
         plt.ylabel('expected return')
         plt.legend();
```

---

9 For further details, see Jones (2012, ch. 9).

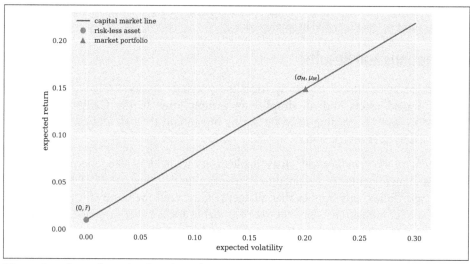

Figure 3-5. Capital market line (CML)

If σ_M, μ_M are the expected volatility and return of the market portfolio, the capital market line relating the expected portfolio return μ to the expected volatility σ is defined by the following:

$$\mu = \bar{r} + \frac{\mu_M - \bar{r}}{\sigma_M}\sigma$$

The following expression is called the *market price of risk*:

$$\frac{\mu_M - \bar{r}}{\sigma_M}$$

It expresses how much more expected return in equilibrium is needed for an agent to bear one unit more of risk.

The CAPM then relates the expected return of any tradable risky asset $n = 1, 2, ..., N$ to the expected return of the market portfolio as follows:

$$\mu^n = \bar{r} + \beta_n(\mu_M - \bar{r})$$

Here, β_n is defined by the covariance of the market portfolio with the risky asset n divided by the variance of the market portfolio itself:

$$\beta_n = \frac{\sigma_{M,n}}{\sigma_M^2}$$

When $\beta_n = 0$, the expected return according to the CAPM formula is the risk-free rate. The higher β_n is, the higher the expected return for the risky asset will be. β_n measures *risk that is nondiversifiable*. This type of risk is also called *market risk* or *systemic risk*. According to the CAPM, this is the only risk for which an agent should be rewarded with a higher expected return.

Numerical Example

Assume the static model economy with three possible future states from before $\mathcal{M}^3 = (\{\Omega, \mathcal{F}, P\}, \mathbb{A})$ with the opportunity to borrow and lend at a risk-free rate of $\bar{r} = 0.0025$. The two risky assets S, T are available in quantities of 0.8 and 0.2, respectively.

Capital market line

Figure 3-6 shows the efficient frontier, the market portfolio, the risk-less asset, and the resulting capital market line in risk-return space:

```
In [75]: phi_M = np.array((0.8, 0.2))

In [76]: mu_M = mu_phi(phi_M)
         mu_M
Out[76]: 0.10666666666666666

In [77]: sigma_M = sigma_phi(phi_M)
         sigma_M
Out[77]: 0.39474323581566567

In [78]: r = 0.0025

In [79]: plt.figure(figsize=(10, 6))
         plt.plot(frontier[:, 0], frontier[:, 1], 'm.', ms=5,
                 label='efficient frontier')
         plt.plot(0, r, 'o', ms=9, label='risk-less asset')
         plt.plot(sigma_M, mu_M, '^', ms=9, label='market portfolio')
         plt.plot((0, 0.6), (r, r + ((mu_M - r) / sigma_M) * 0.6),
                 'r', label='capital market line', lw=2.0)
         plt.annotate('$(0, \\bar{r})$', (0, r), (-0.015, r + 0.01))
         plt.annotate('$(\sigma_M, \mu_M)$', (sigma_M, mu_M),
                 (sigma_M - 0.025, mu_M + 0.01))
         plt.xlabel('expected volatility')
```

```
plt.ylabel('expected return')
plt.legend();
```

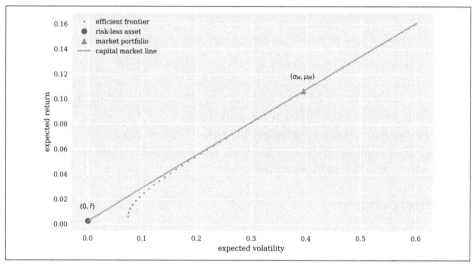

Figure 3-6. Capital market line with two risky assets

Optimal portfolio

Assume an agent with an expected utility function defined over future payoffs as follows:

$$U: \mathbb{X} \to \mathbb{R}_+, x \mapsto \mathbf{E}^P(u(x)) = \mathbf{E}^P\left(x - \frac{b}{2}x^2\right)$$

Here, $b > 0$. After some transformations, the expected utility function can then be expressed over risk-return combinations:

$$U: \mathbb{R}_+ \times \mathbb{R}_+ \to \mathbb{R}, (\sigma, \mu) \mapsto \mu - \frac{b}{2}\left(\sigma^2 + \mu^2\right)$$

Specific Quadratic Utility Function

Although the MVP theory and the CAPM both assume that investors only care about one period portfolio risk and return, this assumption is in general only consistent with the EUT when a specific form of the Bernoulli utility function is given: the quadratic utility. This type of Bernoulli function is almost exclusively mentioned and used in the context of MVP theory. Beyond that, its particular form and characteristics are usually considered inappropriate. Neither the assumption of normally distributed asset returns nor the quadratic utility function seems to be an "elegant" way of reconciling the inconsistency between EUT on the one hand and MVP theory and the CAPM on the other hand.

What portfolio combination would the agent choose on the CML? A straightforward utility maximization, implemented in Python, yields the answer. To this end, fix the parameter $b = 1$:

```
In [80]: def U(p):
             mu, sigma = p
             return mu - 1 / 2 * (sigma ** 2 + mu ** 2)  ❶

In [81]: cons = {'type': 'eq',
                 'fun': lambda p: p[0] - (r + (mu_M - r) / sigma_M * p[1])}  ❷

In [82]: opt = minimize(lambda p: -U(p), (0.1, 0.3), constraints=cons)

In [83]: opt
Out[83]:      fun: -0.034885186826739426
              jac: array([-0.93256102,  0.24608851])
          message: 'Optimization terminated successfully.'
             nfev: 8
              nit: 2
             njev: 2
           status: 0
          success: True
                x: array([0.06743897, 0.2460885 ])
```

❶ The utility function in risk-return space

❷ The condition that the portfolio be on the CML

Indifference curves

A visual analysis can illustrate the optimal decision making of the agent. Fixing a utility level for the agent, one can plot *indifference curves* in risk-return space. An optimal portfolio is found when an indifference curve is tangent to the CML. Any other indifference curve (not touching the CML or cutting the CML twice) cannot identify an optimal portfolio.

First, here is some symbolic Python code that transforms the utility function in risk-
return space into a functional relationship between μ and σ for a fixed utility level v
and a fixed parameter value b. Figure 3-7 shows two indifference curves. Every (σ, μ)
combination on such an indifference curve yields the same utility; the agent is indifferent between such portfolios:

```
In [84]: from sympy import *
         init_printing(use_unicode=False, use_latex=False)

In [85]: mu, sigma, b, v = symbols('mu sigma b v')   ❶

In [86]: sol = solve('mu - b / 2 * (sigma ** 2 + mu ** 2) - v', mu)   ❷

In [87]: sol   ❷
Out[87]:
                _____      _____
               /      2    2             /      2    2
         1 - \/  - b *sigma  - 2*b*v + 1  \/  - b *sigma  - 2*b*v + 1  + 1
         [-----------------------------, -------------------------------]
                       b                               b

In [88]: u1 = sol[0].subs({'b': 1, 'v': 0.1})   ❸
         u1
Out[88]:
               _____
              /           2
         1 - \/  0.8 - sigma

In [89]: u2 = sol[0].subs({'b': 1, 'v': 0.125})   ❸
         u2
Out[89]:
               _____
              /            2
         1 - \/  0.75 - sigma

In [90]: f1 = lambdify(sigma, u1)   ❹
         f2 = lambdify(sigma, u2)   ❹

In [91]: sigma_ = np.linspace(0.0, 0.5)   ❺
         u1_ = f1(sigma_)   ❻
         u2_ = f2(sigma_)   ❻

In [92]: plt.figure(figsize=(10, 6))
         plt.plot(sigma_, u1_, label='$v=0.1$')
         plt.plot(sigma_, u2_, '--', label='$v=0.125$')
         plt.xlabel('expected volatility')
         plt.ylabel('expected return')
         plt.legend();
```

❶ Defines SymPy symbols

❷ Solves the utility function for μ

❸ Substitutes numerical values for b, v

❹ Generates callable functions from the resulting equations

❺ Specifies values for σ over which to evaluate the functions

❻ Evaluates the callable functions for the two different utility levels

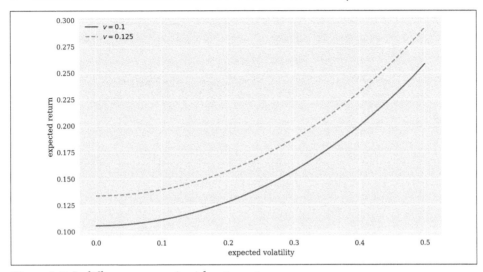

Figure 3-7. Indifference curves in risk-return space

In a next step, the indifference curves need to be combined with the CML to find out visually what the optimal portfolio choice of the agent is. Making use of the previous numerical optimization results, Figure 3-8 shows the optimal portfolio—the point at which the indifference curve is tangent to the CML. Figure 3-8 shows that the agent indeed chooses a mixture of the market portfolio and the risk-less asset:

```
In [93]: u = sol[0].subs({'b': 1, 'v': -opt['fun']})   ❶
         u
Out[93]:
                 _____
                /                        2
         1 - \/  0.930229626346521 - sigma

In [94]: f = lambdify(sigma, u)

In [95]: u_ = f(sigma_)   ❷

In [96]: plt.figure(figsize=(10, 6))
         plt.plot(0, r, 'o', ms=9, label='risk-less asset')
         plt.plot(sigma_M, mu_M, '^', ms=9, label='market portfolio')
         plt.plot(opt['x'][1], opt['x'][0], 'v', ms=9, label='optimal portfolio')
         plt.plot((0, 0.5), (r, r + (mu_M - r) / sigma_M * 0.5),
```

```
                   label='capital market line', lw=2.0)
     plt.plot(sigma_, u_, '--', label='$v={}$'.format(-round(opt['fun'], 3)))
     plt.xlabel('expected volatility')
     plt.ylabel('expected return')
     plt.legend();
```

❶   Defines the indifference curve for the optimal utility level

❷   Derives numerical values to plot the indifference curve

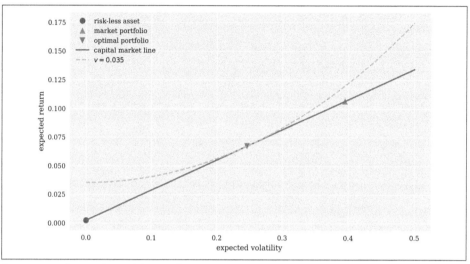

Figure 3-8. Optimal portfolio on the CML

The topics presented in this sub-section are usually discussed under *capital market theory* (CMT). The CAPM is part of that theory and shall be illustrated by the use of real financial time series data in the next chapter.

Arbitrage Pricing Theory

Early on, shortcomings of the CAPM were observed and then addressed in the finance literature. One of the major generalizations of the CAPM is the arbitrage pricing theory (APT) as proposed in Ross (1971) and Ross (1976). Ross (1976) introduces his paper as follows:

> The purpose of this paper is to examine rigorously the arbitrage model of capital asset pricing developed in Ross (1971). The arbitrage model was proposed as an alternative to the mean variance capital asset pricing model, introduced by Sharpe, Lintner, and Treynor, that has become the major analytic tool for explaining phenomena observed in capital markets for risky assets.

Assumptions and Results

The APT is a generalization of the CAPM to multiple risk factors. In that sense, APT does not assume that the market portfolio is the only relevant risk factor; there are rather multiple types of risk that together are assumed to drive the performance (expected returns) of a stock. Such risk factors might include size, volatility, value, and momentum.[10] Beyond this major difference, the model relies on similar assumptions, such as that markets are perfect, that (unlimited) borrowing and lending are possible at the same constant rate, and so on.

In its original dynamic version, as found in Ross (1976), the APT takes on the following form:

$$y_t = a + Bf_t + \epsilon_t$$

Here, y_t is the vector of M observed variables—say, the expected returns of M different stocks—at time t:

$$y_t = \begin{bmatrix} y_t^1 \\ y_t^2 \\ \vdots \\ y_t^M \end{bmatrix}$$

a is the vector of M constant terms:

$$a = \begin{bmatrix} a^1 \\ a^2 \\ \vdots \\ a^M \end{bmatrix}$$

---

10 See Bender et al. (2013) for more background information about factors used in practice.

f_t is the vector of F factors at time t:

$$f_t = \begin{bmatrix} f_t^1 \\ f_t^2 \\ \vdots \\ f_t^F \end{bmatrix}$$

B is the $M \times F$ matrix of the so-called factor loadings:

$$B = \begin{bmatrix} b_{11} & b_{12} & \cdots & b_{1F} \\ b_{21} & b_{22} & \cdots & b_{2F} \\ \vdots & \vdots & \ddots & \vdots \\ b_{M1} & b_{M2} & \cdots & b_{MF} \end{bmatrix}$$

Finally, ϵ_t is the vector of M sufficiently independent residual terms:

$$\epsilon_t = \begin{bmatrix} \epsilon_t^1 \\ \epsilon_t^2 \\ \vdots \\ \epsilon_t^M \end{bmatrix}$$

Jones (2012, ch. 9) describes the difference between the CAPM and the APT as follows:

> Similar to the CAPM, or any other asset pricing model, APT posits a relationship between expected return and risk. It does so, however, using different assumptions and procedures. Very importantly, APT is not critically dependent on an underlying market portfolio as is the CAPM, which predicts that only market risk influences expected returns. Instead, APT recognizes that several types of risk may affect security returns.

Both the CAPM and the APT relate the output variables with the relevant input factors in *linear* fashion. From an econometric point of view, both models are implemented based on linear ordinary least-squares (OLS) regression. While the CAPM can be implemented based on *univariate* linear OLS regression, the APT requires *multivariate* OLS regression.

Numerical Example

The following numerical example casts the APT in a static model, although the formulation given previously is a dynamic one. Assume the static model economy with three possible future states from the previous section, $\mathcal{M}^3 = (\{\Omega, \mathcal{F}, P\}, \mathbb{A})$. Assume that the two risky assets are now the relevant risk factors in the economy and introduce a third asset V with the following future payoff:

$$V_1 = \begin{bmatrix} 12 \\ 15 \\ 7 \end{bmatrix}$$

Although two linearly independent vectors, such as S_1, T_1, cannot form a basis of $\mathbb{R}^3$, they can nevertheless be used for an OLS regression to approximate the payoff V_1. The following Python code implements the OLS regression:

```
In [97]: M1
Out[97]: array([[20,  1],
                [10, 12],
                [ 5, 13]])

In [98]: M0
Out[98]: array([10, 10])

In [99]: V1 = np.array((12, 15, 7))

In [100]: reg = np.linalg.lstsq(M1, V1, rcond=-1)[0]    ❶
          reg    ❶
Out[100]: array([0.6141665 , 0.50030531])

In [101]: np.dot(M1, reg)
Out[101]: array([12.78363525, 12.14532872,  9.57480155])

In [102]: np.dot(M1, reg) - V1    ❷
Out[102]: array([ 0.78363525, -2.85467128,  2.57480155])

In [103]: V0 = np.dot(M0, reg)    ❸
          V0    ❸
Out[103]: 11.144718094850402
```

❶ The optimal regression parameters can be interpreted as factor loadings.

❷ The two factors are not enough to explain the payoff V_1; the replication is imperfect, and the residual values are nonzero.

❸ The factor loadings can be used to estimate an arbitrage-free price V_0 for the risky asset V.

Obviously, the two factors are not enough to fully "explain" the payoff V_1. This is not too surprising given standard results from linear algebra.[11] What about adding a third risk factor U to the model economy? Assume that the third risk factor U is defined by $U_0 = 10$ and the following:

$$U_1 = \begin{bmatrix} 12 \\ 5 \\ 11 \end{bmatrix}$$

Now, the three risk factors together can explain (replicate) the payoff V_1 fully (exactly):

```
In [104]: U0 = 10
          U1 = np.array((12, 5, 11))

In [105]: M0_ = np.array((S0, T0, U0))   ❶

In [106]: M1_ = np.concatenate((M1.T, np.array([U1,]))).T   ❷

In [107]: M1_   ❷
Out[107]: array([[20,  1, 12],
                 [10, 12,  5],
                 [ 5, 13, 11]])

In [108]: np.linalg.matrix_rank(M1_)   ❷
Out[108]: 3

In [109]: reg = np.linalg.lstsq(M1_, V1, rcond=-1)[0]
          reg
Out[109]: array([ 0.9575179 ,  0.72553699, -0.65632458])

In [110]: np.allclose(np.dot(M1_, reg), V1)   ❸
Out[110]: True

In [111]: V0_ = np.dot(M0_, reg)
          V0_   ❹
Out[111]: 10.267303102625307
```

❶ Augmented market price vector.

❷ Augmented market payoff matrix with full rank.

---

11 Of course, the payoff V_1 might lie (incidentally) in the span of the two factor payoff vectors S_1, T_1.

---

❸ Exact replication of V_1. Residual values are zero.

❹ Unique arbitrage-free price for the risky asset V.

The example here resembles the one presented in "Uncertainty and Risk" on page 62 in that enough risk factors (tradable assets) can be used to derive an arbitrage-free price for a traded asset. APT does not necessarily require that perfect replication is possible; its very model formulation contains residual values. However, if perfect replication is possible, then the residual terms are zero, as in the previous example with three risk factors.

Conclusions

Some of the early theories and models from the 1940s through the 1970s, in particular those presented in this chapter, are still central topics of finance textbooks and are still used in financial practice. One reason for this is that many of those mostly normative theories and models have a strong intellectual appeal to students, academics, and practitioners alike. They somehow "simply seem to make sense." Using Python, numerical examples for the models presented are easily created, analyzed, and visualized.

Despite theories and models such as MVP and CAPM being intellectually appealing, easy to implement, and mathematically elegant, it is surprising that they are still so popular today, for a few reasons. First, the popular theories and models presented in this chapter have hardly any meaningful empirical support. Second, some of the theories and models are even theoretically inconsistent with each other in a number of ways. Third, there has been continuous progress on the theoretical and modeling fronts of finance, such that alternative theories and models are available. Fourth, modern computational and empirical finance can rely on almost unlimited data sources and almost unlimited computational power, making concise, parsimonious, and elegant mathematical models and results less and less relevant.

The next chapter analyzes some of the theories and models introduced in this chapter on the basis of real financial data. While in the early years of quantitative finance, data was a scarce resource, today even students have access to a wealth of financial data and open source tools that allow the comprehensive analysis of financial theories and models based on real-world data. Empirical finance has always been an important sister discipline to theoretical finance. However, financial theory has usually driven empirical finance to a large extent. The new area of *data-driven finance* might lead to a lasting shift in the relative importance of theory as compared to data in finance.

References

Books and papers cited in this chapter:

Bender, Jennifer et al. 2013. "Foundations of Factor Investing." *MSCI Research Insight*. *http://bit.ly/aiif_factor_invest*.

Calvello, Angelo. 2020. "Fund Managers Must Embrace AI Disruption." *Financial Times*, January 15, 2020. *http://bit.ly/aiif_ai_disrupt*.

Eichberger, Jürgen, and Ian R. Harper. 1997. *Financial Economics.* New York: Oxford University Press.

Fishburn, Peter. 1968. "Utility Theory." *Management Science* 14 (5): 335-378.

Fama, Eugene F. and Kenneth R. French. 2004. "The Capital Asset Pricing Model: Theory and Evidence." *Journal of Economic Perspectives* 18 (3): 25-46.

Halevy, Alon, Peter Norvig, and Fernando Pereira. 2009. "The Unreasonable Effectiveness of Data." *IEEE Intelligent Systems*, Expert Opinion.

Hilpisch, Yves. 2015. *Derivatives Analytics with Python: Data Analysis, Models, Simulation, Calibration, and Hedging.* Wiley Finance.

Jacod, Jean, and Philip Protter. 2004. *Probability Essentials.* 2nd ed. Berlin: Springer.

Johnstone, David and Dennis Lindley. 2013. "Mean-Variance and Expected Utility: The Borch Paradox." *Statistical Science* 28 (2): 223-237.

Jones, Charles P. 2012. *Investments: Analysis and Management.* 12th ed. Hoboken: John Wiley & Sons.

Karni, Edi. 2014. "Axiomatic Foundations of Expected Utility and Subjective Probability." In *Handbook of the Economics of Risk and Uncertainty*, edited by Mark J. Machina and W. Kip Viscusi, 1-39. Oxford: North Holland.

Lintner, John. 1965. "The Valuation of Risk Assets and the Selection of Risky Investments in Stock Portfolios and Capital Budgets." *Review of Economics and Statistics* 47 (1): 13-37.

Markowitz, Harry. 1952. "Portfolio Selection." *Journal of Finance* 7 (1): 77-91.

Pratt, John W. 1964. "Risk Aversion in the Small and in the Large." *Econometrica* 32 (1/2): 122-136.

Ross, Stephen A. 1971. "Portfolio and Capital Market Theory with Arbitrary Preferences and Distributions: The General Validity of the Mean-Variance Approach in Large Markets." Working Paper No. 12-72, Rodney L. White Center for Financial Research.

———. 1976. "The Arbitrage Theory of Capital Asset Pricing." *Journal of Economic Theory* 13: 341-360.

Rubinstein, Mark. 2006. *A History of the Theory of Investments—My Annotated Bibliography*. Hoboken: Wiley Finance.

Sharpe, William F. 1964. "Capital Asset Prices: A Theory of Market Equilibrium under Conditions of Risk." *Journal of Finance* 19 (3): 425-442.

———. 1966. "Mutual Fund Performance." *Journal of Business* 39 (1): 119-138.

Varian, Hal R. 2010. *Intermediate Microeconomics: A Modern Approach*. 8th ed. New York & London: W.W. Norton & Company.

von Neumann, John, and Oskar Morgenstern. 1944. *Theory of Games and Economic Behavior*. Princeton: Princeton University Press.

## CHAPTER 4

Data-Driven Finance

If artificial intelligence is the new electricity, big data is the oil that powers the generators.

—Kai-Fu Lee (2018)

Nowadays, analysts sift through non-traditional information such as satellite imagery and credit card data, or use artificial intelligence techniques such as machine learning and natural language processing to glean fresh insights from traditional sources such as economic data and earnings-call transcripts.

—Robin Wigglesworth (2019)

This chapter discusses central aspects of data-driven finance. For the purposes of this book, *data-driven finance* is understood to be a financial context (theory, model, application, and so on) that is primarily driven by and based on insights gained from data.

"Scientific Method" on page 100 discusses the scientific method, which is about generally accepted principles that should guide scientific effort. "Financial Econometrics and Regression" on page 101 is about financial econometrics and related topics. "Data Availability" on page 104 sheds light on which types of (financial) data are available today and in what quality and quantity via programmatic APIs. "Normative Theories Revisited" on page 117 revisits the normative theories of Chapter 3 and analyzes them based on real financial time series data. Also based on real financial data, "Debunking Central Assumptions" on page 143 debunks two of the most commonly found assumptions in financial models and theories: *normality of returns* and *linear relationships*.

Scientific Method

The *scientific method* refers to a set of generally accepted principles that should guide any scientific project. Wikipedia (*https://oreil.ly/AX8jv*) defines the scientific method as follows:

> The scientific method is an empirical method of acquiring knowledge that has characterized the development of science since at least the 17th century. It involves careful observation, applying rigorous skepticism about what is observed, given that cognitive assumptions can distort how one interprets the observation. It involves formulating hypotheses, via induction, based on such observations; experimental and measurement-based testing of deductions drawn from the hypotheses; and refinement (or elimination) of the hypotheses based on the experimental findings. These are principles of the scientific method, as distinguished from a definitive series of steps applicable to all scientific enterprises.

Given this definition, normative finance, as discussed in Chapter 3, is in stark contrast to the scientific method. Normative financial theories mostly rely on assumptions and axioms in combination with *deduction* as the major analytical method to arrive at their central results.

- Expected utility theory (EUT) *assumes* that agents have the same utility function no matter what state of the world unfolds and that they maximize expected utility under conditions of uncertainty.

- Mean-variance portfolio (MVP) theory describes how investors *should* invest under conditions of uncertainty *assuming* that only the expected return and the expected volatility of a portfolio over one period count.

- The capital asset pricing model (CAPM) *assumes* that only the nondiversifiable market risk *explains* the expected return and the expected volatility of a stock over one period.

- Arbitrage pricing theory (APT) *assumes* that a number of identifiable risk factors *explains* the expected return and the expected volatility of a stock over time; admittedly, compared to the other theories, the formulation of APT is rather broad and allows for wide-ranging interpretations.

What characterizes the aforementioned normative financial theories is that they were originally derived under certain assumptions and axioms using "pen and paper" only, without any recourse to real-world data or observations. From a historical point of view, many of these theories were rigorously tested against real-world data only long after their publication dates. This can be explained primarily with better data availability and increased computational capabilities over time. After all, data and computation are the main ingredients for the application of statistical methods in practice. The discipline at the intersection of mathematics, statistics, and finance that applies such methods to financial market data is typically called *financial econometrics*, the topic of the next section.

Financial Econometrics and Regression

Adapting the definition provided by Investopedia (*https://oreil.ly/QErpB*) for *econometrics*, one can define *financial econometrics* as follows:

> [Financial] econometrics is the quantitative application of statistical and mathematical models using [financial] data to develop financial theories or test existing hypotheses in finance and to forecast future trends from historical data. It subjects real-world [financial] data to statistical trials and then compares and contrasts the results against the [financial] theory or theories being tested.

Alexander (2008b) provides a thorough and broad introduction to the field of financial econometrics. The second chapter of the book covers single- and multifactor models, such as the CAPM and APT. Alexander (2008b) is part of a series of four books called *Market Risk Analysis*. The first in the series, Alexander (2008a), covers theoretical background concepts, topics, and methods, such as MVP theory and the CAPM themselves. The book by Campbell (2018) is another comprehensive resource for financial theory and related econometric research.

One of the major tools in financial econometrics is *regression*, in both its univariate and multivariate forms. Regression is also a central tool in *statistical learning* in general. What is the difference between traditional mathematics and statistical learning? Although there is no general answer to this question (after all, statistics is a sub-field of mathematics), a simple example should emphasize a major difference relevant to the context of this book.

First is the standard mathematical way. Assume a mathematical function is given as follows:

$$f:\mathbb{R} \to \mathbb{R}_+, x \mapsto 2 + \frac{1}{2}x$$

Given multiple values of $x_i, i = 1, 2, ..., n$, one can derive function values for f by applying the above definition:

$$y_i = f(x_i), i = 1, 2, ..., n$$

The following Python code illustrates this based on a simple numerical example:

```
In [1]: import numpy as np

In [2]: def f(x):
            return 2 + 1 / 2 * x
```

```
In [3]: x = np.arange(-4, 5)
        x
Out[3]: array([-4, -3, -2, -1,  0,  1,  2,  3,  4])

In [4]: y = f(x)
        y
Out[4]: array([0. , 0.5, 1. , 1.5, 2. , 2.5, 3. , 3.5, 4. ])
```

Second is the approach taken in statistical learning. Whereas in the preceding example, the function comes first and then the data is derived, this sequence is reversed in statistical learning. Here, the data is generally given and a functional relationship is to be found. In this context, x is often called the *independent* variable and y the *dependent* variable. Consequently, consider the following data:

$$(x_i, y_i), i = 1, 2, ..., n$$

The problem is to find, for example, parameters α, β such that:

$$\hat{f}(x_i) \equiv \alpha + \beta x_i = \hat{y}_i \approx y_i, i = 1, 2, ..., n$$

Another way of writing this is by including residual values $\epsilon_i, i = 1, 2, ..., n$:

$$\alpha + \beta x_i + \epsilon_i = y_i, i = 1, 2, ..., n$$

In the context of ordinary least-squares (OLS) regression, α, β are chosen to minimize the mean-squared error between the approximated values $\hat{y}_i$ and the real values y_i. The minimization problem, then, is as follows:

$$\min_{\alpha, \beta} \frac{1}{n} \sum_i^n (\hat{y}_i - y_i)^2$$

In the case of *simple OLS regression*, as described previously, the optimal solutions are known in closed form and are as follows:

$$\begin{cases} \beta = \dfrac{\text{Cov}(x, y)}{\text{Var}(x)} \\ \alpha = \bar{y} - \beta \bar{x} \end{cases}$$

Here, Cov() stands for the *covariance*, Var() for the *variance*, and $\bar{x}, \bar{y}$ for the *mean values* of x, y.

Returning to the preceding numerical example, these insights can be used to derive optimal parameters α, β and, in this particular case, to recover the original definition of $f(x)$:

```
In [5]: x
Out[5]: array([-4, -3, -2, -1,  0,  1,  2,  3,  4])

In [6]: y
Out[6]: array([0. , 0.5, 1. , 1.5, 2. , 2.5, 3. , 3.5, 4. ])

In [7]: beta = np.cov(x, y, ddof=0)[0, 1] / x.var()    ❶
        beta    ❶
Out[7]: 0.49999999999999994

In [8]: alpha = y.mean() - beta * x.mean()    ❷
        alpha    ❷
Out[8]: 2.0

In [9]: y_ = alpha + beta * x    ❸

In [10]: np.allclose(y_, y)    ❹
Out[10]: True
```

❶ β as derived from the covariance matrix and the variance

❷ α as derived from β and the mean values

❸ Estimated values $\hat{y}_i, i = 1, 2, ..., n$, given α, β

❹ Checks whether $\hat{y}_i, y_i$ values are numerically equal

The preceding example and those in Chapter 1 illustrate that the application of OLS regression to a given data set is in general straightforward. There are more reasons why OLS regression has become one of the central tools in econometrics and financial econometrics. Among them are the following:

Centuries old
    The least-squares approach, particularly in combination with regression, has been used for more than 200 years.[1]

Simplicity
    The mathematics behind OLS regression is easy to understand and easy to implement in programming.

---

1 See, for example, Kopf (2015).

Scalability

There is basically no limit regarding the data size to which OLS regression can be applied.

Flexibility

OLS regression can be applied to a wide range of problems and data sets.

Speed

OLS regression is fast to evaluate, even on larger data sets.

Availability

Efficient implementations in Python and many other programming languages are readily available.

However, as easy and straightforward as the application of OLS regression might be in general, the method rests on a number of assumptions—most of them related to the residuals—that are not always satisfied in practice.

Linearity

The model is linear in its parameters, with regard to both the coefficients and the residuals.

Independence

Independent variables are not perfectly (to a high degree) correlated with each other (no *multicollinearity*).

Zero mean

The mean value of the residuals is (close to) zero.

No correlation

Residuals are not (strongly) correlated with the independent variables.

Homoscedasticity

The standard deviation of the residuals is (almost) constant.

No autocorrelation

The residuals are not (strongly) correlated with each other.

In practice, it is in general quite simple to test for the validity of the assumptions given a specific data set.

Data Availability

Financial econometrics is driven by statistical methods, such as regression, and the availability of financial data. From the 1950s to the 1990s, and even into the early 2000s, theoretical and empirical financial research was mainly driven by relatively small data sets compared to today's standards, and was mostly comprised of

---

end-of-day (EOD) data. Data availability is something that has changed dramatically over the last decade or so, with more and more types of financial and other data available in ever increasing granularity, quantity, and velocity.

Programmatic APIs

With regard to data-driven finance, what is important is not only what data is available but also how it can be accessed and processed. For quite a while now, finance professionals have relied on data terminals from companies such as Refinitiv (see Eikon Terminal (*https://oreil.ly/gcBey*)) or Bloomberg (see Bloomberg Terminal (*https://oreil.ly/Y1dEC*)), to mention just two of the leading providers. Newspapers, magazines, financial reports, and the like have long been replaced by such terminals as the primary source for financial information. However, the sheer volume and variety of data provided by such terminals cannot be consumed systematically by a single user or even large groups of finance professionals. Therefore, the major breakthrough in data-driven finance is to be seen in the *programmatic availability* of data via application programming interfaces (APIs) that allow the usage of computer code to select, retrieve, and process arbitrary data sets.

The remainder of this section is devoted to the illustration of such APIs by which even academics and retail investors can retrieve a wealth of different data sets. Before such examples are provided, Table 4-1 offers an overview of categories of data that are in general relevant in a financial context, as well as typical examples. In the table, *structured* data refers to numerical data types that often come in tabular structures, while *unstructured* data refers to data in the form of standard text that often has no structure beyond headers or paragraphs, for example. *Alternative* data refers to data types that are typically *not* considered financial data.

Table 4-1. Relevant types of financial data

Time	Structured data	Unstructured data	Alternative data
Historical	Prices, fundamentals	News, texts	Web, social media, satellites
Streaming	Prices, volumes	News, filings	Web, social media, satellites, Internet of Things

Structured Historical Data

First, structured historical data types will be retrieved programmatically. To this end, the following Python code uses the Eikon Data API (*https://oreil.ly/uDMSk*).[2]

---

2 This data service is only available via a paid subscription.

To access data via the Eikon Data API, a local application, such as Refinitiv Workspace (*https://oreil.ly/NPEav*), must be running and the API access must be configured on the Python level:

```
In [11]: import eikon as ek
         import configparser
```

```
In [12]: c = configparser.ConfigParser()
         c.read('../aiif.cfg')
         ek.set_app_key(c['eikon']['app_id'])
         2020-08-04 10:30:18,059 P[14938] [MainThread 4521459136] Error on handshake
             port 9000 : ReadTimeout(ReadTimeout())
```

If these requirements are met, historical structured data can be retrieved via a single function call. For example, the following Python code retrieves EOD data for a set of symbols and a specified time interval:

```
In [14]: symbols = ['AAPL.O', 'MSFT.O', 'NFLX.O', 'AMZN.O']   ❶
```

```
In [15]: data = ek.get_timeseries(symbols,
                                   fields='CLOSE',
                                   start_date='2019-07-01',
                                   end_date='2020-07-01')   ❷
```

```
In [16]: data.info()   ❸
         <class 'pandas.core.frame.DataFrame'>
         DatetimeIndex: 254 entries, 2019-07-01 to 2020-07-01
         Data columns (total 4 columns):
          #   Column   Non-Null Count  Dtype
         ---  ------   --------------  -----
          0   AAPL.O   254 non-null    float64
          1   MSFT.O   254 non-null    float64
          2   NFLX.O   254 non-null    float64
          3   AMZN.O   254 non-null    float64
         dtypes: float64(4)
         memory usage: 9.9 KB
```

```
In [17]: data.tail()   ❹
Out[17]: CLOSE        AAPL.O   MSFT.O   NFLX.O    AMZN.O
         Date
         2020-06-25   364.84   200.34   465.91   2754.58
         2020-06-26   353.63   196.33   443.40   2692.87
         2020-06-29   361.78   198.44   447.24   2680.38
         2020-06-30   364.80   203.51   455.04   2758.82
         2020-07-01   364.11   204.70   485.64   2878.70
```

❶ Defines a list of `RICs` (symbols) to retrieve data for[3]

❷ Retrieves EOD `Close` prices for the list of `RICs`

❸ Shows the meta information for the returned `DataFrame` object

❹ Shows the final rows of the `DataFrame` object

Similarly, one-minute bars with `OHLC` fields can be retrieved with appropriate adjustments of the parameters:

```
In [18]: data = ek.get_timeseries('AMZN.O',
                                   fields='*',
                                   start_date='2020-08-03',
                                   end_date='2020-08-04',
                                   interval='minute')  ❶
```

```
In [19]: data.info()
         <class 'pandas.core.frame.DataFrame'>
         DatetimeIndex: 911 entries, 2020-08-03 08:01:00 to 2020-08-04 00:00:00
         Data columns (total 6 columns):
          #   Column  Non-Null Count  Dtype
         ---  ------  --------------  -----
          0   HIGH    911 non-null    float64
          1   LOW     911 non-null    float64
          2   OPEN    911 non-null    float64
          3   CLOSE   911 non-null    float64
          4   COUNT   911 non-null    float64
          5   VOLUME  911 non-null    float64
         dtypes: float64(6)
         memory usage: 49.8 KB
```

```
In [20]: data.head()
Out[20]: AMZN.O                 HIGH     LOW     OPEN    CLOSE  COUNT  VOLUME
         Date
         2020-08-03 08:01:00  3190.00  3176.03  3176.03  3178.17   18.0   383.0
         2020-08-03 08:02:00  3183.02  3176.03  3180.00  3177.01   15.0   513.0
         2020-08-03 08:03:00  3179.91  3177.05  3179.91  3177.05    5.0    14.0
         2020-08-03 08:04:00  3184.00  3179.91  3179.91  3184.00    8.0   102.0
         2020-08-03 08:05:00  3184.91  3182.91  3183.30  3184.00   12.0   403.0
```

❶ Retrieves one-minute bars with all available fields for a single `RIC`

---

3 RIC stands for *Reuters Instrument Code*.

One can retrieve more than structured financial time series data from the Eikon Data API. Fundamental data can also be retrieved for a number of RICs and a number of different data fields at the same time, as the following Python code illustrates:

```
In [21]: data_grid, err = ek.get_data(['AAPL.O', 'IBM', 'GOOG.O', 'AMZN.O'],
                                       ['TR.TotalReturnYTD', 'TR.WACCBeta',
                                        'YRHIGH', 'YRLOW',
                                        'TR.Ebitda', 'TR.GrossProfit'])  ❶

In [22]: data_grid
Out[22]:    Instrument  YTD Total Return      Beta   YRHIGH      YRLOW        EBITDA  \
         0       AAPL.O         49.141271  1.221249   425.66   192.5800  7.647700e+10
         1          IBM         -5.019570  1.208156   158.75    90.5600  1.898600e+10
         2       GOOG.O         10.278829  1.067084  1586.99  1013.5361  4.757900e+10
         3       AMZN.O         68.406897  1.338106  3344.29  1626.0318  3.025600e+10

            Gross Profit
         0   98392000000
         1   36488000000
         2   89961000000
         3  114986000000
```

❶ Retrieves data for multiple RICs and multiple data fields

Programmatic Data Availability

Basically all structured financial data is available nowadays in programmatic fashion. Financial time series data, in this context, is the paramount example. However, other structured data types such as fundamental data are available in the same way, simplifying the work of quantitative analysts, traders, portfolio managers, and the like significantly.

Structured Streaming Data

Many applications in finance require real-time structured data, such as in algorithmic trading or market risk management. The following Python code makes use of the API of the Oanda Trading Platform (*http://oanda.com*) and streams in real time a number of time stamps, bid quotes, and ask quotes for the Bitcoin price in USD:

```
In [23]: import tpqoa

In [24]: oa = tpqoa.tpqoa('../aiif.cfg')  ❶

In [25]: oa.stream_data('BTC_USD', stop=5)  ❷
         2020-08-04T08:30:38.621075583Z 11298.8 11334.8
         2020-08-04T08:30:50.485678488Z 11298.3 11334.3
         2020-08-04T08:30:50.801666847Z 11297.3 11333.3
```

```
2020-08-04T08:30:51.326269990Z 11296.0 11332.0
2020-08-04T08:30:54.423973431Z 11296.6 11332.6
```

❶ Connects to the Oanda API

❷ Streams a fixed number of ticks for a given symbol

Printing out the streamed data fields is, of course, only for illustration. Certain financial applications might require sophisticated processing of the retrieved data and the generation of signals or statistics, for instance. Particularly during weekdays and trading hours, the number of price ticks streamed for financial instruments increases steadily, demanding powerful data processing capabilities on the end of financial institutions that need to process such data in real time or at least in near-real time ("near time").

The significance of this observation becomes clear when looking at Apple Inc. stock prices. One can calculate that there are roughly $252 \cdot 40 = 10,080$ EOD closing quotes for the Apple stock over a period of 40 years. (Apple Inc. went public on December 12, 1980.) The following code retrieves *tick data* for the Apple stock price for one hour only. The retrieved data set, which might not even be complete for the given time interval, has 50,000 data rows, or five times as many tick quotes as the EOD quotes accumulated over 40 years of trading:

```
In [26]: data = ek.get_timeseries('AAPL.O',
                                  fields='*',
                                  start_date='2020-08-03 15:00:00',
                                  end_date='2020-08-03 16:00:00',
                                  interval='tick')  ❶

In [27]: data.info()
         <class 'pandas.core.frame.DataFrame'>
         DatetimeIndex: 50000 entries, 2020-08-03 15:26:24.889000 to 2020-08-03
          15:59:59.762000
         Data columns (total 2 columns):
          #   Column  Non-Null Count  Dtype
         ---  ------  --------------  -----
          0   VALUE   49953 non-null  float64
          1   VOLUME  50000 non-null  float64
         dtypes: float64(2)
         memory usage: 1.1 MB

In [28]: data.head()
Out[28]: AAPL.O                   VALUE  VOLUME
         Date
         2020-08-03 15:26:24.889  439.06   175.0
         2020-08-03 15:26:24.889  439.08     3.0
         2020-08-03 15:26:24.890  439.08   100.0
         2020-08-03 15:26:24.890  439.08     5.0
         2020-08-03 15:26:24.899  439.10    35.0
```

❶ Retrieves tick data for the Apple stock price

EOD Versus Tick Data

Most of the financial theories still applied today have their origin in when EOD data was basically the only type of financial data available. Today, financial institutions, and even retail traders and investors, are confronted with never-ending streams of real-time data. The example of Apple stock illustrates that for a single stock during one trading hour, there might be four times as many ticks coming in as the amount of EOD data accumulated over a period of 40 years. This not only challenges actors in financial markets, but also puts into question whether existing financial theories can be applied to such an environment at all.

Unstructured Historical Data

Many important data sources in finance provide unstructured data only, such as financial news or company filings. Undoubtedly, machines are much better and faster than humans at crunching large amounts of structured, numerical data. However, recent advances in *natural language processing* (NLP) make machines better and faster at processing financial news too, for example. In 2020, data service providers ingest roughly 1.5 million news articles on a daily basis. It is clear that this vast amount of text-based data cannot be processed properly by human beings.

Fortunately, unstructured data is also to a large extent available these days via programmatic APIs. The following Python code retrieves a number of news articles from the Eikon Data API related to the company Tesla, Inc. and its production. One article is selected and shown in full:

```
In [29]: news = ek.get_news_headlines('R:TSLA.O PRODUCTION',
                                       date_from='2020-06-01',
                                       date_to='2020-08-01',
                                       count=7
                                       ) ❶
```

```
In [30]: news
Out[30]:                                            versionCreated  \
         2020-07-29 11:02:31.276  2020-07-29 11:02:31.276000+00:00
         2020-07-28 00:59:48.000       2020-07-28 00:59:48+00:00
         2020-07-23 21:20:36.090  2020-07-23 21:20:36.090000+00:00
         2020-07-23 08:22:17.000       2020-07-23 08:22:17+00:00
         2020-07-23 07:08:48.000       2020-07-23 07:46:56+00:00
         2020-07-23 00:55:54.000       2020-07-23 00:55:54+00:00
         2020-07-22 21:35:42.640  2020-07-22 22:13:26.597000+00:00


                                                               text  \
         2020-07-29 11:02:31.276  Tesla Launches Hiring Spree in China as It Pre...
```

```
2020-07-28 00:59:48.000      Tesla hiring in Shanghai as production ramps up
2020-07-23 21:20:36.090     Tesla speeds up Model 3 production in Shanghai
2020-07-23 08:22:17.000   UPDATE 1-'Please mine more nickel,' Musk urges...
2020-07-23 07:08:48.000   'Please mine more nickel,' Musk urges as Tesla...
2020-07-23 00:55:54.000   USA-Tesla choisit le Texas pour la production ...
2020-07-22 21:35:42.640   TESLA INC - THE REAL LIMITATION ON TESLA GROWT...

                                                                  storyId  \
2020-07-29 11:02:31.276   urn:newsml:reuters.com:20200729:nCXG3W8s9X:1
2020-07-28 00:59:48.000   urn:newsml:reuters.com:20200728:nL3N2EY3PG:8
2020-07-23 21:20:36.090   urn:newsml:reuters.com:20200723:nNRAcf1v8f:1
2020-07-23 08:22:17.000   urn:newsml:reuters.com:20200723:nL3N2EU1P9:1
2020-07-23 07:08:48.000   urn:newsml:reuters.com:20200723:nL3N2EU0HH:1
2020-07-23 00:55:54.000   urn:newsml:reuters.com:20200723:nL5N2EU03M:1
2020-07-22 21:35:42.640   urn:newsml:reuters.com:20200722:nFWN2ET120:2

                                        sourceCode
2020-07-29 11:02:31.276   NS:CAIXIN
2020-07-28 00:59:48.000     NS:RTRS
2020-07-23 21:20:36.090   NS:SOUTHC
2020-07-23 08:22:17.000     NS:RTRS
2020-07-23 07:08:48.000     NS:RTRS
2020-07-23 00:55:54.000     NS:RTRS
2020-07-22 21:35:42.640     NS:RTRS

In [31]: storyId = news['storyId'][1]  ❷

In [32]: from IPython.display import HTML

In [33]: HTML(ek.get_news_story(storyId)[:1148])  ❸
Out[33]: <IPython.core.display.HTML object>

Jan 06, 2020

Tesla, Inc.TSLA registered record production and deliveries of 104,891 and
112,000 vehicles, respectively, in the fourth quarter of 2019.

Notably, the company's Model S/X and Model 3 reported record production and
deliveries in the fourth quarter. The Model S/X division recorded production
and delivery volume of 17,933 and 19,450 vehicles, respectively. The Model 3
division registered production of 86,958 vehicles, while 92,550 vehicles were
delivered.

In 2019, Tesla delivered 367,500 vehicles, reflecting an increase of 50%, year
over year, and nearly in line with the company's full-year guidance of 360,000
vehicles.
```

❶ Retrieves metadata for a number of news articles that fall in the parameter range

❷ Selects one storyId for which to retrieve the full text

❸ Retrieves the full text for the selected article and shows it

Unstructured Streaming Data

In the same way that historical unstructured data is retrieved, programmatic APIs can be used to stream unstructured news data, for example, in real time or at least near time. One such API is available for DNA (*https://oreil.ly/kVm18*): the Data, News, Analytics platform from Dow Jones. Figure 4-1 shows the screenshot of a web application that streams "Commodity and Financial News" articles and processes these with NLP techniques in real time.

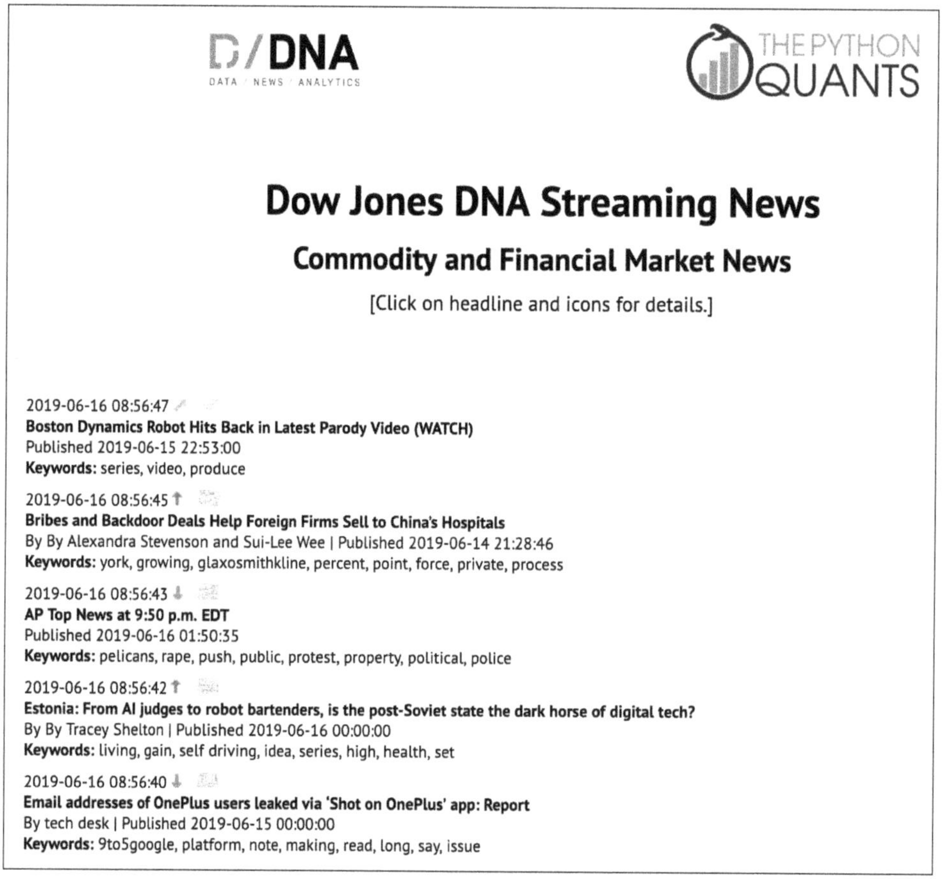

Dow Jones DNA Streaming News

Commodity and Financial Market News

[Click on headline and icons for details.]

2019-06-16 08:56:47
Boston Dynamics Robot Hits Back in Latest Parody Video (WATCH)
Published 2019-06-15 22:53:00
Keywords: series, video, produce

2019-06-16 08:56:45
Bribes and Backdoor Deals Help Foreign Firms Sell to China's Hospitals
By By Alexandra Stevenson and Sui-Lee Wee | Published 2019-06-14 21:28:46
Keywords: york, growing, glaxosmithkline, percent, point, force, private, process

2019-06-16 08:56:43
AP Top News at 9:50 p.m. EDT
Published 2019-06-16 01:50:35
Keywords: pelicans, rape, push, public, protest, property, political, police

2019-06-16 08:56:42
Estonia: From AI judges to robot bartenders, is the post-Soviet state the dark horse of digital tech?
By By Tracey Shelton | Published 2019-06-16 00:00:00
Keywords: living, gain, self driving, idea, series, high, health, set

2019-06-16 08:56:40
Email addresses of OnePlus users leaked via 'Shot on OnePlus' app: Report
By tech desk | Published 2019-06-15 00:00:00
Keywords: 9to5google, platform, note, making, read, long, say, issue

Figure 4-1. News-streaming application based on DNA (Dow Jones)

The news-streaming application has the following main features:

Full text
The full text of each article is available by clicking on the article header.

Keyword summary
A keyword summary is created and printed on the screen.

Sentiment analysis

Sentiment scores are calculated and visualized as colored arrows. Details become visible through a click on the arrows.

Word cloud

A word cloud summary bitmap is created, shown as a thumbnail and visible after a click on the thumbnail (see Figure 4-2).

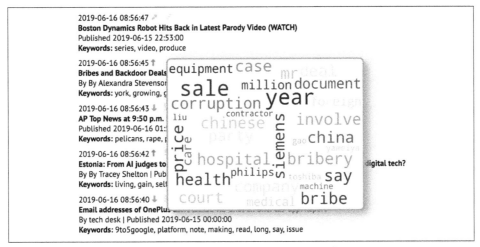

2019-06-16 08:56:47
Boston Dynamics Robot Hits Back in Latest Parody Video (WATCH)
Published 2019-06-15 22:53:00
Keywords: series, video, produce

2019-06-16 08:56:45 ↑
Bribes and Backdoor Deals
By By Alexandra Stevenson
Keywords: york, growing,

2019-06-16 08:56:43 ↓
AP Top News at 9:50 p.m.
Published 2019-06-16 01:
Keywords: pelicans, rape,

2019-06-16 08:56:42 ↑
Estonia: From AI judges to
By By Tracey Shelton | Pub
Keywords: living, gain, self

2019-06-16 08:56:40 ↓
Email addresses of OnePlu
By tech desk | Published 2019-06-15 00:00:00
Keywords: 9to5google, platform, note, making, read, long, say, issue

Figure 4-2. Word cloud bitmap shown in news-streaming application

Alternative Data

Nowadays, financial institutions, and in particular hedge funds, systematically mine a number of alternative data sources to gain an edge in trading and investing. A recent article by Bloomberg (*http://bit.ly/aiif_alt_data*) lists, among others, the following alternative data sources:

- Web-scraped data
- Crowd-sourced data
- Credit cards and point-of-sales (POS) systems
- Social media sentiment
- Search trends
- Web traffic
- Supply chain data
- Energy production data
- Consumer profiles
- Satellite imagery/geospacial data

- App installs

- Ocean vessel tracking

- Wearables, drones, Internet of Things (IoT) sensors

In the following, the usage of alternative data is illustrated by two examples. The first retrieves and processes Apple Inc. press releases in the form of HTML pages. The following Python code makes use of a set of helper functions as shown in "Python Code" on page 156. In the code, a list of URLs is defined, each representing an HTML page with a press release from Apple Inc. The raw HTML code is then retrieved for each press release. Then the raw code is cleaned up, and an excerpt for one press release is printed:

```
In [34]: import nlp        ❶
         import requests

In [35]: sources = [
             'https://nr.apple.com/dE0b1T5G3u',   # iPad Pro
             'https://nr.apple.com/dE4c7T6g1K',   # MacBook Air
             'https://nr.apple.com/dE4q4r8A2A',   # Mac Mini
         ]    ❷

In [36]: html = [requests.get(url).text for url in sources]    ❸

In [37]: data = [nlp.clean_up_text(t) for t in html]    ❹

In [38]: data[0][536:1001]    ❺
Out[38]: ' display, powerful a12x bionic chip and face id introducing the new ipad pro
         with all-screen design and next-generation performance. new york apple today
         introduced the new ipad pro with all-screen design and next-generation
         performance, marking the biggest change to ipad ever. the all-new design
         pushes 11-inch and 12.9-inch liquid retina displays to the edges of ipad pro
         and integrates face id to securely unlock ipad with just a glance.1 the a12x
         bionic chip w'
```

❶ Imports the NLP helper functions

❷ Defines the URLs for the three press releases

❸ Retrieves the raw HTML codes for the three press releases

❹ Cleans up the raw HTML codes (for example, HTML tags are removed)

❺ Prints an excerpt from one press release

Of course, defining alternative data as broadly as is done in this section implies that there is a limitless amount of data that one can retrieve and process for financial purposes. At its core, this is the business of search engines such as the one from Google

LLC. In a financial context, it would be of paramount importance to specify exactly what unstructured alternative data sources to tap into.

The second example is about the retrieval of data from the social network Twitter, Inc. To this end, Twitter provides API access to tweets on its platform, provided one has set up a Twitter account appropriately. The following Python code connects to the Twitter API and retrieves and prints the five most recent tweets from my home timeline and user timeline, respectively:

```
In [39]: from twitter import Twitter, OAuth

In [40]: t = Twitter(auth=OAuth(c['twitter']['access_token'],
                                c['twitter']['access_secret_token'],
                                c['twitter']['api_key'],
                                c['twitter']['api_secret_key']),
                     retry=True)  ❶

In [41]: l = t.statuses.home_timeline(count=5)  ❷

In [42]: for e in l:
             print(e['text'])  ❷
         The Bank of England is effectively subsidizing polluting industries in its
          pandemic rescue program, a think tank sa… https://t.co/Fq5jl2CIcp
         Cool shared task: mining scientific contributions (by @SeeTedTalk @SoerenAuer
          and Jennifer D'Souza)
         https://t.co/dm56DMUrWm
         Twelve people were hospitalized in Wyoming on Monday after a hot air balloon
          crash, officials said.

         Three hot air… https://t.co/EaNBBRXVar
         President Trump directed controversial Pentagon pick into new role with
          similar duties after nomination failed https://t.co/ZyXpPcJkcQ
         Company announcement: Revolut launches Open Banking for its 400,000 Italian...
          https://t.co/OfvbgwbeJW #fintech

In [43]: l = t.statuses.user_timeline(screen_name='dyjh', count=5)  ❸

In [44]: for e in l:
             print(e['text'])  ❸
         #Python for #AlgoTrading (focus on the process) &amp; #AI in #Finance (focus
          on prediction methods) will complement eac… https://t.co/P1s8fXCp42
         Currently putting finishing touches on #AI in #Finance (@OReillyMedia). Book
          going into production shortly. https://t.co/JsOSA3sfBL
         Chinatown Is Coming Back, One Noodle at a Time https://t.co/In5kXNeVc5
         Alt data industry balloons as hedge funds strive for Covid edge via @FT |
          "We remain of the view that alternative d… https://t.co/9HtUOjoEdz
         @Wolf_Of_BTC Just follow me on Twitter (or LinkedIn). Then you will notice for
          sure when it is out.
```

❶ Connects to the Twitter API

❷ Retrieves and prints five (most recent) tweets from home timeline

❸ Retrieves and prints five (most recent) tweets from user timeline

The Twitter API allows also for searches, based on which most recent tweets can be retrieved and processed:

```
In [45]: d = t.search.tweets(q='#Python', count=7)   ❶
```

```
In [46]: for e in d['statuses']:
             print(e['text'])   ❶
         RT @KirkDBorne: #AI is Reshaping Programming — Tips on How to Stay on Top:
          https://t.co/CFNu1i352C
         ―
         Courses:
         1: #MachineLearning — Jupyte…
         RT @reuvenmlerner: Today, a #Python student's code didn't print:

         x = 5
         if x == 5:
             print: ('yes!')

         There was a typo, namely : after pr…
         RT @GavLaaaaaaaa: Javascript Does Not Need a StringBuilder
          https://t.co/aS7NzHLO65 #programming #softwareengineering #bigdata
          #datascience…
         RT @CodeFlawCo: It is necessary to publish regular updates on Twitter
          #programmer #coder #developer #technology RT @pak_aims: Learning to C…
         RT @GavLaaaaaaaa: Javascript Does Not Need a StringBuilder
          https://t.co/aS7NzHLO65 #programming #softwareengineering #bigdata
          #datascience…
```

❶ Searches for tweets with hashtag "Python" and prints the five most recent ones

One can also collect a larger number of tweets from a Twitter user and create a summary in the form of a word cloud (see Figure 4-3). The following Python code again makes use of the NLP helper functions as shown in "Python Code" on page 156:

```
In [47]: l = t.statuses.user_timeline(screen_name='elonmusk', count=50)   ❶
```

```
In [48]: tl = [e['text'] for e in l]   ❷
```

```
In [49]: tl[:5]   ❸
Out[49]: ['@flcnhvy @Lindw0rm @cleantechnica True',
          '@Lindw0rm @cleantechnica Highly likely down the road',
          '@cleantechnica True fact',
          '@NASASpaceflight Scrubbed for the day. A Raptor turbopump spin start valve
           didn't open, triggering an automatic abo… https://t.co/QDdlNXFgJg',
```

```
                    '@Erdayastronaut I'm in the Boca control room. Hop attempt in ~33 minutes.']

In [50]: wc = nlp.generate_word_cloud(' '.join(tl), 35,
                 name='../../images/ch04/musk_twitter_wc.png'
                 ) ❹
```

❶ Retrieves the 50 most recent tweets for the user `elonmusk`

❷ Collects the texts in a `list` object

❸ Shows excerpts for the final five tweets

❹ Generates a word cloud summary and shows it

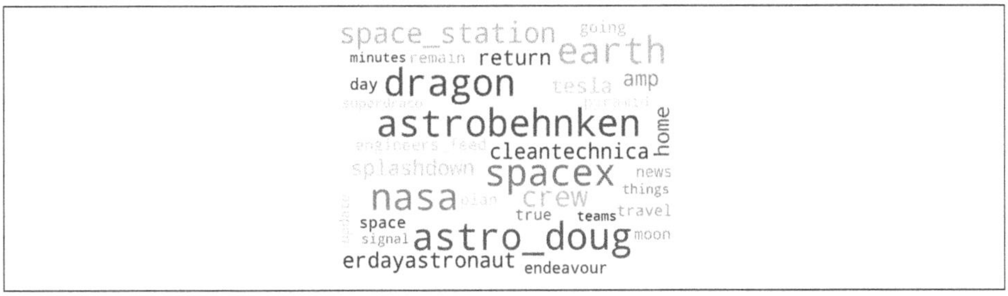

Figure 4-3. Word cloud as summary for larger number of tweets

Once a financial practitioner defines the "relevant financial data" to go beyond structured financial time series data, the data sources seem limitless in terms of volume, variety, and velocity. The way the tweets are retrieved from the Twitter API is almost in near time since the most recent tweets are accessed in the examples. These and similar API-based data sources therefore provide a never-ending stream of alternative data for which, as previously pointed out, it is important to specify exactly what one is looking for. Otherwise, any financial data science effort might easily drown in too much data and/or too noisy data.

Normative Theories Revisited

Chapter 3 introduces normative financial theories such as the MVP theory or the CAPM. For quite a long time, students and academics learning and studying such theories were more or less constrained to the theory itself. With all the available financial data, as discussed and illustrated in the previous section, in combination with powerful open source software for data analysis—such as Python, `NumPy`, `pandas`, and so on—it has become pretty easy and straightforward to put financial theories to real-world tests. It does not require small teams and larger studies anymore to do so. A typical notebook, internet access, and a standard Python environment suffice. This is what this section is about. However, before diving into data-driven finance, the following sub-section discusses briefly some famous paradoxes in the context of EUT and how corporations model and predict the behavior of individuals in practice.

Expected Utility and Reality

In economics, *risk* describes a situation in which possible future states and probabilities for those states to unfold are known in advance to the decision maker. This is the standard assumption in finance and the context of EUT. On the other hand, *ambiguity* describes situations in economics in which probabilities, or even possible future states, are not known in advance to a decision maker. *Uncertainty* subsumes the two different decision-making situations.

There is a long tradition of analyzing the concrete decision-making behavior of individuals ("agents") under uncertainty. Innumerable studies and experiments have been conducted to observe and analyze how agents behave when faced with uncertainty as compared to what theories such as EUT predict. For centuries, *paradoxa* have played an important role in decision-making theory and research.

One such paradox, the *St. Petersburg paradox*, gave rise to the invention of utility functions and EUT in the first place. Daniel Bernoulli presented the paradox—and a solution to it—in 1738. The paradox is based on the following coin tossing game G. An agent is faced with a game during which a (perfect) coin is tossed potentially infinitely many times. If after the first toss heads prevails, the agent receives a payoff of 1 (currency unit). As long as heads is observed, the coin is tossed again. Otherwise the game ends. If heads prevails a second time, the agent receives an additional payoff of 2. If it does a third time, the additional payoff is 4. For the fourth time it is 8, and so on. This is a situation of risk since all possible future states, as well as their associated probabilities, are known in advance.

The expected payoff of this game is *infinite*. This can be seen from the following infinite sum of which every element is strictly positive:

$$\mathbf{E}(G) = \frac{1}{2} \cdot 1 + \frac{1}{4} \cdot 2 + \frac{1}{8} \cdot 4 + \frac{1}{16} \cdot 8 + \dots = \sum_{k=1}^{\infty} \frac{1}{2^k} 2^{k-1} = \sum_{k=1}^{\infty} \frac{1}{2} = \infty$$

However, faced with such a game, a decision maker in general would be willing to pay a *finite* sum only to play the game. A major reason for this is the fact that relatively large payoffs only happen with a relatively small probability. Consider the potential payoff $W = 511$:

$$W = 1 + 2 + 4 + 8 + 16 + 32 + 64 + 128 + 256 = 511$$

The probability of winning such a payoff is pretty low. To be exact, it is only $P(x = W) = \frac{1}{512} = 0.001953125$. The probability for such a payoff or a smaller one, on the other hand, is pretty high:

$$P(x \leq W) = \sum_{k=1}^{9} \frac{1}{2^k} = 0.998046875$$

In other words, in 998 out of 1,000 games the payoff is 511 or smaller. Therefore, an agent would probably not wager much more than 511 to play this game. The way out of this paradox is the introduction of a utility function with *positive but decreasing marginal utility*. In the context of the St. Petersburg paradox, this means that there is a function $u: \mathbb{R}_+ \rightarrow \mathbb{R}$ that assigns to every positive payoff x a real value $u(x)$. Positive but decreasing marginal utility then formally translates into the following:

$$\frac{\partial u}{\partial x} > 0$$

$$\frac{\partial^2 u}{\partial x^2} < 0$$

As seen in Chapter 3, one such candidate function is $u(x) = \ln(x)$ with:

$$\frac{\partial u}{\partial x} = \frac{1}{x}$$

$$\frac{\partial^2 u}{\partial x^2} = -\frac{1}{x^2}$$

The expected utility then is *finite*, as the calculation of the following infinite sum illustrates:

$$\mathbf{E}(u(G)) = \sum_{k=1}^{\infty} \frac{1}{2^k} u\left(2^{k-1}\right) = \sum_{k=1}^{\infty} \frac{\ln\left(2^{k-1}\right)}{2^k} = \left(\sum_{k=1}^{\infty} \frac{(k-1)}{2^k}\right) \cdot \ln(2) = \ln(2) < \infty$$

The expected utility of $\ln(2) = 0.693147$ is obviously a pretty small number in comparison to the expected payoff of infinity. Bernoulli utility functions and EUT resolve the St. Petersburg paradox.

Other paradoxa, such as the *Allais paradox* published in Allais (1953), address the EUT itself. This paradox is based on an experiment with four different games that test subjects should rank. Table 4-2 shows the four games (A, B, A', B'). The ranking is to be done for the two pairs (A, B) and (A', B'). The *independence axiom* postulates that the first row in the table should not have any influence on the ordering of (A', B') since the payoff is the same for both games.

Table 4-2. Games in Allais paradox

Probability	Game A	Game B	Game A'	Game B'
0.66	2,400	2,400	0	0
0.33	2,500	2,400	2,500	2,400
0.01	0	2,400	0	2,400

In experiments, the majority of decision makers rank the games as follows: $B \succ A$ and $A' \succ B'$. The ranking $B \succ A$ leads to the following inequalities, where $u_1 \equiv u(2400), u_2 \equiv u(2500), u_3 \equiv u(0)$:

$$u_1 > 0.66 \cdot u_1 + 0.33 \cdot u_2 + 0.01 \cdot u_3$$
$$0.34 \cdot u_1 > 0.33 \cdot u_2 + 0.01 \cdot u_3$$

The ranking $A' \succ B'$ in turn leads to the following inequalities:

$$0.33 \cdot u_2 + 0.01 \cdot u_3 > 0.33 \cdot u_1 + 0.01 \cdot u_1$$
$$0.34 \cdot u_1 < 0.33 \cdot u_2 + 0.01 \cdot u_3$$

These inequalities obviously contradict each other and lead to the Allais paradox. One possible explanation is that decision makers in general value certainty higher than the typical models, such as EUT, predict. Most people would probably rather choose to receive $1 million with certainty than play a game in which they can win $100 million with a probability of 5%, although there are a number of suitable utility functions available that under EUT would have the decision maker choose the game instead of the certain amount.

Another explanation lies in *framing* decisions and the psychology of decision makers. It is well known that more people would accept a surgery if it has a "95% chance of success" than a "5% chance of death." Simply changing the wording might lead to behavior that is inconsistent with decision-making theories such as EUT.

Another famous paradox addressing shortcomings of EUT in its subjective form, according to Savage (1954, 1972), is the *Ellsberg paradox*, which dates back to the seminal paper by Ellsberg (1961). It addresses the importance of ambiguity in many real-world decision situations. A standard setting for this paradox comprises two different urns, both of which contain exactly 100 balls. For urn 1, it is known that it contains exactly 50 black and 50 red balls. For urn 2, it is only known that it contains black and red balls but not in which proportion.

Test subjects can choose among the following game options:

- Game 1: red 1, black 1, or indifferent
- Game 2: red 2, black 2, or indifferent
- Game 3: red 1, red 2, or indifferent
- Game 4: black 1, black 2, or indifferent

Here, "red 1," for example, means that a red ball is drawn from urn 1. Typically, a test subject would answer as follows:

- Game 1: indifferent
- Game 2: indifferent
- Game 3: red 1
- Game 4: black 1

This set of decisions—which is not the only one to be observed but is a common one —exemplifies what is called *ambiguity aversion*. Since the probabilities for black and red balls, respectively, are not known for urn 2, decision makers prefer a situation of *risk* instead of *ambiguity*.

The two paradoxa of Allais and Ellsberg show that real test subjects quite often behave contrary to what well-established decision theories in economics predict. In other words, human beings as decision makers can in general not be compared to machines that carefully collect data and then crunch the numbers to make a decision under uncertainty, be it in the form of risk or ambiguity. Human behavior is more complex than most, if not all, theories currently suggest. How difficult and complex it can be to explain human behavior is clear after reading, for example, the 800-page book *Behave* by Sapolsky (2018). It covers multiple facets of this topic, ranging from biochemical processes to genetics, human evolution, tribes, language, religion, and more, in an integrative manner.

If standard economic decision paradigms such as EUT do not explain real-world decision making too well, what alternatives are available? Economic experiments that build the basis for the Allais and Ellsberg paradoxa are a good starting point in learning how decision makers behave in specific, controlled situations. Such experiments and their sometimes surprising and paradoxical results have indeed motivated a great number of researchers to come up with alternative theories and models that resolve the paradoxa. The book *The Experiment in the History of Economics* by Fontaine and Leonard (2005) is about the historical role of experiments in economics. There is, for example, a whole string of literature that addresses issues arising from the Ellsberg paradox. This literature deals with, among other topics, nonadditive probabilities, Choquet integrals, and decision heuristics such as *maximizing the minimum payoff* ("max-min") or *minimizing the maximum loss* ("min-max"). These alternative approaches have proven superior to EUT, at least in certain decision-making scenarios. But they are far from being mainstream in finance.

What, after all, has proven to be useful in practice? Not too surprisingly, the answer lies in *data and machine learning algorithms.* The internet, with its billions of users, generates a treasure trove of data describing real-world human behavior, or what is sometimes called *revealed preferences.* The big data generated on the web has a scale that is multiple orders of magnitude larger than what single experiments can generate. Companies such as Amazon, Facebook, Google, and Twitter are able to make billions of dollars by recording user behavior (that is, their revealed preferences) and capitalizing on the insights generated by ML algorithms trained on this data.

The default ML approach taken in this context is supervised learning. The algorithms themselves are in general *theory- and model-free*; variants of neural networks are often applied. Therefore, when companies today predict the behavior of their users or customers, more often than not a model-free ML algorithm is deployed. Traditional decision theories like EUT or one of its successors generally do not play a role at all. This makes it somewhat surprising that such theories still, at the beginning of the 2020s, are a cornerstone of most economic and financial theories applied in practice. And this is not even to mention the large number of financial textbooks that cover traditional decision theories in detail. If one of the most fundamental building blocks of financial theory seems to lack meaningful empirical support or practical benefits, what about the financial models that build on top of it? More on this appears in subsequent sections and chapters.

Data-Driven Predictions of Behavior

Standard economic decision theories are intellectually appealing to many, even to those who, faced with a concrete decision under uncertainty, would behave in contrast to the theories' predictions. On the other hand, big data and model-free, supervised learning approaches prove useful and successful in practice for predicting user and customer behavior. In a financial context, this might imply that one should not really worry about why and how financial agents decide the way they decide. One should rather focus on their indirectly revealed preferences based on features data (new information) that describes the state of a financial market and labels data (outcomes) that reflects the impact of the decisions made by financial agents. This leads to a data-driven instead of a theory- or model-driven view of decision making in financial markets. Financial agents become data-processing organisms that can be much better modeled, for example, by complex neural networks than, say, a simple utility function in combination with an assumed probability distribution.

Mean-Variance Portfolio Theory

Assume a data-driven investor wants to apply MVP theory to invest in a portfolio of technology stocks and wants to add a gold-related exchange-traded fund (ETF) for diversification. Probably, the investor would access relevant historical price data via an API to a trading platform or a data provider. To make the following analysis reproducible, it relies on a CSV data file stored in a remote location. The following Python code retrieves the data file, selects a number of symbols given the investor's goal, and calculates log returns from the price time series data. Figure 4-4 compares the normalized price time series for the selected symbols:

```
In [51]: import numpy as np
         import pandas as pd
         from pylab import plt, mpl
         from scipy.optimize import minimize
         plt.style.use('seaborn')
         mpl.rcParams['savefig.dpi'] = 300
         mpl.rcParams['font.family'] = 'serif'
         np.set_printoptions(precision=5, suppress=True,
                             formatter={'float': lambda x: f'{x:6.3f}'})

In [52]: url = 'http://hilpisch.com/aiif_eikon_eod_data.csv'   ❶

In [53]: raw = pd.read_csv(url, index_col=0, parse_dates=True).dropna()   ❶

In [54]: raw.info()   ❶
         <class 'pandas.core.frame.DataFrame'>
         DatetimeIndex: 2516 entries, 2010-01-04 to 2019-12-31
         Data columns (total 12 columns):
          #   Column  Non-Null Count  Dtype
         ---  ------  --------------  -----
          0   AAPL.O  2516 non-null   float64
          1   MSFT.O  2516 non-null   float64
          2   INTC.O  2516 non-null   float64
          3   AMZN.O  2516 non-null   float64
          4   GS.N    2516 non-null   float64
          5   SPY     2516 non-null   float64
          6   .SPX    2516 non-null   float64
          7   .VIX    2516 non-null   float64
          8   EUR=    2516 non-null   float64
          9   XAU=    2516 non-null   float64
          10  GDX     2516 non-null   float64
          11  GLD     2516 non-null   float64
         dtypes: float64(12)
         memory usage: 255.5 KB

In [55]: symbols = ['AAPL.O', 'MSFT.O', 'INTC.O', 'AMZN.O', 'GLD']   ❷

In [56]: rets = np.log(raw[symbols] / raw[symbols].shift(1)).dropna()   ❸

In [57]: (raw[symbols] / raw[symbols].iloc[0]).plot(figsize=(10, 6));   ❹
```

❶ Retrieves historical EOD data from a remote location

❷ Specifies the symbols (`RICs`) to be invested in

❸ Calculates the log returns for all time series

❹ Plots the normalized financial time series for the selected symbols

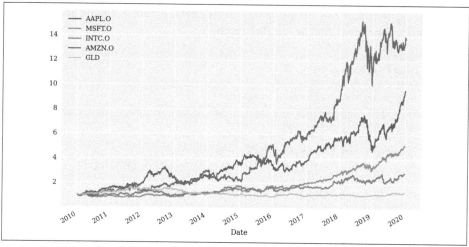

Figure 4-4. Normalized financial time series data

The data-driven investor wants to first set a baseline for performance as given by an equally weighted portfolio over the whole period of the available data. To this end, the following Python code defines functions to calculate the portfolio return, the portfolio volatility, and the portfolio Sharpe ratio given a set of weights for the selected symbols:

```
In [58]: weights = len(rets.columns) * [1 / len(rets.columns)]   ❶

In [59]: def port_return(rets, weights):
             return np.dot(rets.mean(), weights) * 252   ❷

In [60]: port_return(rets, weights)   ❷
Out[60]: 0.15694764653018106

In [61]: def port_volatility(rets, weights):
             return np.dot(weights, np.dot(rets.cov() * 252 , weights)) ** 0.5   ❸

In [62]: port_volatility(rets, weights)   ❸
Out[62]: 0.16106507848480675

In [63]: def port_sharpe(rets, weights):
             return port_return(rets, weights) / port_volatility(rets, weights)   ❹
```

```
In [64]: port_sharpe(rets, weights)  ❹
Out[64]: 0.97443622172255
```

❶ Equally weighted portfolio

❷ Portfolio return

❸ Portfolio volatility

❹ Portfolio Sharpe ratio (with zero short rate)

The investor also wants to analyze which combinations of portfolio risk and return—and consequently Sharpe ratio—are roughly possible by applying Monte Carlo simulation to randomize the portfolio weights. Short sales are excluded, and the portfolio weights are assumed to add up to 100%. The following Python code implements the simulation and visualizes the results (see Figure 4-5):

```
In [65]: w = np.random.random((1000, len(symbols)))  ❶
         w = (w.T / w.sum(axis=1)).T  ❶

In [66]: w[:5]  ❶
Out[66]: array([[ 0.184,  0.157,  0.227,  0.353,  0.079],
               [ 0.207,  0.282,  0.258,  0.023,  0.230],
               [ 0.313,  0.284,  0.051,  0.340,  0.012],
               [ 0.238,  0.181,  0.145,  0.191,  0.245],
               [ 0.246,  0.256,  0.315,  0.181,  0.002]])

In [67]: pvr = [(port_volatility(rets[symbols], weights),
               port_return(rets[symbols], weights))
               for weights in w]  ❷
         pvr = np.array(pvr)  ❷

In [68]: psr = pvr[:, 1] / pvr[:, 0]  ❸

In [69]: plt.figure(figsize=(10, 6))
         fig = plt.scatter(pvr[:, 0], pvr[:, 1],
                           c=psr, cmap='coolwarm')
         cb = plt.colorbar(fig)
         cb.set_label('Sharpe ratio')
         plt.xlabel('expected volatility')
         plt.ylabel('expected return')
         plt.title(' | '.join(symbols));
```

❶ Simulates portfolio weights adding up to 100%

❷ Derives the resulting portfolio volatilities and returns

❸ Calculates the resulting Sharpe ratios

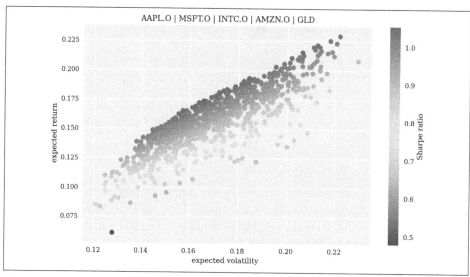

Figure 4-5. Simulated portfolio volatilities, returns, and Sharpe ratios

The data-driven investor now wants to backtest the performance of a portfolio that was set up at the beginning of 2011. The optimal portfolio composition was derived from the financial time series data available from 2010. At the beginning of 2012, the portfolio composition was adjusted given the available data from 2011, and so on. To this end, the following Python code derives the *portfolio weights* for every relevant year that *maximizes the Sharpe ratio*:

```
In [70]: bnds = len(symbols) * [(0, 1),]   ❶
         bnds   ❶
Out[70]: [(0, 1), (0, 1), (0, 1), (0, 1), (0, 1)]

In [71]: cons = {'type': 'eq', 'fun': lambda weights: weights.sum() - 1}   ❷

In [72]: opt_weights = {}
         for year in range(2010, 2019):
             rets_ = rets[symbols].loc[f'{year}-01-01':f'{year}-12-31']   ❸
             ow = minimize(lambda weights: -port_sharpe(rets_, weights),
                           len(symbols) * [1 / len(symbols)],
                           bounds=bnds,
                           constraints=cons)['x']   ❹
             opt_weights[year] = ow   ❺

In [73]: opt_weights   ❺
Out[73]: {2010: array([ 0.366,  0.000,  0.000,  0.056,  0.578]),
          2011: array([ 0.543,  0.000,  0.077,  0.000,  0.380]),
          2012: array([ 0.324,  0.000,  0.000,  0.471,  0.205]),
          2013: array([ 0.012,  0.305,  0.219,  0.464,  0.000]),
          2014: array([ 0.452,  0.115,  0.419,  0.000,  0.015]),
          2015: array([ 0.000,  0.000,  0.000,  1.000,  0.000]),
```

```
       2016: array([ 0.150,  0.260,  0.000,  0.058,  0.533]),
       2017: array([ 0.231,  0.203,  0.031,  0.109,  0.426]),
       2018: array([ 0.000,  0.295,  0.000,  0.705,  0.000])}
```

❶ Specifies the bounds for the single asset weights

❷ Specifies that all weights need to add up to 100%

❸ Selects the relevant data set for the given year

❹ Derives the portfolio weights that maximize the Sharpe ratio

❺ Stores these weights in a `dict` object

The optimal portfolio compositions as derived for the relevant years illustrate that MVP theory in its original form quite often leads to (relative) extreme situations in the sense that one or more assets are not included at all or that even a single asset makes up 100% of the portfolio. Of course, this can be actively avoided by setting, for example, a minimum weight for every asset considered. The results also indicate that this approach leads to significant rebalancings in the portfolio, driven by the previous year's realized statistics and correlations.

To complete the backtest, the following code compares the expected portfolio statistics (from the optimal composition of the previous year applied to the previous year's data) with the realized portfolio statistics for the current year (from the optimal composition from the previous year applied to the current year's data):

```
In [74]: res = pd.DataFrame()
         for year in range(2010, 2019):
             rets_ = rets[symbols].loc[f'{year}-01-01':f'{year}-12-31']
             epv = port_volatility(rets_, opt_weights[year])    ❶
             epr = port_return(rets_, opt_weights[year])    ❶
             esr = epr / epv    ❶
             rets_ = rets[symbols].loc[f'{year + 1}-01-01':f'{year + 1}-12-31']
             rpv = port_volatility(rets_, opt_weights[year])    ❷
             rpr = port_return(rets_, opt_weights[year])    ❷
             rsr = rpr / rpv    ❷
             res = res.append(pd.DataFrame({'epv': epv, 'epr': epr, 'esr': esr,
                                            'rpv': rpv, 'rpr': rpr, 'rsr': rsr},
                                           index=[year + 1]))

In [75]: res
Out[75]:          epv       epr       esr       rpv       rpr       rsr
         2011  0.157440  0.303003  1.924564  0.160622  0.133836  0.833235
         2012  0.173279  0.169321  0.977156  0.182292  0.161375  0.885256
         2013  0.202460  0.278459  1.375378  0.168714  0.166897  0.989228
         2014  0.181544  0.368961  2.032353  0.197798  0.026830  0.135645
         2015  0.160340  0.309486  1.930190  0.211368 -0.024560 -0.116194
         2016  0.326730  0.778330  2.382179  0.296565  0.103870  0.350242
```

```
       2017  0.106148  0.090933  0.856663  0.079521  0.230630  2.900235
       2018  0.086548  0.260702  3.012226  0.157337  0.038234  0.243004
       2019  0.323796  0.228008  0.704174  0.207672  0.275819  1.328147

In [76]: res.mean()
Out[76]: epv    0.190920
         epr    0.309689
         esr    1.688320
         rpv    0.184654
         rpr    0.123659
         rsr    0.838755
         dtype: float64
```

❶ Expected portfolio statistics

❷ Realized portfolio statistics

Figure 4-6 compares the expected and realized portfolio volatilities for the single years. MVP theory does quite a good job in predicting the portfolio volatility. This is also supported by a relatively high correlation between the two time series:

```
In [77]: res[['epv', 'rpv']].corr()
Out[77]:           epv       rpv
         epv  1.000000  0.765733
         rpv  0.765733  1.000000

In [78]: res[['epv', 'rpv']].plot(kind='bar', figsize=(10, 6),
              title='Expected vs. Realized Portfolio Volatility');
```

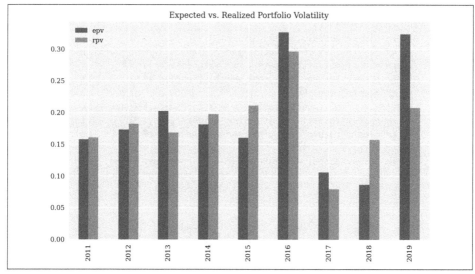

Figure 4-6. Expected versus realized portfolio volatilities

However, the conclusions are the opposite when comparing the expected with the realized portfolio returns (see Figure 4-7). MVP theory obviously fails in predicting the portfolio returns, as is confirmed by the negative correlation between the two time series:

```
In [79]: res[['epr', 'rpr']].corr()
Out[79]:           epr        rpr
         epr   1.000000  -0.350437
         rpr  -0.350437   1.000000

In [80]: res[['epr', 'rpr']].plot(kind='bar', figsize=(10, 6),
             title='Expected vs. Realized Portfolio Return');
```

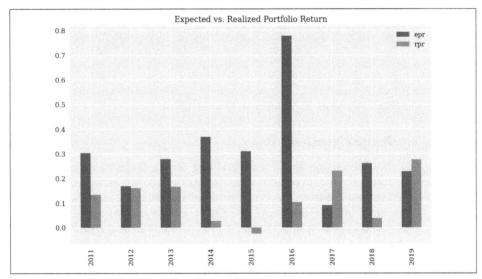

Figure 4-7. Expected versus realized portfolio returns

Similar, or even worse, conclusions need to be drawn with regard to the Sharpe ratio (see Figure 4-8). For the data-driven investor who aims at maximizing the Sharpe ratio of the portfolio, the theory's predictions are generally significantly off from the realized values. The correlation between the two time series is even lower than for the returns:

```
In [81]: res[['esr', 'rsr']].corr()
Out[81]:           esr        rsr
         esr   1.000000  -0.698607
         rsr  -0.698607   1.000000

In [82]: res[['esr', 'rsr']].plot(kind='bar', figsize=(10, 6),
             title='Expected vs. Realized Sharpe Ratio');
```

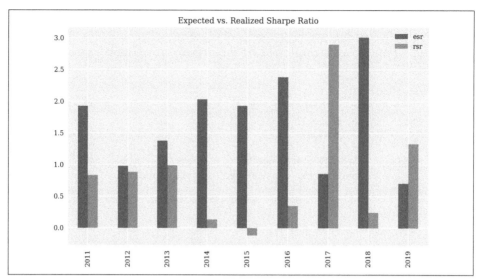

Figure 4-8. Expected versus realized portfolio Sharpe ratios

Predictive Power of MVP Theory

MVP theory applied to real-world data reveals its practical short-comings. Without additional constraints, optimal portfolio compositions and rebalancings can be extreme. The predictive power with regard to portfolio return and Sharpe ratio is pretty bad in the numerical example, whereas the predictive power with regard to portfolio risk seems acceptable. However, investors generally are interested in risk-adjusted performance measures, such as the Sharpe ratio, and this is the statistic for which MVP theory fails worst in the example.

Capital Asset Pricing Model

A similar approach can be applied to put the CAPM to a real-world test. Assume that the data-driven technology investor from before wants to apply the CAPM to derive expected returns for the four technology stocks from before. The following Python code first derives the beta for every stock for a given year, and then calculates the expected return for the stock in the next year, given its beta and the performance of the market portfolio. The market portfolio is approximated by the S&P 500 stock index:

```
In [83]: r = 0.005   ❶

In [84]: market = '.SPX'   ❷

In [85]: rets = np.log(raw / raw.shift(1)).dropna()
```

```
In [86]: res = pd.DataFrame()

In [87]: for sym in rets.columns[:4]:
             print('\n' + sym)
             print(54 * '=')
             for year in range(2010, 2019):
                 rets_ = rets.loc[f'{year}-01-01':f'{year}-12-31']
                 muM = rets_[market].mean() * 252
                 cov = rets_.cov().loc[sym, market]    ❸
                 var = rets_[market].var()    ❸
                 beta = cov / var    ❸
                 rets_ = rets.loc[f'{year + 1}-01-01':f'{year + 1}-12-31']
                 muM = rets_[market].mean() * 252
                 mu_capm = r + beta * (muM - r)    ❹
                 mu_real = rets_[sym].mean() * 252    ❺
                 res = res.append(pd.DataFrame({'symbol': sym,
                                                'mu_capm': mu_capm,
                                                'mu_real': mu_real},
                                               index=[year + 1]),
                                 sort=True)    ❻
                 print('{} | beta: {:.3f} | mu_capm: {:6.3f} | mu_real: {:6.3f}'
                       .format(year + 1, beta, mu_capm, mu_real))    ❻
```

❶ Specifies the risk-less short rate

❷ Defines the market portfolio

❸ Derives the beta of the stock

❹ Calculates the expected return given previous year's beta and current year market
    portfolio performance

❺ Calculates the realized performance of the stock for the current year

❻ Collects and prints all results

The preceding code provides the following output:

```
AAPL.O
======================================================
2011 | beta: 1.052 | mu_capm: -0.000 | mu_real:  0.228
2012 | beta: 0.764 | mu_capm:  0.098 | mu_real:  0.275
2013 | beta: 1.266 | mu_capm:  0.327 | mu_real:  0.053
2014 | beta: 0.630 | mu_capm:  0.070 | mu_real:  0.320
2015 | beta: 0.833 | mu_capm: -0.005 | mu_real: -0.047
2016 | beta: 1.144 | mu_capm:  0.103 | mu_real:  0.096
2017 | beta: 1.009 | mu_capm:  0.180 | mu_real:  0.381
2018 | beta: 1.379 | mu_capm: -0.091 | mu_real: -0.071
2019 | beta: 1.252 | mu_capm:  0.316 | mu_real:  0.621
```

```
MSFT.O
==================================================
2011 | beta: 0.890 | mu_capm:   0.001 | mu_real: -0.072
2012 | beta: 0.816 | mu_capm:   0.104 | mu_real:  0.029
2013 | beta: 1.109 | mu_capm:   0.287 | mu_real:  0.337
2014 | beta: 0.876 | mu_capm:   0.095 | mu_real:  0.216
2015 | beta: 0.955 | mu_capm:  -0.007 | mu_real:  0.178
2016 | beta: 1.249 | mu_capm:   0.113 | mu_real:  0.113
2017 | beta: 1.224 | mu_capm:   0.217 | mu_real:  0.321
2018 | beta: 1.303 | mu_capm:  -0.086 | mu_real:  0.172
2019 | beta: 1.442 | mu_capm:   0.364 | mu_real:  0.440

INTC.O
==================================================
2011 | beta: 1.081 | mu_capm:  -0.000 | mu_real:  0.142
2012 | beta: 0.842 | mu_capm:   0.108 | mu_real: -0.163
2013 | beta: 1.081 | mu_capm:   0.280 | mu_real:  0.230
2014 | beta: 0.883 | mu_capm:   0.096 | mu_real:  0.335
2015 | beta: 1.055 | mu_capm:  -0.008 | mu_real: -0.052
2016 | beta: 1.009 | mu_capm:   0.092 | mu_real:  0.051
2017 | beta: 1.261 | mu_capm:   0.223 | mu_real:  0.242
2018 | beta: 1.163 | mu_capm:  -0.076 | mu_real:  0.017
2019 | beta: 1.376 | mu_capm:   0.347 | mu_real:  0.243

AMZN.O
==================================================
2011 | beta: 1.102 | mu_capm:  -0.001 | mu_real: -0.039
2012 | beta: 0.958 | mu_capm:   0.122 | mu_real:  0.374
2013 | beta: 1.116 | mu_capm:   0.289 | mu_real:  0.464
2014 | beta: 1.262 | mu_capm:   0.135 | mu_real: -0.251
2015 | beta: 1.473 | mu_capm:  -0.013 | mu_real:  0.778
2016 | beta: 1.122 | mu_capm:   0.102 | mu_real:  0.104
2017 | beta: 1.118 | mu_capm:   0.199 | mu_real:  0.446
2018 | beta: 1.300 | mu_capm:  -0.086 | mu_real:  0.251
2019 | beta: 1.619 | mu_capm:   0.408 | mu_real:  0.207
```

Figure 4-9 compares the predicted (expected) return for a single stock, given the beta from the previous year and market portfolio performance of the current year, with the realized return of the stock for the current year. Obviously, the CAPM in its original form does not prove really useful in predicting a stock's performance based on beta only:

```
In [88]: sym = 'AMZN.O'

In [89]: res[res['symbol'] == sym].corr()
Out[89]:           mu_capm    mu_real
         mu_capm  1.000000  -0.004826
         mu_real -0.004826   1.000000

In [90]: res[res['symbol'] == sym].plot(kind='bar',
                     figsize=(10, 6), title=sym);
```

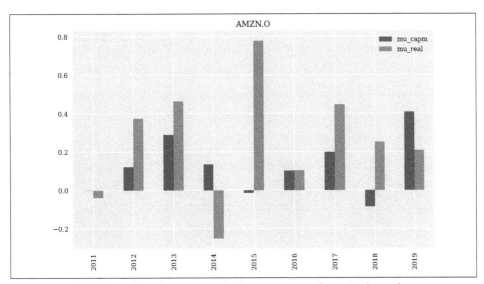

Figure 4-9. CAPM-predicted versus realized stock returns for a single stock

Figure 4-10 compares the averages of the CAPM-predicted stock returns with the averages of the realized returns. Also here, the CAPM does not do a good job.

What is easy to see is that the CAPM predictions do not vary that much on average for the stocks analyzed; they are between 12.2% and 14.4%. However, the realized average returns of the stocks show a high variability; these are between 9.4% and 29.2%. Market portfolio performance and beta alone obviously cannot account for the observed returns of the (technology) stocks:

```
In [91]: grouped = res.groupby('symbol').mean()
         grouped
Out[91]:         mu_capm    mu_real
         symbol
         AAPL.O  0.110855   0.206158
         AMZN.O  0.128223   0.259395
         INTC.O  0.117929   0.116180
         MSFT.O  0.120844   0.192655

In [92]: grouped.plot(kind='bar', figsize=(10, 6), title='Average Values');
```

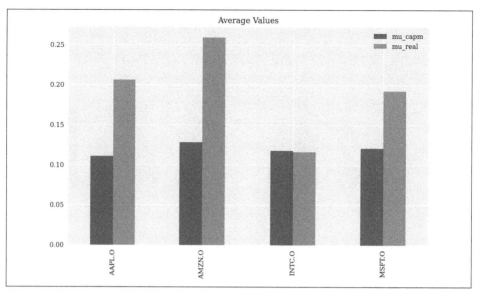

Figure 4-10. Average CAPM-predicted versus average realized stock returns for multiple stocks

Predictive Power of the CAPM

The predictive power of the CAPM with regard to the future per-formance of stocks, relative to the market portfolio, is pretty low or even nonexistent for certain stocks. One of the reasons is probably the fact that the CAPM rests on the same central assumptions as MVP theory, namely that investors care about only the (expected) return and (expected) volatility of a portfolio and/or stock. From a modeling point of view, one can ask whether the single risk factor is enough to explain variability in stock returns or whether there might be a nonlinear relationship between a stock's return and the market portfolio performance.

Arbitrage Pricing Theory

The predictive power of the CAPM seems quite limited given the results from the previous numerical example. A valid question is whether the market portfolio perfor-mance alone is enough to explain variability in stock returns. The answer of the APT is *no*—there can be more (even many more) factors that together explain variability in stock returns. "Arbitrage Pricing Theory" on page 90 formally describes the frame-work of APT that also relies on a linear relationship between the factors and a stock's return.

The data-driven investor recognizes that the CAPM is not sufficient to reliably predict a stock's performance relative to the market portfolio performance. Therefore, the investor decides to add to the market portfolio three additional factors that might drive a stock's performance:

- Market volatility (as represented by the VIX index, .VIX)
- Exchange rates (as represented by the EUR/USD rate, EUR=)
- Commodity prices (as represented by the gold price, XAU=)

The following Python code implements a simple APT approach by using the four factors in combination with multivariate regression to explain a stock's future performance in relation to the factors:

```
In [93]: factors = ['.SPX', '.VIX', 'EUR=', 'XAU='] ❶

In [94]: res = pd.DataFrame()

In [95]: np.set_printoptions(formatter={'float': lambda x: f'{x:5.2f}'})

In [96]: for sym in rets.columns[:4]:
             print('\n' + sym)
             print(71 * '=')
             for year in range(2010, 2019):
                 rets_ = rets.loc[f'{year}-01-01':f'{year}-12-31']
                 reg = np.linalg.lstsq(rets_[factors],
                                       rets_[sym], rcond=-1)[0] ❷
                 rets_ = rets.loc[f'{year + 1}-01-01':f'{year + 1}-12-31']
                 mu_apt = np.dot(rets_[factors].mean() * 252, reg) ❸
                 mu_real =  rets_[sym].mean() * 252 ❹
                 res = res.append(pd.DataFrame({'symbol': sym,
                                     'mu_apt': mu_apt, 'mu_real': mu_real},
                                     index=[year + 1]))
                 print('{} | fl: {} | mu_apt: {:6.3f} | mu_real: {:6.3f}'
                       .format(year + 1, reg.round(2), mu_apt, mu_real))
```

❶ The four factors

❷ The multivariate regression

❸ The APT-predicted return of the stock

❹ The realized return of the stock

The preceding code provides the following output:

```
AAPL.O
=======================================================================
2011 | fl: [ 0.91 -0.04 -0.35  0.12] | mu_apt:  0.011 | mu_real:  0.228
2012 | fl: [ 0.76 -0.02 -0.24  0.05] | mu_apt:  0.099 | mu_real:  0.275
```

```
2013 | fl: [ 1.67  0.04 -0.56  0.10] | mu_apt:  0.366 | mu_real:  0.053
2014 | fl: [ 0.53 -0.00  0.02  0.16] | mu_apt:  0.050 | mu_real:  0.320
2015 | fl: [ 1.07  0.02  0.25  0.01] | mu_apt: -0.038 | mu_real: -0.047
2016 | fl: [ 1.21  0.01 -0.14 -0.02] | mu_apt:  0.110 | mu_real:  0.096
2017 | fl: [ 1.10  0.01 -0.15 -0.02] | mu_apt:  0.170 | mu_real:  0.381
2018 | fl: [ 1.06 -0.03 -0.15  0.12] | mu_apt: -0.088 | mu_real: -0.071
2019 | fl: [ 1.37  0.01 -0.20  0.13] | mu_apt:  0.364 | mu_real:  0.621

MSFT.O
=====================================================================
2011 | fl: [ 0.98  0.01  0.02 -0.11] | mu_apt: -0.008 | mu_real: -0.072
2012 | fl: [ 0.82  0.00 -0.03 -0.01] | mu_apt:  0.103 | mu_real:  0.029
2013 | fl: [ 1.14  0.00 -0.07 -0.01] | mu_apt:  0.294 | mu_real:  0.337
2014 | fl: [ 1.28  0.05  0.04  0.07] | mu_apt:  0.149 | mu_real:  0.216
2015 | fl: [ 1.20  0.03  0.05  0.01] | mu_apt: -0.016 | mu_real:  0.178
2016 | fl: [ 1.44  0.03 -0.17 -0.02] | mu_apt:  0.127 | mu_real:  0.113
2017 | fl: [ 1.33  0.01 -0.14  0.00] | mu_apt:  0.216 | mu_real:  0.321
2018 | fl: [ 1.10 -0.02 -0.14  0.22] | mu_apt: -0.087 | mu_real:  0.172
2019 | fl: [ 1.51  0.01 -0.16 -0.02] | mu_apt:  0.378 | mu_real:  0.440

INTC.O
=====================================================================
2011 | fl: [ 1.17  0.01  0.05 -0.13] | mu_apt: -0.010 | mu_real:  0.142
2012 | fl: [ 1.03  0.04  0.01  0.03] | mu_apt:  0.122 | mu_real: -0.163
2013 | fl: [ 1.06 -0.01 -0.10  0.01] | mu_apt:  0.267 | mu_real:  0.230
2014 | fl: [ 0.96  0.02  0.36 -0.02] | mu_apt:  0.063 | mu_real:  0.335
2015 | fl: [ 0.93 -0.01 -0.09  0.02] | mu_apt:  0.001 | mu_real: -0.052
2016 | fl: [ 1.02  0.00 -0.05  0.06] | mu_apt:  0.099 | mu_real:  0.051
2017 | fl: [ 1.41  0.02 -0.18  0.03] | mu_apt:  0.226 | mu_real:  0.242
2018 | fl: [ 1.12 -0.01 -0.11  0.17] | mu_apt: -0.076 | mu_real:  0.017
2019 | fl: [ 1.50  0.01 -0.34  0.30] | mu_apt:  0.431 | mu_real:  0.243

AMZN.O
=====================================================================
2011 | fl: [ 1.02 -0.03 -0.18 -0.14] | mu_apt: -0.016 | mu_real: -0.039
2012 | fl: [ 0.98 -0.01 -0.17 -0.09] | mu_apt:  0.117 | mu_real:  0.374
2013 | fl: [ 1.07 -0.00  0.09  0.00] | mu_apt:  0.282 | mu_real:  0.464
2014 | fl: [ 1.54  0.03  0.01 -0.08] | mu_apt:  0.176 | mu_real: -0.251
2015 | fl: [ 1.26 -0.02  0.45 -0.11] | mu_apt: -0.044 | mu_real:  0.778
2016 | fl: [ 1.06 -0.00 -0.15 -0.04] | mu_apt:  0.099 | mu_real:  0.104
2017 | fl: [ 0.94 -0.02  0.12 -0.03] | mu_apt:  0.185 | mu_real:  0.446
2018 | fl: [ 0.90 -0.04 -0.25  0.28] | mu_apt: -0.085 | mu_real:  0.251
2019 | fl: [ 1.99  0.05 -0.37  0.12] | mu_apt:  0.506 | mu_real:  0.207
```

Figure 4-11 compares the APT-predicted returns for a stock and its realized stock returns over time. Compared to the single-factor CAPM, there seems to be hardly any improvement:

```
In [97]: sym = 'AMZN.O'

In [98]: res[res['symbol'] == sym].corr()
Out[98]:          mu_apt    mu_real
```

```
       mu_apt   1.000000 -0.098281
       mu_real -0.098281  1.000000

In [99]: res[res['symbol'] == sym].plot(kind='bar',
                          figsize=(10, 6), title=sym);
```

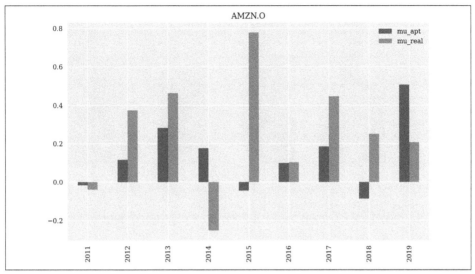

Figure 4-11. APT-predicted versus realized stock returns for a stock

The same picture arises in Figure 4-12, produced by the following snippet, which compares the averages for multiple stocks. Because there is hardly any variation in the average APT predictions, there are large average differences to the realized returns:

```
In [100]: grouped = res.groupby('symbol').mean()
          grouped
Out[100]:          mu_apt    mu_real
          symbol
          AAPL.O   0.116116   0.206158
          AMZN.O   0.135528   0.259395
          INTC.O   0.124811   0.116180
          MSFT.O   0.128441   0.192655

In [101]: grouped.plot(kind='bar', figsize=(10, 6), title='Average Values');
```

Of course, the selection of the risk factors is of paramount importance in this context. The data-driven investor decides to find out what risk factors are typically considered relevant ones for stocks. After studying the paper by Bender et al. (2013), the investor replaces the original risk factors with a new set. In particular, the investor chooses the set as presented in Table 4-3.

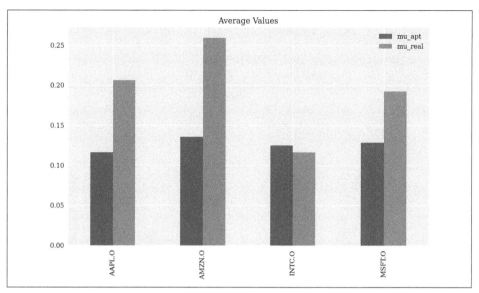

Figure 4-12. Average APT-predicted versus average realized stock returns for multiple stocks

Table 4-3. Risk factors for APT

Factor	Description	RIC
Market	MSCI World Gross Return Daily USD (PUS = Price Return)	.dMIWO00000GUS
Size	MSCI World Equal Weight Price Net Index EOD	.dMIWO0000ENUS
Volatility	MSCI World Minimum Volatility Net Return	.dMIWO0000YNUS
Value	MSCI World Value Weighted Gross (NUS for Net)	.dMIWO000PkGUS
Risk	MSCI World Risk Weighted Gross USD EOD	.dMIWO000PlGUS
Growth	MSCI World Quality Net Return USD	.MIWO0000vNUS
Momentum	MSCI World Momentum Gross Index USD EOD	.dMIWO0000NGUS

The following Python code retrieves a respective data set from a remote location and visualizes the normalized time series data (see Figure 4-13). Already a brief look reveals that the time series seem to be highly positively correlated:

```
In [102]: factors = pd.read_csv('http://hilpisch.com/aiif_eikon_eod_factors.csv',
                                index_col=0, parse_dates=True)  ❶

In [103]: (factors / factors.iloc[0]).plot(figsize=(10, 6));  ❷
```

❶ Retrieves factors time series data

❷ Normalizes and plots the data

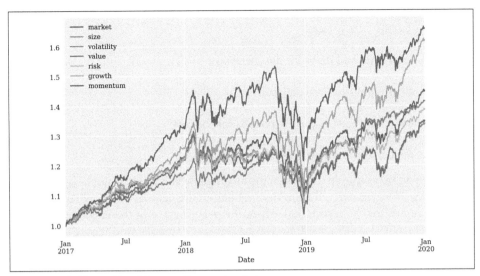

Figure 4-13. Normalized factors time series data

This impression is confirmed by the following calculation and the resulting correlation matrix for the factor returns. All correlation factors are about 0.75 or higher:

```
In [104]: start = '2017-01-01'  ❶
          end = '2020-01-01'  ❶

In [105]: retsd = rets.loc[start:end].copy()  ❷
          retsd.dropna(inplace=True)  ❷

In [106]: retsf = np.log(factors / factors.shift(1))  ❸
          retsf = retsf.loc[start:end]  ❸
          retsf.dropna(inplace=True)  ❸
          retsf = retsf.loc[retsd.index].dropna()  ❸

In [107]: retsf.corr()  ❹
Out[107]:             market      size  volatility      value      risk    growth  \
          market    1.000000  0.935867    0.845010   0.964124  0.947150  0.959038
          size      0.935867  1.000000    0.791767   0.965739  0.983238  0.835477
          volatility 0.845010 0.791767    1.000000   0.778294  0.865467  0.818280
          value     0.964124  0.965739    0.778294   1.000000  0.958359  0.864222
          risk      0.947150  0.983238    0.865467   0.958359  1.000000  0.858546
          growth    0.959038  0.835477    0.818280   0.864222  0.858546  1.000000
          momentum  0.928705  0.796420    0.819585   0.818796  0.825563  0.952956

                    momentum
          market    0.928705
          size      0.796420
          volatility 0.819585
          value     0.818796
          risk      0.825563
```

```
growth        0.952956
momentum      1.000000
```

❶ Defines start and end dates for data selection

❷ Selects the relevant returns data sub-set

❸ Calculates and processes the log returns for the factors

❹ Shows the correlation matrix for the factors

The following Python code derives factor loadings for the original stocks but with the new factors. They are derived from the first half of the data set and applied to predict the stock return for the second half given the performance of the single factors. The realized return is also calculated. Both time series are compared in Figure 4-14. As to be expected given the high correlation of the factors, the explanatory power of the APT approach is not much higher compared to the CAPM:

```
In [108]: res = pd.DataFrame()

In [109]: np.set_printoptions(formatter={'float': lambda x: f'{x:5.2f}'})

In [110]: split = int(len(retsf) * 0.5)
          for sym in rets.columns[:4]:
              print('\n' + sym)
              print(74 * '=')
              retsf_, retsd_ = retsf.iloc[:split], retsd.iloc[:split]
              reg = np.linalg.lstsq(retsf_, retsd_[sym], rcond=-1)[0]
              retsf_, retsd_ = retsf.iloc[split:], retsd.iloc[split:]
              mu_apt = np.dot(retsf_.mean() * 252, reg)
              mu_real =  retsd_[sym].mean() * 252
              res = res.append(pd.DataFrame({'mu_apt': mu_apt,
                              'mu_real': mu_real}, index=[sym,]),
                              sort=True)
              print('fl: {} | apt: {:.3f} | real: {:.3f}'
                    .format(reg.round(1), mu_apt, mu_real))


          AAPL.O
          ==========================================================================
          fl: [ 2.30  2.80 -0.70 -1.40 -4.20  2.00 -0.20] | apt: 0.115 | real: 0.301

          MSFT.O
          ==========================================================================
          fl: [ 1.50  0.00  0.10 -1.30 -1.40  0.80  1.00] | apt: 0.181 | real: 0.304

          INTC.O
          ==========================================================================
          fl: [-3.10  1.60  0.40  1.30 -2.60  2.50  1.10] | apt: 0.186 | real: 0.118
```

```
          AMZN.O
          ===========================================================================
          fl: [ 9.10  3.30 -1.00 -7.10 -3.10 -1.80  1.20] | apt: 0.019 | real: 0.050
```

```
In [111]: res.plot(kind='bar', figsize=(10, 6));
```

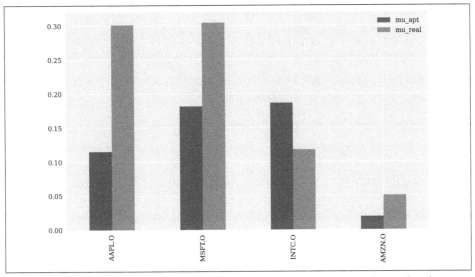

Figure 4-14. APT-predicted returns based on typical factors compared to realized returns

The data-driven investor is not willing to dismiss the APT completely. Therefore, an additional test might shed some more light on the explanatory power of APT. To this end, the factor loadings are used to test whether APT can explain movements of the stock price over time (correctly). And indeed, although APT does not predict the absolute performance correctly (it is off by 10+ percentage points), it predicts the direction of the stock price movement correctly in the majority of cases (see Figure 4-15). The correlation between the predicted and realized returns is also pretty high at around 85%. However, the analysis uses realized factor returns to generate the APT predictions—something, of course, not available in practice a day before the relevant trading day:

```
In [112]: sym
Out[112]: 'AMZN.O'

In [113]: rets_sym = np.dot(retsf_, reg)   ❶

In [114]: rets_sym = pd.DataFrame(rets_sym,
                                  columns=[sym + '_apt'],
                                  index=retsf_.index)   ❷

In [115]: rets_sym[sym + '_real'] = retsd_[sym]   ❸
```

```
In [116]: rets_sym.mean() * 252    ❹
Out[116]: AMZN.O_apt      0.019401
          AMZN.O_real     0.050344
          dtype: float64

In [117]: rets_sym.std() * 252 ** 0.5    ❺
Out[117]: AMZN.O_apt      0.270995
          AMZN.O_real     0.307653
          dtype: float64

In [118]: rets_sym.corr()    ❻
Out[118]:             AMZN.O_apt  AMZN.O_real
          AMZN.O_apt    1.000000     0.832218
          AMZN.O_real   0.832218     1.000000

In [119]: rets_sym.cumsum().apply(np.exp).plot(figsize=(10, 6));
```

❶ Predicts the daily stock price returns given the realized factor returns

❷ Stores the results in a `DataFrame` object and adds column and index data

❸ Adds the realized stock price returns to the `DataFrame` object

❹ Calculates the annualized returns

❺ Calculates the annualized volatility

❻ Calculates the correlation factor

Figure 4-15. APT-predicted performance and real performance over time (gross)

How accurately does APT predict the direction of the stock price movement given the realized factor returns? The following Python code shows that the accuracy score is a bit better than 75%:

```
In [120]: rets_sym['same'] = (np.sign(rets_sym[sym + '_apt']) ==
                              np.sign(rets_sym[sym + '_real']))

In [121]: rets_sym['same'].value_counts()
Out[121]: True     288
          False     89
          Name: same, dtype: int64

In [122]: rets_sym['same'].value_counts()[True] / len(rets_sym)
Out[122]: 0.7639257294429708
```

Debunking Central Assumptions

The previous section provides a number of numerical, real-world examples showing how popular normative financial theories might fail in practice. This section argues that one of the major reasons is that central assumptions of these popular financial theories are invalid; that is, they simply do not describe the reality of financial markets. The two assumptions analyzed are *normally distributed returns* and *linear relationships*.

Normally Distributed Returns

As a matter of fact, only a normal distribution is completely specified through its first (expectation) and second moment (standard deviation).

Sample data sets

For illustration, consider a randomly generated set of standard normally distributed numbers as generated by the following Python code.[4] Figure 4-16 shows the typical bell shape of the resulting histogram:

```
In [1]: import numpy as np
        import pandas as pd
        from pylab import plt, mpl
        np.random.seed(100)
        plt.style.use('seaborn')
        mpl.rcParams['savefig.dpi'] = 300
        mpl.rcParams['font.family'] = 'serif'

In [2]: N = 10000
```

---

4 Numbers generated by the random number generator of NumPy are *pseudorandom numbers*, although they are referenced throughout the book as *random numbers*.

```
In [3]: snrn = np.random.standard_normal(N)  ❶
        snrn -= snrn.mean()  ❷
        snrn /= snrn.std()  ❸

In [4]: round(snrn.mean(), 4)  ❷
Out[4]: -0.0

In [5]: round(snrn.std(), 4)  ❸
Out[5]: 1.0

In [6]: plt.figure(figsize=(10, 6))
        plt.hist(snrn, bins=35);
```

❶ Draws standard normally distributed random numbers

❷ Corrects the first moment (expectation) to 0.0

❸ Corrects the second moment (standard deviation) to 1.0

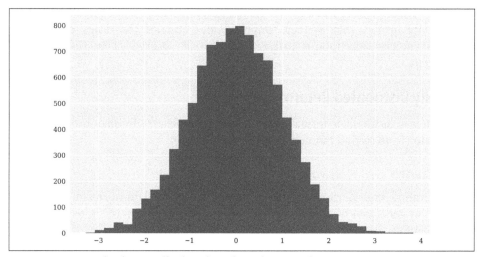

Figure 4-16. Standard normally distributed random numbers

Now consider a set of random numbers that share the same first and second moment values but have a completely different distribution than Figure 4-17 illustrates. Although the moments are the same, this distribution only consists of three discrete values:

```
In [7]: numbers = np.ones(N) * 1.5  ❶
        split = int(0.25 * N)  ❶
        numbers[split:3 * split] = -1  ❶
        numbers[3 * split:4 * split] = 0  ❶

In [8]: numbers -= numbers.mean()  ❷
```

```
         numbers /= numbers.std()   ❸

In [9]: round(numbers.mean(), 4)   ❷
Out[9]: 0.0

In [10]: round(numbers.std(), 4)   ❸
Out[10]: 1.0

In [11]: plt.figure(figsize=(10, 6))
         plt.hist(numbers, bins=35);
```

❶ A set of numbers with three discrete values only

❷ Corrects the first moment (expectation) to 0.0

❸ Corrects the second moment (standard deviation) to 1.0

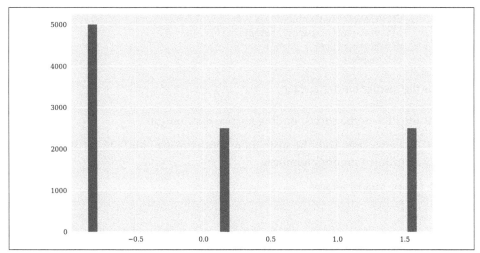

Figure 4-17. Distribution with first and second moment of 0.0 and 1.0, respectively

First and Second Moment

The first and second moment of a probability distribution only describe a normal distribution completely. There are infinitely many other distributions that might share the first two moments with a normal distribution while being completely different.

In preparation for a test of real financial returns, consider the following Python functions that allow one to visualize data as a histogram and to add a probability density function (PDF) of a normal distribution with the first two moments of the data:

```
In [12]: import math
         import scipy.stats as scs
```

```
         import statsmodels.api as sm

In [13]: def dN(x, mu, sigma):
             ''' Probability density function of a normal random variable x.
             '''
             z = (x - mu) / sigma
             pdf = np.exp(-0.5 * z ** 2) / math.sqrt(2 * math.pi * sigma ** 2)
             return pdf

In [14]: def return_histogram(rets, title=''):
             ''' Plots a histogram of the returns.
             '''
             plt.figure(figsize=(10, 6))
             x = np.linspace(min(rets), max(rets), 100)
             plt.hist(np.array(rets), bins=50,
                     density=True, label='frequency')    ❶
             y = dN(x, np.mean(rets), np.std(rets))    ❷
             plt.plot(x, y, linewidth=2, label='PDF')    ❷
             plt.xlabel('log returns')
             plt.ylabel('frequency/probability')
             plt.title(title)
             plt.legend()
```

❶ Plots the histogram of the data

❷ Plots the PDF of the corresponding normal distribution

Figure 4-18 shows how well the histogram approximates the PDF for the standard normally distributed random numbers:

```
In [15]: return_histogram(snrn)
```

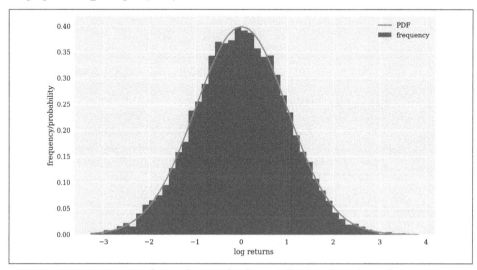

Figure 4-18. Histogram and PDF for standard normally distributed numbers

By contrast, Figure 4-19 illustrates that the PDF of the normal distribution has nothing to do with the data shown as a histogram:

```
In [16]: return_histogram(numbers)
```

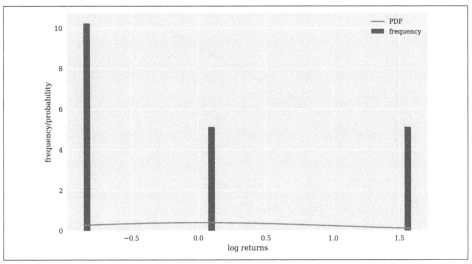

Figure 4-19. Histogram and normal PDF for discrete numbers

Another way of comparing a normal distribution to data is the Quantile-Quantile (Q-Q) plot. As Figure 4-20 shows, for normally distributed numbers, the numbers themselves lie (mostly) on a straight line in the Q-Q plane:

```
In [17]: def return_qqplot(rets, title=''):
             ''' Generates a Q-Q plot of the returns.
             '''
             fig = sm.qqplot(rets, line='s', alpha=0.5)
             fig.set_size_inches(10, 6)
             plt.title(title)
             plt.xlabel('theoretical quantiles')
             plt.ylabel('sample quantiles')

In [18]: return_qqplot(snrn)
```

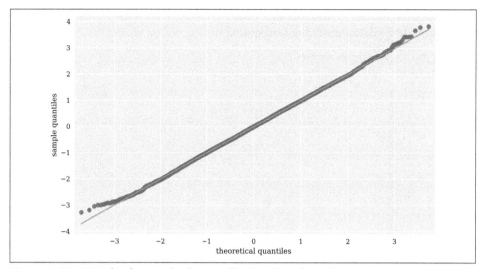

Figure 4-20. Q-Q plot for standard normally distributed numbers

Again, the Q-Q plot as shown in Figure 4-21 for the discrete numbers looks completely different to the one in Figure 4-20:

```
In [19]: return_qqplot(numbers)
```

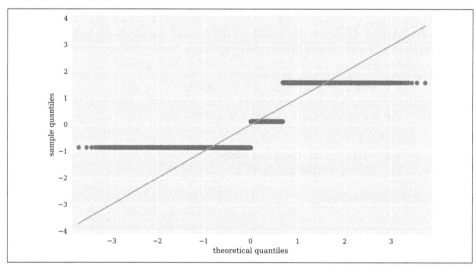

Figure 4-21. Q-Q plot for discrete numbers

Finally, one can also use statistical tests to check whether a set of numbers is normally distributed or not.

The following Python function implements three tests:

- Test for normal skew.
- Test for normal kurtosis.
- Test for normal skew and kurtosis combined.

A p-value below 0.05 is generally considered to be a counter-indicator for normality; that is, the hypothesis that the numbers are normally distributed is rejected. In that sense, as in the preceding figures, the p-values for the two data sets speak for themselves:

```
In [20]: def print_statistics(rets):
             print('RETURN SAMPLE STATISTICS')
             print('---------------------------------------------')
             print('Skew of Sample Log Returns {:9.6f}'.format(
                     scs.skew(rets)))
             print('Skew Normal Test p-value   {:9.6f}'.format(
                     scs.skewtest(rets)[1]))
             print('---------------------------------------------')
             print('Kurt of Sample Log Returns {:9.6f}'.format(
                     scs.kurtosis(rets)))
             print('Kurt Normal Test p-value   {:9.6f}'.format(
                     scs.kurtosistest(rets)[1]))
             print('---------------------------------------------')
             print('Normal Test p-value        {:9.6f}'.format(
                     scs.normaltest(rets)[1]))
             print('---------------------------------------------')

In [21]: print_statistics(snrn)
         RETURN SAMPLE STATISTICS
         ---------------------------------------------
         Skew of Sample Log Returns  0.016793
         Skew Normal Test p-value    0.492685
         ---------------------------------------------
         Kurt of Sample Log Returns -0.024540
         Kurt Normal Test p-value    0.637637
         ---------------------------------------------
         Normal Test p-value         0.707334
         ---------------------------------------------

In [22]: print_statistics(numbers)
         RETURN SAMPLE STATISTICS
         ---------------------------------------------
         Skew of Sample Log Returns  0.689254
         Skew Normal Test p-value    0.000000
         ---------------------------------------------
         Kurt of Sample Log Returns -1.141902
         Kurt Normal Test p-value    0.000000
         ---------------------------------------------
         Normal Test p-value         0.000000
         ---------------------------------------------
```

Real financial returns

The following Python code retrieves EOD data from a remote source, as done earlier in the chapter, and calculates the log returns for all financial time series contained in the data set. Figure 4-22 shows that the log returns of the S&P 500 stock index represented as a histogram show a much higher peak and fatter tails when compared to the normal PDF with the sample expectation and standard deviation. These two insights are *stylized facts* because they can be consistently observed for different financial instruments:

```
In [23]: raw = pd.read_csv('http://hilpisch.com/aiif_eikon_eod_data.csv',
                           index_col=0, parse_dates=True).dropna()

In [24]: rets = np.log(raw / raw.shift(1)).dropna()

In [25]: symbol = '.SPX'

In [26]: return_histogram(rets[symbol].values, symbol)
```

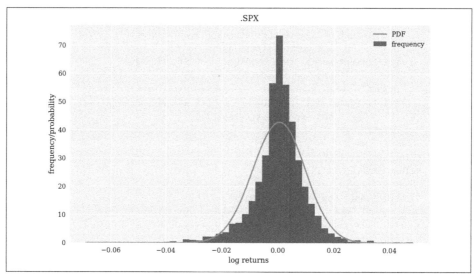

Figure 4-22. Frequency distribution and normal PDF for S&P 500 log returns

Similar insights can be gained when considering the Q-Q plot for the S&P 500 log returns in Figure 4-23. In particular, the Q-Q plot visualizes the fat tails pretty well (points below the straight line to the left and above the straight line to the right):

```
In [27]: return_qqplot(rets[symbol].values, symbol)
```

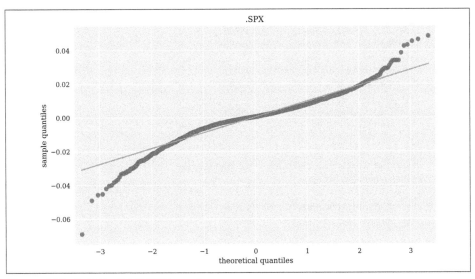

Figure 4-23. Q-Q for S&P 500 log returns

The Python code that follows conducts the statistical tests regarding the normality of the real financial returns for a selection of the financial time series from the data set. Real financial returns regularly fail such tests. Therefore, it is safe to conclude that the normality assumption about financial returns hardly, if at all, describes financial reality:

```
In [28]: symbols = ['.SPX', 'AMZN.O', 'EUR=', 'GLD']

In [29]: for sym in symbols:
             print('\n{}'.format(sym))
             print(45 * '=')
             print_statistics(rets[sym].values)

         .SPX
         =============================================
         RETURN SAMPLE STATISTICS
         ---------------------------------------------
         Skew of Sample Log Returns -0.497160
         Skew Normal Test p-value    0.000000
         ---------------------------------------------
         Kurt of Sample Log Returns  4.598167
         Kurt Normal Test p-value    0.000000
         ---------------------------------------------
         Normal Test p-value         0.000000
         ---------------------------------------------

         AMZN.O
         =============================================
         RETURN SAMPLE STATISTICS
```

```
--------------------------------------------------
Skew of Sample Log Returns  0.135268
Skew Normal Test p-value     0.005689
--------------------------------------------------
Kurt of Sample Log Returns  7.344837
Kurt Normal Test p-value     0.000000
--------------------------------------------------
Normal Test p-value          0.000000
--------------------------------------------------

EUR=
==================================================
RETURN SAMPLE STATISTICS
--------------------------------------------------
Skew of Sample Log Returns  -0.053959
Skew Normal Test p-value     0.268203
--------------------------------------------------
Kurt of Sample Log Returns  1.780899
Kurt Normal Test p-value     0.000000
--------------------------------------------------
Normal Test p-value          0.000000
--------------------------------------------------

GLD
==================================================
RETURN SAMPLE STATISTICS
--------------------------------------------------
Skew of Sample Log Returns  -0.581025
Skew Normal Test p-value     0.000000
--------------------------------------------------
Kurt of Sample Log Returns  5.899701
Kurt Normal Test p-value     0.000000
--------------------------------------------------
Normal Test p-value          0.000000
--------------------------------------------------
```

Normality Assumption

Although the normality assumption is a good approximation for many real-world phenomena, such as in physics, it is not appropriate and can even be dangerous when it comes to financial returns. Almost no financial return sample data set passes statistical normality tests. Beyond the fact that it has proven useful in other domains, a major reason why this assumption is found in so many financial models is that it leads to elegant and relatively simple mathematical models, calculations, and proofs.

Linear Relationships

Similar to the "omnipresence" of the normality assumption in financial models and theories, *linear relationships* between variables seem to be another widespread benchmark. This sub-section considers an important one, namely the assumed linear relationship in the CAPM between the beta of a stock and its expected (realized) return. Generally speaking, the higher the beta is, the higher the expected return given a positive market performance will be—in a fixed proportional way as given by the beta value itself.

Recall the calculation of the betas, the CAPM expected returns, and the realized returns for a selection of technology stocks from the previous section, which is repeated in the following Python code for convenience. This time, the beta values are added to the results' DataFrame object as well.

```
In [30]: r = 0.005

In [31]: market = '.SPX'

In [32]: res = pd.DataFrame()

In [33]: for sym in rets.columns[:4]:
             for year in range(2010, 2019):
                 rets_ = rets.loc[f'{year}-01-01':f'{year}-12-31']
                 muM = rets_[market].mean() * 252
                 cov = rets_.cov().loc[sym, market]
                 var = rets_[market].var()
                 beta = cov / var
                 rets_ = rets.loc[f'{year + 1}-01-01':f'{year + 1}-12-31']
                 muM = rets_[market].mean() * 252
                 mu_capm = r + beta * (muM - r)
                 mu_real = rets_[sym].mean() * 252
                 res = res.append(pd.DataFrame({'symbol': sym,
                                                'beta': beta,
                                                'mu_capm': mu_capm,
                                                'mu_real': mu_real},
                                                index=[year + 1]),
                                                sort=True)
```

The following analysis calculates the R^2 score for a linear regression for which the beta is the independent variable and the *expected CAPM return*, given the market portfolio performance, is the dependent variable. R^2 refers to the *coefficient of determination* and measures how well a model performs compared to a baseline predictor in the form of a simple mean value. The linear regression can only explain around 10% of the variability in the expected CAPM return, a pretty low value, which is also confirmed through Figure 4-24:

```
In [34]: from sklearn.metrics import r2_score
```

```
In [35]: reg = np.polyfit(res['beta'], res['mu_capm'], deg=1)
         res['mu_capm_ols'] = np.polyval(reg, res['beta'])

In [36]: r2_score(res['mu_capm'], res['mu_capm_ols'])
Out[36]: 0.09272355783573516

In [37]: res.plot(kind='scatter', x='beta', y='mu_capm', figsize=(10, 6))
         x = np.linspace(res['beta'].min(), res['beta'].max())
         plt.plot(x, np.polyval(reg, x), 'g--', label='regression')
         plt.legend();
```

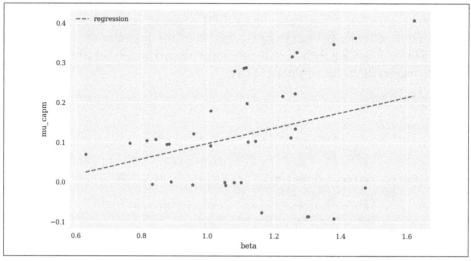

Figure 4-24. Expected CAPM return versus beta (including linear regression)

For the *realized return*, the explanatory power of the linear regression is even lower, with about 4.5% (see Figure 4-25). The linear regressions recover the positive relationship between beta and stock returns—"the higher the beta, the higher the return given the (positive) market portfolio performance"—as indicated by the positive slope of the regression lines. However, they only explain a small part of the observed overall variability in the stock returns:

```
In [38]: reg = np.polyfit(res['beta'], res['mu_real'], deg=1)
         res['mu_real_ols'] = np.polyval(reg, res['beta'])

In [39]: r2_score(res['mu_real'], res['mu_real_ols'])
Out[39]: 0.04466919444752959

In [40]: res.plot(kind='scatter', x='beta', y='mu_real', figsize=(10, 6))
         x = np.linspace(res['beta'].min(), res['beta'].max())
         plt.plot(x, np.polyval(reg, x), 'g--', label='regression')
         plt.legend();
```

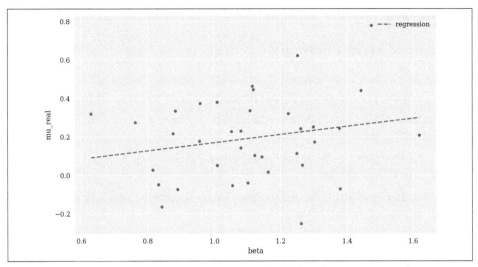

Figure 4-25. Expected CAPM return versus beta (including linear regression)

Linear Relationships

As with the normality assumptions, linear relationships can often be observed in the physical world. However, in finance there are hardly any cases in which variables depend on each other in a clearly linear way. From a modeling point of view, linear relationships lead, as does the normality assumption, to elegant and relatively simple mathematical models, calculations, and proofs. In addition, the standard tool in financial econometrics, OLS regression, is well suited to dealing with linear relationships in data. These are major reasons why normality and linearity are often deliberately chosen as convenient building blocks of financial models and theories.

Conclusions

Science has been driven for centuries by the rigorous generation and analysis of data. However, finance used to be characterized by normative theories based on simplified mathematical models of the financial markets, relying on assumptions such as normality of returns and linear relationships. The almost universal and comprehensive availability of (financial) data has led to a shift in focus from a *theory-first* approach to *data-driven* finance. Several examples based on real financial data illustrate that many popular financial models and theories cannot survive a confrontation with financial market realities. Although elegant, they might be too simplistic to capture the complexities, changing nature, and nonlinearities of financial markets.

References

Books and papers cited in this chapter:

Allais, M. 1953. "Le Comportement de l'Homme Rationnel devant le Risque: Critique des Postulats et Axiomes de l'Ecole Americaine." *Econometrica* 21 (4): 503-546.

Alexander, Carol. 2008a. *Quantitative Methods in Finance*. Market Risk Analysis I, West Sussex: John Wiley & Sons.

————. 2008b. *Practical Financial Econometrics*. Market Risk Analysis II, West Sussex: John Wiley & Sons.

Bender, Jennifer et al. 2013. "Foundations of Factor Investing." *MSCI Research Insight*. *http://bit.ly/aiif_factor_invest*.

Campbell, John Y. 2018. *Financial Decisions and Markets: A Course in Asset Pricing*. Princeton and Oxford: Princeton University Press.

Ellsberg, Daniel. 1961. "Risk, Ambiguity, and the Savage Axioms." *Quarterly Journal of Economics* 75 (4): 643-669.

Fontaine, Philippe and Robert Leonard. 2005. *The Experiment in the History of Economics*. London and New York: Routledge.

Kopf, Dan. 2015. "The Discovery of Statistical Regression." *Priceonomics*, November 6, 2015. *http://bit.ly/aiif_ols*.

Lee, Kai-Fu. 2018. *AI Superpowers: China, Silicon Valley, and the New World Order*. Boston and New York: Houghton Mifflin Harcourt.

Sapolsky, Robert M. 2018. *Behave: The Biology of Humans at Our Best and Worst*. New York: Penguin Books.

Savage, Leonard J. (1954) 1972. *The Foundations of Statistics*. 2nd ed. New York: Dover Publications.

Wigglesworth, Robin. 2019. "How Investment Analysts Became Data Miners." *Financial Times*, November 28, 2019. *https://oreil.ly/QJGtd*.

Python Code

The following Python file contains a number of helper functions to simplify certain tasks in NLP:

```
#
# NLP Helper Functions
#
# Artificial Intelligence in Finance
# (c) Dr Yves J Hilpisch
# The Python Quants GmbH
#
```

```
import re
import nltk
import string
import pandas as pd
from pylab import plt
from wordcloud import WordCloud
from nltk.corpus import stopwords
from nltk.corpus import wordnet as wn
from lxml.html.clean import Cleaner
from sklearn.feature_extraction.text import TfidfVectorizer
plt.style.use('seaborn')

cleaner = Cleaner(style=True, links=True, allow_tags=[''],
                  remove_unknown_tags=False)

stop_words = stopwords.words('english')
stop_words.extend(['new', 'old', 'pro', 'open', 'menu', 'close'])


def remove_non_ascii(s):
    ''' Removes all non-ascii characters.
    '''
    return ''.join(i for i in s if ord(i) < 128)

def clean_up_html(t):
    t = cleaner.clean_html(t)
    t = re.sub('[\n\t\r]', ' ', t)
    t = re.sub(' +', ' ', t)
    t = re.sub('<.*?>', '', t)
    t = remove_non_ascii(t)
    return t

def clean_up_text(t, numbers=False, punctuation=False):
    ''' Cleans up a text, e.g. HTML document,
        from HTML tags and also cleans up the
        text body.
    '''
    try:
        t = clean_up_html(t)
    except:
        pass
    t = t.lower()
    t = re.sub(r"what's", "what is ", t)
    t = t.replace('(ap)', '')
    t = re.sub(r"\'ve", " have ", t)
    t = re.sub(r"can't", "cannot ", t)
    t = re.sub(r"n't", " not ", t)
    t = re.sub(r"i'm", "i am ", t)
    t = re.sub(r"\'s", "", t)
    t = re.sub(r"\'re", " are ", t)
    t = re.sub(r"\'d", " would ", t)
    t = re.sub(r"\'ll", " will ", t)
```

```python
        t = re.sub(r'\s+', ' ', t)
        t = re.sub(r"\\", "", t)
        t = re.sub(r"\'", "", t)
        t = re.sub(r"\"", "", t)
        if numbers:
            t = re.sub('[^a-zA-Z ?!]+', '', t)
        if punctuation:
            t = re.sub(r'\W+', ' ', t)
        t = remove_non_ascii(t)
        t = t.strip()
        return t

def nltk_lemma(word):
    ''' If one exists, returns the lemma of a word.
        I.e. the base or dictionary version of it.
    '''
    lemma = wn.morphy(word)
    if lemma is None:
        return word
    else:
        return lemma

def tokenize(text, min_char=3, lemma=True, stop=True,
             numbers=False):
    ''' Tokenizes a text and implements some
        transformations.
    '''
    tokens = nltk.word_tokenize(text)
    tokens = [t for t in tokens if len(t) >= min_char]
    if numbers:
        tokens = [t for t in tokens if t[0].lower()
                  in string.ascii_lowercase]
    if stop:
        tokens = [t for t in tokens if t not in stop_words]
    if lemma:
        tokens = [nltk_lemma(t) for t in tokens]
    return tokens

def generate_word_cloud(text, no, name=None, show=True):
    ''' Generates a word cloud bitmap given a
        text document (string).
        It uses the Term Frequency (TF) and
        Inverse Document Frequency (IDF)
        vectorization approach to derive the
        importance of a word -- represented
        by the size of the word in the word cloud.

    Parameters
    ==========
    text: str
        text as the basis
    no: int
```

```
        number of words to be included
    name: str
        path to save the image
    show: bool
        whether to show the generated image or not
    '''
    tokens = tokenize(text)
    vec = TfidfVectorizer(min_df=2,
                    analyzer='word',
                    ngram_range=(1, 2),
                    stop_words='english'
                    )
    vec.fit_transform(tokens)
    wc = pd.DataFrame({'words': vec.get_feature_names(),
                    'tfidf': vec.idf_})
    words = ' '.join(wc.sort_values('tfidf', ascending=True)['words'].head(no))
    wordcloud = WordCloud(max_font_size=110,
                    background_color='white',
                    width=1024, height=768,
                    margin=10, max_words=150).generate(words)
    if show:
        plt.figure(figsize=(10, 10))
        plt.imshow(wordcloud, interpolation='bilinear')
        plt.axis('off')
        plt.show()
    if name is not None:
        wordcloud.to_file(name)


def generate_key_words(text, no):
    try:
        tokens = tokenize(text)
        vec = TfidfVectorizer(min_df=2,
                    analyzer='word',
                    ngram_range=(1, 2),
                    stop_words='english'
                    )

        vec.fit_transform(tokens)
        wc = pd.DataFrame({'words': vec.get_feature_names(),
                    'tfidf': vec.idf_})
        words = wc.sort_values('tfidf', ascending=False)['words'].values
        words = [ a for a in words if not a.isnumeric()][:no]
    except:
        words = list()
    return words
```

## CHAPTER 5

Machine Learning

> Dataism says that the universe consists of data flows, and the value of any phenomenon or entity is determined by its contribution to data processing....Dataism thereby collapses the barrier between animals [humans] and machines, and expects electronic algorithms to eventually decipher and outperform biochemical algorithms.
>
> —Yuval Noah Harari (2015)

> Machine learning is the scientific method on steroids. It follows the same process of generating, testing, and discarding or refining hypotheses. But while a scientist may spend his or her whole life coming up with and testing a few hundred hypotheses, a machine learning system can do the same in a second. Machine learning automates discovery. It's no surprise, then, that it's revolutionizing science as much as it's revolutionizing business.
>
> —Pedro Domingos (2015)

This chapter is about *machine learning as a process*. Although it uses specific algorithms and specific data for illustration, the notions and approaches discussed in this chapter are general in nature. The goal is to present the most important elements of machine learning in a single place and in an easy-to-understand and easy-to-visualize manner. The approach of this chapter is practical and illustrative in nature, omitting most technical details throughout. In that sense, the chapter provides a kind of blueprint for later, more realistic machine learning applications.

"Learning" on page 162 briefly discusses the very notion of a machine that *learns*. "Data" on page 162 imports and preprocesses the sample data used in later sections. The sample data is based on a time series for the EUR/USD exchange rate. "Success" on page 165 implements OLS regression and neural network estimation given the sample data and uses the mean-squared error as the measure of success. "Capacity" on page 169 discusses the role of the model capacity in making models more successful in the context of estimation problems. "Evaluation" on page

172 explains the role that model evaluation, typically based on a validation data subset, plays in the machine-learning process. "Bias and Variance" on page 178 discusses the notions of *high bias* and *high variance* models and their typical characteristics in the context of estimation problems. "Cross-Validation" on page 180 illustrates the concept of cross-validation to avoid, among other things, overfitting due to a too-large model capacity.

VanderPlas (2017, ch. 5) discusses topics similar to the ones covered in this chapter, making use primarily of the `scikit-learn` Python package. Chollet (2017, ch. 4) also provides an overview similar to the one provided here, but primarily makes use of the `Keras` deep learning package. Goodfellow et al. (2016, ch. 5) give a more technical and mathematical overview of machine learning and related important concepts.

Learning

On a formal, more abstract level, *learning* by an algorithm or computer program can be defined as in Mitchell (1997):

> A computer program is said to learn from experience *E* with respect to some class of tasks *T* and performance measure *P*, if its performance at tasks in *T*, as measured by *P*, improves with experience *E*.

There is a class of tasks that are to be performed (for example, *estimation* or *classification*). Then there is a performance measure, such as the *mean-squared error* (MSE) or the *accuracy ratio*. Then there is *learning* as measured by the improvement in performance given the experience of the algorithm with the task. The class of tasks at hand is described in general based on the given data set, which includes the features data and the labels data in the case of supervised learning, or only the features data in the case of unsupervised learning.

Learning Task Versus Task to Learn

In the definition of learning through an algorithm or computer program, it is important to note the difference between the task of learning and the tasks to be learned. *Learning* means to learn how to (best) execute a certain task, such as estimation or classification.

Data

This section introduces the sample data set to be used in the sections to follow. The sample data is created based on a real financial time series for the EUR/USD exchange rate. First, the data is imported from a CSV file, and then the data is resampled to monthly data and stored in a `Series` object:

```
In [1]: import numpy as np
        import pandas as pd
```

```
         from pylab import plt, mpl
         np.random.seed(100)
         plt.style.use('seaborn')
         mpl.rcParams['savefig.dpi'] = 300
         mpl.rcParams['font.family'] = 'serif'

In [2]: url = 'http://hilpisch.com/aiif_eikon_eod_data.csv'   ❶

In [3]: raw = pd.read_csv(url, index_col=0, parse_dates=True)['EUR=']   ❶

In [4]: raw.head()
Out[4]: Date
        2010-01-01    1.4323
        2010-01-04    1.4411
        2010-01-05    1.4368
        2010-01-06    1.4412
        2010-01-07    1.4318
        Name: EUR=, dtype: float64

In [5]: raw.tail()
Out[5]: Date
        2019-12-26    1.1096
        2019-12-27    1.1175
        2019-12-30    1.1197
        2019-12-31    1.1210
        2020-01-01    1.1210
        Name: EUR=, dtype: float64

In [6]: l = raw.resample('1M').last()   ❷

In [7]: l.plot(figsize=(10, 6), title='EUR/USD monthly');
```

❶   Imports the financial time series data

❷   Resamples the data to monthly time intervals

Figure 5-1 shows the financial time series.

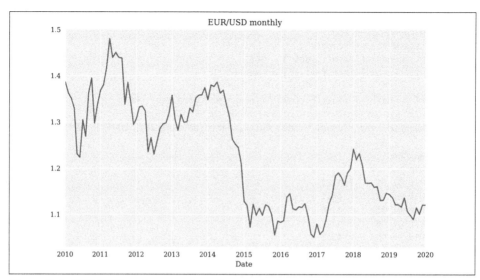

Figure 5-1. EUR/USD exchange rate as time series (monthly)

To have a single feature only, the following Python code creates a synthetic feature vector. This allows for simple visualizations in two dimensions. The synthetic feature (independent variable), of course, does not have any explanatory power for the EUR/USD exchange rate (labels data, dependent variable). In what follows, it is also abstracted from the fact that the labels data is sequential and temporal in nature. The sample data set is treated in this chapter as a general data set composed of a one-dimensional features vector and a one-dimensional labels vector. Figure 5-2 visualizes the sample data set that implies an *estimation problem* is the task at hand:

```
In [8]: l = l.values        ❶
        l -= l.mean()        ❷

In [9]: f = np.linspace(-2, 2, len(l))   ❸

In [10]: plt.figure(figsize=(10, 6))
         plt.plot(f, l, 'ro')
         plt.title('Sample Data Set')
         plt.xlabel('features')
         plt.ylabel('labels');
```

❶ Transforms the labels data to an `ndarray` object

❷ Subtracts the mean value from the data element-wise

❸ Creates a synthetic feature as an `ndarray` object

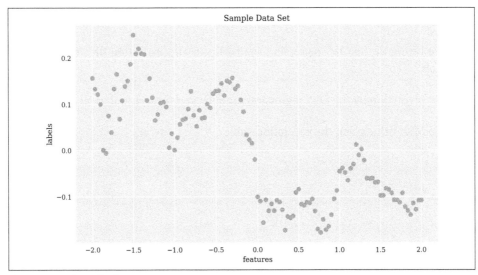

Figure 5-2. Sample data set

Success

The measure of success for estimation problems in general is the MSE, as used in Chapter 1. Based on the MSE, success is judged given the labels data as the relevant benchmark and the predicted values of an algorithm after having been exposed to the data set or parts of it. As in Chapter 1, two algorithms are considered in this and the following sections: OLS regression and neural networks.

First is OLS regression. The application is straightforward, as the following Python code illustrates. The regression result is shown in Figure 5-3 for a regression including monomials up to the fifth order. The resulting MSE is also calculated:

```
In [11]: def MSE(l, p):
             return np.mean((l - p) ** 2)    ❶

In [12]: reg = np.polyfit(f, l, deg=5)    ❷
         reg    ❷
Out[12]: array([-0.01910626, -0.0147182 ,  0.10990388,  0.06007211, -0.20833598,
                -0.03275423])

In [13]: p = np.polyval(reg, f)    ❸

In [14]: MSE(l, p)    ❹
Out[14]: 0.0034166422957371025

In [15]: plt.figure(figsize=(10, 6))
         plt.plot(f, l, 'ro', label='sample data')
         plt.plot(f, p, '--', label='regression')
         plt.legend();
```

① The function MSE calculates the mean-squared error.

② The fitting of the OLS regression model up to and including fifth-order monomials.

③ The prediction by the OLS regression model given the optimal parameters.

④ The MSE value given the prediction values.

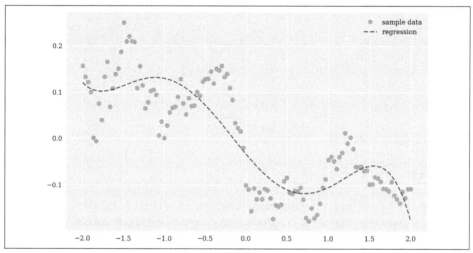

Figure 5-3. Sample data and cubic regression line

OLS regression is generally solved analytically. Therefore, no iterated learning takes place. However, one can simulate a learning procedure by gradually exposing the algorithm to more data. The following Python code implements OLS regression and prediction, starting with a few samples only and gradually increasing the number to finally reach the complete length of the data set. The regression step is implemented based on the smaller sub-sets, whereas the prediction steps are implemented based on the whole features data in each case. In general, the MSE drops significantly when increasing the training data set:

```
In [16]: for i in range(10, len(f) + 1, 20):
             reg = np.polyfit(f[:i], l[:i], deg=3)   ①
             p = np.polyval(reg, f)   ②
             mse = MSE(l, p)   ③
             print(f'{i:3d} | MSE={mse}')
          10 | MSE=248628.10681642237
          30 | MSE=731.9382249304651
          50 | MSE=12.236088505004465
          70 | MSE=0.7410590619743301
          90 | MSE=0.0057430617304093275
         110 | MSE=0.006492800939555582
```

❶ Regression step based on data sub-set

❷ Prediction step based on the complete data set

❸ Resulting MSE value

Second is the neural network. The application to the sample data is again straightforward and similar to the case in Chapter 1. Figure 5-4 shows how the neural network approximates the sample data:

```
In [17]: import logging
         import tensorflow as tf
         tf.random.set_seed(100)
         tf.get_logger().setLevel(logging.ERROR)

In [18]: from keras.layers import Dense
         from keras.models import Sequential
         Using TensorFlow backend.

In [19]: model = Sequential()
         model.add(Dense(256, activation='relu', input_dim=1))   ❶
         model.add(Dense(1, activation='linear'))   ❶
         model.compile(loss='mse', optimizer='rmsprop')

In [20]: model.summary()
         Model: "sequential_1"
```

Layer (type)	Output Shape	Param #
dense_1 (Dense)	(None, 256)	512
dense_2 (Dense)	(None, 1)	257

```
         Total params: 769
         Trainable params: 769
         Non-trainable params: 0
```

```
In [21]: %time h = model.fit(f, l, epochs=1500, verbose=False)   ❷
         CPU times: user 5.89 s, sys: 761 ms, total: 6.66 s
         Wall time: 4.43 s
Out[21]: <keras.callbacks.callbacks.History at 0x7fc05d599d90>

In [22]: p = model.predict(f).flatten()   ❸

In [23]: MSE(l, p)   ❹
Out[23]: 0.0020217512014360102

In [24]: plt.figure(figsize=(10, 6))
         plt.plot(f, l, 'ro', label='sample data')
```

```
plt.plot(f, p, '--', label='DNN approximation')
plt.legend();
```

❶ The neural network is a shallow network with a single hidden layer.

❷ The fitting step with a relatively high number of epochs.

❸ The prediction step that also flattens the `ndarray` object.

❹ The resulting MSE value for the DNN prediction.

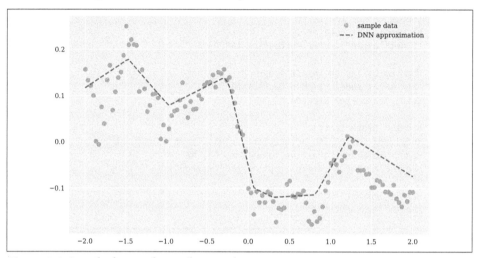

Figure 5-4. Sample data and neural network approximation

With the `Keras` package, the MSE values are stored after every learning step. Figure 5-5 shows how the MSE value ("loss") decreases on average (as far as one can tell from the plot) with the increasing number of epochs over which the neural network is trained:

```
In [25]: import pandas as pd
In [26]: res = pd.DataFrame(h.history)

In [27]: res.tail()
Out[27]:          loss
         1495  0.001547
         1496  0.001520
         1497  0.001456
         1498  0.001356
         1499  0.001325

In [28]: res.iloc[100:].plot(figsize=(10, 6))
         plt.ylabel('MSE')
         plt.xlabel('epochs');
```

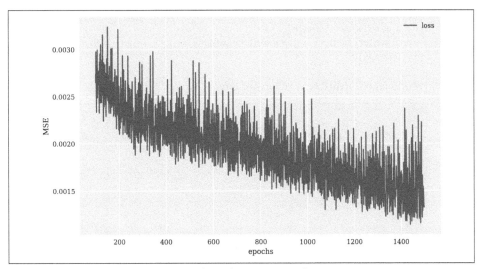

Figure 5-5. MSE values against number of training epochs

Capacity

The *capacity* of a model or algorithm defines what types of functions or relationships the model or algorithm can basically learn. In the case of OLS regression based on monomials only, there is only one parameter that defines the capacity of the model: the degree of the highest monomial to be used. If this degree parameter is set to deg=3, the OLS regression model can learn functional relationships of constant, linear, quadratic, or cubic type. The higher the parameter deg is, the higher the capacity of the OLS regression model will be.

The following Python code starts at deg=1 and increases the degree in increments of two. The MSE values monotonically decrease with the increasing degree parameter. Figure 5-6 shows the regression lines for all degrees considered:

```
In [29]: reg = {}
         for d in range(1, 12, 2):
             reg[d] = np.polyfit(f, l, deg=d)   ❶
             p = np.polyval(reg[d], f)
             mse = MSE(l, p)
             print(f'{d:2d} | MSE={mse}')
          1 | MSE=0.005322474034260403
          3 | MSE=0.004353110724143185
          5 | MSE=0.0034166422957371025
          7 | MSE=0.0027389501772354025
          9 | MSE=0.001411961626330845
         11 | MSE=0.0012651237868752322

In [30]: plt.figure(figsize=(10, 6))
         plt.plot(f, l, 'ro', label='sample data')
```

```
for d in reg:
    p = np.polyval(reg[d], f)
    plt.plot(f, p, '--', label=f'deg={d}')
plt.legend();
```

❶ Regression step for different values for deg

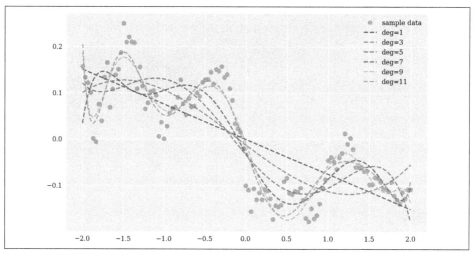

Figure 5-6. Regression lines for different highest degrees

The capacity of a neural network depends on a number of *hyperparameters*. Among them are, in general, the following:

- Number of hidden layers
- Number of hidden units for each hidden layer

Together, these two hyperparameters define the number of trainable parameters (weights) in the neural network. The neural network model in the previous section has a relatively low number of trainable parameters. Adding, for example, just one more layer of the same size increases the number of trainable parameters significantly. Although the number of training epochs may need to be increased, the MSE value decreases significantly for the neural network with the higher capacity, and the fit also seems much better visually, as Figure 5-7 shows:

```
In [31]: def create_dnn_model(hl=1, hu=256):
             ''' Function to create Keras DNN model.

             Parameters
             ==========
             hl: int
                 number of hidden layers
             hu: int
```

```
            number of hidden units (per layer)
        '''
        model = Sequential()
        for _ in range(hl):
            model.add(Dense(hu, activation='relu', input_dim=1))   ❶
        model.add(Dense(1, activation='linear'))
        model.compile(loss='mse', optimizer='rmsprop')
        return model

In [32]: model = create_dnn_model(3)   ❷

In [33]: model.summary()   ❸
        Model: "sequential_2"
```

Layer (type)	Output Shape	Param #
dense_3 (Dense)	(None, 256)	512
dense_4 (Dense)	(None, 256)	65792
dense_5 (Dense)	(None, 256)	65792
dense_6 (Dense)	(None, 1)	257

```
        Total params: 132,353
        Trainable params: 132,353
        Non-trainable params: 0
```

```
In [34]: %time model.fit(f, l, epochs=2500, verbose=False)
        CPU times: user 34.9 s, sys: 5.91 s, total: 40.8 s
        Wall time: 15.5 s

Out[34]: <keras.callbacks.callbacks.History at 0x7fc03fc18890>

In [35]: p = model.predict(f).flatten()

In [36]: MSE(l, p)
Out[36]: 0.00046612284916401614

In [37]: plt.figure(figsize=(10, 6))
        plt.plot(f, l, 'ro', label='sample data')
        plt.plot(f, p, '--', label='DNN approximation')
        plt.legend();
```

❶ Adds potentially many layers to the neural network

❷ A deep neural network with three hidden layers

❸ The summary shows the increased number of trainable parameters (increased capacity)

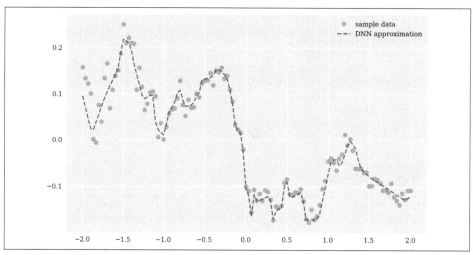

Figure 5-7. Sample data and DNN approximation (higher capacity)

Evaluation

In the previous sections, the analysis focuses on the performance of estimation algorithms on the sample data set as a whole. As a general rule, the capacity of the model or algorithm directly influences its performance when training and evaluating it on the same data set. However, this is the "simple and easy case" in ML. The more complex and interesting case is when a trained model or algorithm shall be used for a generalization on data that the model or algorithm has not seen before. Such a generalization can, for example, be the prediction (estimation) of a future stock price, given the history of stock prices, or the classification of potential debtors as "creditworthy" or "not creditworthy," given the data from existing debtors.

Although the term *prediction* is often used freely in the context of estimations, given the features data set used for training, a real prediction probably entails predicting something not known up front and never seen before. Again, the prediction of a future stock price is a good example for a real prediction in a temporal sense.

In general, a given data set is divided into sub-sets that each have different purposes:

Training data set
    This is the sub-set used for the training of the algorithm.

Validation data set
    This is the sub-set used for validating the performance of the algorithm during training—and this data set is different from the training data set.

Test data set

This is the sub-set on which the trained algorithm is only tested after the training is finished.

Insights that are gained by applying a (currently) trained algorithm on the validation data set might reflect on the training itself (for example, by adjusting the hyperparameters of a model). On the other hand, the idea is that insights from testing the trained algorithm on the test data set shall not be reflected in the training itself or the hyperparameters.

The following Python code chooses, somewhat arbitrarily, 25% of the sample data for testing; the model or algorithm will not see this data before the training (learning) is finished. Similarly, 25% of the sample data is reserved for validation; this data is used to monitor performance during the training step and possibly during many learning iterations. The remaining 50% is used for the training (learning) itself.[1] Given the sample data set, it makes sense to apply shuffling techniques to populate all sample data sub-sets randomly:

```
In [38]: te = int(0.25 * len(f))   ❶
         va = int(0.25 * len(f))   ❷

In [39]: np.random.seed(100)
         ind = np.arange(len(f))   ❸
         np.random.shuffle(ind)    ❸

In [40]: ind_te = np.sort(ind[:te])        ❹
         ind_va = np.sort(ind[te:te + va]) ❹
         ind_tr = np.sort(ind[te + va:])   ❹

In [41]: f_te = f[ind_te]   ❺
         f_va = f[ind_va]   ❺
         f_tr = f[ind_tr]   ❺

In [42]: l_te = l[ind_te]   ❻
         l_va = l[ind_va]   ❻
         l_tr = l[ind_tr]   ❻
```

❶ Number of test data set samples

❷ Number of validation data set samples

❸ Randomized index for complete data set

❹ Resulting sorted indexes for the data sub-sets

---

1 Often, the rule of thumb mentioned in this context is "60%, 20%, 20%" for the split of a given data set into training, validation, and testing data sub-sets.

❺ Resulting features data sub-sets

❻ Resulting labels data sub-sets

Randomized Sampling

The randomized population of training, validation, and test data sets is a common and useful technique for data sets that are neither sequence-like nor temporal in nature. However, when one is dealing, say, with a financial time series, shuffling the data is generally to be avoided because it breaks up temporal structures and sneaks foresight bias into the process by using, for example, later samples for training and implementing the testing on earlier samples.

Based on the training and validation data sub-sets, the following Python code implements a regression for different `deg` parameter values and calculates the MSE values for the predictions on both data sub-sets. Although the MSE values on the training data set decrease monotonically, the MSE values on the validation data set often reach a minimum for a certain parameter value and then increase again. This phenomenon indicates what is called *overfitting*. Figure 5-8 shows the regression fits for the different values of `deg` and compares the fits for both the training data and validation data sets:

```
In [43]: reg = {}
         mse = {}
         for d in range(1, 22, 4):
             reg[d] = np.polyfit(f_tr, l_tr, deg=d)
             p = np.polyval(reg[d], f_tr)
             mse_tr = MSE(l_tr, p)    ❶
             p = np.polyval(reg[d], f_va)
             mse_va = MSE(l_va, p)    ❷
             mse[d] = (mse_tr, mse_va)
             print(f'{d:2d} | MSE_tr={mse_tr:7.5f} | MSE_va={mse_va:7.5f}')
          1 | MSE_tr=0.00574 | MSE_va=0.00492
          5 | MSE_tr=0.00375 | MSE_va=0.00273
          9 | MSE_tr=0.00132 | MSE_va=0.00243
         13 | MSE_tr=0.00094 | MSE_va=0.00183
         17 | MSE_tr=0.00060 | MSE_va=0.00153
         21 | MSE_tr=0.00046 | MSE_va=0.00837

In [44]: fig, ax = plt.subplots(2, 1, figsize=(10, 8), sharex=True)
         ax[0].plot(f_tr, l_tr, 'ro', label='training data')
         ax[1].plot(f_va, l_va, 'go', label='validation data')
         for d in reg:
             p = np.polyval(reg[d], f_tr)
             ax[0].plot(f_tr, p, '--', label=f'deg={d} (tr)')
             p = np.polyval(reg[d], f_va)
             plt.plot(f_va, p, '--', label=f'deg={d} (va)')
```

```
ax[0].legend()
ax[1].legend();
```

❶ MSE value for the training data set

❷ MSE value for the validation data set

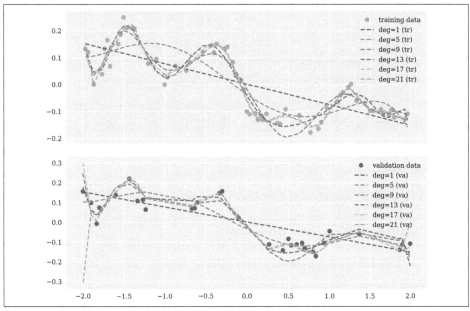

Figure 5-8. Training and validation data including regression fits

With `Keras` and the neural network model, the validation data set performance can be monitored for every single learning step. One can also use callback functions to stop the model training early when no further improvements, say, in the performance on the training data set, are observed. The following Python code makes use of such a callback function. Figure 5-9 shows the predictions of the neural network for the training and validation data sets:

```
In [45]: from keras.callbacks import EarlyStopping

In [46]: model = create_dnn_model(2, 256)

In [47]: callbacks = [EarlyStopping(monitor='loss',    ❶
                                    patience=100,       ❷
                                    restore_best_weights=True)]  ❸

In [48]: %%time
         h = model.fit(f_tr, l_tr, epochs=3000, verbose=False,
                       validation_data=(f_va, l_va),    ❹
                       callbacks=callbacks)    ❺
```

```
        CPU times: user 8.07 s, sys: 1.33 s, total: 9.4 s
        Wall time: 4.81 s

Out[48]: <keras.callbacks.callbacks.History at 0x7fc0438b47d0>

In [49]: fig, ax = plt.subplots(2, 1, sharex=True, figsize=(10, 8))
         ax[0].plot(f_tr, l_tr, 'ro', label='training data')
         p = model.predict(f_tr)
         ax[0].plot(f_tr, p, '--', label=f'DNN (tr)')
         ax[0].legend()
         ax[1].plot(f_va, l_va, 'go', label='validation data')
         p = model.predict(f_va)
         ax[1].plot(f_va, p, '--', label=f'DNN (va)')
         ax[1].legend();
```

❶ Learning is stopped based on training data MSE value.

❷ It is only stopped after a certain number of epochs that do not show an improvement.

❸ The best weights are restored when the learning is stopped.

❹ The validation data sub-sets are specified.

❺ The callback function is passed to the `fit()` method.

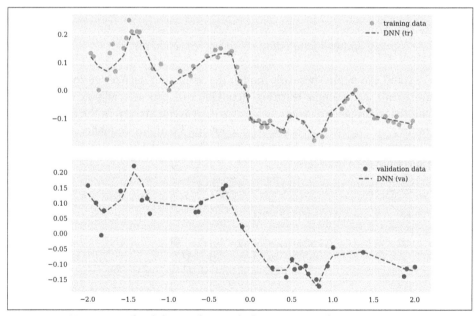

Figure 5-9. Training and validation data including DNN predictions

---

Keras allows analysis of the change in the MSE values on both data sets for every single epoch the model has been trained in. Figure 5-10 shows that the MSE values decrease with the increasing number of training epochs, although only on average and not monotonically:

```
In [50]: res = pd.DataFrame(h.history)

In [51]: res.tail()
Out[51]:       val_loss      loss
         1375  0.000854  0.000544
         1376  0.000685  0.000473
         1377  0.001326  0.000942
         1378  0.001026  0.000867
         1379  0.000710  0.000500

In [52]: res.iloc[35::25].plot(figsize=(10, 6))
         plt.ylabel('MSE')
         plt.xlabel('epochs');
```

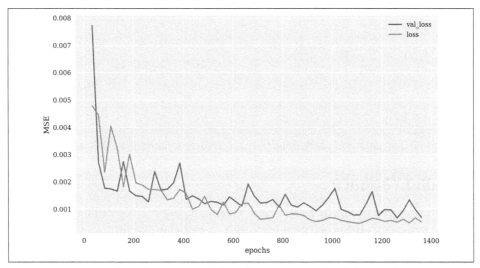

Figure 5-10. MSE values for DNN model on the training and validation data sets

In the case of OLS regression, one would probably choose a high—but not too high—value for the degree parameter, such as deg=9. The parameterization of the neural network model automatically gives the best model configuration at the end of the training. Figure 5-10 compares the predictions of both models to each other and to the test data set. Given the nature of the sample data, the somewhat better test data set performance of the neural network should not come as a surprise:

```
In [53]: p_ols = np.polyval(reg[5], f_te)
         p_dnn = model.predict(f_te).flatten()

In [54]: MSE(l_te, p_ols)
```

```
Out[54]: 0.0038960346771028356

In [55]: MSE(l_te, p_dnn)
Out[55]: 0.000705705678438721

In [56]: plt.figure(figsize=(10, 6))
         plt.plot(f_te, l_te, 'ro', label='test data')
         plt.plot(f_te, p_ols, '--', label='OLS prediction')
         plt.plot(f_te, p_dnn, '-.', label='DNN prediction');
         plt.legend();
```

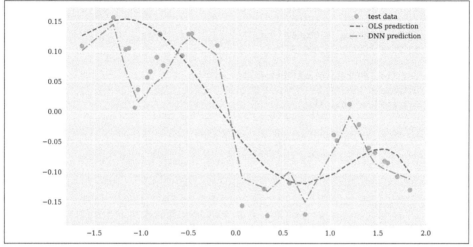

Figure 5-11. Test data and predictions from OLS regression and the DNN model

Bias and Variance

A major problem in ML in general and when applying ML algorithms to financial data in particular is the problem of *overfitting*. A model is overfitting its training data when the performance is worse on the validation and test data than on the training data. An example using OLS regression can illustrate the problem both visually and numerically.

The following Python code uses smaller sub-sets for both training and validation and implements a linear regression, as well as one of higher order. The linear regression fit, as shown in Figure 5-12, has a *high bias* on the training data set; absolute differences between predictions and labels data are relatively high. The higher-order fit shows a *high variance*. It hits all training data points exactly, but the fit itself varies significantly to achieve the perfect fit:

```
In [57]: f_tr = f[:20:2]   ❶
         l_tr = l[:20:2]   ❶

In [58]: f_va = f[1:20:2]  ❷
```

```
        l_va = l[1:20:2]  ❷

In [59]: reg_b = np.polyfit(f_tr, l_tr, deg=1)  ❸

In [60]: reg_v = np.polyfit(f_tr, l_tr, deg=9, full=True)[0]  ❹

In [61]: f_ = np.linspace(f_tr.min(), f_va.max(), 75)  ❺

In [62]: plt.figure(figsize=(10, 6))
         plt.plot(f_tr, l_tr, 'ro', label='training data')
         plt.plot(f_va, l_va, 'go', label='validation data')
         plt.plot(f_, np.polyval(reg_b, f_), '--', label='high bias')
         plt.plot(f_, np.polyval(reg_v, f_), '--', label='high variance')
         plt.ylim(-0.2)
         plt.legend(loc=2);
```

❶ Smaller features data sub-set

❷ Smaller labels data sub-set

❸ High bias OLS regression (linear)

❹ High variance OLS regression (higher order)

❺ Enlarged features data set for plotting

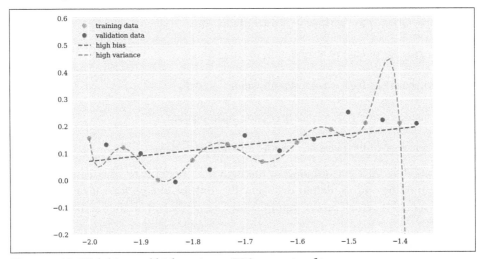

Figure 5-12. High bias and high variance OLS regression fits

Figure 5-12 shows that a high bias fit performs worse in the example than a high variance fit on the training data. But the high variance fit, which is overfitting here to a large extent, performs much worse on the validation data. This can be illustrated by comparing performance measures for all cases. The following Python code calculates not only the MSE values, but also the R^2 values:

```
In [63]: from sklearn.metrics import r2_score

In [64]: def evaluate(reg, f, l):
             p = np.polyval(reg, f)
             bias = np.abs(l - p).mean()    ❶
             var = p.var()    ❷
             msg = f'MSE={MSE(l, p):.4f} | R2={r2_score(l, p):9.4f} | '
             msg += f'bias={bias:.4f} | var={var:.4f}'
             print(msg)

In [65]: evaluate(reg_b, f_tr, l_tr)    ❸
         MSE=0.0026 | R2=   0.3484 | bias=0.0423 | var=0.0014

In [66]: evaluate(reg_b, f_va, l_va)    ❹
         MSE=0.0032 | R2=   0.4498 | bias=0.0460 | var=0.0014

In [67]: evaluate(reg_v, f_tr, l_tr)    ❺
         MSE=0.0000 | R2=   1.0000 | bias=0.0000 | var=0.0040

In [68]: evaluate(reg_v, f_va, l_va)    ❻
         MSE=0.8752 | R2=-149.2658 | bias=0.3565 | var=0.7539
```

❶ Model bias as mean absolute differences

❷ Model variance as variance of model predictions

❸ Performance of *high bias* model on *training data*

❹ Performance of *high bias* model on *validation data*

❺ Performance of *high variance* model on *training data*

❻ Performance of *high variance* model on *validation data*

The results show that performance of the high bias model is roughly comparable on both the training and validation data sets. By contrast, the performance of the high variance model is perfect on the training data and pretty bad on the validation data.

Cross-Validation

A standard approach to avoid overfitting is *cross-validation*, during which multiple training and validation data populations are tested. The scikit-learn package provides functionality to implement cross-validation in a standardized way. The function cross_val_score can be applied to any scikit-learn model object.

The following code implements the OLS regression approach on the complete sample data set, using a polynomial OLS regression model from `scikit-learn`. The five-fold cross-validation is implemented for different degrees for the highest polynomial. The cross-validation scores become, on average, worse the higher the highest degree is in the regression. Particularly bad results are observed when the first 20% of the data is used for validation (data on the left-hand side in Figure 5-3) or the final 20% of the data is used (data on the right-hand side in Figure 5-3). Similarly, the best validation scores are observed for the middle 20% of the sample data set:

```
In [69]: from sklearn.model_selection import cross_val_score
         from sklearn.preprocessing import PolynomialFeatures
         from sklearn.linear_model import LinearRegression
         from sklearn.pipeline import make_pipeline

In [70]: def PolynomialRegression(degree=None, **kwargs):
             return make_pipeline(PolynomialFeatures(degree),
                       LinearRegression(**kwargs))   ❶

In [71]: np.set_printoptions(suppress=True,
                 formatter={'float': lambda x: f'{x:12.2f}'})   ❷

In [72]: print('\nCross-validation scores')
         print(74 * '=')
         for deg in range(0, 10, 1):
             model = PolynomialRegression(deg)
             cvs = cross_val_score(model, f.reshape(-1, 1), l, cv=5)   ❸
             print(f'deg={deg} | ' + str(cvs.round(2)))

         Cross-validation scores
         ==========================================================================
         deg=0 | [        -6.07        -7.34        -0.09        -6.32        -8.69]
         deg=1 | [        -0.28        -1.40         0.16        -1.66        -4.62]
         deg=2 | [        -3.48        -2.45         0.19        -1.57       -12.94]
         deg=3 | [        -0.00        -1.24         0.32        -0.48       -43.62]
         deg=4 | [      -222.81        -2.88         0.37        -0.32      -496.61]
         deg=5 | [      -143.67        -5.85         0.49         0.12     -1241.04]
         deg=6 | [     -4038.96       -14.71         0.49        -0.33      -317.32]
         deg=7 | [     -9937.83       -13.98         0.64         0.22    -18725.61]
         deg=8 | [     -3514.36       -11.22        -0.15        -6.29   -298744.18]
         deg=9 | [     -7454.15        -0.91         0.15        -0.41    -13580.75]
```

❶ Creates a polynomial regression model class

❷ Adjusts the default printing settings for numpy

❸ Implements the five-fold cross-validation

Keras provides wrapper classes to use Keras model objects with `scikit-learn` functionality, such as the `cross_val_score` function. The following example uses the

KerasRegressor class to wrap the neural network models and to apply the cross-validation to them. The cross-validation scores are better throughout for the two networks tested when compared to the OLS regression cross-validation scores. The neural network capacity does not play too large a role in this example:

```
In [73]: np.random.seed(100)
         tf.random.set_seed(100)
         from keras.wrappers.scikit_learn import KerasRegressor

In [74]: model = KerasRegressor(build_fn=create_dnn_model,
                            verbose=False, epochs=1000,
                            hl=1, hu=36)   ❶

In [75]: %time cross_val_score(model, f, l, cv=5)   ❷
         CPU times: user 18.6 s, sys: 2.17 s, total: 20.8 s
         Wall time: 14.6 s

Out[75]: array([      -0.02,         -0.01,         -0.00,         -0.00,
                      -0.01])

In [76]: model = KerasRegressor(build_fn=create_dnn_model,
                            verbose=False, epochs=1000,
                            hl=3, hu=256)   ❸

In [77]: %time cross_val_score(model, f, l, cv=5)   ❹
         CPU times: user 1min 5s, sys: 11.6 s, total: 1min 16s
         Wall time: 30.1 s

Out[77]: array([      -0.08,         -0.00,         -0.00,         -0.00,
                      -0.05])
```

❶ Wrapper class for neural network with *low* capacity

❷ Cross-validation for neural network with *low* capacity

❸ Wrapper class for neural network with *high* capacity

❹ Cross-validation for neural network with *high* capacity

Avoiding Overfitting

Overfitting—when a model performs much better on a training data set than on the validation and test data sets—is to be avoided in ML in general and in finance in particular. Proper evaluation procedures and analyses, such as cross-validation, help in preventing overfitting and in finding, for example, an adequate model capacity.

Conclusions

This chapter presents a blueprint for a machine learning process. The main elements presented are as follows:

Learning
> What exactly is meant by machine *learning*?

Data
> What raw data and what (preprocessed) features and labels data is to be used?

Success
> Given the problem as defined indirectly by the data (estimation, classification, etc.), what is the appropriate measure of success?

Capacity
> Which role does the model capacity play, and what might be an adequate capacity given the problem at hand?

Evaluation
> How shall the model performance be evaluated given the purpose of the trained model?

Bias and variance
> Which models are better suited for the problem at hand: those with rather high bias or rather high variance?

Cross-validation
> For non-sequence-like data sets, how does the model perform when cross-validated on different configurations for the training and validation data sub-sets used?

This blueprint is applied loosely in subsequent chapters to a number of real-world financial use cases. For more background information and details about machine learning as a process, refer to the references listed at the end of this chapter.

References

Books and papers cited in this chapter:

Chollet, François. 2017. *Deep Learning with Python*. Shelter Island: Manning.

Domingos, Pedro. 2015. *The Master Algorithm: How the Quest for the Ultimate Learning Machine Will Remake Our World*. New York: Basic Books.

Goodfellow, Ian, Yoshua Bengio, and Aaron Courville. 2016. *Deep Learning*. Cambridge: MIT Press. *http://deeplearningbook.org*.

Harari, Yuval Noah. 2015. *Homo Deus: A Brief History of Tomorrow.* London: Harvill Secker.

Mitchell, Tom M. 1997. *Machine Learning.* New York: McGraw-Hill.

VanderPlas, Jake. 2017. *Python Data Science Handbook.* Sebastopol: O'Reilly.

## CHAPTER 6

AI-First Finance

> A computation takes information and transforms it, implementing what mathemati-
> cians call a *function*....If you're in possession of a function that inputs all the world's
> financial data and outputs the best stocks to buy, you'll soon be extremely rich.
>
> —Max Tegmark (2017)

This chapter sets out to combine data-driven finance with the machine learning approach from the previous chapter. It only represents the beginning of this endeavor in that, for the first time, neural networks are used to discover statistical inefficiencies. "Efficient Markets" on page 186 discusses the efficient market hypothesis and uses OLS regression to illustrate it based on financial time series data. "Market Prediction Based on Returns Data" on page 192 for the first time applies neural networks, alongside OLS regression, to predict the future direction of a financial instrument's price ("market direction"). The analysis relies on returns data only. "Market Prediction with More Features" on page 199 adds more features to the mix, such as typical financial indicators. In this context, first results indicate that statistical inefficiencies might indeed be present. This is confirmed in "Market Prediction Intraday" on page 204, which works with intraday data as compared to end-of-day data. Finally, "Conclusions" on page 205 discusses the effectiveness of big data in combination with AI in certain domains and argues that AI-first, theory-free finance might represent a way out of the theory fallacies in traditional finance.

Efficient Markets

One of the hypotheses with the strongest empirical support is the *efficient market hypothesis* (EMH). It is also called the *random walk hypothesis* (RWH).[1] Simply speaking, the hypothesis says that the prices of financial instruments at a certain point in time reflect all available information at this point in time. If the EMH holds true, a discussion about whether the price of a stock is too high or too low would be pointless. The price of a stock, given the EMH, is at all times exactly on its appropriate level given the available information.

Lots of effort has been put into refining and formalizing the idea of efficient markets since the formulation and first discussions of the EMH in the 1960s. The definitions as presented in Jensen (1978) are still used today. Jensen defines an efficient market as follows:

> A market is efficient with respect to an information set θ_t if it is impossible to make economic profits by trading on the basis of information set θ_t. By economic profits, we mean the risk adjusted returns net of all costs.

In this context, Jensen distinguishes three forms of market efficiency:

Weak form of EMH
  In this case, the information set θ_t only encompasses the past price and return history of the market.

Semi-strong form of EMH
  In this case, the information set θ_t is taken to be all publicly available information, including not only the past price and return history but also financial reports, news articles, weather data, and so on.

Strong form of EMH
  This case is given when the information set θ_t includes all information available to anyone (that is, even private information).

No matter which form is assumed, the implications of the EMH are far reaching. In his pioneering article on the EMH, Fama (1965) concludes the following:

> For many years, economists, statisticians, and teachers of finance have been interested in developing and testing models of stock price behavior. One important model that has evolved from this research is the theory of random walks. This theory casts serious doubt on many other methods for describing and predicting stock price behavior—methods that have considerable popularity outside the academic world. For example, we shall see later that, if the random-walk theory is an accurate description of reality,

---

[1] For the purposes of this chapter and the book, the two hypotheses are treated as equal, although the RWH is somewhat stronger than the EMH. See, for instance, Copeland et al. (2005, ch. 10).

---

then the various "technical" or "chartist" procedures for predicting stock prices are completely without value.

In other words, if the EMH holds true, then any kind of research or data analysis for the purposes of achieving above-market returns should be useless in practice. On the other hand, a multitrillion-dollar asset management industry has evolved that promises such above-market returns due to rigorous research and the active management of capital. In particular, the hedge fund industry is based on promises to deliver *alpha* —that is, returns that are above-market and even independent, at least to a large extent, of the market returns. How hard it is to live up to such a promise is shown by the data from a recent study by Preqin (*https://oreil.ly/C38Tl*). The study reports a drop in the Preqin All-Strategies Hedge Fund index of –3.42% for the year 2018. Close to 40% of all hedge funds covered by the study experienced losses of 5% or greater for that year.

If a stock price (or the price of any other financial instrument) follows a standard random walk, then the returns are normally distributed with zero mean. The stock price goes up with 50% probability and down with 50% probability. In such a context, the best predictor of tomorrow's stock price, in a least-squares sense, is today's stock price. This is due to the Markov property of random walks, namely that the distribution of the future stock prices is independent of the history of the price process; it only depends on the current price level. Therefore, in the context of a random walk, the analysis of the historical prices (or returns) is useless for predicting future prices.

Against this background, a semiformal test for efficient markets can be implemented as follows.[2] Take a financial time series, lag the price data multiple times, and use the lagged price data as features data for an OLS regression that uses the current price level as the labels data. This is similar in spirit to charting techniques that rely on historical price formations to predict future prices.

The following Python code implements such an analysis based on lagged price data for a number of financial instruments—both tradable ones and nontradable ones. First, import the data and its visualization (see Figure 6-1):

```
In [1]: import numpy as np
        import pandas as pd
        from pylab import plt, mpl
        plt.style.use('seaborn')
        mpl.rcParams['savefig.dpi'] = 300
        mpl.rcParams['font.family'] = 'serif'
        pd.set_option('precision', 4)
        np.set_printoptions(suppress=True, precision=4)

In [2]: url = 'http://hilpisch.com/aiif_eikon_eod_data.csv'  ❶
```

---

2 See also Hilpisch (2018, ch. 15).

```
In [3]: data = pd.read_csv(url, index_col=0, parse_dates=True).dropna()    ❶

In [4]: (data / data.iloc[0]).plot(figsize=(10, 6), cmap='coolwarm');    ❷
```

❶   Reads the data into a `DataFrame` object

❷   Plots the normalized time series data

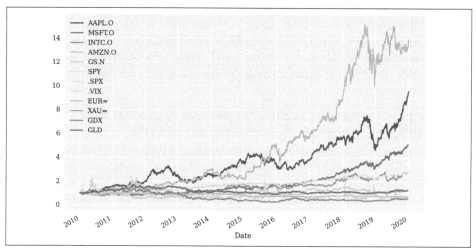

Figure 6-1. Normalized time series data (end-of-day)

Second, the price data for all financial time series is lagged and stored in `DataFrame` objects:

```
In [5]: lags = 7    ❶

In [6]: def add_lags(data, ric, lags):
            cols = []
            df = pd.DataFrame(data[ric])
            for lag in range(1, lags + 1):
                col = 'lag_{}'.format(lag)    ❷
                df[col] = df[ric].shift(lag)    ❸
                cols.append(col)    ❹
            df.dropna(inplace=True)    ❺
            return df, cols

In [7]: dfs = {}
        for sym in data.columns:
            df, cols = add_lags(data, sym, lags)    ❻
            dfs[sym] = df    ❼

In [8]: dfs[sym].head(7)    ❽
Out[8]:                 GLD    lag_1    lag_2    lag_3    lag_4    lag_5    lag_6    lag_7
```

```
Date
2010-01-13  111.54  110.49  112.85  111.37  110.82  111.51  109.70  109.80
2010-01-14  112.03  111.54  110.49  112.85  111.37  110.82  111.51  109.70
2010-01-15  110.86  112.03  111.54  110.49  112.85  111.37  110.82  111.51
2010-01-19  111.52  110.86  112.03  111.54  110.49  112.85  111.37  110.82
2010-01-20  108.94  111.52  110.86  112.03  111.54  110.49  112.85  111.37
2010-01-21  107.37  108.94  111.52  110.86  112.03  111.54  110.49  112.85
2010-01-22  107.17  107.37  108.94  111.52  110.86  112.03  111.54  110.49
```

❶ The number of lags (in trading days)

❷ Creates a column name

❸ Lags the price data

❹ Adds the column name to a list object

❺ Deletes all incomplete data rows

❻ Creates the lagged data for every financial time series

❼ Stores the results in a dict object

❽ Shows a sample of the lagged price data

Third, with the data prepared, the OLS regression analysis is straightforward to conduct. Figure 6-2 shows the average optimal regression results. Without a doubt, the price data that is lagged by only one day has the highest explanatory power. Its weight is close to 1, supporting the idea that the best predictor for tomorrow's price of a financial instrument is its price today. This also holds true for the single regression results obtained per financial time series:

```
In [9]: regs = {}
        for sym in data.columns:
            df = dfs[sym]  ❶
            reg = np.linalg.lstsq(df[cols], df[sym], rcond=-1)[0]  ❷
            regs[sym] = reg  ❸

In [10]: rega = np.stack(tuple(regs.values()))  ❹

In [11]: regd = pd.DataFrame(rega, columns=cols, index=data.columns)  ❺

In [12]: regd  ❺
Out[12]:        lag_1    lag_2    lag_3   lag_4    lag_5   lag_6    lag_7
        AAPL.O  1.0106  -0.0592  0.0258  0.0535  -0.0172  0.0060  -0.0184
        MSFT.O  0.8928   0.0112  0.1175 -0.0832  -0.0258  0.0567   0.0323
        INTC.O  0.9519   0.0579  0.0490 -0.0772  -0.0373  0.0449   0.0112
        AMZN.O  0.9799  -0.0134  0.0206  0.0007   0.0525 -0.0452   0.0056
        GS.N    0.9806   0.0342 -0.0172  0.0042  -0.0387  0.0585  -0.0215
```

```
SPY     0.9692   0.0067   0.0228  -0.0244  -0.0237   0.0379   0.0121
.SPX    0.9672   0.0106   0.0219  -0.0252  -0.0318   0.0515   0.0063
.VIX    0.8823   0.0591  -0.0289   0.0284  -0.0256   0.0511   0.0306
EUR=    0.9859   0.0239  -0.0484   0.0508  -0.0217   0.0149  -0.0055
XAU=    0.9864   0.0069   0.0166  -0.0215   0.0044   0.0198  -0.0125
GDX     0.9765   0.0096  -0.0039   0.0223  -0.0364   0.0379  -0.0065
GLD     0.9766   0.0246   0.0060  -0.0142  -0.0047   0.0223  -0.0106
```

```
In [13]: regd.mean().plot(kind='bar', figsize=(10, 6));  ❻
```

❶ Gets the data for the current time series

❷ Implements the regression analysis

❸ Stores the optimal regression parameters in a `dict` object

❹ Combines the optimal results into a single `ndarray` object

❺ Puts the results into a `DataFrame` object and shows them

❻ Visualizes the average optimal regression parameters (weights) for every lag

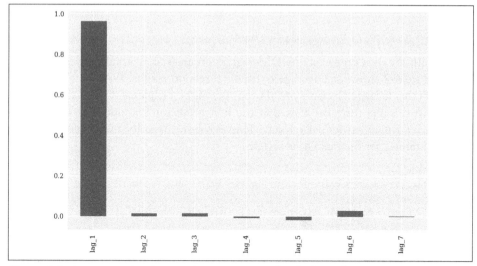

Figure 6-2. Average optimal regression parameters for the lagged prices

Given this semiformal analysis, there seems to be strong supporting evidence for the EMH in its weak form, at least. It is noteworthy that the OLS regression analysis as implemented here violates several assumptions. Among those is that the features are assumed to be noncorrelated among each other, whereas they should ideally be highly correlated with the labels data. However, the lagged price data leads to highly correlated features. The following Python code presents the correlation data, which shows a close-to-perfect correlation between all features. This explains why only one feature ("lag 1") is enough to accomplish the approximation and prediction based on the OLS regression approach. Adding more, highly correlated features does not yield any improvements. Another fundamental assumption violated is the *stationarity* of the time series data, which the following code also tests for:[3]

```
In [14]: dfs[sym].corr()  ❶
Out[14]:          GLD    lag_1   lag_2   lag_3   lag_4   lag_5   lag_6   lag_7
         GLD    1.0000  0.9972  0.9946  0.9920  0.9893  0.9867  0.9841  0.9815
         lag_1  0.9972  1.0000  0.9972  0.9946  0.9920  0.9893  0.9867  0.9842
         lag_2  0.9946  0.9972  1.0000  0.9972  0.9946  0.9920  0.9893  0.9867
         lag_3  0.9920  0.9946  0.9972  1.0000  0.9972  0.9946  0.9920  0.9893
         lag_4  0.9893  0.9920  0.9946  0.9972  1.0000  0.9972  0.9946  0.9920
         lag_5  0.9867  0.9893  0.9920  0.9946  0.9972  1.0000  0.9972  0.9946
         lag_6  0.9841  0.9867  0.9893  0.9920  0.9946  0.9972  1.0000  0.9972
         lag_7  0.9815  0.9842  0.9867  0.9893  0.9920  0.9946  0.9972  1.0000

In [15]: from statsmodels.tsa.stattools import adfuller  ❷

In [16]: adfuller(data[sym].dropna())  ❷
Out[16]: (-1.9488969577009954,
          0.3094193074034718,
          0,
          2515,
          {'1%': -3.4329527780962255,
           '5%': -2.8626898965523724,
           '10%': -2.567382133955709},
          8446.683102944744)
```

❶ Shows the correlations between the lagged time series

❷ Tests for stationarity using the Augmented Dickey-Fuller (*https://oreil.ly/rfdaC*) test

In summary, if the EMH holds true, active or algorithmic portfolio management or trading would not make economic sense. Simply investing in a stock or an efficient portfolio in the MVP sense, say, and passively holding the investment over a long period would yield without any effort at least the same, if not superior, returns. According to the CAPM and the MVP, the higher the risk the investor is willing to bear, the higher the expected return should be. In fact, as Copeland et al. (2005, ch. 10) point out, the CAPM and the EMH form a joint hypothesis about financial markets: if the EMH is rejected, then the CAPM must be rejected as well, since its derivation assumes the EMH to hold true.

---

3 For details on *stationarity* in financial time series, see Tsay (2005, sec. 2.1). Tsay points out: "The foundation of time series analysis is stationarity."

Market Prediction Based on Returns Data

As Chapter 2 shows, ML and, in particular, DL algorithms have generated break-throughs in recent years in fields that have proven resistant over pretty long periods of time to standard statistical or mathematical methods. What about the financial markets? Might ML and DL algorithms be capable of discovering inefficiencies where traditional financial econometrics methods, such as OLS regression, fail? Of course, there are no simple and concise answers to these questions yet.

However, some concrete examples might shed light on possible answers. To this end, the same data as in the previous section is used to derive log returns from the price data. The idea is to compare the performance of OLS regression to the performance of neural networks in predicting the next day's direction of movement for the different time series. The goal at this stage is to discover *statistical inefficiencies* as compared to *economic inefficiencies*. Statistical inefficiencies are given when a model is able to predict the direction of the future price movement with a certain edge (say, the prediction is correct in 55% or 60% of the cases). Economic inefficiencies would only be given if the statistical inefficiencies can be exploited profitably through a trading strategy that takes into account, for example, transaction costs.

The first step in the analysis is to create data sets with lagged log returns data. The normalized lagged log returns data is also tested for stationarity (given), and the features are tested for correlation (not correlated). Since the following analyses rely on time-series-related data only, they are dealing with *weak form market efficiency*:

```
In [17]: rets = np.log(data / data.shift(1))   ❶

In [18]: rets.dropna(inplace=True)

In [19]: dfs = {}
         for sym in data:
             df, cols = add_lags(rets, sym, lags)   ❷
             mu, std = df[cols].mean(), df[cols].std()   ❸
             df[cols] = (df[cols] - mu) / std   ❸
             dfs[sym] = df

In [20]: dfs[sym].head()   ❹
Out[20]:                GLD    lag_1    lag_2    lag_3    lag_4    lag_5    lag_6    lag_7
         Date
         2010-01-14  0.0044   0.9570  -2.1692   1.3386   0.4959  -0.6434   1.6613  -0.1028
         2010-01-15 -0.0105   0.4379   0.9571  -2.1689   1.3388   0.4966  -0.6436   1.6614
         2010-01-19  0.0059  -1.0842   0.4385   0.9562  -2.1690   1.3395   0.4958  -0.6435
         2010-01-20 -0.0234   0.5967  -1.0823   0.4378   0.9564  -2.1686   1.3383   0.4958
         2010-01-21 -0.0145  -2.4045   0.5971  -1.0825   0.4379   0.9571  -2.1680   1.3384

In [21]: adfuller(dfs[sym]['lag_1'])   ❺
Out[21]: (-51.568251505825536,
          0.0,
```

```
0,
2507,
{'1%': -3.4329610922579095,
 '5%': -2.8626935681060375,
 '10%': -2.567384088736619},
7017.165474260225)
```

In [22]: dfs[sym].corr() ❻
Out[22]:
```
              GLD    lag_1    lag_2       lag_3   lag_4       lag_5   lag_6    lag_7
GLD       1.0000  -0.0297   0.0003  1.2635e-02  -0.0026  -5.9392e-03   0.0099  -0.0013
lag_1    -0.0297   1.0000  -0.0305  8.1418e-04   0.0128  -2.8765e-03  -0.0053   0.0098
lag_2     0.0003  -0.0305   1.0000 -3.1617e-02   0.0003   1.3234e-02  -0.0043  -0.0052
lag_3     0.0126   0.0008  -0.0316  1.0000e+00  -0.0313  -6.8542e-06   0.0141  -0.0044
lag_4    -0.0026   0.0128   0.0003 -3.1329e-02   1.0000  -3.1761e-02   0.0002   0.0141
lag_5    -0.0059  -0.0029   0.0132 -6.8542e-06  -0.0318   1.0000e+00  -0.0323   0.0002
lag_6     0.0099  -0.0053  -0.0043  1.4115e-02   0.0002  -3.2289e-02   1.0000  -0.0324
lag_7    -0.0013   0.0098  -0.0052 -4.3869e-03   0.0141   2.1707e-04  -0.0324   1.0000
```

❶ Derives the log returns from the price data

❷ Lags the log returns data

❸ Applies *Gaussian normalization* to the features data[4]

❹ Shows a sample of the lagged returns data

❺ Tests for stationarity of the time series data

❻ Shows the correlation data for the features

First, the OLS regression is implemented and the predictions resulting from the regression are generated. The analysis is implemented on the complete data set. It shall show how well the algorithms perform in-sample. The accuracy with which OLS regression predicts the next day's direction of movement is slightly, or even a few percentage points, above 50% with one exception:

In [23]: from sklearn.metrics import accuracy_score

In [24]: %%time
         for sym in data:
             df = dfs[sym]
             reg = np.linalg.lstsq(df[cols], df[sym], rcond=-1)[0]   ❶
             pred = np.dot(df[cols], reg)   ❷
             acc = accuracy_score(np.sign(df[sym]), np.sign(pred))   ❸
             print(f'OLS | {sym:10s} | acc={acc:.4f}')
         OLS | AAPL.O | acc=0.5056

---

4 Another term for the approach is *z-score normalization*.

```
OLS | MSFT.O     | acc=0.5088
OLS | INTC.O     | acc=0.5040
OLS | AMZN.O     | acc=0.5048
OLS | GS.N       | acc=0.5080
OLS | SPY        | acc=0.5080
OLS | .SPX       | acc=0.5167
OLS | .VIX       | acc=0.5291
OLS | EUR=       | acc=0.4984
OLS | XAU=       | acc=0.5207
OLS | GDX        | acc=0.5307
OLS | GLD        | acc=0.5072
CPU times: user 201 ms, sys: 65.8 ms, total: 267 ms
Wall time: 60.8 ms
```

❶ The regression step

❷ The prediction step

❸ The accuracy of the prediction

Second, the same analysis is done again but this time with a neural network from
scikit-learn as the model for learning and predicting. The prediction accuracy in-
sample is significantly above 50% throughout and above 60% in a few cases:

```
In [25]: from sklearn.neural_network import MLPRegressor

In [26]: %%time
         for sym in data.columns:
             df = dfs[sym]
             model = MLPRegressor(hidden_layer_sizes=[512],
                                  random_state=100,
                                  max_iter=1000,
                                  early_stopping=True,
                                  validation_fraction=0.15,
                                  shuffle=False)   ❶
             model.fit(df[cols], df[sym])   ❷
             pred = model.predict(df[cols])   ❸
             acc = accuracy_score(np.sign(df[sym]), np.sign(pred))   ❹
             print(f'MLP | {sym:10s} | acc={acc:.4f}')
         MLP | AAPL.O     | acc=0.6005
         MLP | MSFT.O     | acc=0.5853
         MLP | INTC.O     | acc=0.5766
         MLP | AMZN.O     | acc=0.5510
         MLP | GS.N       | acc=0.6527
         MLP | SPY        | acc=0.5419
         MLP | .SPX       | acc=0.5399
         MLP | .VIX       | acc=0.6579
         MLP | EUR=       | acc=0.5642
         MLP | XAU=       | acc=0.5522
         MLP | GDX        | acc=0.6029
         MLP | GLD        | acc=0.5259
```

```
CPU times: user 1min 37s, sys: 6.74 s, total: 1min 44s
Wall time: 14 s
```

❶ Model instantiation

❷ Model fitting

❸ Prediction step

❹ Accuracy calculation

Third, the same analysis again but with a neural network from the Keras package. The accuracy results are similar to those from the MLPRegressor, but with a higher average accuracy:

```
In [27]: import tensorflow as tf
         from keras.layers import Dense
         from keras.models import Sequential
         Using TensorFlow backend.

In [28]: np.random.seed(100)
         tf.random.set_seed(100)

In [29]: def create_model(problem='regression'):        ❶
             model = Sequential()
             model.add(Dense(512, input_dim=len(cols),
                             activation='relu'))
             if problem == 'regression':
                 model.add(Dense(1, activation='linear'))
                 model.compile(loss='mse', optimizer='adam')
             else:
                 model.add(Dense(1, activation='sigmoid'))
                 model.compile(loss='binary_crossentropy', optimizer='adam')
             return model

In [30]: %%time
         for sym in data.columns[:]:
             df = dfs[sym]
             model = create_model()        ❷
             model.fit(df[cols], df[sym], epochs=25, verbose=False)        ❸
             pred = model.predict(df[cols])        ❹
             acc = accuracy_score(np.sign(df[sym]), np.sign(pred))        ❺
             print(f'DNN | {sym:10s} | acc={acc:.4f}')
         DNN | AAPL.O     | acc=0.6292
         DNN | MSFT.O     | acc=0.5981
         DNN | INTC.O     | acc=0.6073
         DNN | AMZN.O     | acc=0.5781
         DNN | GS.N       | acc=0.6196
         DNN | SPY        | acc=0.5829
         DNN | .SPX       | acc=0.6077
         DNN | .VIX       | acc=0.6392
```

```
DNN | EUR=       | acc=0.5845
DNN | XAU=       | acc=0.5881
DNN | GDX        | acc=0.5829
DNN | GLD        | acc=0.5666
CPU times: user 34.3 s, sys: 5.34 s, total: 39.6 s
Wall time: 23.1 s
```

❶ Model creation function

❷ Model instantiation

❸ Model fitting

❹ Prediction step

❺ Accuracy calculation

This simple example shows that neural networks can outperform OLS regression significantly *in-sample* in predicting the next day's direction of price movements. However, how does the picture change when testing for the *out-of-sample* performance of the two model types?

To this end, the analyses are repeated, but the training (fitting) step is implemented on the first 80% of the data while the performance is tested on the remaining 20%. OLS regression is implemented first. Out-of-sample OLS regression shows similar accuracy levels as in-sample—around 50%:

```
In [31]: split = int(len(dfs[sym]) * 0.8)

In [32]: %%time
         for sym in data.columns:
             df = dfs[sym]
             train = df.iloc[:split]    ❶
             reg = np.linalg.lstsq(train[cols], train[sym], rcond=-1)[0]
             test = df.iloc[split:]     ❷
             pred = np.dot(test[cols], reg)
             acc = accuracy_score(np.sign(test[sym]), np.sign(pred))
             print(f'OLS | {sym:10s} | acc={acc:.4f}')
         OLS | AAPL.O     | acc=0.5219
         OLS | MSFT.O     | acc=0.4960
         OLS | INTC.O     | acc=0.5418
         OLS | AMZN.O     | acc=0.4841
         OLS | GS.N       | acc=0.4980
         OLS | SPY        | acc=0.5020
         OLS | .SPX       | acc=0.5120
         OLS | .VIX       | acc=0.5458
         OLS | EUR=       | acc=0.4482
         OLS | XAU=       | acc=0.5299
         OLS | GDX        | acc=0.5159
         OLS | GLD        | acc=0.5100
```

```
CPU times: user 200 ms, sys: 60.6 ms, total: 261 ms
Wall time: 61.7 ms
```

❶ Creates the *training* data sub-set

❷ Creates the *test* data sub-set

The performance of the `MLPRegressor` model is out-of-sample much worse when
compared to the in-sample numbers and similar to the OLS regression results:

```
In [34]: %%time
         for sym in data.columns:
             df = dfs[sym]
             train = df.iloc[:split]
             model = MLPRegressor(hidden_layer_sizes=[512],
                                  random_state=100,
                                  max_iter=1000,
                                  early_stopping=True,
                                  validation_fraction=0.15,
                                  shuffle=False)
             model.fit(train[cols], train[sym])
             test = df.iloc[split:]
             pred = model.predict(test[cols])
             acc = accuracy_score(np.sign(test[sym]), np.sign(pred))
             print(f'MLP | {sym:10s} | acc={acc:.4f}')
         MLP | AAPL.O     | acc=0.4920
         MLP | MSFT.O     | acc=0.5279
         MLP | INTC.O     | acc=0.5279
         MLP | AMZN.O     | acc=0.4641
         MLP | GS.N       | acc=0.5040
         MLP | SPY        | acc=0.5259
         MLP | .SPX       | acc=0.5478
         MLP | .VIX       | acc=0.5279
         MLP | EUR=       | acc=0.4980
         MLP | XAU=       | acc=0.5239
         MLP | GDX        | acc=0.4880
         MLP | GLD        | acc=0.5000
         CPU times: user 1min 39s, sys: 4.98 s, total: 1min 44s
         Wall time: 13.7 s
```

The same holds true for the `Sequential` model from `Keras` for which the out-of-
sample numbers also show accuracy values between a few percentage points above
and below the 50% threshold:

```
In [35]: %%time
         for sym in data.columns:
             df = dfs[sym]
             train = df.iloc[:split]
             model = create_model()
             model.fit(train[cols], train[sym], epochs=50, verbose=False)
             test = df.iloc[split:]
             pred = model.predict(test[cols])
```

```
    acc = accuracy_score(np.sign(test[sym]), np.sign(pred))
    print(f'DNN | {sym:10s} | acc={acc:.4f}')
DNN | AAPL.O     | acc=0.5179
DNN | MSFT.O     | acc=0.5598
DNN | INTC.O     | acc=0.4821
DNN | AMZN.O     | acc=0.4920
DNN | GS.N       | acc=0.5179
DNN | SPY        | acc=0.4861
DNN | .SPX       | acc=0.5100
DNN | .VIX       | acc=0.5378
DNN | EUR=       | acc=0.4661
DNN | XAU=       | acc=0.4602
DNN | GDX        | acc=0.4841
DNN | GLD        | acc=0.5378
CPU times: user 50.4 s, sys: 7.52 s, total: 57.9 s
Wall time: 32.9 s
```

Weak Form Market Efficiency

Although the labeling as *weak form* market efficiency might suggest otherwise, it is the hardest form in the sense that only time-series-related data can be used to identify statistical inefficiencies. With the semi-strong form, any other source of publicly available data could be added to improve prediction accuracy.

Based on the approaches chosen in this section, markets seem to be at least efficient in the weak form. Just analyzing historical return patterns based on OLS regression or neural networks might not be enough to discover statistical inefficiencies.

There are two major elements of the approach chosen in this section that can be adjusted in the hope of improving prediction results:

Features

In addition to vanilla price-and-returns data, other features can be added to the data, such as technical indicators (for example, simple moving averages, or SMAs for short). The hope is, in the technical chartist's tradition, that such indicators improve the prediction accuracy.

Bar length

Instead of working with end-of-day data, intraday data might allow for higher prediction accuracies. Here, the hope is that one is more likely to discover statistical inefficiencies during the day as compared to at end of day, when all market participants in general pay the highest attention to making their final trades—by taking into account all available information.

The following two sections address these elements.

Market Prediction with More Features

In trading, there is a long tradition of using technical indicators to generate, based on observed patterns, buy or sell signals. Such technical indicators, basically of any kind, can also be used as features for the training of neural networks.

The following Python code uses an SMA, rolling minimum and maximum values, momentum, and rolling volatility as features:

```
In [36]: url = 'http://hilpisch.com/aiif_eikon_eod_data.csv'

In [37]: data = pd.read_csv(url, index_col=0, parse_dates=True).dropna()

In [38]: def add_lags(data, ric, lags, window=50):
             cols = []
             df = pd.DataFrame(data[ric])
             df.dropna(inplace=True)
             df['r'] = np.log(df / df.shift())
             df['sma'] = df[ric].rolling(window).mean()    ❶
             df['min'] = df[ric].rolling(window).min()     ❷
             df['max'] = df[ric].rolling(window).max()     ❸
             df['mom'] = df['r'].rolling(window).mean()    ❹
             df['vol'] = df['r'].rolling(window).std()     ❺
             df.dropna(inplace=True)
             df['d'] = np.where(df['r'] > 0, 1, 0)         ❻
             features = [ric, 'r', 'd', 'sma', 'min', 'max', 'mom', 'vol']
             for f in features:
                 for lag in range(1, lags + 1):
                     col = f'{f}_lag_{lag}'
                     df[col] = df[f].shift(lag)
                     cols.append(col)
             df.dropna(inplace=True)
             return df, cols

In [39]: lags = 5

In [40]: dfs = {}
         for ric in data:
             df, cols = add_lags(data, ric, lags)
             dfs[ric] = df.dropna(), cols
```

❶ Simple moving average (SMA)

❷ Rolling minimum

❸ Rolling maximum

❹ Momentum as average of log returns

❺ Rolling volatility

---

❻   Direction as binary feature

Technical Indicators as Features

As the preceding examples show, basically any traditional technical indicator used for investing or intraday trading can be used as a feature to train ML algorithms. In that sense, AI and ML do not necessarily render such indicators obsolete, rather they can indeed enrich the ML-driven derivation of trading strategies.

In-sample, the performance of the `MLPClassifier` model is now much better when taking into account the new features and normalizing them for training. The `Sequential` model of `Keras` reaches accuracies of around 70% for the number of epochs trained. From experience, these can be easily increased by increasing the number of epochs and/or the capacity of the neural network:

```
In [41]: from sklearn.neural_network import MLPClassifier

In [42]: %%time
         for ric in data:
             model = MLPClassifier(hidden_layer_sizes=[512],
                                   random_state=100,
                                   max_iter=1000,
                                   early_stopping=True,
                                   validation_fraction=0.15,
                                   shuffle=False)
             df, cols = dfs[ric]
             df[cols] = (df[cols] - df[cols].mean()) / df[cols].std()  ❶
             model.fit(df[cols], df['d'])
             pred = model.predict(df[cols])
             acc = accuracy_score(df['d'], pred)
             print(f'IN-SAMPLE | {ric:7s} | acc={acc:.4f}')
         IN-SAMPLE | AAPL.O  | acc=0.5510
         IN-SAMPLE | MSFT.O  | acc=0.5376
         IN-SAMPLE | INTC.O  | acc=0.5607
         IN-SAMPLE | AMZN.O  | acc=0.5559
         IN-SAMPLE | GS.N    | acc=0.5794
         IN-SAMPLE | SPY     | acc=0.5729
         IN-SAMPLE | .SPX    | acc=0.5941
         IN-SAMPLE | .VIX    | acc=0.6940
         IN-SAMPLE | EUR=    | acc=0.5766
         IN-SAMPLE | XAU=    | acc=0.5672
         IN-SAMPLE | GDX     | acc=0.5847
         IN-SAMPLE | GLD     | acc=0.5567
         CPU times: user 1min 1s, sys: 4.5 s, total: 1min 6s
         Wall time: 9.05 s

In [43]: %%time
         for ric in data:
```

```
      model = create_model('classification')
      df, cols = dfs[ric]
      df[cols] = (df[cols] - df[cols].mean()) / df[cols].std()  ❶
      model.fit(df[cols], df['d'], epochs=50, verbose=False)
      pred = np.where(model.predict(df[cols]) > 0.5, 1, 0)
      acc = accuracy_score(df['d'], pred)
      print(f'IN-SAMPLE | {ric:7s} | acc={acc:.4f}')
IN-SAMPLE | AAPL.O  | acc=0.7156
IN-SAMPLE | MSFT.O  | acc=0.7156
IN-SAMPLE | INTC.O  | acc=0.7046
IN-SAMPLE | AMZN.O  | acc=0.6640
IN-SAMPLE | GS.N    | acc=0.6855
IN-SAMPLE | SPY     | acc=0.6696
IN-SAMPLE | .SPX    | acc=0.6579
IN-SAMPLE | .VIX    | acc=0.7489
IN-SAMPLE | EUR=    | acc=0.6737
IN-SAMPLE | XAU=    | acc=0.7143
IN-SAMPLE | GDX     | acc=0.6826
IN-SAMPLE | GLD     | acc=0.7078
CPU times: user 1min 5s, sys: 7.06 s, total: 1min 12s
Wall time: 44.3 s
```

❶ Normalizes the features data

Are these improvements to be transferred to the out-of-sample prediction accuracies? The following Python code repeats the analysis, this time with the training and test split as used before. Unfortunately, the picture is mixed at best. The numbers do not represent real improvements when compared to the approach, relying only on lagged returns data as features. For selected instruments, there seems to be an edge of a few percentage points in the prediction accuracy compared to the 50% benchmark. For others, however, the accuracy is still below 50%—as illustrated for the MLPClassifier model:

```
In [44]: def train_test_model(model):
             for ric in data:
                 df, cols = dfs[ric]
                 split = int(len(df) * 0.85)
                 train = df.iloc[:split].copy()
                 mu, std = train[cols].mean(), train[cols].std()  ❶
                 train[cols] = (train[cols] - mu) / std
                 model.fit(train[cols], train['d'])
                 test = df.iloc[split:].copy()
                 test[cols] = (test[cols] - mu) / std
                 pred = model.predict(test[cols])
                 acc = accuracy_score(test['d'], pred)
                 print(f'OUT-OF-SAMPLE | {ric:7s} | acc={acc:.4f}')

In [45]: model_mlp = MLPClassifier(hidden_layer_sizes=[512],
                                   random_state=100,
                                   max_iter=1000,
                                   early_stopping=True,
```

```
                          validation_fraction=0.15,
                          shuffle=False)

In [46]: %time train_test_model(model_mlp)
         OUT-OF-SAMPLE | AAPL.O | acc=0.4432
         OUT-OF-SAMPLE | MSFT.O | acc=0.4595
         OUT-OF-SAMPLE | INTC.O | acc=0.5000
         OUT-OF-SAMPLE | AMZN.O | acc=0.5270
         OUT-OF-SAMPLE | GS.N   | acc=0.4838
         OUT-OF-SAMPLE | SPY    | acc=0.4811
         OUT-OF-SAMPLE | .SPX   | acc=0.5027
         OUT-OF-SAMPLE | .VIX   | acc=0.5676
         OUT-OF-SAMPLE | EUR=   | acc=0.4649
         OUT-OF-SAMPLE | XAU=   | acc=0.5514
         OUT-OF-SAMPLE | GDX    | acc=0.5162
         OUT-OF-SAMPLE | GLD    | acc=0.4946
         CPU times: user 44.9 s, sys: 2.64 s, total: 47.5 s
         Wall time: 6.37 s
```

❶ Training data set statistics are used for normalization.

The good in-sample performance and the not-so-good out-of-sample performance
suggest that overfitting of the neural network might play a crucial role. One approach
to avoid overfitting is to use ensemble methods that combine multiple trained models
of the same type to come up with a more robust meta model and better out-of-sample
predictions. One such method is called *bagging*. scikit-learn has an implementation of this approach in the form of the BaggingClassifier class (*https://oreil.ly/
gQLFZ*). Using multiple estimators allows for training every one of them without
exposing them to the complete training data set or all features. This should help in
avoiding overfitting.

The following Python code implements a bagging approach based on a number of
base estimators of the same type (MLPClassifier). The prediction accuracies are now
consistently above 50%. Some accuracy values are above 55%, which can be considered pretty high in this context. Overall, bagging seems to avoid, at least to some
extent, overfitting and seems to improve the predictions noticeably:

```
In [47]: from sklearn.ensemble import BaggingClassifier

In [48]: base_estimator = MLPClassifier(hidden_layer_sizes=[256],
                                        random_state=100,
                                        max_iter=1000,
                                        early_stopping=True,
                                        validation_fraction=0.15,
                                        shuffle=False)      ❶

In [49]: model_bag = BaggingClassifier(base_estimator=base_estimator,  ❶
                                       n_estimators=35,     ❷
                                       max_samples=0.25,    ❸
                                       max_features=0.5,    ❹
```

```
                         bootstrap=False,    ❺
                         bootstrap_features=True,   ❻
                         n_jobs=8,   ❼
                         random_state=100
                      )

In [50]: %time train_test_model(model_bag)
         OUT-OF-SAMPLE | AAPL.O | acc=0.5243
         OUT-OF-SAMPLE | MSFT.O | acc=0.5703
         OUT-OF-SAMPLE | INTC.O | acc=0.5027
         OUT-OF-SAMPLE | AMZN.O | acc=0.5270
         OUT-OF-SAMPLE | GS.N   | acc=0.5243
         OUT-OF-SAMPLE | SPY    | acc=0.5595
         OUT-OF-SAMPLE | .SPX   | acc=0.5514
         OUT-OF-SAMPLE | .VIX   | acc=0.5649
         OUT-OF-SAMPLE | EUR=   | acc=0.5108
         OUT-OF-SAMPLE | XAU=   | acc=0.5378
         OUT-OF-SAMPLE | GDX    | acc=0.5162
         OUT-OF-SAMPLE | GLD    | acc=0.5432
         CPU times: user 2.55 s, sys: 494 ms, total: 3.05 s
         Wall time: 11.1 s
```

❶ The base estimator

❷ The number of estimators used

❸ Maximum percentage of training data used per estimator

❹ Maximum number of features used per estimator

❺ Whether to bootstrap (reuse) data

❻ Whether to bootstrap (reuse) features

❼ Number of parallel jobs

End-of-Day Market Efficiency

The efficient market hypothesis dates back to the 1960s and 1970s, periods during which end-of-day data was basically the only available time series data. Back in those days (and still today), it could be assumed that market players paid particularly close attention to their positions and trades the closer the end of the trading session came. This might be more true for stocks, say, and a bit less so for currencies, which are traded in principle around the clock.

Market Prediction Intraday

This chapter has not produced conclusive evidence, but the analyses implemented so far point more in the direction that markets are weakly efficient on an end-of-day basis. What about intraday markets? Are there more consistent statistical inefficiencies to be spotted? To work toward an answer of this question, another data set is necessary. The following Python code uses a data set that is composed of the same instruments as in the end-of-day data set, but now contains hourly closing prices. Since trading hours might differ from instrument to instrument, the data set is incomplete. This is no problem, though, since the analyses are implemented time series by time series.

The technical implementation for the hourly data is essentially the same as before, relying on the same code as the end-of-day analysis:

```
In [51]: url = 'http://hilpisch.com/aiif_eikon_id_data.csv'

In [52]: data = pd.read_csv(url, index_col=0, parse_dates=True)

In [53]: data.info()
         <class 'pandas.core.frame.DataFrame'>
         DatetimeIndex: 5529 entries, 2019-03-01 00:00:00 to 2020-01-01 00:00:00
         Data columns (total 12 columns):
          #   Column  Non-Null Count  Dtype
         ---  ------  --------------  -----
          0   AAPL.O  3384 non-null   float64
          1   MSFT.O  3378 non-null   float64
          2   INTC.O  3275 non-null   float64
          3   AMZN.O  3381 non-null   float64
          4   GS.N    1686 non-null   float64
          5   SPY     3388 non-null   float64
          6   .SPX    1802 non-null   float64
          7   .VIX    2959 non-null   float64
          8   EUR=    5429 non-null   float64
          9   XAU=    5149 non-null   float64
          10  GDX     3173 non-null   float64
          11  GLD     3351 non-null   float64
         dtypes: float64(12)
         memory usage: 561.5 KB

In [54]: lags = 5

In [55]: dfs = {}
         for ric in data:
             df, cols = add_lags(data, ric, lags)
             dfs[ric] = df, cols
```

The prediction accuracies intraday are again distributed around 50% with a relatively wide spread for the single neural network. On the positive side, some accuracy values are above 55%. The bagging meta model shows a more consistent out-of-sample performance, though, with many of the observed accuracy values a few percentage points above the 50% benchmark:

```
In [56]: %time train_test_model(model_mlp)
         OUT-OF-SAMPLE | AAPL.O | acc=0.5420
         OUT-OF-SAMPLE | MSFT.O | acc=0.4930
         OUT-OF-SAMPLE | INTC.O | acc=0.5549
         OUT-OF-SAMPLE | AMZN.O | acc=0.4709
         OUT-OF-SAMPLE | GS.N   | acc=0.5184
         OUT-OF-SAMPLE | SPY    | acc=0.4860
         OUT-OF-SAMPLE | .SPX   | acc=0.5019
         OUT-OF-SAMPLE | .VIX   | acc=0.4885
         OUT-OF-SAMPLE | EUR=   | acc=0.5130
         OUT-OF-SAMPLE | XAU=   | acc=0.4824
         OUT-OF-SAMPLE | GDX    | acc=0.4765
         OUT-OF-SAMPLE | GLD    | acc=0.5455
         CPU times: user 1min 4s, sys: 5.05 s, total: 1min 9s
         Wall time: 9.56 s

In [57]: %time train_test_model(model_bag)
         OUT-OF-SAMPLE | AAPL.O | acc=0.5660
         OUT-OF-SAMPLE | MSFT.O | acc=0.5431
         OUT-OF-SAMPLE | INTC.O | acc=0.5072
         OUT-OF-SAMPLE | AMZN.O | acc=0.5110
         OUT-OF-SAMPLE | GS.N   | acc=0.5020
         OUT-OF-SAMPLE | SPY    | acc=0.5120
         OUT-OF-SAMPLE | .SPX   | acc=0.4677
         OUT-OF-SAMPLE | .VIX   | acc=0.5092
         OUT-OF-SAMPLE | EUR=   | acc=0.5242
         OUT-OF-SAMPLE | XAU=   | acc=0.5255
         OUT-OF-SAMPLE | GDX    | acc=0.5085
         OUT-OF-SAMPLE | GLD    | acc=0.5374
         CPU times: user 2.64 s, sys: 439 ms, total: 3.08 s
         Wall time: 12.4 s
```

Intraday Market Efficiency

Even if markets are *weakly efficient on an end-of-day basis*, they can nevertheless be *weakly inefficient intraday*. Such statistical inefficiencies might result from temporary imbalances, buy or sell pressures, market overreactions, technically driven buy or sell orders, and so on. The central question is whether such statistical inefficiencies, once discovered, can be exploited profitably via specific trading strategies.

Conclusions

In their widely cited article "The Unreasonable Effectiveness of Data," Halevy et al. (2009) point out that economists suffer from what they call *physics envy*. By that, they mean the inability to explain human behavior in the same mathematically elegant way that physicists are able to describe even complex real-world phenomena. One such example is Albert Einstein's probably best-known formula $E = mc^2$, which equates energy with the mass of an object times the speed of light squared.

In economics and finance, researchers for decades have tried to emulate the physical approach in deriving and proving simple, elegant equations to explain economic and financial phenomena. But as Chapter 3 and Chapter 4 together show, many of the most elegant financial theories have hardly any supporting evidence in the real financial world in which the simplifying assumptions, such as normal distributions and linear relationships, do not hold.

As Halevy et al. (2009) explain in their article, there might be domains, such as natural languages and the rules they follow, that defy the derivation and formulation of concise, elegant theories. Researchers might simply need to rely on complex theories and models that are driven by data. For language in particular, the World Wide Web represents a treasure trove of *big data*. And big data seems to be required to train ML and DL algorithms on certain tasks, such as natural language processing or translation on a human level.

After all, finance might be a discipline that has more in common with natural language than with physics. Maybe there are, after all, no simple, elegant formulas that describe important financial phenomena, such as the daily change in a currency rate or the price of a stock.[5] Maybe the truth might be found only in the big data that nowadays is available in programmatic fashion to financial researchers and academics alike.

This chapter presents the beginning of the quest to uncover the truth, to discover the holy grail of finance: proving that markets are not that efficient after all. The relatively simple neural network approaches of this chapter only rely on time-series-related features for the training. The labels are simple and straightforward: whether the market (financial instrument's price) goes up or down. The goal is to discover *statistical inefficiencies* in predicting the future market direction. This in turn represents the first step in exploiting such inefficiencies economically through an implementable trading strategy.

Agrawal et al. (2018) explain in detail, with many examples, that predictions themselves are only one side of the coin. Decision and implementation rules that specify in detail how a certain prediction is dealt with are equally important. The same holds true in an algorithmic trading context: the signal (prediction) is only the beginning.

---

5 There are, of course, more simple financial aspects that allow the modeling by a simple formula. An example might be the derivation of a continuous discount factor D for a period of two years $T = 2$ if the relevant log return is $r = 0.01$. It is given by $D(r, T) = \exp(-rT) = \exp(-0.01 \cdot 2) = 0.9802$. AI or ML cannot offer any benefits here.

The hard part is to optimally execute an appropriate trade, to monitor active trades, to implement appropriate risk measures—such as stop loss and take profit orders—and so on.

In its quest for statistical inefficiencies, this chapter relies on data and neural networks only. There is no theory involved, and there are no assumptions about how market participants might behave, or similar reasonings. The major modeling effort is done with regard to preparing the features, which of course represent what the modeler considers important. One implicit assumption in the approach taken is that statistical inefficiencies can be discovered based on time-series-related data only. This is to say that markets are not even weakly efficient—the most difficult form of the three to disprove.

Relying on financial data only and applying general ML and DL algorithms and models to it are what this book considers *AI-first finance*. No theories needed, no modeling of human behavior, no assumptions about distributions or the nature of relationships—just data and algorithms. In that sense, AI-first finance could also be labeled *theory-free* or *model-free finance*.

References

Books and papers cited in this chapter:

Agrawal, Ajay, Joshua Gans, and Avi Goldfarb. 2018. *Prediction Machines: The Simple Economics of Artificial Intelligence*. Boston: Harvard Business Review Press.

Copeland, Thomas, Fred Weston, and Kuldeep Shastri. 2005. *Financial Theory and Corporate Policy*. 4th ed. Boston: Pearson.

Fama, Eugene. 1965. "Random Walks in Stock Market Prices." *Financial Analysts Journal* (September/October): 55-59.

Halevy, Alon, Peter Norvig, and Fernando Pereira. 2009. "The Unreasonable Effectiveness of Data." *IEEE Intelligent Systems*, Expert Opinion.

Hilpisch, Yves. 2018. *Python for Finance: Mastering Data-Driven Finance*. 2nd ed. Sebastopol: O'Reilly.

Jensen, Michael. 1978. "Some Anomalous Evidence Regarding Market Efficiency." *Journal of Financial Economics* 6 (2/3): 95-101.

Tegmark, Max. 2017. *Life 3.0: Being Human in the Age of Artificial Intelligence*. United Kingdom: Penguin Random House.

Tsay, Ruey S. 2005. *Analysis of Financial Time Series*. Hoboken: Wiley.

## PART III

Statistical Inefficiencies

"There are patterns in the market," Simons told a colleague. "I know we can find them."[1]

—Gregory Zuckerman (2019)

The major goal of this part is to apply neural networks and reinforcement learning to discover statistical inefficiencies in financial markets (data). A *statistical inefficiency*, for the purposes of this book, is found when a *predictor* (a model or algorithm in general or a neural network in particular) predicts markets significantly better than a random predictor assigning equal probability to upwards and downwards movements. In an algorithmic trading context, to have such a predictor available is a prerequisite for the generation of *alpha* or above-market returns.

This part consists of three chapters that provide more background, details, and examples related to dense neural networks (DNNs), recurrent neural networks (RNNs), and reinforcement learning (RL):

- Chapter 7 covers DNNs in some more detail and applies them to the problem of predicting the direction of financial market movements. Historical data is used to generate lagged features data and to generate binary labels data. Such data sets are then used to train DNNs via supervised learning. The focus lies on identifying statistical inefficiencies in financial markets. In some of the examples, the DNN achieves an out-of-sample prediction accuracy of more than 60%.

---

1 Gregory Zuckerman. 2019. *The Man Who Solved the Market.* New York: Penguin Random House.

- Chapter 8 is about RNNs, which are designed to accommodate the specific nature of sequential data, such as textual data or time series data. The idea is to add some form of memory to the network that carries previous (historical) information through the network (layers). The approach taken in this chapter is close to the one in Chapter 7, with the same goal of discovering statistical inefficiencies in the financial market data. As numerical examples illustrate, RNNs also can reach prediction accuracies out-of-sample of more than 60%.

- Chapter 9 discusses RL as one of the major success stories in AI. The chapter discusses different RL agents applied to both a simulated physical environment from the OpenAI Gym and financial market environments as developed in the chapter. The algorithm of choice in RL often is Q-learning, which is discussed in detail and applied to train a trading bot. The trading bot shows respectable out-of-sample financial performance, which is generally an even more important yardstick than prediction accuracy alone. In that sense, the chapter builds a natural bridge to Part IV, which is concerned with exploiting statistical inefficiencies economically.

Although they are quite an important type of a neural network, *convolutional neural networks* (CNNs) are not discussed in detail in this part. Appendix C illustrates the application of CNNs in a concise way. In many cases, CNNs can also be applied to the problems that DNNs and RNNs are applied to in this part of the book.

The approach in this part is a practical one, leaving out many important details with regard to the algorithms and techniques applied. This seems justified since there are a number of good resources in book form and otherwise available that can be consulted for technical details and background information. The chapters to follow provide references to a select few, generally comprehensive, resources when appropriate.

## CHAPTER 7

Dense Neural Networks

> [I]f you're trying to predict the movements of a stock on the stock market given its recent price history, you're unlikely to succeed, because price history doesn't contain much predictive information.
>
> —François Chollet (2017)

This chapter is about important aspects of *dense neural networks*. Previous chapters have already made use of this type of neural network. In particular, the `MLPClassifier` and `MLPRegressor` models from `scikit-learn` and the `Sequential` model from `Keras` for classification and estimation are dense neural networks (DNNs). This chapter exclusively focuses on `Keras` since it gives more freedom and flexibility in modeling DNNs.[1]

"The Data" on page 212 introduces the foreign exchange (FX) data set that the other sections in this chapter use. "Baseline Prediction" on page 214 generates a baseline, in-sample prediction on the new data set. Normalization of training and test data is introduced in "Normalization" on page 218. As means to avoid overfitting, "Dropout" on page 220 and "Regularization" on page 222 discuss dropout and regularization as popular methods. Bagging, as another method to avoid overfitting and already used in Chapter 6, is revisited in "Bagging" on page 225. Finally, "Optimizers" on page 227 compares the performance of different optimizers that can be used with `Keras` DNN models.

Although the introductory quote for the chapter might give little reason for hope, the main goal for this chapter—as well as for Part III as a whole—is to discover statistical inefficiencies in financial markets (time series) by applying neural networks. The

---

1 See Chollet (2017) for more details and background information on the `Keras` package. See Goodfellow et al. (2016) for a comprehensive treatment of neural networks and related methods.

numerical results presented in this chapter, such as prediction accuracies of 60% and more in certain cases, indicate that at least some hope is justified.

The Data

Chapter 6 discovers hints for statistical inefficiencies for, among other time series, the intraday price series of the EUR/USD currency pair. This chapter and the following ones focus on foreign exchange (FX) as an asset class and specifically on the EUR/USD currency pair. Among other reasons, economically exploiting statistical inefficiencies for FX is in general not as involved as for other asset classes, such as for volatility products like the VIX volatility index. Free and comprehensive data availability is also often given for FX. The following data set is from the Refinitiv Eikon Data API. The data set has been retrieved via the API. The data set contains open, high, low, and close values. Figure 7-1 visualizes the closing prices:

```
In [1]: import os
        import numpy as np
        import pandas as pd
        from pylab import plt, mpl
        plt.style.use('seaborn')
        mpl.rcParams['savefig.dpi'] = 300
        mpl.rcParams['font.family'] = 'serif'
        pd.set_option('precision', 4)
        np.set_printoptions(suppress=True, precision=4)
        os.environ['PYTHONHASHSEED'] = '0'

In [2]: url = 'http://hilpisch.com/aiif_eikon_id_eur_usd.csv'  ❶

In [3]: symbol = 'EUR_USD'

In [4]: raw = pd.read_csv(url, index_col=0, parse_dates=True)  ❶

In [5]: raw.head()
Out[5]:                       HIGH     LOW    OPEN   CLOSE
        Date
        2019-10-01 00:00:00  1.0899  1.0897  1.0897  1.0899
        2019-10-01 00:01:00  1.0899  1.0896  1.0899  1.0898
        2019-10-01 00:02:00  1.0898  1.0896  1.0898  1.0896
        2019-10-01 00:03:00  1.0898  1.0896  1.0897  1.0898
        2019-10-01 00:04:00  1.0898  1.0896  1.0897  1.0898

In [6]: raw.info()
        <class 'pandas.core.frame.DataFrame'>
        DatetimeIndex: 96526 entries, 2019-10-01 00:00:00 to 2019-12-31 23:06:00
        Data columns (total 4 columns):
         #   Column  Non-Null Count   Dtype
        ---  ------  --------------   -----
         0   HIGH    96526 non-null   float64
         1   LOW     96526 non-null   float64
```

```
   2   OPEN    96526 non-null  float64
   3   CLOSE   96526 non-null  float64
dtypes: float64(4)
memory usage: 3.7 MB

In [7]: data = pd.DataFrame(raw['CLOSE'].loc[:])  ❷
        data.columns = [symbol]  ❷

In [8]: data = data.resample('1h', label='right').last().ffill()  ❷

In [9]: data.info()
        <class 'pandas.core.frame.DataFrame'>
        DatetimeIndex: 2208 entries, 2019-10-01 01:00:00 to 2020-01-01 00:00:00
        Freq: H
        Data columns (total 1 columns):
         #   Column   Non-Null Count   Dtype
        ---  ------   --------------   -----
         0   EUR_USD  2208 non-null    float64
        dtypes: float64(1)
        memory usage: 34.5 KB

In [10]: data.plot(figsize=(10, 6));  ❷
```

❶ Reads the data into a `DataFrame` object

❷ Selects, resamples, and plots the closing prices

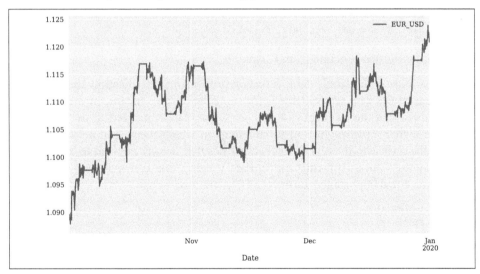

Figure 7-1. Mid-closing prices for EUR/USD (intraday)

Baseline Prediction

Based on the new data set, the prediction approach from Chapter 6 is repeated. First is the creation of the lagged features:

```
In [11]: lags = 5

In [12]: def add_lags(data, symbol, lags, window=20):   ❶
             cols = []
             df = data.copy()
             df.dropna(inplace=True)
             df['r'] = np.log(df / df.shift())
             df['sma'] = df[symbol].rolling(window).mean()
             df['min'] = df[symbol].rolling(window).min()
             df['max'] = df[symbol].rolling(window).max()
             df['mom'] = df['r'].rolling(window).mean()
             df['vol'] = df['r'].rolling(window).std()
             df.dropna(inplace=True)
             df['d'] = np.where(df['r'] > 0, 1, 0)
             features = [symbol, 'r', 'd', 'sma', 'min', 'max', 'mom', 'vol']
             for f in features:
                 for lag in range(1, lags + 1):
                     col = f'{f}_lag_{lag}'
                     df[col] = df[f].shift(lag)
                     cols.append(col)
             df.dropna(inplace=True)
             return df, cols

In [13]: data, cols = add_lags(data, symbol, lags)
```

❶ Slightly adjusted function from Chapter 6

Second, a look at the labels data. A major problem in classification that can arise depending on the data set available is *class imbalance*. This means, in the context of binary labels, that the frequency of one particular class compared to the other class might be higher. This might lead to situations in which the neural network simply predicts the class with the higher frequency since this already can lead to low loss and high accuracy values. Applying appropriate weights, one can make sure that both classes gain equal importance during the DNN training step:[2]

```
In [14]: len(data)
Out[14]: 2183

In [15]: c = data['d'].value_counts()   ❶
         c   ❶
Out[15]: 0    1445
         1     738
```

---

2 See this blog post (*https://oreil.ly/3X1Qk*), which discusses solutions to class imbalance with Keras.

```
          Name: d, dtype: int64

In [16]: def cw(df):  ❷
             c0, c1 = np.bincount(df['d'])
             w0 = (1 / c0) * (len(df)) / 2
             w1 = (1 / c1) * (len(df)) / 2
             return {0: w0, 1: w1}

In [17]: class_weight = cw(data)  ❷

In [18]: class_weight  ❷
Out[18]: {0: 0.755363321799308, 1: 1.4789972899728998}

In [19]: class_weight[0] * c[0]  ❸
Out[19]: 1091.5

In [20]: class_weight[1] * c[1]  ❸
Out[20]: 1091.5
```

❶ Shows the frequency of the two classes

❷ Calculates appropriate weights to reach an equal weighting

❸ With the calculated weights, both classes gain equal weight

Third is the creation of the DNN model with Keras and the training of the model on the complete data set. The baseline performance in-sample is around 60%:

```
In [21]: import random
         import tensorflow as tf
         from keras.layers import Dense
         from keras.models import Sequential
         from keras.optimizers import Adam
         from sklearn.metrics import accuracy_score
         Using TensorFlow backend.

In [22]: def set_seeds(seed=100):
             random.seed(seed)  ❶
             np.random.seed(seed)  ❷
             tf.random.set_seed(seed)  ❸

In [23]: optimizer = Adam(lr=0.001)  ❹

In [24]: def create_model(hl=1, hu=128, optimizer=optimizer):
             model = Sequential()
             model.add(Dense(hu, input_dim=len(cols),
                             activation='relu'))  ❺
             for _ in range(hl):
                 model.add(Dense(hu, activation='relu'))  ❻
             model.add(Dense(1, activation='sigmoid'))  ❼
             model.compile(loss='binary_crossentropy',  ❽
```

```
                        optimizer=optimizer,   ❾
                        metrics=['accuracy'])  ❿
            return model

In [25]: set_seeds()
         model = create_model(hl=1, hu=128)

In [26]: %%time
         model.fit(data[cols], data['d'], epochs=50,
                   verbose=False, class_weight=cw(data))
         CPU times: user 6.44 s, sys: 939 ms, total: 7.38 s
         Wall time: 4.07 s

Out[26]: <keras.callbacks.callbacks.History at 0x7fbfc2ee6690>

In [27]: model.evaluate(data[cols], data['d'])
         2183/2183 [==============================] - 0s 24us/step

Out[27]: [0.582192026280068, 0.6087952256202698]

In [28]: data['p'] = np.where(model.predict(data[cols]) > 0.5, 1, 0)

In [29]: data['p'].value_counts()
Out[29]: 1    1340
         0     843
         Name: p, dtype: int64
```

❶ Python random number seed

❷ NumPy random number seed

❸ TensorFlow random number seed

❹ Default optimizer (see *https://oreil.ly/atpu8*)

❺ First layer

❻ Additional layers

❼ Output layer

❽ Loss function (see *https://oreil.ly/cVGVf*)

❾ Optimizer to be used

❿ Additional metrics to be collected

The same holds true for the performance of the model out-of-sample. It is still well above 60%. This can be considered already quite good:

```
In [30]: split = int(len(data) * 0.8)   ❶

In [31]: train = data.iloc[:split].copy()   ❷

In [32]: test = data.iloc[split:].copy()   ❸

In [33]: set_seeds()
         model = create_model(hl=1, hu=128)

In [34]: %%time
         h = model.fit(train[cols], train['d'],
                  epochs=50, verbose=False,
                  validation_split=0.2, shuffle=False,
                  class_weight=cw(train))
         CPU times: user 4.72 s, sys: 686 ms, total: 5.41 s
         Wall time: 3.14 s

Out[34]: <keras.callbacks.callbacks.History at 0x7fbfc3231250>

In [35]: model.evaluate(train[cols], train['d'])   ❹
         1746/1746 [==============================] - 0s 13us/step

Out[35]: [0.612861613500842, 0.5853379368782043]

In [36]: model.evaluate(test[cols], test['d'])   ❺
         437/437 [==============================] - 0s 16us/step

Out[36]: [0.5946959675858714, 0.6247139573097229]

In [37]: test['p'] = np.where(model.predict(test[cols]) > 0.5, 1, 0)

In [38]: test['p'].value_counts()
Out[38]: 1    291
         0    146
         Name: p, dtype: int64
```

❶ Splits the whole data set…

❷ …into the training data set…

❸ …and the test data set.

❹ Evaluates the *in-sample* performance.

❺ Evaluates the *out-of-sample* performance.

Figure 7-2 shows how the accuracy on the training and validation data sub-sets changes over the training epochs:

```
In [39]: res = pd.DataFrame(h.history)

In [40]: res[['accuracy', 'val_accuracy']].plot(figsize=(10, 6), style='--');
```

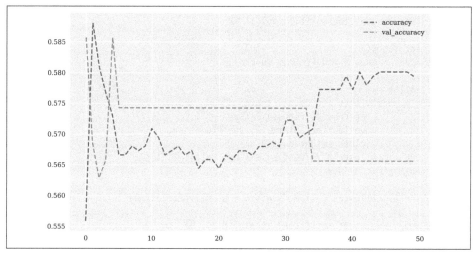

Figure 7-2. Training and validation accuracy values

The analysis in this section sets the stage for the more elaborate use of DNNs with Keras. It presents a baseline market prediction approach. The following sections add different elements that are primarily supposed to improve the out-of-sample model performance and to avoid overfitting of the model to the training data.

Normalization

The baseline prediction in "Baseline Prediction" on page 214 takes the lagged features as they are. In Chapter 6, the features data is normalized by subtracting the mean of the training data for every feature and dividing it by the standard deviation of the training data. This normalization technique is called *Gaussian normalization* and proves often, if not always, to be an important aspect when training a neural network. As the following Python code and its results illustrate, the in-sample performance increases significantly when working with normalized features data. The out-of-sample performance also slightly increases. However, there is no guarantee that the out-of-sample performance increases through features normalization:

```
In [41]: mu, std = train.mean(), train.std()    ❶

In [42]: train_ = (train - mu) / std    ❷

In [43]: set_seeds()
```

```
        model = create_model(hl=2, hu=128)

In [44]: %%time
        h = model.fit(train_[cols], train['d'],
                epochs=50, verbose=False,
                validation_split=0.2, shuffle=False,
                class_weight=cw(train))
        CPU times: user 5.81 s, sys: 879 ms, total: 6.69 s
        Wall time: 3.53 s

Out[44]: <keras.callbacks.callbacks.History at 0x7fbfa51353d0>

In [45]: model.evaluate(train_[cols], train['d'])  ❸
        1746/1746 [==============================] - 0s 14us/step

Out[45]: [0.4253406366728084, 0.887170672416687]

In [46]: test_ = (test - mu) / std  ❹

In [47]: model.evaluate(test_[cols], test['d'])  ❺
        437/437 [==============================] - 0s 24us/step

Out[47]: [1.1377735263422917, 0.681922197341919]

In [48]: test['p'] = np.where(model.predict(test_[cols]) > 0.5, 1, 0)

In [49]: test['p'].value_counts()
Out[49]: 0    281
        1    156
        Name: p, dtype: int64
```

❶ Calculates the mean and standard deviation for all *training features*

❷ Normalizes the *training data* set based on Gaussian normalization

❸ Evaluates the *in-sample* performance

❹ Normalizes the *test data* set based on Gaussian normalization

❺ Evaluates the *out-of-sample* performance

A major problem that often arises is *overfitting*. It is impressively visualized in Figure 7-3, which shows a steadily improving training accuracy while the validation accuracy decreases slowly:

```
In [50]: res = pd.DataFrame(h.history)

In [51]: res[['accuracy', 'val_accuracy']].plot(figsize=(10, 6), style='--');
```

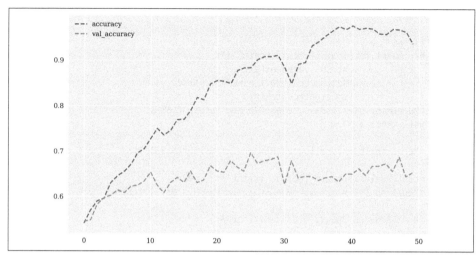

Figure 7-3. Training and validation accuracy values (normalized features data)

Three candidate methods to avoid overfitting are *dropout, regularization,* and *bagging.* The following sections discuss these methods. The impact of the chosen optimizer is also discussed later in this chapter.

Dropout

The idea of *dropout* is that neural networks should not use all hidden units during the training stage. The analogy to the human brain is that a human being regularly forgets information that was previously learned. This, so to say, keeps the human brain "open minded." Ideally, a neural network should behave similarly: the connections in the DNN should not become too strong in order to avoid overfitting to the training data.

Technically, a `Keras` model has additional layers between the hidden layers that manage the dropout. The major parameter is the rate with which the hidden units of a layer get dropped. These drops in general happen in randomized fashion. This can be avoided by fixing the `seed` parameter. While the in-sample performance decreases, the out-of-sample performance slightly decreases as well. However, the difference between the two performance measures is smaller, which is in general a desirable situation:

```
In [52]: from keras.layers import Dropout

In [53]: def create_model(hl=1, hu=128, dropout=True, rate=0.3,
                           optimizer=optimizer):
             model = Sequential()
             model.add(Dense(hu, input_dim=len(cols),
                             activation='relu'))
```

```
        if dropout:
            model.add(Dropout(rate, seed=100))  ❶
        for _ in range(hl):
            model.add(Dense(hu, activation='relu'))
            if dropout:
                model.add(Dropout(rate, seed=100))  ❶
        model.add(Dense(1, activation='sigmoid'))
        model.compile(loss='binary_crossentropy', optimizer=optimizer,
                      metrics=['accuracy'])
        return model

In [54]: set_seeds()
         model = create_model(hl=1, hu=128, rate=0.3)

In [55]: %%time
         h = model.fit(train_[cols], train['d'],
                   epochs=50, verbose=False,
                   validation_split=0.15, shuffle=False,
                   class_weight=cw(train))
         CPU times: user 5.46 s, sys: 758 ms, total: 6.21 s
         Wall time: 3.53 s

Out[55]: <keras.callbacks.callbacks.History at 0x7fbfa6386550>

In [56]: model.evaluate(train_[cols], train['d'])
         1746/1746 [==============================] - 0s 20us/step

Out[56]: [0.4423361133190911, 0.7840778827667236]

In [57]: model.evaluate(test_[cols], test['d'])
         437/437 [==============================] - 0s 34us/step

Out[57]: [0.5875822428434883, 0.6430205702781677]
```

❶ Adds dropout after each layer

As Figure 7-4 illustrates, the training accuracy and validation accuracy now do not drift apart as fast as before:

```
In [58]: res = pd.DataFrame(h.history)

In [59]: res[['accuracy', 'val_accuracy']].plot(figsize=(10, 6), style='--');
```

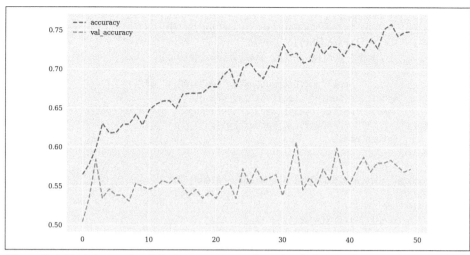

Figure 7-4. Training and validation accuracy values (with dropout)

Intentional Forgetting

Dropout in the Sequential model of Keras emulates what all human beings experience: forgetting previously memorized information. This is accomplished by deactivating certain hidden units of a hidden layer during training. In effect, this often avoids, to a larger extent, overfitting a neural network to the training data.

Regularization

Another means to avoid overfitting is *regularization*. With regularization, large weights in the neural network get penalized in the calculation of the loss (function). This avoids the situation where certain connections in the DNN become too strong and dominant. Regularization can be introduced in a Keras DNN through a parameter in the Dense layers. Depending on the regularization parameter chosen, training and test accuracy can be kept quite close together. Two regularizers are in general used, one based on the linear norm, l1, and one based on the Euclidean norm, l2. The following Python code adds regularization to the model creation function:

```
In [60]: from keras.regularizers import l1, l2

In [61]: def create_model(hl=1, hu=128, dropout=False, rate=0.3,
                          regularize=False, reg=l1(0.0005),
                          optimizer=optimizer, input_dim=len(cols)):
            if not regularize:
                reg = None
            model = Sequential()
            model.add(Dense(hu, input_dim=input_dim,
```

```
                        activity_regularizer=reg,  ❶
                        activation='relu'))
            if dropout:
                model.add(Dropout(rate, seed=100))
            for _ in range(hl):
                model.add(Dense(hu, activation='relu',
                            activity_regularizer=reg))  ❶
                if dropout:
                    model.add(Dropout(rate, seed=100))
            model.add(Dense(1, activation='sigmoid'))
            model.compile(loss='binary_crossentropy', optimizer=optimizer,
                        metrics=['accuracy'])
            return model

In [62]: set_seeds()
         model = create_model(hl=1, hu=128, regularize=True)

In [63]: %%time
         h = model.fit(train_[cols], train['d'],
                    epochs=50, verbose=False,
                    validation_split=0.2, shuffle=False,
                    class_weight=cw(train))
         CPU times: user 5.49 s, sys: 1.05 s, total: 6.54 s
         Wall time: 3.15 s

Out[63]: <keras.callbacks.callbacks.History at 0x7fbfa6b8e110>

In [64]: model.evaluate(train_[cols], train['d'])
         1746/1746 [==============================] - 0s 15us/step

Out[64]: [0.5307255412568205, 0.7691867351531982]

In [65]: model.evaluate(test_[cols], test['d'])
         437/437 [==============================] - 0s 22us/step

Out[65]: [0.8428352184644826, 0.6590389013290405]
```

❶ Regularization is added to each layer.

Figure 7-5 shows the training and validation accuracy under regularization. The two performance measures are much closer together than previously seen:

```
In [66]: res = pd.DataFrame(h.history)

In [67]: res[['accuracy', 'val_accuracy']].plot(figsize=(10, 6), style='--');
```

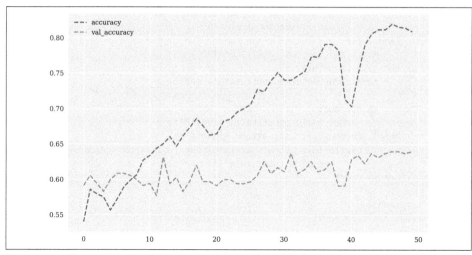

Figure 7-5. Training and validation accuracy values (with regularization)

Of course, dropout and regularization can be used together. The idea is that the two measures combined even better avoid overfitting and bring the in-sample and out-of-sample accuracy values closer together. And indeed the difference between the two measures is lowest in this case:

```
In [68]: set_seeds()
         model = create_model(hl=2, hu=128,
                         dropout=True, rate=0.3,    ❶
                         regularize=True, reg=l2(0.001),    ❷
                         )

In [69]: %%time
         h = model.fit(train_[cols], train['d'],
                     epochs=50, verbose=False,
                     validation_split=0.2, shuffle=False,
                     class_weight=cw(train))
         CPU times: user 7.06 s, sys: 958 ms, total: 8.01 s
         Wall time: 4.28 s

Out[69]: <keras.callbacks.callbacks.History at 0x7fbfa701cb50>

In [70]: model.evaluate(train_[cols], train['d'])
         1746/1746 [==============================] - 0s 18us/step

Out[70]: [0.5007762827004764, 0.7691867351531982]

In [71]: model.evaluate(test_[cols], test['d'])
         437/437 [==============================] - 0s 23us/step

Out[71]: [0.6191965124699835, 0.6864988803863525]
```

❶ Dropout is added to the model creation.

❷ Regularization is added to the model creation.

Figure 7-6 shows the training and validation accuracy when combining dropout with regularization. The difference between training and validation data accuracy over the training epochs is some four percentage points only on average:

```
In [72]: res = pd.DataFrame(h.history)

In [73]: res[['accuracy', 'val_accuracy']].plot(figsize=(10, 6), style='--');
```

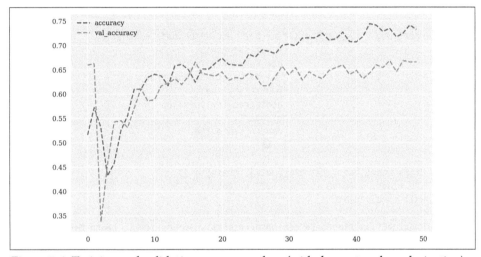

Figure 7-6. Training and validation accuracy values (with dropout and regularization)

Penalizing Large Weights

Regularization avoids overfitting by penalizing large weights in a neural network. Single weights cannot get that large enough to dominate a neural network. The penalties keep weights on a comparable level.

Bagging

The bagging method to avoid overfitting is already used in Chapter 6, although only for the scikit-learn MLPRegressor model. There is also a wrapper for a Keras DNN classification model to expose it in scikit-learn fashion, namely the KerasClassifier class. The following Python code combines the Keras DNN modeling based on the wrapper with the BaggingClassifier from scikit-learn. The in-sample and out-of-sample performance measures are relatively high, around 70%. However, the result is driven by the class imbalance, as addressed previously, and as reflected here in the high frequency of the 0 predictions:

```
In [75]: from sklearn.ensemble import BaggingClassifier
         from keras.wrappers.scikit_learn import KerasClassifier

In [76]: max_features = 0.75

In [77]: set_seeds()
         base_estimator = KerasClassifier(build_fn=create_model,
                           verbose=False, epochs=20, hl=1, hu=128,
                           dropout=True, regularize=False,
                           input_dim=int(len(cols) * max_features))  ❶

In [78]: model_bag = BaggingClassifier(base_estimator=base_estimator,
                           n_estimators=15,
                           max_samples=0.75,
                           max_features=max_features,
                           bootstrap=True,
                           bootstrap_features=True,
                           n_jobs=1,
                           random_state=100,
                       )  ❷

In [79]: %time model_bag.fit(train_[cols], train['d'])
         CPU times: user 40 s, sys: 5.23 s, total: 45.3 s
         Wall time: 26.3 s

Out[79]: BaggingClassifier(base_estimator=<keras.wrappers.scikit_learn.KerasClassifier
            object at 0x7fbfa7cc7b90>,
            bootstrap_features=True, max_features=0.75, max_samples=0.75,
                        n_estimators=15, n_jobs=1, random_state=100)

In [80]: model_bag.score(train_[cols], train['d'])
Out[80]: 0.720504009163803

In [81]: model_bag.score(test_[cols], test['d'])
Out[81]: 0.6704805491990846

In [82]: test['p'] = model_bag.predict(test_[cols])

In [83]: test['p'].value_counts()
Out[83]: 0    408
         1     29
         Name: p, dtype: int64
```

❶ The base estimator, here a Keras Sequential model, is instantiated.

❷ The BaggingClassifier model is instantiated for a number of equal base estimators.

Distributing Learning

Bagging, in a sense, distributes learning among a number of neural networks (or other models) in that each neural network, for example, only sees certain parts of the training data set and only a selection of the features. This avoids the risk that a single neural network overfits the complete training data set. The prediction is based on all selectively trained neural networks together.

Optimizers

The `Keras` package offers a selection of optimizers that can be used in combination with the `Sequential` model (see *https://oreil.ly/atpu8*). Different optimizers might show different performances, with regard to both the time the training takes and the prediction accuracy. The following Python code uses different optimizers and benchmarks their performance. In all cases, the default parametrization of `Keras` is used. The out-of-sample performance does not vary that much. However, the in-sample performance, given the different optimizers, varies by a wide margin:

```
In [84]: import time

In [85]: optimizers = ['sgd', 'rmsprop', 'adagrad', 'adadelta',
                       'adam', 'adamax', 'nadam']

In [86]: %%time
         for optimizer in optimizers:
             set_seeds()
             model = create_model(hl=1, hu=128,
                          dropout=True, rate=0.3,
                          regularize=False, reg=l2(0.001),
                          optimizer=optimizer
                          )  ❶
             t0 = time.time()
             model.fit(train_[cols], train['d'],
                     epochs=50, verbose=False,
                     validation_split=0.2, shuffle=False,
                     class_weight=cw(train))  ❷
             t1 = time.time()
             t = t1 - t0
             acc_tr = model.evaluate(train_[cols], train['d'], verbose=False)[1]  ❸
             acc_te = model.evaluate(test_[cols], test['d'], verbose=False)[1]  ❹
             out = f'{optimizer:10s} | time[s]: {t:.4f} | in-sample={acc_tr:.4f}'
             out += f' | out-of-sample={acc_te:.4f}'
             print(out)
         sgd        | time[s]: 2.8092 | in-sample=0.6363 | out-of-sample=0.6568
         rmsprop    | time[s]: 2.9480 | in-sample=0.7600 | out-of-sample=0.6613
         adagrad    | time[s]: 2.8472 | in-sample=0.6747 | out-of-sample=0.6499
         adadelta   | time[s]: 3.2068 | in-sample=0.7279 | out-of-sample=0.6522
         adam       | time[s]: 3.2364 | in-sample=0.7365 | out-of-sample=0.6545
```

```
adamax     | time[s]: 3.2465 | in-sample=0.6982 | out-of-sample=0.6476
nadam      | time[s]: 4.1275 | in-sample=0.7944 | out-of-sample=0.6590
CPU times: user 35.9 s, sys: 4.55 s, total: 40.4 s
Wall time: 23.1 s
```

❶ Instantiates the DNN model for the given optimizer

❷ Fits the model with the given optimizer

❸ Evaluates the *in-sample* performance

❹ Evaluates the *out-of-sample* performance

Conclusions

This chapter dives deeper into the world of DNNs and uses Keras as the primary package. Keras offers a high degree of flexibility in composing DNNs. The results in this chapter are promising in that both in-sample and out-of-sample performance—with regard to the prediction accuracy—are consistently 60% and higher. However, prediction accuracy is just one side of the coin. An appropriate trading strategy must be available and implementable to economically profit from the predictions, or "signals." This topic of paramount importance in the context of algorithmic trading is discussed in detail in Part IV. The next two chapters first illustrate the use of different neural networks (recurrent and convolutional neural networks) and learning techniques (reinforcement learning).

References

Keras is a powerful and comprehensive package for deep learning with TensforFlow as its primary backend. The project is also evolving fast. Make sure to stay up to date via the main project page (*http://keras.io*). The major resources about Keras in book form are the following:

Chollet, Francois. 2017. *Deep Learning with Python*. Shelter Island: Manning.

Goodfellow, Ian, Yoshua Bengio, and Aaron Courville. 2016. *Deep Learning*. Cambridge: MIT Press. *http://deeplearningbook.org*.

## CHAPTER 8

Recurrent Neural Networks

History never repeats itself, but it rhymes.

　　—Mark Twain (probably)

My life seemed to be a series of events and accidents. Yet when I look back, I see a pattern.

　　—Bernoît Mandelbrot

This chapter is about *recurrent neural networks* (RNNs). This type of network is specifically designed to learn about sequential data, such as text or time series data. The discussion in this chapter takes, as before, a practical approach and relies mainly on worked-out Python examples, making use of `Keras`.[1]

"First Example" on page 230 and "Second Example" on page 234 introduce RNNs on the basis of two simple examples with sample numerical data. The application of RNNs to predict sequential data is illustrated. "Financial Price Series" on page 237 then works with financial price series data and applies the RNN approach to predict such a series directly via estimation. "Financial Return Series" on page 240 then works with returns data to predict the future direction of the price of a financial instrument also via an estimation approach. "Financial Features" on page 242 adds financial features to the mix—in addition to price and return data—to predict the market direction. Three different approaches are illustrated in this section: prediction via a shallow RNN for both estimation and classification, as well as prediction via a deep RNN for classification.

---

1 For technical details of RNNs, refer to Goodfellow et al. (2016, ch. 10). For the practical implementation, refer to Chollet (2017, ch. 6).

The chapter shows that the application of RNNs to financial time series data can achieve a prediction accuracy of well above 60% out-of-sample in the context of directional market predictions. However, the results obtained cannot fully keep up with those seen in Chapter 7. This might come as a surprise, since RNNs are meant to work well with financial time series data, which is the primary focus of this book.

First Example

To illustrate the training and usage of RNNs, consider a simple example based on a sequence of integers. First, some imports and configurations:

```
In [1]: import os
        import random
        import numpy as np
        import pandas as pd
        import tensorflow as tf
        from pprint import pprint
        from pylab import plt, mpl
        plt.style.use('seaborn')
        mpl.rcParams['savefig.dpi'] = 300
        mpl.rcParams['font.family'] = 'serif'
        pd.set_option('precision', 4)
        np.set_printoptions(suppress=True, precision=4)
        os.environ['PYTHONHASHSEED'] = '0'
```

```
In [2]: def set_seeds(seed=100):  ❶
            random.seed(seed)
            np.random.seed(seed)
            tf.random.set_seed(seed)
        set_seeds()  ❶
```

❶ Function to set all seed values

Second is the simple data set that is transformed into an appropriate shape:

```
In [3]: a = np.arange(100)  ❶
        a
Out[3]: array([ 0,  1,  2,  3,  4,  5,  6,  7,  8,  9, 10, 11, 12, 13, 14, 15, 16,
               17, 18, 19, 20, 21, 22, 23, 24, 25, 26, 27, 28, 29, 30, 31, 32, 33,
               34, 35, 36, 37, 38, 39, 40, 41, 42, 43, 44, 45, 46, 47, 48, 49, 50,
               51, 52, 53, 54, 55, 56, 57, 58, 59, 60, 61, 62, 63, 64, 65, 66, 67,
               68, 69, 70, 71, 72, 73, 74, 75, 76, 77, 78, 79, 80, 81, 82, 83, 84,
               85, 86, 87, 88, 89, 90, 91, 92, 93, 94, 95, 96, 97, 98, 99])
```

```
In [4]: a = a.reshape((len(a), -1))  ❷
```

```
In [5]: a.shape  ❷
Out[5]: (100, 1)
```

```
In [6]: a[:5]  ❷
Out[6]: array([[0],
```

```
             [1],
             [2],
             [3],
             [4]])
```

❶ Sample data

❷ Reshaping to two dimensions

Using the `TimeseriesGenerator`, the raw data can be transformed into an object suited for the training of an RNN. The idea is to use a certain number of lags of the original data to train the model to predict the next value in the sequence. For example, 0, 1, 2 are the three lagged values (features) used to predict the value 3 (label). In the same way, 1, 2, 3 are used to predict 4:

```
In [7]: from keras.preprocessing.sequence import TimeseriesGenerator
        Using TensorFlow backend.

In [8]: lags = 3

In [9]: g = TimeseriesGenerator(a, a, length=lags, batch_size=5)  ❶

In [10]: pprint(list(g)[0])  ❶
         (array([[[0],
                  [1],
                  [2]],

                 [[1],
                  [2],
                  [3]],

                 [[2],
                  [3],
                  [4]],

                 [[3],
                  [4],
                  [5]],

                 [[4],
                  [5],
                  [6]]]),
          array([[3],
                 [4],
                 [5],
                 [6],
                 [7]]))
```

❶ `TimeseriesGenerator` creates batches of lagged sequential data.

The creation of the RNN model is similar to DNNs. The following Python code uses a single hidden layer of type `SimpleRNN` (Chollet 2017, ch. 6; also see Keras recurrent layers (*https://oreil.ly/kpuqA*)). Even with relatively few hidden units, the number of trainable parameters is quite large. The `.fit()` method takes as input generator objects such as those created with `TimeseriesGenerator`:

```
In [11]: from keras.models import Sequential
         from keras.layers import SimpleRNN, LSTM, Dense

In [12]: model = Sequential()
         model.add(SimpleRNN(100, activation='relu',
                             input_shape=(lags, 1)))  ❶
         model.add(Dense(1, activation='linear'))
         model.compile(optimizer='adagrad', loss='mse',
                       metrics=['mae'])

In [13]: model.summary()  ❷
         Model: "sequential_1"

         _____
         Layer (type)                 Output Shape              Param #
         =================================================================
         simple_rnn_1 (SimpleRNN)     (None, 100)               10200
         _____
         dense_1 (Dense)              (None, 1)                 101
         =================================================================
         Total params: 10,301
         Trainable params: 10,301
         Non-trainable params: 0
         _____

In [14]: %%time
         h = model.fit(g, epochs=1000, steps_per_epoch=5,
                       verbose=False)  ❸
         CPU times: user 17.4 s, sys: 3.9 s, total: 21.3 s
         Wall time: 30.8 s

Out[14]: <keras.callbacks.callbacks.History at 0x7f7f079058d0>
```

❶ The single hidden layer is of type `SimpleRNN`.

❷ The summary of the shallow RNN.

❸ The fitting of the RNN based on the generator object.

The performance metrics might show relatively erratic behavior when training RNNs (see Figure 8-1):

```
In [15]: res = pd.DataFrame(h.history)

In [16]: res.tail(3)
Out[16]:          loss     mae
         997  0.0001  0.0109
         998  0.0007  0.0211
         999  0.0001  0.0101

In [17]: res.iloc[10:].plot(figsize=(10, 6), style=['--', '--']);
```

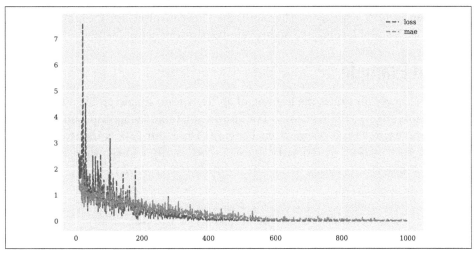

Figure 8-1. Performance metrics during RNN training

Having a trained RNN available, the following Python code generates in-sample and out-of-sample predictions:

```
In [18]: x = np.array([21, 22, 23]).reshape((1, lags, 1))
         y = model.predict(x, verbose=False)    ❶
         int(round(y[0, 0]))
Out[18]: 24

In [19]: x = np.array([87, 88, 89]).reshape((1, lags, 1))
         y = model.predict(x, verbose=False)    ❶
         int(round(y[0, 0]))
Out[19]: 90

In [20]: x = np.array([187, 188, 189]).reshape((1, lags, 1))
         y = model.predict(x, verbose=False)    ❷
         int(round(y[0, 0]))
Out[20]: 190

In [21]: x = np.array([1187, 1188, 1189]).reshape((1, lags, 1))
```

```
        y = model.predict(x, verbose=False)  ❸
        int(round(y[0, 0]))
Out[21]: 1194
```

❶   In-sample prediction

❷   Out-of-sample prediction

❸   Far-out-of-sample prediction

Even for far-out-of-sample predictions, the results are good in general in this simple
case. However, the problem at hand could, for example, be perfectly solved by the
application of OLS regression. Therefore, the effort involved for the training of an
RNN for such a problem is quite high given the performance of the RNN.

Second Example

The first example illustrates the training of an RNN for a simple problem that is easy
to solve not only by OLS regression but also by a human being inspecting the data.
The second example is a bit more challenging. The input data is transformed by a
quadratic term and a trigonometric term, as well as by adding white noise to it.
Figure 8-2 shows the resulting sequence for the interval $[-2\pi, 2\pi]$:

```
In [22]: def transform(x):
            y = 0.05 * x ** 2 + 0.2 * x + np.sin(x) + 5  ❶
            y += np.random.standard_normal(len(x)) * 0.2  ❷
            return y

In [23]: x = np.linspace(-2 * np.pi, 2 * np.pi, 500)
         a = transform(x)

In [24]: plt.figure(figsize=(10, 6))
         plt.plot(x, a);
```

❶   Deterministic transformation

❷   Stochastic transformation

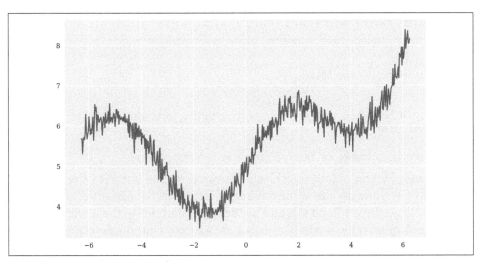

Figure 8-2. Sample sequence data

As before, the raw data is reshaped, `TimeseriesGenerator` is applied, and the RNN with a single hidden layer is trained:

```
In [25]: a = a.reshape((len(a), -1))

In [26]: a[:5]
Out[26]: array([[5.6736],
                [5.68  ],
                [5.3127],
                [5.645 ],
                [5.7118]])

In [27]: lags = 5

In [28]: g = TimeseriesGenerator(a, a, length=lags, batch_size=5)

In [29]: model = Sequential()
         model.add(SimpleRNN(500, activation='relu', input_shape=(lags, 1)))
         model.add(Dense(1, activation='linear'))
         model.compile(optimizer='rmsprop', loss='mse', metrics=['mae'])

In [30]: model.summary()
         Model: "sequential_2"
```

Layer (type)	Output Shape	Param #
simple_rnn_2 (SimpleRNN)	(None, 500)	251000
dense_2 (Dense)	(None, 1)	501

```
         Total params: 251,501
         Trainable params: 251,501
```

```
Non-trainable params: 0
```

```
In [31]: %%time
         model.fit(g, epochs=500,
                            steps_per_epoch=10,
                            verbose=False)
         CPU times: user 1min 6s, sys: 14.6 s, total: 1min 20s
         Wall time: 23.1 s

Out[31]: <keras.callbacks.callbacks.History at 0x7f7f09c11810>
```

The following Python code predicts sequence values for the interval $[-6\pi, 6\pi]$. This interval is three times the size of the training interval and contains out-of-sample predictions both on the left-hand side and on the right-hand side of the training interval. Figure 8-3 shows that the model performs quite well, even out-of-sample:

```
In [32]: x = np.linspace(-6 * np.pi, 6 * np.pi, 1000)    ❶
         d = transform(x)
```

```
In [33]: g_ = TimeseriesGenerator(d, d, length=lags, batch_size=len(d))    ❶
```

```
In [34]: f = list(g_)[0][0].reshape((len(d) - lags, lags, 1))    ❶
```

```
In [35]: y = model.predict(f, verbose=False)    ❷
```

```
In [36]: plt.figure(figsize=(10, 6))
         plt.plot(x[lags:], d[lags:], label='data', alpha=0.75)
         plt.plot(x[lags:], y, 'r.', label='pred', ms=3)
         plt.axvline(-2 * np.pi, c='g', ls='--')
         plt.axvline(2 * np.pi, c='g', ls='--')
         plt.text(-15, 22, 'out-of-sample')
         plt.text(-2, 22, 'in-sample')
         plt.text(10, 22, 'out-of-sample')
         plt.legend();
```

❶ Enlarges the sample data set

❷ In-sample *and* out-of-sample prediction

Simplicity of Examples

The first two examples are deliberately chosen to be simple. Both problems posed in the examples can be solved more efficiently with OLS regression, for example, by allowing for trigonometric basis functions in the second example. However, the training of RNNs for nontrivial sequence data, such as financial time series data, is basically the same. In such a context, OLS regression, for instance, can in general not keep up with the capabilities of RNNs.

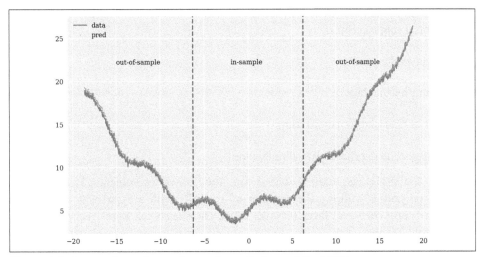

Figure 8-3. In-sample and out-of-sample predictions of the RNN

Financial Price Series

As a first application of RNNs to financial time series data, consider intraday EUR/USD quotes. With the approach introduced in the previous two sections, the training of the RNN on the financial time series is straightforward. First, the data is imported and resampled. The data is also normalized and transformed into the appropriate ndarray object:

```
In [37]: url = 'http://hilpisch.com/aiif_eikon_id_eur_usd.csv'

In [38]: symbol = 'EUR_USD'

In [39]: raw = pd.read_csv(url, index_col=0, parse_dates=True)

In [40]: def generate_data():
             data = pd.DataFrame(raw['CLOSE'])       ❶
             data.columns = [symbol]                 ❷
             data = data.resample('30min', label='right').last().ffill()   ❸
             return data

In [41]: data = generate_data()

In [42]: data = (data - data.mean()) / data.std()   ❹

In [43]: p = data[symbol].values                     ❺

In [44]: p = p.reshape((len(p), -1))                 ❺
```

❶ Selects a single column

❷ Renames the column

❸ Resamples the data

❹ Applies Gaussian normalization

❺ Reshapes the data set to two dimensions

Second, the RNN is trained based on the generator object. The function create_rnn_model() allows the creation of an RNN with a SimpleRNN or an LSTM (*long short-term memory*) layer (Chollet 2017, ch. 6; also see Keras recurrent layers (*https://oreil.ly/kpuqA*)).

```
In [45]: lags = 5

In [46]: g = TimeseriesGenerator(p, p, length=lags, batch_size=5)

In [47]: def create_rnn_model(hu=100, lags=lags, layer='SimpleRNN',
                              features=1, algorithm='estimation'):
             model = Sequential()
             if layer == 'SimpleRNN':
                 model.add(SimpleRNN(hu, activation='relu',
                                 input_shape=(lags, features)))   ❶
             else:
                 model.add(LSTM(hu, activation='relu',
                             input_shape=(lags, features)))   ❶
             if algorithm == 'estimation':
                 model.add(Dense(1, activation='linear'))   ❷
                 model.compile(optimizer='adam', loss='mse', metrics=['mae'])
             else:
                 model.add(Dense(1, activation='sigmoid'))   ❷
                 model.compile(optimizer='adam', loss='mse', metrics=['accuracy'])
             return model

In [48]: model = create_rnn_model()

In [49]: %%time
         model.fit(g, epochs=500, steps_per_epoch=10,
                         verbose=False)
         CPU times: user 20.8 s, sys: 4.66 s, total: 25.5 s
         Wall time: 11.2 s

Out[49]: <keras.callbacks.callbacks.History at 0x7f7ef6716590>
```

❶ Adds a SimpleRNN layer or LSTM layer

❷ Adds an output layer for *estimation* or *classification*

Third, the in-sample prediction is generated. As Figure 8-4 illustrates, the RNN is capable of capturing the structure of the normalized financial time series data. Based on this visualization, the prediction accuracy seems quite good:

```
In [50]: y = model.predict(g, verbose=False)

In [51]: data['pred'] = np.nan
         data['pred'].iloc[lags:] = y.flatten()

In [52]: data[[symbol, 'pred']].plot(
                    figsize=(10, 6), style=['b', 'r-.'],
                    alpha=0.75);
```

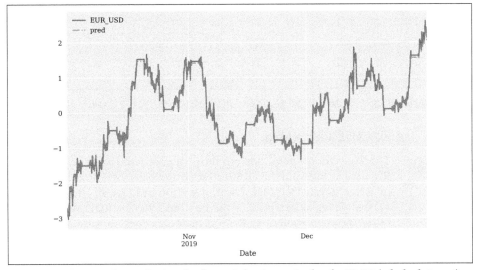

Figure 8-4. In-sample prediction for financial price series by the RNN (whole data set)

However, the visualization suggests a result that does not hold up upon closer inspection. Figure 8-5 zooms in and only shows 50 data points from the original data set and of the prediction. It becomes clear that the prediction values from the RNN are basically just the most previous lag, shifted by one time interval. Visually speaking, the prediction line is the financial time series itself, moved one time interval to the right:

```
In [53]: data[[symbol, 'pred']].iloc[50:100].plot(
                    figsize=(10, 6), style=['b', 'r-.'],
                    alpha=0.75);
```

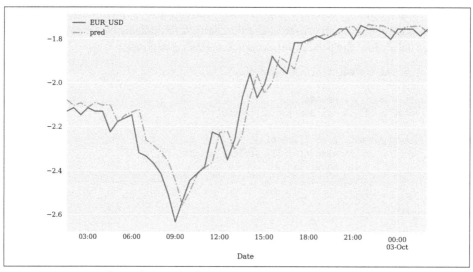

Figure 8-5. In-sample prediction for financial price series by the RNN (data sub-set)

RNNs and Efficient Markets

The results for the prediction of a financial price series based on an RNN are in line with the OLS regression approach used in Chapter 6 to illustrate the EMH. There, it is illustrated that, in a least-squares sense, today's price is the best predictor for tomorrow's price. The application of an RNN to price data does not yield any other insight.

Financial Return Series

As previous analyses have shown, it might be easier to predict returns instead of prices. Therefore, the following Python code repeats the preceding analysis based on log returns:

```
In [54]: data = generate_data()

In [55]: data['r'] = np.log(data / data.shift(1))

In [56]: data.dropna(inplace=True)

In [57]: data = (data - data.mean()) / data.std()

In [58]: r = data['r'].values

In [59]: r = r.reshape((len(r), -1))

In [60]: g = TimeseriesGenerator(r, r, length=lags, batch_size=5)
```

```
In [61]: model = create_rnn_model()

In [62]: %%time
         model.fit(g, epochs=500, steps_per_epoch=10,
                            verbose=False)
         CPU times: user 20.4 s, sys: 4.2 s, total: 24.6 s
         Wall time: 11.3 s

Out[62]: <keras.callbacks.callbacks.History at 0x7f7ef47a8dd0>
```

As Figure 8-6 shows, the RNN's predictions are not too good in absolute terms. However, they seem to get the market direction (sign of the return) somehow right:

```
In [63]: y = model.predict(g, verbose=False)

In [64]: data['pred'] = np.nan
         data['pred'].iloc[lags:] = y.flatten()
         data.dropna(inplace=True)

In [65]: data[['r', 'pred']].iloc[50:100].plot(
                    figsize=(10, 6), style=['b', 'r-.'],
                    alpha=0.75);
         plt.axhline(0, c='grey', ls='--')
```

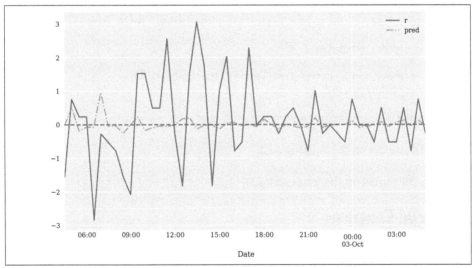

Figure 8-6. In-sample prediction for financial return series by the RNN (data sub-set)

While Figure 8-6 only provides an indication, the relatively high accuracy score supports the assumption that the RNN might perform better on a return than on a price series:

```
In [66]: from sklearn.metrics import accuracy_score
```

```
In [67]: accuracy_score(np.sign(data['r']), np.sign(data['pred']))
Out[67]: 0.6806532093445226
```

However, to get a realistic picture, a train-test split is in order. The accuracy score out-of-sample is not as high as the one seen for the whole data set in-sample, but it is still high for the problem at hand:

```
In [68]: split = int(len(r) * 0.8)  ❶
```

```
In [69]: train = r[:split]  ❶
```

```
In [70]: test = r[split:]  ❶
```

```
In [71]: g = TimeseriesGenerator(train, train, length=lags, batch_size=5)  ❷
```

```
In [72]: set_seeds()
         model = create_rnn_model(hu=100)
```

```
In [73]: %%time
         model.fit(g, epochs=100, steps_per_epoch=10, verbose=False)  ❷
         CPU times: user 5.67 s, sys: 1.09 s, total: 6.75 s
         Wall time: 2.95 s
```

```
Out[73]: <keras.callbacks.callbacks.History at 0x7f7ef5482dd0>
```

```
In [74]: g_ = TimeseriesGenerator(test, test, length=lags, batch_size=5)  ❸
```

```
In [75]: y = model.predict(g_)  ❸
```

```
In [76]: accuracy_score(np.sign(test[lags:]), np.sign(y))  ❸
Out[76]: 0.6708428246013668
```

❶ Splits the data into train and test data sub-sets

❷ Fits the model on the training data

❸ Tests the model on the testing data

Financial Features

The application of RNNs is not restricted to the raw price or return data. Additional features can also be included to improve the prediction of the RNN. The following Python code adds typical financial features to the data set:

```
In [77]: data = generate_data()
```

```
In [78]: data['r'] = np.log(data / data.shift(1))
```

```
In [79]: window = 20
         data['mom'] = data['r'].rolling(window).mean()  ❶
```

```
              data['vol'] = data['r'].rolling(window).std()  ❷

In [80]: data.dropna(inplace=True)
```

❶ Adds a time series *momentum* feature

❷ Adds a rolling *volatility* feature

Estimation

The out-of-sample accuracy, maybe somewhat surprisingly, drops significantly in the
estimation case. In other words, there is no improvement observed from adding
financial features in this particular case:

```
In [81]: split = int(len(data) * 0.8)

In [82]: train = data.iloc[:split].copy()

In [83]: mu, std = train.mean(), train.std()  ❶

In [84]: train = (train - mu) / std  ❷

In [85]: test = data.iloc[split:].copy()

In [86]: test = (test - mu) / std  ❸

In [87]: g = TimeseriesGenerator(train.values, train['r'].values,
                                 length=lags, batch_size=5)  ❹

In [88]: set_seeds()
         model = create_rnn_model(hu=100, features=len(data.columns),
                                  layer='SimpleRNN')

In [89]: %%time
         model.fit(g, epochs=100, steps_per_epoch=10,
                           verbose=False)  ❹
         CPU times: user 5.24 s, sys: 1.08 s, total: 6.32 s
         Wall time: 2.73 s

Out[89]: <keras.callbacks.callbacks.History at 0x7f7ef313c950>

In [90]: g_ = TimeseriesGenerator(test.values, test['r'].values,
                                  length=lags, batch_size=5)  ❺

In [91]: y = model.predict(g_).flatten()  ❺

In [92]: accuracy_score(np.sign(test['r'].iloc[lags:]), np.sign(y))  ❺
Out[92]: 0.37299771167048057
```

❶ Calculates the first and second moment of the training data

❷ Applies Gaussian normalization to the training data

❸ Applies Gaussian normalization to the testing data—based on the statistics from the training data

❹ Fits the model on the training data

❺ Tests the model on the testing data

Classification

The analyses so far use a `Keras` RNN model for *estimation* to predict the future direction of the price of the financial instrument. The problem at hand is probably better cast directly into a *classification* setting. The following Python code works with binary labels data and predicts the direction of the price movement directly. It also works this time with an LSTM layer. The out-of-sample accuracy is quite high even for a relatively small number of hidden units and only a few training epochs. The approach again takes class imbalance into account by adjusting the class weights appropriately. The prediction accuracy is quite high in this case with around 65%:

```
In [93]: set_seeds()
         model = create_rnn_model(hu=50,
                     features=len(data.columns),
                     layer='LSTM',
                     algorithm='classification')   ❶

In [94]: train_y = np.where(train['r'] > 0, 1, 0)   ❷

In [95]: np.bincount(train_y)   ❸
Out[95]: array([2374, 1142])

In [96]: def cw(a):
             c0, c1 = np.bincount(a)
             w0 = (1 / c0) * (len(a)) / 2
             w1 = (1 / c1) * (len(a)) / 2
             return {0: w0, 1: w1}

In [97]: g = TimeseriesGenerator(train.values, train_y,
                     length=lags, batch_size=5)

In [98]: %%time
         model.fit(g, epochs=5, steps_per_epoch=10,
                     verbose=False, class_weight=cw(train_y))
         CPU times: user 1.25 s, sys: 159 ms, total: 1.41 s
         Wall time: 947 ms
```

```
Out[98]: <keras.callbacks.callbacks.History at 0x7f7ef43baf90>

In [99]: test_y = np.where(test['r'] > 0, 1, 0)  ❹

In [100]: g_ = TimeseriesGenerator(test.values, test_y,
                                   length=lags, batch_size=5)

In [101]: y = np.where(model.predict(g_, batch_size=None) > 0.5, 1, 0).flatten()

In [102]: np.bincount(y)
Out[102]: array([492, 382])

In [103]: accuracy_score(test_y[lags:], y)
Out[103]: 0.6498855835240275
```

❶ RNN model for classification

❷ Binary training labels

❸ Class frequency for training labels

❹ Binary testing labels

Deep RNNs

Finally, consider deep RNNs, which are RNNs with multiple hidden layers. They are as easily created as deep DNNs. The only requirement is that for the nonfinal hidden layers, the parameter return_sequences is set to True. The following Python function to create a deep RNN also allows for the addition of Dropout layers to potentially avoid overfitting. The prediction accuracy is comparable to the one seen in the previous sub-section:

```
In [104]: from keras.layers import Dropout

In [105]: def create_deep_rnn_model(hl=2, hu=100, layer='SimpleRNN',
                                    optimizer='rmsprop', features=1,
                                    dropout=False, rate=0.3, seed=100):
              if hl <= 2: hl = 2  ❶
              if layer == 'SimpleRNN':
                  layer = SimpleRNN
              else:
                  layer = LSTM
              model = Sequential()
              model.add(layer(hu, input_shape=(lags, features),
                              return_sequences=True,
                          ))  ❷
              if dropout:
                  model.add(Dropout(rate, seed=seed))  ❸
              for _ in range(2, hl):
                  model.add(layer(hu, return_sequences=True))
```

```
            if dropout:
                model.add(Dropout(rate, seed=seed))    ❸
            model.add(layer(hu))    ❹
            model.add(Dense(1, activation='sigmoid'))    ❺
            model.compile(optimizer=optimizer,
                          loss='binary_crossentropy',
                          metrics=['accuracy'])
            return model

In [106]: set_seeds()
          model = create_deep_rnn_model(
                      hl=2, hu=50, layer='SimpleRNN',
                      features=len(data.columns),
                      dropout=True, rate=0.3)    ❶

In [107]: %%time
          model.fit(g, epochs=200, steps_per_epoch=10,
                        verbose=False, class_weight=cw(train_y))
          CPU times: user 14.2 s, sys: 2.85 s, total: 17.1 s
          Wall time: 7.09 s

Out[107]: <keras.callbacks.callbacks.History at 0x7f7ef6428790>

In [108]: y = np.where(model.predict(g_, batch_size=None) > 0.5, 1, 0).flatten()

In [109]: np.bincount(y)
Out[109]: array([550, 324])

In [110]: accuracy_score(test_y[lags:], y)
Out[110]: 0.6430205949656751
```

❶ A minimum of two hidden layers is ensured.

❷ The first hidden layer.

❸ The Dropout layers.

❹ The final hidden layer.

❺ The model is built for classification.

Conclusions

This chapter introduces RNNs with Keras and illustrates the application of such neural networks to financial time series data. On the Python level, working with RNNs is not too different from working with DNNs. One major difference is that the training and test data must necessarily be presented in a sequential form to the respective methods. However, this is made easy by the application of the TimeseriesGenerator function, which transforms sequential data into a generator object that `Keras` RNNs can work with.

The examples in this chapter work with both financial price series and financial return series. In addition, financial features, such as time series momentum, can also be added easily. The functions presented for model creation allow, among other things, for one to use `SimpleRNN` or `LSTM` layers as well as different optimizers. They also allow one to model estimation and classification problems in the context of shallow and deep neural networks.

The out-of-sample prediction accuracy, when predicting market direction, is relatively high for the classification examples—but it's not that high and can even be quite low for the estimation examples.

References

Books and papers cited in this chapter:

Chollet, François. 2017. *Deep Learning with Python*. Shelter Island: Manning.

Goodfellow, Ian, Yoshua Bengio, and Aaron Courville. 2016. *Deep Learning*. Cambridge: MIT Press. *http://deeplearningbook.org*.

## CHAPTER 9

Reinforcement Learning

> Like a human, our agents learn for themselves to achieve successful strategies that lead
> to the greatest long-term rewards. This paradigm of learning by trial-and-error, solely
> from rewards or punishments, is known as reinforcement learning.[1]
>
> —DeepMind (2016)

The learning algorithms applied in Chapters 7 and 8 fall into the category of *supervised learning*. These methods require that there is a data set available with features and labels that allows the algorithms to learn relationships between the features and labels to succeed at estimation or classification tasks. As the simple example in Chapter 1 illustrates, *reinforcement learning* (RL) works differently. To begin with, there is no need for a comprehensive data set of features and labels to be given up front. The data is rather generated by the learning agent while interacting with the environment of interest. This chapter covers RL in some detail and introduces fundamental notions, as well as one of the most popular algorithms used in the field: *Q-learning* (QL). Neural networks are not replaced by RL algorithms; they generally play an important role in this context as well.

"Fundamental Notions" on page 250 explains fundamental notions in RL, such as environments, states, and agents. "OpenAI Gym" on page 251 introduces the OpenAI Gym suite of RL environments of which the `CartPole` environment is used as an example. In this environment, which Chapter 2 introduces and discusses briefly, agents must learn how to balance a pole on a cart by moving the cart to the left or to the right. "Monte Carlo Agent" on page 255 shows how to solve the `CartPole` problem by the use of dimensionality reduction and Monte Carlo simulation. Standard supervised learning algorithms such as DNNs are in general not suited to solve

---

1 See Deep Reinforcement Learning (*https://oreil.ly/h-EFL*).

problems such as the CartPole one since they lack a notion of delayed reward. This problem is illustrated in "Neural Network Agent" on page 257. "DQL Agent" on page 260 discusses a QL agent that explicitly takes into account delayed rewards and is able to solve the CartPole problem. The same agent is applied in "Simple Finance Gym" on page 264 to a simple financial market environment. Although the agent does not perform too well in this setting, the example shows that QL agents can also learn to trade and to become what is often called a *trading bot*. To improve the learning of QL agents, "Better Finance Gym" on page 268 presents an improved financial market environment that, among other benefits, allows the use of more than one type of feature to describe the state of the environment. Based on this improved environment, "FQL Agent" on page 271 introduces and applies an improved financial QL agent that performs better as a trading bot.

Fundamental Notions

This section gives a brief overview of the fundamental notions in RL. Among them are the following:

Environment

The *environment* defines the problem at hand. This can be a computer game to be played or a financial market to be traded in.

State

A *state* subsumes all relevant parameters that describe the current state of the environment. In a computer game, this might be the whole screen with all its pixels. In a financial market, this might include current and historical price levels or financial indicators such as moving averages, macroeconomic variables, and so on.

Agent

The term *agent* subsumes all elements of the RL algorithm that interacts with the environment and that learns from these interactions. In a gaming context, the agent might represent a player playing the game. In a financial context, the agent could represent a trader placing bets on rising or falling markets.

Action

An agent can choose one *action* from a (limited) set of allowed actions. In a computer game, movements to the left or right might be allowed actions, whereas in a financial market, going long or short could be admissible actions.

Step

Given an action of an agent, the state of the environment is updated. One such update is generally called a *step*. The concept of a step is general enough to encompass both heterogeneous and homogeneous time intervals between two steps. While in computer games, real-time interaction with the game environment is simulated by rather short, homogeneous time intervals ("game clock"), a trading bot interacting with a financial market environment could take actions at longer, heterogeneous time intervals, for instance.

Reward

Depending on the action an agent chooses, a *reward* (or penalty) is awarded. For a computer game, points are a typical reward. In a financial context, profit (or loss) is a standard reward (or penalty).

Target

The *target* specifies what the agent tries to maximize. In a computer game, this in general is the score reached by the agent. For a financial trading bot, this might be the accumulated trading profit.

Policy

The *policy* defines which action an agent takes given a certain state of the environment. Given a certain state of a computer game, represented by all the pixels that make up the current scene, the policy might specify that the agent chooses "move right" as the action. A trading bot that observes three price increases in a row might decide, according to its policy, to short the market.

Episode

An *episode* is a set of steps from the initial state of the environment until success is achieved or failure is observed. In a game, this is from the start of the game until a win or loss. In the financial world, for example, this is from the beginning of the year to the end of the year or to bankruptcy.

Sutton and Barto (2018) provide a detailed introduction to the RL field. The book discusses the preceding notions in detail and illustrates them on the basis of a multitude of concrete examples. The following sections again choose a practical, implementation-oriented approach to RL. The examples discussed illustrate all of the preceding notions on the basis of Python code.

OpenAI Gym

In most of the success stories as presented in Chapter 2, RL plays a dominant role. This has spurred widespread interest in RL as an algorithm. OpenAI is an organization that strives to facilitate research in AI in general and in RL in particular. OpenAI has developed and open sourced a suite of environments, called OpenAI Gym (*https://gym.openai.com*), that allows the training of RL agents via a standardized API.

Among the many environments, there is the CartPole (*https://oreil.ly/f6tAK*) environment (or game) that simulates a classical RL problem. A pole is standing upright on a cart, and the goal is to learn a policy to balance the pole on the cart by moving the cart either to the right or to the left. The state of the environment is given by four parameters, describing the following physical measurements: cart position, cart velocity, pole angle, and pole velocity (at tip). Figure 9-1 shows a visualization of the environment.

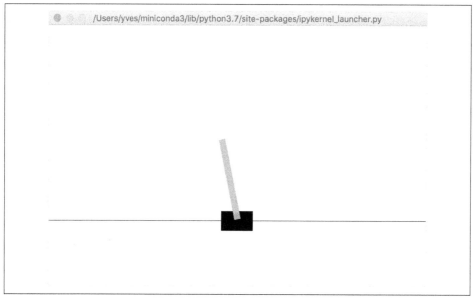

Figure 9-1. CartPole environment of OpenAI Gym

Consider the following Python code that instantiates an environment object for CartPole and inspects the *observation space*. The observation space is a model for the state of the environment:

```
In [1]: import os
        import math
        import random
        import numpy as np
        import pandas as pd
        from pylab import plt, mpl
        plt.style.use('seaborn')
        mpl.rcParams['savefig.dpi'] = 300
        mpl.rcParams['font.family'] = 'serif'
        np.set_printoptions(precision=4, suppress=True)
        os.environ['PYTHONHASHSEED'] = '0'
In [2]: import gym

In [3]: env = gym.make('CartPole-v0')   ❶

In [4]: env.seed(100)   ❶
        env.action_space.seed(100)   ❶
Out[4]: [100]
```

```
In [5]: env.observation_space  ❷
Out[5]: Box(4,)

In [6]: env.observation_space.low.astype(np.float16)  ❷
Out[6]: array([-4.8  ,   -inf, -0.419,   -inf], dtype=float16)

In [7]: env.observation_space.high.astype(np.float16)  ❷
Out[7]: array([4.8  ,   inf, 0.419,   inf], dtype=float16)

In [8]: state = env.reset()  ❸

In [9]: state  ❹
Out[9]: array([-0.0163,  0.0238, -0.0392, -0.0148])
```

❶　The environment object, with fixed seed values

❷　The observation space with minimal and maximal values

❸　Reset of the environment

❹　Initial state: cart position, cart velocity, pole angle, pole angular velocity

In the following environment, the allowed actions are described by the *action space*. In this case there are two, and they are represented by 0 (push cart to the left) and 1 (push cart to the right):

```
In [10]: env.action_space  ❶
Out[10]: Discrete(2)

In [11]: env.action_space.n  ❶
Out[11]: 2

In [12]: env.action_space.sample()  ❷
Out[12]: 1

In [13]: env.action_space.sample()  ❷
Out[13]: 0

In [14]: a = env.action_space.sample()  ❷
         a  ❷
Out[14]: 1

In [15]: state, reward, done, info = env.step(a)  ❸
         state, reward, done, info  ❹
Out[15]: (array([-0.0158,  0.2195, -0.0395, -0.3196]), 1.0, False, {})
```

❶　The action space

❷　Random actions sampled from the action space

❸ Step forward based on random action

❹ New state of the environment, reward, success/failure, additional information

As long as done=False, the agent is still in the game and can choose another action. Success is achieved when the agent reaches a total of 200 steps in a row or a total reward of 200 (reward of 1.0 per step). A failure is observed when the pole on the cart reaches a certain angle that would lead to the pole falling from the cart. In that case, done=True is returned.

A simple agent is one that follows a completely random policy: no matter what state is observed, the agent chooses a random action. This is what the following code implements. The number of steps the agent can go only depends in such a case on how lucky it is. No learning in the form of updating the policy is taking place:

```
In [16]: env.reset()
         for e in range(1, 200):
             a = env.action_space.sample()  ❶
             state, reward, done, info = env.step(a)  ❷
             print(f'step={e:2d} | state={state} | action={a} | reward={reward}')
             if done and (e + 1) < 200:  ❸
                 print('*** FAILED ***')  ❸
                 break
         step= 1 | state=[-0.0423  0.1982  0.0256 -0.2476] | action=1 | reward=1.0
         step= 2 | state=[-0.0383  0.0028  0.0206  0.0531] | action=0 | reward=1.0
         step= 3 | state=[-0.0383  0.1976  0.0217 -0.2331] | action=1 | reward=1.0
         step= 4 | state=[-0.0343  0.0022  0.017   0.0664] | action=0 | reward=1.0
         step= 5 | state=[-0.0343  0.197   0.0184 -0.2209] | action=1 | reward=1.0
         step= 6 | state=[-0.0304  0.0016  0.0139  0.0775] | action=0 | reward=1.0
         step= 7 | state=[-0.0303  0.1966  0.0155 -0.2107] | action=1 | reward=1.0
         step= 8 | state=[-0.0264  0.0012  0.0113  0.0868] | action=0 | reward=1.0
         step= 9 | state=[-0.0264  0.1962  0.013  -0.2023] | action=1 | reward=1.0
         step=10 | state=[-0.0224  0.3911  0.009  -0.4908] | action=1 | reward=1.0
         step=11 | state=[-0.0146  0.5861 -0.0009 -0.7807] | action=1 | reward=1.0
         step=12 | state=[-0.0029  0.7812 -0.0165 -1.0736] | action=1 | reward=1.0
         step=13 | state=[ 0.0127  0.9766 -0.0379 -1.3714] | action=1 | reward=1.0
         step=14 | state=[ 0.0323  1.1722 -0.0654 -1.6758] | action=1 | reward=1.0
         step=15 | state=[ 0.0557  0.9779 -0.0989 -1.4041] | action=0 | reward=1.0
         step=16 | state=[ 0.0753  0.7841 -0.127  -1.1439] | action=0 | reward=1.0
         step=17 | state=[ 0.0909  0.5908 -0.1498 -0.8936] | action=0 | reward=1.0
         step=18 | state=[ 0.1028  0.7876 -0.1677 -1.2294] | action=1 | reward=1.0
         step=19 | state=[ 0.1185  0.9845 -0.1923 -1.5696] | action=1 | reward=1.0
         step=20 | state=[ 0.1382  0.7921 -0.2237 -1.3425] | action=0 | reward=1.0
         *** FAILED ***

In [17]: done
Out[17]: True
```

❶ Random action policy

❷ Stepping forward one step

❸ Failure if less than 200 steps

Data Through Interaction

Whereas in supervised learning the training, validation, and test data sets are assumed to exist before the training begins, in RL the agent generates its data itself by interacting with the environment. In many contexts, such as in games, this is a huge simplification. Consider the game of chess: instead of loading thousands of historical human-played chess games into a computer, an RL agent can generate thousands or millions of games itself by playing against another chess engine or another version of itself, for instance.

Monte Carlo Agent

The `CartPole` problem does not necessarily require a full-fledged RL approach nor some neural network to be solved. This section presents a simple solution to the problem based on Monte Carlo simulation. To this end, a specific policy is defined that makes use of *dimensionality reduction*. In that case, the four parameters defining a state of the environment are collapsed, via a linear combination, into a single real-valued parameter.[2] The following Python code implements this idea:

```
In [18]: np.random.seed(100)  ❶

In [19]: weights = np.random.random(4) * 2 - 1  ❶

In [20]: weights  ❶
Out[20]: array([ 0.0868, -0.4433, -0.151 ,  0.6896])

In [21]: state = env.reset()  ❷

In [22]: state  ❷
Out[22]: array([-0.0347, -0.0103,  0.047 , -0.0315])

In [23]: s = np.dot(state, weights)  ❸
         s  ❸
Out[23]: -0.02725361929630797
```

❶ Random weights for fixed seed value

---

2 See, for example, this blog post (*https://oreil.ly/84RwE*).

❷ Initial state of the environment

❸ Dot product of state and weights

The policy is then defined based on the sign of the single state parameter s:

```
In [24]: if s < 0:
             a = 0
         else:
             a = 1

In [25]: a
Out[25]: 0
```

This policy can then be used to play an episode of the CartPole game. Given the random nature of the weights applied, the results are in general not better than those of the random action policy of the previous section:

```
In [26]: def run_episode(env, weights):
             state = env.reset()
             treward = 0
             for _ in range(200):
                 s = np.dot(state, weights)
                 a = 0 if s < 0 else 1
                 state, reward, done, info = env.step(a)
                 treward += reward
                 if done:
                     break
             return treward

In [27]: run_episode(env, weights)
Out[27]: 41.0
```

Therefore, Monte Carlo simulation is applied to test a large number of different weights. The following code simulates a large number of weights, checks them for success or failure, and then chooses the weights that yield success:

```
In [28]: def set_seeds(seed=100):
             random.seed(seed)
             np.random.seed(seed)
             env.seed(seed)

In [29]: set_seeds()
         num_episodes = 1000

In [30]: besttreward = 0
         for e in range(1, num_episodes + 1):
             weights = np.random.rand(4) * 2 - 1    ❶
             treward = run_episode(env, weights)    ❷
             if treward > besttreward:              ❸
                 besttreward = treward              ❹
                 bestweights = weights              ❺
```

```
           if treward == 200:
               print(f'SUCCESS | episode={e}')
               break
           print(f'UPDATE  | episode={e}')
      UPDATE  | episode=1
      UPDATE  | episode=2
      SUCCESS | episode=13

In [31]: weights
Out[31]: array([-0.4282,  0.7048,  0.95  ,  0.7697])
```

❶ Random weights.

❷ Total reward for these weights.

❸ Improvement observed?

❹ Replace best total reward.

❺ Replace best weights.

The CartPole problem is considered solved by an agent if the average total reward over 100 consecutive episodes is 195 or higher. As the following code demonstrates, this is indeed the case for the Monte Carlo agent:

```
In [32]: res = []
         for _ in range(100):
             treward = run_episode(env, weights)
             res.append(treward)
         res[:10]
Out[32]: [200.0, 200.0, 200.0, 200.0, 200.0, 200.0, 200.0, 200.0, 200.0, 200.0]

In [33]: sum(res) / len(res)
Out[33]: 200.0
```

This is, of course, a strong benchmark that other, more sophisticated approaches are up against.

Neural Network Agent

The CartPole game can be cast into a classification setting as well. The state of an environment consists of four feature values. The correct action given the feature values is the label. By interacting with the environment, a neural network agent can collect a data set consisting of combinations of feature values and labels. Given this incrementally growing data set, a neural network can be trained to learn the correct action given a state of the environment. The neural network represents the policy in this case. The agent updates the policy based on new experiences.

First, some imports:

```
In [34]: import tensorflow as tf
         from keras.layers import Dense, Dropout
         from keras.models import Sequential
         from keras.optimizers import Adam, RMSprop
         from sklearn.metrics import accuracy_score
         Using TensorFlow backend.
```

```
In [35]: def set_seeds(seed=100):
             random.seed(seed)
             np.random.seed(seed)
             tf.random.set_seed(seed)
             env.seed(seed)
             env.action_space.seed(100)
```

Second is the NNAgent class that combines the major elements of the agent: the neural network model for the policy, choosing an action given the policy, updating the policy (training the neural network), and the learning process itself over a number of episodes. The agent uses both *exploration* and *exploitation* to choose an action. Exploration refers to a random action, independent of the current policy. Exploitation refers to an action as derived from the current policy. The idea is that some degree of exploration ensures a richer experience and thereby improved learning for the agent:

```
In [36]: class NNAgent:
             def __init__(self):
                 self.max = 0          ❶
                 self.scores = list()
                 self.memory = list()
                 self.model = self._build_model()

             def _build_model(self):    ❷
                 model = Sequential()
                 model.add(Dense(24, input_dim=4,
                                 activation='relu'))
                 model.add(Dense(1, activation='sigmoid'))
                 model.compile(loss='binary_crossentropy',
                               optimizer=RMSprop(lr=0.001))
                 return model

             def act(self, state):      ❸
                 if random.random() <= 0.5:
                     return env.action_space.sample()
                 action = np.where(self.model.predict(
                     state, batch_size=None)[0, 0] > 0.5, 1, 0)
                 return action

             def train_model(self, state, action):    ❹
                 self.model.fit(state, np.array([action,]),
                                epochs=1, verbose=False)

             def learn(self, episodes):    ❺
```

```
        for e in range(1, episodes + 1):
            state = env.reset()
            for _ in range(201):
                state = np.reshape(state, [1, 4])
                action = self.act(state)
                next_state, reward, done, info = env.step(action)
                if done:
                    score = _ + 1
                    self.scores.append(score)
                    self.max = max(score, self.max)   ❶
                    print('episode: {:4d}/{} | score: {:3d} | max: {:3d}'
                            .format(e, episodes, score, self.max), end='\r')
                    break
                self.memory.append((state, action))
                self.train_model(state, action)   ❹
                state = next_state
```

❶ The maximum total reward

❷ The DNN classification model for the policy

❸ The method to choose an action (exploration and exploitation)

❹ The method to update the policy (train the neural network)

❺ The method to learn from interacting with the environment

The neural network agent does not solve the problem for the configuration shown. The maximum total reward of 200 is not achieved even once:

```
In [37]: set_seeds(100)
         agent = NNAgent()

In [38]: episodes = 500

In [39]: agent.learn(episodes)
         episode:  500/500 | score:  11 | max:  44
In [40]: sum(agent.scores) / len(agent.scores)   ❶
Out[40]: 13.682
```

❶ Average total reward over all episodes

Something seems to be missing with this approach. One major missing element is the idea of looking beyond the current state and action to be chosen. The approach implemented does not, by any means, take into account that success is only achieved when the agent survives 200 consecutive steps. Simply speaking, the agent avoids taking the wrong action but does not learn to win the game.

Analyzing the collected history of states (features) and actions (labels) reveals that the neural network reaches an accuracy of around 75%.

However, this does not translate into a winning policy as seen before:

```
In [41]: f = np.array([[m[0][0] for m in agent.memory])    ❶
            f    ❶
Out[41]: array([[-0.0163,  0.0238, -0.0392, -0.0148],
                [-0.0158,  0.2195, -0.0395, -0.3196],
                [-0.0114,  0.0249, -0.0459, -0.0396],
                ...,
                [ 0.0603,  0.9682, -0.0852, -1.4595],
                [ 0.0797,  1.1642, -0.1144, -1.7776],
                [ 0.103 ,  1.3604, -0.15  , -2.1035]])

In [42]: l = np.array([[m[1] for m in agent.memory])    ❷
            l    ❷
Out[42]: array([1, 0, 1, ..., 1, 1, 1])

In [43]: accuracy_score(np.where(agent.model.predict(f) > 0.5, 1, 0), l)
Out[43]: 0.7525626872733008
```

❶ Features (states) from all episodes

❷ Labels (actions) from all episodes

DQL Agent

Q-learning (QL) is an algorithm that takes into account delayed rewards in addition to immediate rewards from an action. The algorithm is due to Watkins (1989) and Watkins and Dayan (1992) and is explained in detail in Sutton and Barto (2018, ch. 6). QL addresses the problem of looking beyond the immediate next reward as encountered with the neural network agent.

The algorithm works roughly as follows. There is an *action-value* policy Q, which assigns a value to every combination of a state and an action. The higher the value is, the better the action from the point of view of the agent will be. If the agent uses the policy Q to choose an action, it selects the action with the highest value.

How is the value of an action derived? The value of an action is composed of its *direct reward* and the *discounted value* of the optimal action in the next state. The following is the formal expression:

$$Q(S_t, A_t) = R_{t+1} + \gamma \max_a Q(S_{t+1}, a)$$

Here, S_t is the state at step (time) t, A_t is the action taken at state S_t, R_{t+1} is the direct reward of action A_t, $0 < \gamma < 1$ is a discount factor, and $\max_a Q(S_{t+1}, a)$ is the maximum delayed reward given the optimal action from the current policy Q.

In a simple environment, with only a limited number of possible states, Q can, for example, be represented by a *table*, listing for every state-action combination the corresponding value. However, in more interesting or complex settings, such as the CartPole environment, the number of states is too large for Q to be written out comprehensively. Therefore, Q is in general understood to be a *function*.

This is where neural networks come into play. In realistic settings and environments, a closed-form solution for the function Q might not exist or might be too hard to derive, say, based on dynamic programming. Therefore, QL algorithms generally target *approximations* only. Neural networks, with their universal approximation capabilities, are a natural choice to accomplish the approximation of Q.

Another critical element of QL is *replay*. The QL agent replays a number of experiences (state-action combinations) to update the policy function Q regularly. This can improve the learning considerably. Furthermore, the QL agent presented in the following—DQLAgent—also alternates between exploration and exploitation during the learning. The alternation is done in a systematic way in that the agent starts with exploration only—in the beginning it could not have learned anything—and slowly but steadily decreases the exploration rate ϵ until it reaches a minimum level:[3]

```
In [44]: from collections import deque
         from keras.optimizers import Adam, RMSprop

In [45]: class DQLAgent:
             def __init__(self, gamma=0.95, hu=24, opt=Adam,
                 lr=0.001, finish=False):
                 self.finish = finish
                 self.epsilon = 1.0      ❶
                 self.epsilon_min = 0.01      ❷
                 self.epsilon_decay = 0.995      ❸
                 self.gamma = gamma      ❹
                 self.batch_size = 32      ❺
                 self.max_treward = 0
                 self.averages = list()
                 self.memory = deque(maxlen=2000)      ❻
                 self.osn = env.observation_space.shape[0]
                 self.model = self._build_model(hu, opt, lr)

             def _build_model(self, hu, opt, lr):
                 model = Sequential()
                 model.add(Dense(hu, input_dim=self.osn,
                             activation='relu'))
                 model.add(Dense(hu, activation='relu'))
                 model.add(Dense(env.action_space.n, activation='linear'))
                 model.compile(loss='mse', optimizer=opt(lr=lr))
                 return model
```

---

3 The implementation is similar to the one found in this blog post (*https://oreil.ly/8mI4m*).

```python
    def act(self, state):
        if random.random() <= self.epsilon:
            return env.action_space.sample()
        action = self.model.predict(state)[0]
        return np.argmax(action)

    def replay(self):
        batch = random.sample(self.memory, self.batch_size)  ❼
        for state, action, reward, next_state, done in batch:
            if not done:
                reward += self.gamma * np.amax(
                    self.model.predict(next_state)[0])  ❽
            target = self.model.predict(state)
            target[0, action] = reward
            self.model.fit(state, target, epochs=1,
                           verbose=False)  ❾
        if self.epsilon > self.epsilon_min:
            self.epsilon *= self.epsilon_decay  ❿

    def learn(self, episodes):
        trewards = []
        for e in range(1, episodes + 1):
            state = env.reset()
            state = np.reshape(state, [1, self.osn])
            for _ in range(5000):
                action = self.act(state)
                next_state, reward, done, info = env.step(action)
                next_state = np.reshape(next_state,
                                        [1, self.osn])
                self.memory.append([state, action, reward,
                                    next_state, done])  ⓫
                state = next_state
                if done:
                    treward = _ + 1
                    trewards.append(treward)
                    av = sum(trewards[-25:]) / 25
                    self.averages.append(av)
                    self.max_treward = max(self.max_treward, treward)
                    templ = 'episode: {:4d}/{} | treward: {:4d} | '
                    templ += 'av: {:6.1f} | max: {:4d}'
                    print(templ.format(e, episodes, treward, av,
                                       self.max_treward), end='\r')
                    break
            if av > 195 and self.finish:
                break
            if len(self.memory) > self.batch_size:
                self.replay()  ⓬
    def test(self, episodes):
        trewards = []
        for e in range(1, episodes + 1):
            state = env.reset()
```

```
                    for _ in range(5001):
                        state = np.reshape(state, [1, self.osn])
                        action = np.argmax(self.model.predict(state)[0])
                        next_state, reward, done, info = env.step(action)
                        state = next_state
                        if done:
                            treward = _ + 1
                            trewards.append(treward)
                            print('episode: {:4d}/{} | treward: {:4d}'
                                  .format(e, episodes, treward), end='\r')
                            break
                return trewards
```

❶ Initial exploration rate

❷ Minimum exploration rate

❸ Decay rate for exploration rate

❹ Discount factor for delayed reward

❺ Batch size for replay

❻ deque collection for limited history

❼ Random selection of history batch for replay

❽ Q value for state-action pair

❾ Update of the neural network for the new action-value pairs

❿ Update of the exploration rate

⓫ Storing the new data

⓬ Replay to update the policy based on past experiences

How does the QL agent perform? As the code that follows shows, it reaches a winning state for CartPole of a total reward of 200. Figure 9-2 shows the moving average of scores and how it increases over time, although not monotonically. To the contrary, the performance of the agent can significantly decrease at times, as Figure 9-2 shows. Among other things, the exploration that is taking place throughout leads to random actions that might not necessarily lead to good results in terms of total rewards but may lead to beneficial experiences for updating the policy network:

```
In [46]: episodes = 1000

In [47]: set_seeds(100)
```

```
         agent = DQLAgent(finish=True)

In [48]: agent.learn(episodes)
         episode:  400/1000 | treward:  200 | av:  195.4 | max:  200
In [49]: plt.figure(figsize=(10, 6))
         x = range(len(agent.averages))
         y = np.polyval(np.polyfit(x, agent.averages, deg=3), x)
         plt.plot(agent.averages, label='moving average')
         plt.plot(x, y, 'r--', label='trend')
         plt.xlabel('episodes')
         plt.ylabel('total reward')
         plt.legend();
```

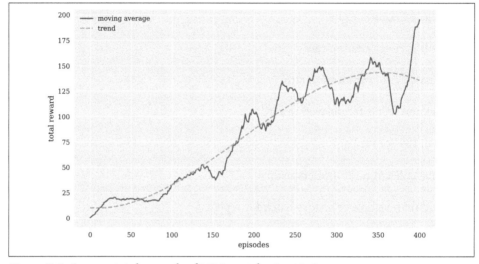

Figure 9-2. Average total rewards of DQLAgent for CartPole

Does the QL agent solve the CartPole problem? In this particular case, it does, given the definition of success by OpenAI Gym:

```
In [50]: trewards = agent.test(100)
         episode:  100/100 | treward:  200
In [51]: sum(trewards) / len(trewards)
Out[51]: 200.0
```

Simple Finance Gym

To transfer the QL approach to the financial domain, this section provides a class that mimics an OpenAI Gym environment, but for a financial market as represented by financial time series data. The idea is that, similar to the CartPole environment, four historical prices represent the state of the financial market. An agent can decide, when presented with the state, whether to go long or to go short. In that case, the two environments are comparable since a state is given by four parameters and an agent can take two different actions.

To mimic the OpenAI Gym API, two helper classes are needed—one for the observation space, and one for the action space:

```
In [52]: class observation_space:
             def __init__(self, n):
                 self.shape = (n,)
```

```
In [53]: class action_space:
             def __init__(self, n):
                 self.n = n
             def seed(self, seed):
                 pass
             def sample(self):
                 return random.randint(0, self.n - 1)
```

The following Python code defines the `Finance` class. It retrieves end-of-day historical prices for a number of symbols. The major methods of the class are `.reset()` and `.step()`. The `.step()` method checks whether the right action has been taken, defines the reward accordingly, and checks for success or failure. A success is achieved when the agent is able to correctly trade through the whole data set. This can, of course, be defined differently (say, a success is achieved when the agent trades successfully for 1,000 steps). A failure is defined as an accuracy ratio of less than 50% (total rewards divided by total number of steps). However, this is only checked for after a certain number of steps to avoid the high initial variance of this metric:

```
In [54]: class Finance:
             url = 'http://hilpisch.com/aiif_eikon_eod_data.csv'
             def __init__(self, symbol, features):
                 self.symbol = symbol
                 self.features = features
                 self.observation_space = observation_space(4)
                 self.osn = self.observation_space.shape[0]
                 self.action_space = action_space(2)
                 self.min_accuracy = 0.475     ❶
                 self._get_data()
                 self._prepare_data()
             def _get_data(self):
                 self.raw = pd.read_csv(self.url, index_col=0,
                                 parse_dates=True).dropna()
             def _prepare_data(self):
                 self.data = pd.DataFrame(self.raw[self.symbol])
                 self.data['r'] = np.log(self.data / self.data.shift(1))
                 self.data.dropna(inplace=True)
                 self.data = (self.data - self.data.mean()) / self.data.std()
                 self.data['d'] = np.where(self.data['r'] > 0, 1, 0)
             def _get_state(self):
                 return self.data[self.features].iloc[
                     self.bar - self.osn:self.bar].values     ❷
```

```
def seed(self, seed=None):
    pass
def reset(self):  ❸
    self.treward = 0
    self.accuracy = 0
    self.bar = self.osn
    state = self.data[self.features].iloc[
        self.bar - self.osn:self.bar]
    return state.values
def step(self, action):
    correct = action == self.data['d'].iloc[self.bar]  ❹
    reward = 1 if correct else 0  ❺
    self.treward += reward  ❻
    self.bar += 1  ❼
    self.accuracy = self.treward / (self.bar - self.osn)  ❽
    if self.bar >= len(self.data):  ❾
        done = True
    elif reward == 1:  ❿
        done = False
    elif (self.accuracy < self.min_accuracy and
            self.bar > self.osn + 10):  ⓫
        done = True
    else:  ⓬
        done = False
    state = self._get_state()
    info = {}
    return state, reward, done, info
```

❶ Defines the minimum accuracy required.

❷ Selects the data defining the state of the financial market.

❸ Resets the environment to its initial values.

❹ Checks whether the agent has chosen the right action (successful trade).

❺ Defines the reward the agent receives.

❻ Adds the reward to the total reward.

❼ Moves the environment one step forward.

❽ Calculates the accuracy of successful actions (trades) given all steps (trades).

❾ If the agent reaches the end of the data set, success is achieved.

❿ If the agent takes the right action, it can move on.

⓫ If, after some initial steps, the accuracy drops under the minimum level, the episode ends (failure).

⓬ For the remaining cases, the agent can move on.

Instances of the `Finance` class behave like an environment of the OpenAI Gym. In particular, in this base case, the instance behaves exactly like the `CartPole` environment:

```
In [55]: env = Finance('EUR=', 'EUR=')  ❶

In [56]: env.reset()
Out[56]: array([1.819 , 1.8579, 1.7749, 1.8579])

In [57]: a = env.action_space.sample()
         a
Out[57]: 0

In [58]: env.step(a)
Out[58]: (array([1.8579, 1.7749, 1.8579, 1.947 ]), 0, False, {})
```

❶ Specifies which symbol and which type of feature (symbol or log return) to be used to define the data representing the state

Can the `DQLAgent`, as developed for the `CartPole` game, learn to trade in a financial market? Yes, it can, as the following code illustrates. However, although the agent improves its trading skill (on average) over the training episodes, the results are not too impressive (see Figure 9-3):

```
In [59]: set_seeds(100)
         agent = DQLAgent(gamma=0.5, opt=RMSprop)

In [60]: episodes = 1000

In [61]: agent.learn(episodes)
         episode: 1000/1000 | treward: 2511 | av: 1012.7 | max: 2511
In [62]: agent.test(3)
         episode:    3/3 | treward: 2511
Out[62]: [2511, 2511, 2511]

In [63]: plt.figure(figsize=(10, 6))
         x = range(len(agent.averages))
         y = np.polyval(np.polyfit(x, agent.averages, deg=3), x)
         plt.plot(agent.averages, label='moving average')
         plt.plot(x, y, 'r--', label='regression')
         plt.xlabel('episodes')
         plt.ylabel('total reward')
         plt.legend();
```

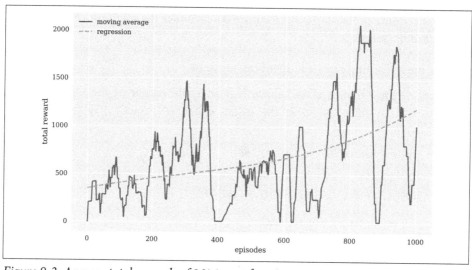

Figure 9-3. Average total rewards of DQLAgent for Finance

General RL Agents

This section provides a class for a financial market environment that mimics the API of an OpenAI Gym environment. It also applies, without any changes to the agent itself, the QL agent to the new financial market environment. Although the performance of the agent in this new environment might not be impressive, it illustrates that the approach of RL, as introduced in this chapter, is rather general. RL agents can in general learn from different environments they interact with. This explains to some extent why AlphaZero from DeepMind is able to master not only the game of Go but also chess and shogi, as discussed in Chapter 2.

Better Finance Gym

The idea in the previous section is to develop a simple class that allows RL within a financial market setting. The major goal in that section is to replicate the API of an OpenAI Gym environment. However, there is no need to restrict such an environment to a single type of feature to describe the state of the financial market nor to use only four lags. This section introduces an improved Finance class that allows for multiple features, a flexible number of lags, and specific start and end points for the base data set used. This, among other things, allows the use of one part of the data set for learning and another one for validation or testing. The Python code presented in the following also allows the use of leverage. This might be helpful when intraday data is considered with relatively small absolute returns:

```
In [64]: class Finance:
             url = 'http://hilpisch.com/aiif_eikon_eod_data.csv'
             def __init__(self, symbol, features, window, lags,
                          leverage=1, min_performance=0.85,
                          start=0, end=None, mu=None, std=None):
                 self.symbol = symbol
                 self.features = features          ❶
                 self.n_features = len(features)
                 self.window = window
                 self.lags = lags                  ❶
                 self.leverage = leverage          ❷
                 self.min_performance = min_performance    ❸
                 self.start = start
                 self.end = end
                 self.mu = mu
                 self.std = std
                 self.observation_space = observation_space(self.lags)
                 self.action_space = action_space(2)
                 self._get_data()
                 self._prepare_data()
             def _get_data(self):
                 self.raw = pd.read_csv(self.url, index_col=0,
                                        parse_dates=True).dropna()
             def _prepare_data(self):
                 self.data = pd.DataFrame(self.raw[self.symbol])
                 self.data = self.data.iloc[self.start:]
                 self.data['r'] = np.log(self.data / self.data.shift(1))
                 self.data.dropna(inplace=True)
                 self.data['s'] = self.data[self.symbol].rolling(
                                             self.window).mean()    ❹
                 self.data['m'] = self.data['r'].rolling(self.window).mean()    ❹
                 self.data['v'] = self.data['r'].rolling(self.window).std()    ❹
                 self.data.dropna(inplace=True)
                 if self.mu is None:
                     self.mu = self.data.mean()    ❺
                     self.std = self.data.std()    ❺
                 self.data_ = (self.data - self.mu) / self.std    ❺
                 self.data_['d'] = np.where(self.data['r'] > 0, 1, 0)
                 self.data_['d'] = self.data_['d'].astype(int)
                 if self.end is not None:
                     self.data = self.data.iloc[:self.end - self.start]
                     self.data_ = self.data_.iloc[:self.end - self.start]
             def _get_state(self):
                 return self.data_[self.features].iloc[self.bar -
                                       self.lags:self.bar]
             def seed(self, seed):
                 random.seed(seed)
                 np.random.seed(seed)
             def reset(self):
                 self.treward = 0
                 self.accuracy = 0
                 self.performance = 1
```

```
            self.bar = self.lags
            state = self.data_[self.features].iloc[self.bar-
                            self.lags:self.bar]
            return state.values
        def step(self, action):
            correct = action == self.data_['d'].iloc[self.bar]
            ret = self.data['r'].iloc[self.bar] * self.leverage   ❻
            reward_1 = 1 if correct else 0
            reward_2 = abs(ret) if correct else -abs(ret)   ❼
            self.treward += reward_1
            self.bar += 1
            self.accuracy = self.treward / (self.bar - self.lags)
            self.performance *= math.exp(reward_2)   ❽
            if self.bar >= len(self.data):
                done = True
            elif reward_1 == 1:
                done = False
            elif (self.performance < self.min_performance and
                    self.bar > self.lags + 5):
                done = True
            else:
                done = False
            state = self._get_state()
            info = {}
            return state.values, reward_1 + reward_2 * 5, done, info
```

❶ The features to define the state

❷ The number of lags to be used

❸ The minimum gross performance required

❹ Additional financial features (simple moving average, momentum, rolling volatility)

❺ Gaussian normalization of the data

❻ The leveraged return for the step

❼ The return-based reward for the step

❽ The gross performance after the step

The new Finance class gives more flexibility for the modeling of the financial market environment. The following code shows an example for two features and five lags:

```
In [65]: env = Finance('EUR=', ['EUR=', 'r'], 10, 5)

In [66]: a = env.action_space.sample()
         a
```

```
Out[66]: 0

In [67]: env.reset()
Out[67]: array([[ 1.7721, -1.0214],
                [ 1.5973, -2.4432],
                [ 1.5876, -0.1208],
                [ 1.6292,  0.6083],
                [ 1.6408,  0.1807]])

In [68]: env.step(a)
Out[68]: (array([[ 1.5973, -2.4432],
                 [ 1.5876, -0.1208],
                 [ 1.6292,  0.6083],
                 [ 1.6408,  0.1807],
                 [ 1.5725, -0.9502]]),
          1.0272827803740798,
          False,
          {})
```

Different Types of Environments and Data

It is important to notice that there is a fundamental difference between the `CartPole` environment and the two versions of the `Finance` environment. In the `CartPole` environment, no data is available up front. Only an initial state is chosen with some degree of randomness. Given this state and the action taken by an agent, deterministic transformations are applied to generate new states (data). This is possible since a physical system is simulated that follows physical laws.

The `Finance` environment, on the other hand, starts with real, historical market data and only presents the available data to the agent in similar fashion as the `CartPole` environment (that is, step by step and state by state). In this case, the action of the agent does not really influence the environment; the environment instead evolves deterministically, and the agent learns how to behave optimally—trade profitably—in that environment.

In that sense, the `Finance` environment is more comparable, say, to the problem of finding the fastest way through a labyrinth. In such a case, the data representing the labyrinth is given up front and the agent is only presented with the relevant sub-set of the data (the current state) as it moves around the labyrinth.

FQL Agent

Relying on the new `Finance` environment, this section improves on the simple DQL agent to improve the performance in the financial market context. The `FQLAgent` class is able to handle multiple features and a flexible number of lags. It also distinguishes the learning environment (`learn_env`) from the validation environment (valid_env). This allows one to gain a more realistic picture of the out-of-sample performance of the agent during training. The basic structure of the class and the RL/QL learning approach is the same for both the DQLAgent class and the FQLAgent class:

```
In [69]: class FQLAgent:
             def __init__(self, hidden_units, learning_rate, learn_env, valid_env):
                 self.learn_env = learn_env
                 self.valid_env = valid_env
                 self.epsilon = 1.0
                 self.epsilon_min = 0.1
                 self.epsilon_decay = 0.98
                 self.learning_rate = learning_rate
                 self.gamma = 0.95
                 self.batch_size = 128
                 self.max_treward = 0
                 self.trewards = list()
                 self.averages = list()
                 self.performances = list()
                 self.aperformances = list()
                 self.vperformances = list()
                 self.memory = deque(maxlen=2000)
                 self.model = self._build_model(hidden_units, learning_rate)

             def _build_model(self, hu, lr):
                 model = Sequential()
                 model.add(Dense(hu, input_shape=(
                     self.learn_env.lags, self.learn_env.n_features),
                             activation='relu'))
                 model.add(Dropout(0.3, seed=100))
                 model.add(Dense(hu, activation='relu'))
                 model.add(Dropout(0.3, seed=100))
                 model.add(Dense(2, activation='linear'))
                 model.compile(
                     loss='mse',
                     optimizer=RMSprop(lr=lr)
                 )
                 return model

             def act(self, state):
                 if random.random() <= self.epsilon:
                     return self.learn_env.action_space.sample()
                 action = self.model.predict(state)[0, 0]
                 return np.argmax(action)

             def replay(self):
                 batch = random.sample(self.memory, self.batch_size)
                 for state, action, reward, next_state, done in batch:
                     if not done:
                         reward += self.gamma * np.amax(
                             self.model.predict(next_state)[0, 0])
                     target = self.model.predict(state)
```

```python
            target[0, 0, action] = reward
            self.model.fit(state, target, epochs=1,
                                verbose=False)
        if self.epsilon > self.epsilon_min:
            self.epsilon *= self.epsilon_decay

    def learn(self, episodes):
        for e in range(1, episodes + 1):
            state = self.learn_env.reset()
            state = np.reshape(state, [1, self.learn_env.lags,
                                        self.learn_env.n_features])
            for _ in range(10000):
                action = self.act(state)
                next_state, reward, done, info = \
                            self.learn_env.step(action)
                next_state = np.reshape(next_state,
                                [1, self.learn_env.lags,
                                  self.learn_env.n_features])
                self.memory.append([state, action, reward,
                                    next_state, done])
                state = next_state
                if done:
                    treward = _ + 1
                    self.trewards.append(treward)
                    av = sum(self.trewards[-25:]) / 25
                    perf = self.learn_env.performance
                    self.averages.append(av)
                    self.performances.append(perf)
                    self.aperformances.append(
                        sum(self.performances[-25:]) / 25)
                    self.max_treward = max(self.max_treward, treward)
                    templ = 'episode: {:2d}/{} | treward: {:4d} | '
                    templ += 'perf: {:5.3f} | av: {:5.1f} | max: {:4d}'
                    print(templ.format(e, episodes, treward, perf,
                                av, self.max_treward), end='\r')
                    break
            self.validate(e, episodes)
            if len(self.memory) > self.batch_size:
                self.replay()
    def validate(self, e, episodes):
        state = self.valid_env.reset()
        state = np.reshape(state, [1, self.valid_env.lags,
                                    self.valid_env.n_features])
        for _ in range(10000):
            action = np.argmax(self.model.predict(state)[0, 0])
            next_state, reward, done, info = self.valid_env.step(action)
            state = np.reshape(next_state, [1, self.valid_env.lags,
                                self.valid_env.n_features])
            if done:
                treward = _ + 1
                perf = self.valid_env.performance
                self.vperformances.append(perf)
```

```
              if e % 20 == 0:
                  templ = 71 * '='
                  templ += '\nepisode: {:2d}/{} | VALIDATION | '
                  templ += 'treward: {:4d} | perf: {:5.3f} | '
                  templ += 'eps: {:.2f}\n'
                  templ += 71 * '='
                  print(templ.format(e, episodes, treward,
                                     perf, self.epsilon))
          break
```

The following Python code shows that the performance of the FQLAgent is substantially better than that of the simple DQLAgent that solves the CartPole problem. This trading bot seems to learn about trading rather consistently through interacting with the financial market environment (see Figure 9-4):

```
In [70]: symbol = 'EUR='
         features = [symbol, 'r', 's', 'm', 'v']

In [71]: a = 0
         b = 2000
         c = 500

In [72]: learn_env = Finance(symbol, features, window=10, lags=6,
                             leverage=1, min_performance=0.85,
                             start=a, end=a + b, mu=None, std=None)

In [73]: learn_env.data.info()
         <class 'pandas.core.frame.DataFrame'>
         DatetimeIndex: 2000 entries, 2010-01-19 to 2017-12-26
         Data columns (total 5 columns):
          #   Column  Non-Null Count  Dtype
         ---  ------  --------------  -----
          0   EUR=    2000 non-null   float64
          1   r       2000 non-null   float64
          2   s       2000 non-null   float64
          3   m       2000 non-null   float64
          4   v       2000 non-null   float64
         dtypes: float64(5)
         memory usage: 93.8 KB

In [74]: valid_env = Finance(symbol, features, window=learn_env.window,
                             lags=learn_env.lags, leverage=learn_env.leverage,
                             min_performance=learn_env.min_performance,
                             start=a + b, end=a + b + c,
                             mu=learn_env.mu, std=learn_env.std)

In [75]: valid_env.data.info()
         <class 'pandas.core.frame.DataFrame'>
         DatetimeIndex: 500 entries, 2017-12-27 to 2019-12-20
         Data columns (total 5 columns):
          #   Column  Non-Null Count  Dtype
         ---  ------  --------------  -----
```

```
        0   EUR=   500 non-null    float64
        1   r      500 non-null    float64
        2   s      500 non-null    float64
        3   m      500 non-null    float64
        4   v      500 non-null    float64
       dtypes: float64(5)
       memory usage: 23.4 KB

In [76]: set_seeds(100)
         agent = FQLAgent(24, 0.0001, learn_env, valid_env)

In [77]: episodes = 61

In [78]: agent.learn(episodes)
         ================================================================
         episode: 20/61 | VALIDATION | treward:  494 | perf: 1.169 | eps: 0.68
         ================================================================
         ================================================================
         episode: 40/61 | VALIDATION | treward:  494 | perf: 1.111 | eps: 0.45
         ================================================================
         ================================================================
         episode: 60/61 | VALIDATION | treward:  494 | perf: 1.089 | eps: 0.30
         ================================================================
         episode: 61/61 | treward: 1994 | perf: 1.268 | av: 1615.1 | max: 1994
In [79]: agent.epsilon
Out[79]: 0.291602079838278

In [80]: plt.figure(figsize=(10, 6))
         x = range(1, len(agent.averages) + 1)
         y = np.polyval(np.polyfit(x, agent.averages, deg=3), x)
         plt.plot(agent.averages, label='moving average')
         plt.plot(x, y, 'r--', label='regression')
         plt.xlabel('episodes')
         plt.ylabel('total reward')
         plt.legend();
```

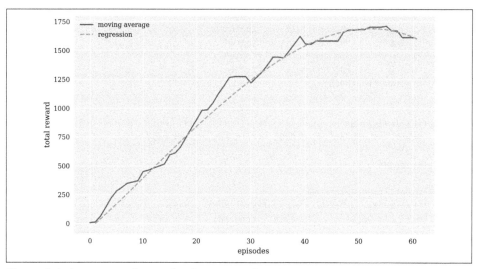

Figure 9-4. Average total rewards of FQLAgent for Finance

An interesting picture also arises for the training and validation performances, as shown in Figure 9-5. The training performance shows a high variance, which is due, for example, to the exploration that is going on in addition to the exploitation of the currently optimal policy. In comparison, the validation performance has a much lower variance because it only relies on the exploitation of the currently optimal policy:

```
In [81]: plt.figure(figsize=(10, 6))
         x = range(1, len(agent.performances) + 1)
         y = np.polyval(np.polyfit(x, agent.performances, deg=3), x)
         y_ = np.polyval(np.polyfit(x, agent.vperformances, deg=3), x)
         plt.plot(agent.performances[:], label='training')
         plt.plot(agent.vperformances[:], label='validation')
         plt.plot(x, y, 'r--', label='regression (train)')
         plt.plot(x, y_, 'r-.', label='regression (valid)')
         plt.xlabel('episodes')
         plt.ylabel('gross performance')
         plt.legend();
```

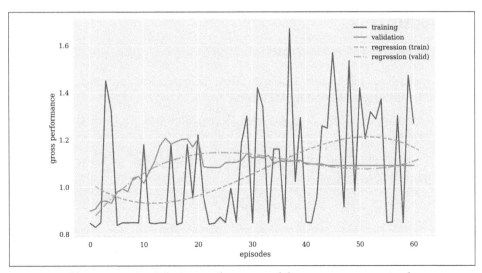

Figure 9-5. Training and validation performance of the FQLAgent per episode

Conclusions

This chapter discusses reinforcement learning as one of the most successful algorithm classes that AI has to offer. Most of the advances and success stories discussed in Chapter 2 have their origin in improvements in the field of RL. In this context, neural networks are not rendered useless. To the contrary, they play an important role in approximating the optimal action policy, usually in the form of a policy Q that, given a certain state, assigns each action a value. The higher the value is, the better the action will be, taking into account both immediate and delayed rewards.

The inclusion of delayed rewards, of course, is relevant in many important contexts. In a gaming context, with multiple actions available in general, it is optimal to choose the one that promises the highest total reward—and probably not just the highest immediate reward. The final total score is what is to be maximized. The same holds true in a financial context. The long-term performance is in general the appropriate goal for trading and investing, not a quick short-term profit that might come at an increased risk of going bankrupt.

The examples in this chapter also demonstrate that the RL approach is rather flexible and general in that it can be applied to different settings equally well. The DQL agent that solves the CartPole problem can also learn how to trade in a financial market, although not too well. Based on improvements of the Finance environment and the FQL agent, the FQL trading bot shows a respectable performance both in-sample (on the training data) and out-of-sample (on the validation data).

References

Books and papers cited in this chapter:

Sutton, Richard S. and Andrew G. Barto. 2018. *Reinforcement Learning: An Introduction*. Cambridge and London: MIT Press.

Watkins, Christopher. 1989. *Learning from Delayed Rewards*. Ph.D. thesis, University of Cambridge.

Watkins, Christopher and Peter Dayan. 1992. "Q-Learning." *Machine Learning* 8 (May): 279-282.

## PART IV

Algorithmic Trading

Success means making profits and avoiding losses.

—Martin Zweig

Part III is concerned with the discovery of *statistical* inefficiencies in financial markets by the use of deep learning and reinforcement learning techniques. This part, by contrast, is concerned with identifying and exploiting *economic* inefficiencies for which statistical inefficiencies are a prerequisite in general. The tool of choice for exploiting economic inefficiencies is *algorithmic trading*, that is, the automated execution of trading strategies based on predictions generated by a trading bot.

Table IV-1 compares in a simplified manner the problem of training and deploying a trading bot with the one of building and deploying a self-driving car.

Table IV-1. Self-driving cars compared to trading bots

Step	Self-Driving Car	Trading Bot
Training	Training AI in virtual and recorded environments	Training AI with simulated and real historical data
Risk management	Adding rules to avoid collisions, crashes, and so on	Adding rules to avoid large losses, to take profits early, and so on
Deployment	Combining AI with car hardware, deploying the car on the street, and monitoring	Combining AI with trading platform, deploying the trading bot for real trading, and monitoring

This part consists of three chapters that are structured along the three steps, as illustrated in Table IV-1, to exploit economic inefficiencies through a trading bot—starting with the vectorized backtesting of trading strategies, covering the analysis of risk management measures through event-based backtesting, and discussing technical details in the context of strategy execution and deployment:

- Chapter 10 is about the *vectorized backtesting* of algorithmic trading strategies, such as those based on a DNN for market prediction. This approach is both efficient and insightful with regard to a first judgment of the economic potential of a trading strategy. It also allows one to assess the impact of transaction costs on economic performance.

- Chapter 11 covers central aspects of managing the risk of algorithmic trading strategies, such as the use of stop loss orders or take profit orders. In addition to vectorized backtesting, this chapter introduces event-based backtesting as a more flexible approach to judge the economic potential of a trading strategy.

- Chapter 12 is primarily about the execution of trading strategies. Topics are the retrieval of historical data, the training of a trading bot based on this data, the streaming of real-time data, and the placement of orders. It introduces Oanda (*http://oanda.com*) and its API as a trading platform well suited to algorithmic trading. It also covers fundamental aspects of deploying AI-powered algorithmic trading strategies in automatic fashion.

Algorithmic Trading Strategies

Algorithmic trading is a vast field and encompasses different types of trading strategies. Some, for example, try to minimize the market impact during the execution of large orders (liquidity algorithms). Others try to replicate the payoff of derivatives instruments as closely as possible (dynamic hedging/replication). These examples illustrate that not all algorithmic trading strategies have the goal of exploiting economic inefficiencies. For the purposes of this book, the focus on algorithmic trading strategies that result from predictions made by a trading bot (for example, in the form of a DNN agent or an RL agent) seems appropriate and useful.

## CHAPTER 10

Vectorized Backtesting

Tesla's chief executive and serial technology entrepreneur, Elon Musk, has said his company's cars will be able to be summoned and drive autonomously across the US to pick up their owners within the next two years.

—Samuel Gibbs (2016)

Big money is made in the stock market by being on the right side of the major moves.

—Martin Zweig

The term *vectorized backtesting* refers to a technical approach to backtesting algorithmic trading strategies, such as those based on a dense neural network (DNN) for market prediction. The books by Hilpisch (2018, ch. 15; 2020, ch. 4) cover vectorized backtesting based on a number of concrete examples. *Vectorized* in this context refers to a programming paradigm that relies heavily or even exclusively on vectorized code (that is, code without any looping on the Python level). Vectorization of code is good practice with such packages such as Numpy or pandas in general and has been used intensively in previous chapters as well. The benefits of vectorized code are more concise and easy-to-read code, as well as faster execution in many important scenarios. On the other hand, it might not be as flexible in backtesting trading strategies as, for example, event-based backtesting, which is introduced and used in Chapter 11.

Having a good AI-powered predictor available that beats a simple baseline predictor is important but is generally not enough to generate *alpha* (that is, above-market returns, possibly adjusted for risk). For example, it is also important for a prediction-based trading strategy to predict the large market movements correctly and not just the majority of the (potentially pretty small) market movements. Vectorized backtesting is an easy and fast way of figuring out the economic potential of a trading strategy.

Compared to autonomous vehicles (AVs), vectorized backtesting is like testing the AI of AVs in virtual environments just to see how it performs "in general" in a risk-free environment. However, for the AI of an AV it is not only important to perform well *on average*, but it is also of paramount importance to see how it masters critical or even extreme situations. Such an AI is supposed to cause "zero casualties" on average, not 0.1 or 0.5. For a financial AI, it is similarly—even if not equally—important to get the large market movements correct. Whereas this chapter focuses on the pure performance of financial AI agents (trading bots), Chapter 11 goes deeper into risk assessment and the backtesting of standard risk measures.

"Backtesting an SMA-Based Strategy" on page 282 introduces vectorized backtesting based on a simple example using simple moving averages as technical indicators and end-of-day (EOD) data. This allows for insightful visualizations and an easier understanding of the approach when getting started. "Backtesting a Daily DNN-Based Strategy" on page 289 trains a DNN based on EOD data and backtests the resulting prediction-based strategy for its economic performance. "Backtesting an Intraday DNN-Based Strategy" on page 295 then does the same with intraday data. In all examples, proportional transaction costs are included in the form of assumed bid-ask spreads.

Backtesting an SMA-Based Strategy

This section introduces vectorized backtesting based on a classical trading strategy that uses simple moving averages (SMAs) as technical indicators. The following code realizes the necessary imports and configurations and retrieves EOD data for the EUR/USD currency pair:

```
In [1]: import os
        import math
        import numpy as np
        import pandas as pd
        from pylab import plt, mpl
        plt.style.use('seaborn')
        mpl.rcParams['savefig.dpi'] = 300
        mpl.rcParams['font.family'] = 'serif'
        pd.set_option('mode.chained_assignment', None)
        pd.set_option('display.float_format', '{:.4f}'.format)
        np.set_printoptions(suppress=True, precision=4)
        os.environ['PYTHONHASHSEED'] = '0'

In [2]: url = 'http://hilpisch.com/aiif_eikon_eod_data.csv'  ❶

In [3]: symbol = 'EUR='  ❶

In [4]: data = pd.DataFrame(pd.read_csv(url, index_col=0,
                            parse_dates=True).dropna()[symbol])  ❶
```

```
In [5]: data.info()  ❶
        <class 'pandas.core.frame.DataFrame'>
        DatetimeIndex: 2516 entries, 2010-01-04 to 2019-12-31
        Data columns (total 1 columns):
         #   Column  Non-Null Count  Dtype
        ---  ------  --------------  -----
         0   EUR=    2516 non-null   float64
        dtypes: float64(1)
        memory usage: 39.3 KB
```

❶ Retrieves EOD data for EUR/USD

The idea of the strategy is the following. Calculate a shorter SMA1, say for 42 days, and a longer SMA2, say for 258 days. Whenever SMA1 is above SMA2, go long on the financial instrument. Whenever SMA1 is below SMA2, go short on the financial instrument. Because the example is based on EUR/USD, going long or short is easily accomplished.

The following Python code calculates in vectorized fashion the SMA values and visualizes the resulting time series alongside the original time series (see Figure 10-1):

```
In [6]: data['SMA1'] = data[symbol].rolling(42).mean()   ❶

In [7]: data['SMA2'] = data[symbol].rolling(258).mean()  ❷

In [8]: data.plot(figsize=(10, 6));  ❸
```

❶ Calculates the shorter SMA1

❷ Calculates the longer SMA2

❸ Visualizes the three time series

Equipped with the SMA time series data, the resulting positions can, again in vectorized fashion, be derived. Note the shift of the resulting position time series by one day to avoid foresight bias in the data. This shift is necessary since the calculation of the SMAs includes the closing values from the same day. Therefore, the position derived from the SMA values from one day needs to be applied to the next day for the whole time series.

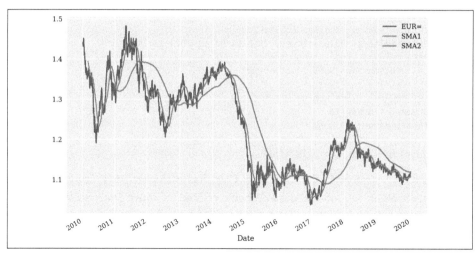

Figure 10-1. Time series data for EUR/USD and SMAs

Figure 10-2 visualizes the resulting positions as an overlay to the other time series:

```
In [9]: data.dropna(inplace=True)   ❶

In [10]: data['p'] = np.where(data['SMA1'] > data['SMA2'], 1, -1)   ❷

In [11]: data['p'] = data['p'].shift(1)   ❸

In [12]: data.dropna(inplace=True)   ❶

In [13]: data.plot(figsize=(10, 6), secondary_y='p');   ❹
```

❶ Deletes rows containing NaN values

❷ Derives the position values based on same-day SMA values

❸ Shifts the position values by one day to avoid foresight bias

❹ Visualizes the position values as derived from the SMAs

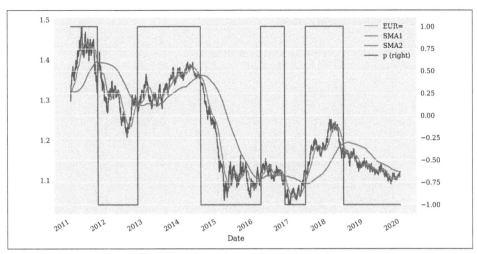

Figure 10-2. Time series data for EUR/USD, SMAs, and resulting positions

One crucial step is missing: the combination of the positions with the returns of the financial instrument. Since positions are conveniently represented by a +1 for a long position and a -1 for a short position, this step boils down to multiplying two columns of the DataFrame object—in vectorized fashion again. The SMA-based trading strategy outperforms the passive benchmark investment by a considerable margin, as Figure 10-3 illustrates:

```
In [14]: data['r'] = np.log(data[symbol] / data[symbol].shift(1))    ❶

In [15]: data.dropna(inplace=True)

In [16]: data['s'] = data['p'] * data['r']    ❷

In [17]: data[['r', 's']].sum().apply(np.exp)    ❸
Out[17]: r    0.8640
         s    1.3773
         dtype: float64

In [18]: data[['r', 's']].sum().apply(np.exp) - 1    ❹
Out[18]: r    -0.1360
         s     0.3773
         dtype: float64

In [19]: data[['r', 's']].cumsum().apply(np.exp).plot(figsize=(10, 6));    ❺
```

❶ Calculates the log returns

❷ Calculates the strategy returns

❸ Calculates the gross performances

❹ Calculates the net performances

❺ Visualizes the gross performances over time

Figure 10-3. Gross performance of passive benchmark investment and SMA strategy

So far, the performance figures are not considering transaction costs. These are, of course, a crucial element when judging the economic potential of a trading strategy. In the current setup, proportional transaction costs can be easily included in the calculations. The idea is to determine when a trade takes place and to reduce the performance of the trading strategy by a certain value to account for the relevant bid-ask spread. As the following calculations show, and as is obvious from Figure 10-2, the trading strategy does not change positions too often. Therefore, in order to have some meaningful effects of transaction costs, they are assumed to be quite a bit higher than typically seen for EUR/USD. The net effect of subtracting transaction costs is a few percentage points under the given assumptions (see Figure 10-4):

```
In [20]: sum(data['p'].diff() != 0) + 2    ❶
Out[20]: 10

In [21]: pc = 0.005    ❷

In [22]: data['s_'] = np.where(data['p'].diff() != 0,
                               data['s'] - pc, data['s'])    ❸

In [23]: data['s_'].iloc[0] -= pc    ❹

In [24]: data['s_'].iloc[-1] -= pc    ❺

In [25]: data[['r', 's', 's_']][data['p'].diff() != 0]    ❻
Out[25]:                      r       s      s_
```

```
         Date
         2011-01-12   0.0123   0.0123   0.0023
         2011-10-10   0.0198  -0.0198  -0.0248
         2012-11-07  -0.0034  -0.0034  -0.0084
         2014-07-24  -0.0001   0.0001  -0.0049
         2016-03-16   0.0102   0.0102   0.0052
         2016-11-10  -0.0018   0.0018  -0.0032
         2017-06-05  -0.0025  -0.0025  -0.0075
         2018-06-15   0.0035  -0.0035  -0.0085

In [26]: data[['r', 's', 's_']].sum().apply(np.exp)
Out[26]: r    0.8640
         s    1.3773
         s_   1.3102
         dtype: float64

In [27]: data[['r', 's', 's_']].sum().apply(np.exp) - 1
Out[27]: r   -0.1360
         s    0.3773
         s_   0.3102
         dtype: float64

In [28]: data[['r', 's', 's_']].cumsum().apply(np.exp).plot(figsize=(10, 6));
```

❶ Calculates the number of trades, including entry and exit trade

❷ Fixes the proportional transaction costs (deliberately set quite high)

❸ Adjusts the strategy performance for the transaction costs

❹ Adjusts the strategy performance for the *entry* trade

❺ Adjusts the strategy performance for the *exit* trade

❻ Shows the adjusted performance values for the regular trades

Figure 10-4. Gross performance of the SMA strategy before and after transaction costs

What about the resulting risk of the trading strategy? For a trading strategy that is based on directional predictions and that takes long or short positions only, the risk, expressed as the volatility (standard deviation of the log returns), is exactly the same as for the passive benchmark investment:

```
In [29]: data[['r', 's', 's_']].std()  ❶
Out[29]: r    0.0054
         s    0.0054
         s_   0.0054
         dtype: float64

In [30]: data[['r', 's', 's_']].std() * math.sqrt(252)  ❷
Out[30]: r    0.0853
         s    0.0853
         s_   0.0855
         dtype: float64
```

❶ Daily volatility

❷ Annualized volatility

Vectorized Backtesting

Vectorized backtesting is a powerful and efficient approach to backtesting the "pure" performance of a prediction-based trading strategy. It can also accommodate proportional transaction costs, for instance. However, it is not well suited to including typical risk management measures, such as (trailing) stop loss orders or take profit orders. This is addressed in Chapter 11.

Backtesting a Daily DNN-Based Strategy

The previous section lays out the blueprint for vectorized backtesting on the basis of a simple, easy-to-visualize trading strategy. The same blueprint can be applied, for example, to DNN-based trading strategies with minimal technical adjustments. The following trains a Keras DNN model, as discussed in Chapter 7. The data that is used is the same as in the previous example. However, as in Chapter 7, different features and lags thereof need to be added to the DataFrame object:

```
In [31]: data = pd.DataFrame(pd.read_csv(url, index_col=0,
                                 parse_dates=True).dropna()[symbol])

In [32]: data.info()
         <class 'pandas.core.frame.DataFrame'>
         DatetimeIndex: 2516 entries, 2010-01-04 to 2019-12-31
         Data columns (total 1 columns):
          #   Column  Non-Null Count  Dtype
         ---  ------  --------------  -----
          0   EUR=    2516 non-null   float64
         dtypes: float64(1)
         memory usage: 39.3 KB

In [33]: lags = 5

In [34]: def add_lags(data, symbol, lags, window=20):
             cols = []
             df = data.copy()
             df.dropna(inplace=True)
             df['r'] = np.log(df / df.shift(1))
             df['sma'] = df[symbol].rolling(window).mean()
             df['min'] = df[symbol].rolling(window).min()
             df['max'] = df[symbol].rolling(window).max()
             df['mom'] = df['r'].rolling(window).mean()
             df['vol'] = df['r'].rolling(window).std()
             df.dropna(inplace=True)
             df['d'] = np.where(df['r'] > 0, 1, 0)
             features = [symbol, 'r', 'd', 'sma', 'min', 'max', 'mom', 'vol']
             for f in features:
                 for lag in range(1, lags + 1):
                     col = f'{f}_lag_{lag}'
                     df[col] = df[f].shift(lag)
                     cols.append(col)
             df.dropna(inplace=True)
             return df, cols

In [35]: data, cols = add_lags(data, symbol, lags, window=20)
```

The following Python code accomplishes additional imports and defines the set_seeds() and create_model() functions:

```
In [36]: import random
         import tensorflow as tf
         from keras.layers import Dense, Dropout
         from keras.models import Sequential
         from keras.regularizers import l1
         from keras.optimizers import Adam
         from sklearn.metrics import accuracy_score
         Using TensorFlow backend.

In [37]: def set_seeds(seed=100):
             random.seed(seed)
             np.random.seed(seed)
             tf.random.set_seed(seed)
         set_seeds()

In [38]: optimizer = Adam(learning_rate=0.0001)

In [39]: def create_model(hl=2, hu=128, dropout=False, rate=0.3,
                          regularize=False, reg=l1(0.0005),
                          optimizer=optimizer, input_dim=len(cols)):
             if not regularize:
                 reg = None
             model = Sequential()
             model.add(Dense(hu, input_dim=input_dim,
                         activity_regularizer=reg,
                         activation='relu'))
             if dropout:
                 model.add(Dropout(rate, seed=100))
             for _ in range(hl):
                 model.add(Dense(hu, activation='relu',
                             activity_regularizer=reg))
                 if dropout:
                     model.add(Dropout(rate, seed=100))
             model.add(Dense(1, activation='sigmoid'))
             model.compile(loss='binary_crossentropy',
                         optimizer=optimizer,
                         metrics=['accuracy'])
             return model
```

Based on a sequential train-test split of the historical data, the following Python code first trains the DNN model based on normalized features data:

```
In [40]: split = '2018-01-01'  ❶

In [41]: train = data.loc[:split].copy()  ❶

In [42]: np.bincount(train['d'])  ❷
Out[42]: array([ 982, 1006])
```

```
In [43]: mu, std = train.mean(), train.std()  ❸

In [44]: train_ = (train - mu) / std  ❸

In [45]: set_seeds()
         model = create_model(hl=2, hu=64)  ❹

In [46]: %%time
         model.fit(train_[cols], train['d'],
                 epochs=20, verbose=False,
                 validation_split=0.2, shuffle=False)  ❺
         CPU times: user 2.93 s, sys: 574 ms, total: 3.5 s
         Wall time: 1.93 s

Out[46]: <keras.callbacks.callbacks.History at 0x7fc9392f38d0>

In [47]: model.evaluate(train_[cols], train['d'])  ❻
         1988/1988 [==============================] - 0s 17us/step

Out[47]: [0.6745863538872549, 0.5925553441047668]
```

❶ Splits the data into training and test data

❷ Shows the frequency of the labels classes

❸ Normalizes the training features data

❹ Creates the DNN model

❺ Trains the DNN model on the training data

❻ Evaluates the performance of the model on the training data

So far, this basically repeats the core approach of Chapter 7. Vectorized backtesting can now be applied to judge the economic performance of the DNN-based trading strategy *in-sample* based on the model's predictions (see Figure 10-5). In this context, an upward prediction is naturally interpreted as a long position and a downward prediction as a short position:

```
In [48]: train['p'] = np.where(model.predict(train_[cols]) > 0.5, 1, 0)  ❶

In [49]: train['p'] = np.where(train['p'] == 1, 1, -1)  ❷

In [50]: train['p'].value_counts()  ❸
Out[50]: -1    1098
          1     890
         Name: p, dtype: int64

In [51]: train['s'] = train['p'] * train['r']  ❹
```

```
In [52]: train[['r', 's']].sum().apply(np.exp)  ❺
Out[52]: r    0.8787
         s    5.0766
         dtype: float64

In [53]: train[['r', 's']].sum().apply(np.exp)  - 1  ❺
Out[53]: r   -0.1213
         s    4.0766
         dtype: float64

In [54]: train[['r', 's']].cumsum().apply(np.exp).plot(figsize=(10, 6));  ❻
```

❶ Generates the binary predictions

❷ Translates the predictions into position values

❸ Shows the number of long and short positions

❹ Calculates the strategy performance values

❺ Calculates the gross and net performances (in-sample)

❻ Visualizes the gross performances over time (in-sample)

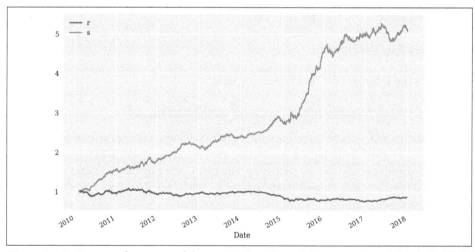

Figure 10-5. Gross performance of the passive benchmark investment and the daily DNN strategy (in-sample)

Next is the same sequence of calculations for the test data set. Whereas the out-performance in-sample is significant, the numbers out-of-sample are not as impressive but are still convincing (see Figure 10-6):

```
In [55]: test = data.loc[split:].copy()  ❶

In [56]: test_ = (test - mu) / std  ❷

In [57]: model.evaluate(test_[cols], test['d'])  ❸
         503/503 [==============================] - 0s 17us/step

Out[57]: [0.6933823573897421, 0.5407554507255554]

In [58]: test['p'] = np.where(model.predict(test_[cols]) > 0.5, 1, -1)

In [59]: test['p'].value_counts()
Out[59]: -1    406
          1     97
         Name: p, dtype: int64

In [60]: test['s'] = test['p'] * test['r']

In [61]: test[['r', 's']].sum().apply(np.exp)
Out[61]: r    0.9345
         s    1.2431
         dtype: float64

In [62]: test[['r', 's']].sum().apply(np.exp) - 1
Out[62]: r    -0.0655
         s     0.2431
         dtype: float64

In [63]: test[['r', 's']].cumsum().apply(np.exp).plot(figsize=(10, 6));
```

❶ Generates the test data sub-set

❷ Normalizes the test data

❸ Evaluates the model performance on the test data

The DNN-based trading strategy leads to a larger number of trades as compared to the SMA-based strategy. This makes the inclusion of transaction costs an even more important aspect when judging the economic performance.

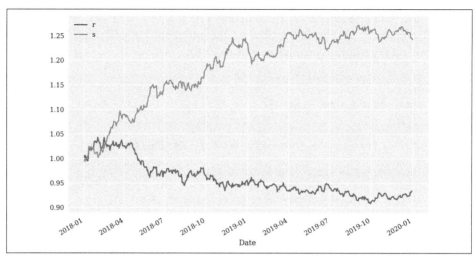

Figure 10-6. Gross performance of the passive benchmark investment and the daily DNN strategy (out-of-sample)

The following code assumes now realistic bid-ask spreads for EUR/USD on the level of 1.2 pips (that is, 0.00012 in terms of currency units).[1] To simplify the calculations, an average value for the proportional transaction costs pc is calculated based on the average closing price for EUR/USD (see Figure 10-7):

```
In [64]: sum(test['p'].diff() != 0)
Out[64]: 147

In [65]: spread = 0.00012        ❶
         pc = spread / data[symbol].mean()    ❷
         print(f'{pc:.6f}')
         0.000098

In [66]: test['s_'] = np.where(test['p'].diff() != 0,
                               test['s'] - pc, test['s'])

In [67]: test['s_'].iloc[0] -= pc

In [68]: test['s_'].iloc[-1] -= pc

In [69]: test[['r', 's', 's_']].sum().apply(np.exp)
Out[69]: r    0.9345
         s    1.2431
         s_   1.2252
         dtype: float64
```

---

1 This, for example, is a typical spread that Oanda (*http://oanda.com*) offers retail traders.

```
In [70]: test[['r', 's', 's_']].sum().apply(np.exp) - 1
Out[70]: r    -0.0655
         s     0.2431
         s_    0.2252
         dtype: float64

In [71]: test[['r', 's', 's_']].cumsum().apply(np.exp).plot(figsize=(10, 6));
```

❶ Fixes the average bid-ask spread

❷ Calculates the average proportional transaction costs

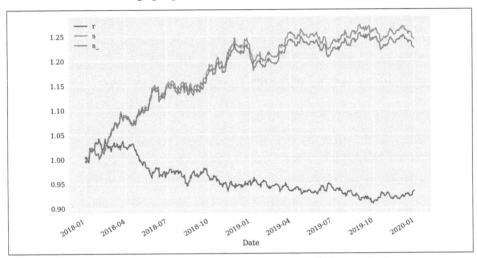

Figure 10-7. Gross performance of the daily DNN strategy before and after transaction costs (out-of-sample)

The DNN-based trading strategy seems promising both before and after typical transaction costs. However, would a similar strategy be economically viable intraday as well, when even more trades are observed? The next section analyzes a DNN-based intraday strategy.

Backtesting an Intraday DNN-Based Strategy

To train and backtest a DNN model on intraday data, another data set is required:

```
In [72]: url = 'http://hilpisch.com/aiif_eikon_id_eur_usd.csv'  ❶

In [73]: symbol = 'EUR='  ❶

In [74]: data = pd.DataFrame(pd.read_csv(url, index_col=0,
                            parse_dates=True).dropna()['CLOSE'])  ❶
         data.columns = [symbol]
```

```
In [75]: data = data.resample('5min', label='right').last().ffill()  ❷

In [76]: data.info()  ❷
         <class 'pandas.core.frame.DataFrame'>
         DatetimeIndex: 26486 entries, 2019-10-01 00:05:00 to 2019-12-31 23:10:00
         Freq: 5T
         Data columns (total 1 columns):
          #   Column  Non-Null Count  Dtype
         ---  ------  --------------  -----
          0   EUR=    26486 non-null  float64
         dtypes: float64(1)
         memory usage: 413.8 KB

In [77]: lags = 5

In [78]: data, cols = add_lags(data, symbol, lags, window=20)
```

❶ Retrieves intraday data for EUR/USD and picks the closing prices

❷ Resamples the data to five-minute bars

The procedure of the previous section can now be repeated with the new data set. First, train the DNN model:

```
In [79]: split = int(len(data) * 0.85)

In [80]: train = data.iloc[:split].copy()

In [81]: np.bincount(train['d'])
Out[81]: array([16284,  6207])

In [82]: def cw(df):
             c0, c1 = np.bincount(df['d'])
             w0 = (1 / c0) * (len(df)) / 2
             w1 = (1 / c1) * (len(df)) / 2
             return {0: w0, 1: w1}

In [83]: mu, std = train.mean(), train.std()

In [84]: train_ = (train - mu) / std

In [85]: set_seeds()
         model = create_model(hl=1, hu=128,
                               reg=True, dropout=False)

In [86]: %%time
         model.fit(train_[cols], train['d'],
                   epochs=40, verbose=False,
                   validation_split=0.2, shuffle=False,
                   class_weight=cw(train))
         CPU times: user 40.6 s, sys: 5.49 s, total: 46 s
         Wall time: 25.2 s
```

```
Out[86]: <keras.callbacks.callbacks.History at 0x7fc91a6b2a90>

In [87]: model.evaluate(train_[cols], train['d'])
         22491/22491 [==============================] - 0s 13us/step

Out[87]: [0.5218664327576152, 0.6729803085327148]
```

In-sample, the performance looks promising, as illustrated in Figure 10-8:

```
In [88]: train['p'] = np.where(model.predict(train_[cols]) > 0.5, 1, -1)

In [89]: train['p'].value_counts()
Out[89]: -1    11519
          1    10972
         Name: p, dtype: int64

In [90]: train['s'] = train['p'] * train['r']

In [91]: train[['r', 's']].sum().apply(np.exp)
Out[91]: r    1.0223
         s    1.6665
         dtype: float64

In [92]: train[['r', 's']].sum().apply(np.exp) - 1
Out[92]: r    0.0223
         s    0.6665
         dtype: float64

In [93]: train[['r', 's']].cumsum().apply(np.exp).plot(figsize=(10, 6));
```

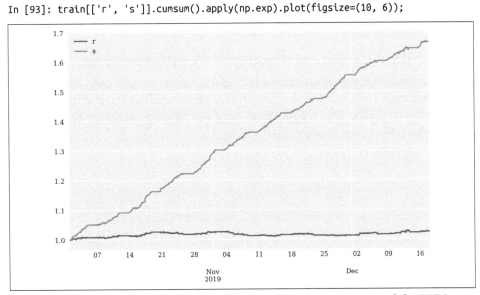

Figure 10-8. Gross performance of the passive benchmark investment and the DNN intraday strategy (in-sample)

Out-of-sample, the performance also looks promising before transaction costs. The strategy seems to systematically outperform the passive benchmark investment (see Figure 10-9):

```
In [94]: test = data.iloc[split:].copy()

In [95]: test_ = (test - mu) / std

In [96]: model.evaluate(test_[cols], test['d'])
         3970/3970 [==============================] - 0s 19us/step

Out[96]: [0.5226116042706168, 0.668513834476471]

In [97]: test['p'] = np.where(model.predict(test_[cols]) > 0.5, 1, -1)

In [98]: test['p'].value_counts()
Out[98]: -1    2273
          1    1697
         Name: p, dtype: int64

In [99]: test['s'] = test['p'] * test['r']

In [100]: test[['r', 's']].sum().apply(np.exp)
Out[100]: r    1.0071
          s    1.0658
          dtype: float64

In [101]: test[['r', 's']].sum().apply(np.exp) - 1
Out[101]: r    0.0071
          s    0.0658
          dtype: float64

In [102]: test[['r', 's']].cumsum().apply(np.exp).plot(figsize=(10, 6));
```

The final litmus test with regard to pure economic performance comes when adding transaction costs. The strategy leads to hundreds of trades over a relatively short period of time. As the following analysis suggests, based on standard retail bid-ask spreads, the DNN-based strategy is not viable.

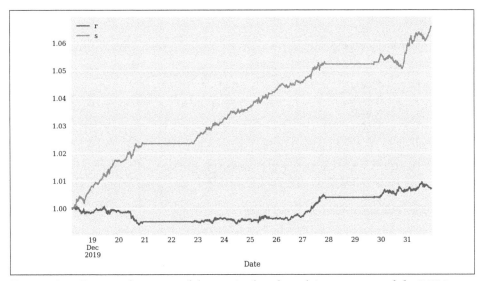

Figure 10-9. Gross performance of the passive benchmark investment and the DNN intraday strategy (out-of-sample)

Reducing the spread to a level that professional, high-volume traders might achieve, the strategy still does not break even but rather loses a large proportion of the profits to the transaction costs (see Figure 10-10):

```
In [103]: sum(test['p'].diff() != 0)
Out[103]: 1303

In [104]: spread = 0.00012  ❶
          pc_1 = spread / test[symbol]  ❶

In [105]: spread = 0.00006  ❷
          pc_2 = spread / test[symbol]  ❷

In [106]: test['s_1'] = np.where(test['p'].diff() != 0,
                                 test['s'] - pc_1, test['s'])  ❶

In [107]: test['s_1'].iloc[0] -= pc_1.iloc[0]  ❶
          test['s_1'].iloc[-1] -= pc_1.iloc[0]  ❶

In [108]: test['s_2'] = np.where(test['p'].diff() != 0,
                                 test['s'] - pc_2, test['s'])  ❷

In [109]: test['s_2'].iloc[0] -= pc_2.iloc[0]  ❷
          test['s_2'].iloc[-1] -= pc_2.iloc[0]  ❷

In [110]: test[['r', 's', 's_1', 's_2']].sum().apply(np.exp)
Out[110]: r    1.0071
          s    1.0658
```

```
          s_1    0.9259
          s_2    0.9934
          dtype: float64

In [111]: test[['r', 's', 's_1', 's_2']].sum().apply(np.exp) - 1
Out[111]: r        0.0071
          s        0.0658
          s_1     -0.0741
          s_2     -0.0066
          dtype: float64

In [112]: test[['r', 's', 's_1', 's_2']].cumsum().apply(
              np.exp).plot(figsize=(10, 6), style=['-', '-', '--', '--']);
```

❶ Assumes bid-ask spread on retail level

❷ Assumes bid-ask spread on professional level

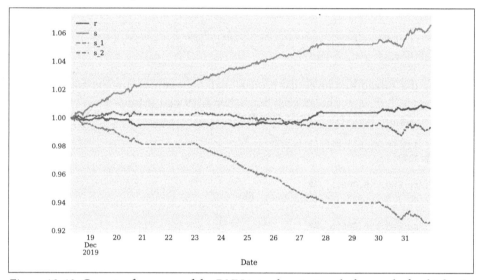

Figure 10-10. Gross performance of the DNN intraday strategy before and after higher/ lower transaction costs (out-of-sample)

Intraday Trading

Intraday algorithmic trading in the form discussed in this chapter often seems appealing from a statistical point of view. Both in-sample and out-of-sample, the DNN model reaches a high accuracy when predicting the market direction. Excluding transaction costs, this also translates both in-sample and out-of-sample into a significant outperformance of the DNN-based strategy when compared to the passive benchmark investment. However, adding transaction costs to the mix reduces the performance of the DNN-based strategy considerably, making it unviable for typical retail bid-ask spreads and not really attractive for lower, high-volume bid-ask spreads.

Conclusions

Vectorized backtesting proves to be an efficient and valuable approach for backtesting the performance of AI-powered algorithmic trading strategies. This chapter first explains the basic idea behind the approach based on a simple example using two SMAs to derive signals. This allows for a simple visualization of the strategy and resulting positions. It then proceeds by backtesting a DNN-based trading strategy, as discussed in detail in Chapter 7, in combination with EOD data. Both before and after transaction costs, the *statistical inefficiencies* as discovered in Chapter 7 translate into *economic inefficiencies*, which means profitable trading strategies. When using the same vectorized backtesting approaches with intraday data, the DNN strategy also shows a significant outperformance both in- and out-of-sample when compared to the passive benchmark investment—at least before transaction costs. Adding transaction costs to the backtesting illustrates that these must be pretty low, on a level often not even achieved by big professional traders, to render the trading strategy economically viable.

References

Books and papers cited in this chapter:

Gibbs Samuel. 2016. "Elon Musk: Tesla Cars Will Be Able to Cross Us with No Driver in Two Years." *The Guardian*. January 11, 2016. *https://oreil.ly/C508Q*.

Hilpisch, Yves. 2018. *Python for Finance: Mastering Data-Driven Finance.* 2nd ed. Sebastopol: O'Reilly.

———. 2020. *Python for Algorithmic Trading: From Idea to Cloud Deployment.* Sebastopol: O'Reilly.

## CHAPTER 11

Risk Management

A significant barrier to deploying autonomous vehicles (AVs) on a massive scale is safety assurance.

—Majid Khonji et al. (2019)

Having better prediction raises the value of judgment. After all, it doesn't help to know the likelihood of rain if you don't know how much you like staying dry or how much you hate carrying an umbrella.

—Ajay Agrawal et al. (2018)

Vectorized backtesting in general enables one to judge the economic potential of a prediction-based algorithmic trading strategy on an as-is basis (that is, in its pure form). Most AI agents applied in practice have more components than just the prediction model. For example, the AI of autonomous vehicles (AVs) comes not standalone but rather with a large number of rules and heuristics that restrict what actions the AI takes or can take. In the context of AVs, this primarily relates to managing risks, such as those resulting from collisions or crashes.

In a financial context, AI agents or trading bots are also not deployed as-is in general. Rather, there are a number of standard risk measures that are typically used, such as *(trailing) stop loss orders* or *take profit orders*. The reasoning is clear. When placing directional bets in financial markets, too-large losses are to be avoided. Similarly, when a certain profit level is reached, the success is to be protected by early close outs. How such risk measures are handled is a matter, more often than not, of human judgment, supported probably by a formal analysis of relevant data and statistics. Conceptually, this is a major point discussed in the book by Agrawal et al. (2018): AI provides improved predictions, but human judgment still plays a role in setting decision rules and action boundaries.

This chapter has a threefold purpose. First, it backtests in both *vectorized* and *event-based* fashion algorithmic trading strategies that result from a trained deep Q-learning agent. Henceforth, such agents are called *trading bots*. Second, it assesses risks related to the financial instrument on which the strategies are implemented. And third, it backtests typical risk measures, such as stop loss orders, using the event-based approach introduced in this chapter. The major benefit of event-based backtesting when compared to vectorized backtesting is a higher degree of flexibility in modeling and analyzing decision rules and risk management measures. In other words, it allows one to zoom in on details that are pushed toward the background when working with vectorized programming approaches.

"Trading Bot" on page 304 introduces and trains the trading bot based on the financial Q-learning agent from Chapter 9. "Vectorized Backtesting" on page 308 uses vectorized backtesting from Chapter 10 to judge the (pure) economic performance of the trading bot. Event-based backtesting is introduced in "Event-Based Backtesting" on page 311. First, a base class is discussed. Second, based on the base class, the backtesting of the trading bot is implemented and conducted. In this context, also see Hilpisch (2020, ch. 6). "Assessing Risk" on page 318 analyzes selected statistical measures important for setting risk management rules, such as *maximum drawdown* and *average true range* (ATR). "Backtesting Risk Measures" on page 322 then backtests the impact of major risk measures on the performance of the trading bot.

Trading Bot

This section presents a trading bot based on the financial Q-learning agent, `FQLAgent`, from Chapter 9. This is the trading bot that is analyzed in subsequent sections. As usual, our imports come first:

```
In [1]: import os
        import numpy as np
        import pandas as pd
        from pylab import plt, mpl
        plt.style.use('seaborn')
        mpl.rcParams['savefig.dpi'] = 300
        mpl.rcParams['font.family'] = 'serif'
        pd.set_option('mode.chained_assignment', None)
        pd.set_option('display.float_format', '{:.4f}'.format)
        np.set_printoptions(suppress=True, precision=4)
        os.environ['PYTHONHASHSEED'] = '0'
```

"Finance Environment" on page 333 presents a Python module with the `Finance` class used in the following. "Trading Bot" on page 304 provides the Python module with the `TradingBot` class and some helper functions for plotting training and validation results. Both classes are pretty close to the ones introduced in Chapter 9, which is why they are used here without further explanations.

The following code trains the trading bot on historical end-of-day (EOD) data, including a sub-set of the data used for validation. Figure 11-1 shows average total rewards as achieved for the different training episodes:

```
In [2]: import finance
        import tradingbot
        Using TensorFlow backend.

In [3]: symbol = 'EUR='
        features = [symbol, 'r', 's', 'm', 'v']

In [4]: a = 0
        b = 1750
        c = 250

In [5]: learn_env = finance.Finance(symbol, features, window=20, lags=3,
                        leverage=1, min_performance=0.9, min_accuracy=0.475,
                        start=a, end=a + b, mu=None, std=None)

In [6]: learn_env.data.info()
        <class 'pandas.core.frame.DataFrame'>
        DatetimeIndex: 1750 entries, 2010-02-02 to 2017-01-12
        Data columns (total 6 columns):
         #   Column  Non-Null Count  Dtype
        ---  ------  --------------  -----
         0   EUR=    1750 non-null   float64
         1   r       1750 non-null   float64
         2   s       1750 non-null   float64
         3   m       1750 non-null   float64
         4   v       1750 non-null   float64
         5   d       1750 non-null   int64
        dtypes: float64(5), int64(1)
        memory usage: 95.7 KB

In [7]: valid_env = finance.Finance(symbol, features=learn_env.features,
                        window=learn_env.window,
                        lags=learn_env.lags,
                        leverage=learn_env.leverage,
                        min_performance=0.0, min_accuracy=0.0,
                        start=a + b, end=a + b + c,
                        mu=learn_env.mu, std=learn_env.std)

In [8]: valid_env.data.info()
        <class 'pandas.core.frame.DataFrame'>
        DatetimeIndex: 250 entries, 2017-01-13 to 2018-01-10
        Data columns (total 6 columns):
         #   Column  Non-Null Count  Dtype
        ---  ------  --------------  -----
         0   EUR=    250 non-null    float64
         1   r       250 non-null    float64
         2   s       250 non-null    float64
         3   m       250 non-null    float64
```

```
    4   v       250 non-null    float64
    5   d       250 non-null    int64
dtypes: float64(5), int64(1)
memory usage: 13.7 KB
```

In [9]: tradingbot.set_seeds(100)
        agent = tradingbot.TradingBot(24, 0.001, learn_env, valid_env)

In [10]: episodes = 61

In [11]: %time agent.learn(episodes)
         ===
         episode: 10/61 | VALIDATION | treward: 247 | perf: 0.936 | eps: 0.95
         ===

         ===
         episode: 20/61 | VALIDATION | treward: 247 | perf: 0.897 | eps: 0.86
         ===

         ===
         episode: 30/61 | VALIDATION | treward: 247 | perf: 1.035 | eps: 0.78
         ===

         ===
         episode: 40/61 | VALIDATION | treward: 247 | perf: 0.935 | eps: 0.70
         ===

         ===
         episode: 50/61 | VALIDATION | treward: 247 | perf: 0.890 | eps: 0.64
         ===

         ===
         episode: 60/61 | VALIDATION | treward: 247 | perf: 0.998 | eps: 0.58
         ===
         episode: 61/61 | treward: 17 | perf: 0.979 | av: 475.1 | max: 1747
         CPU times: user 51.4 s, sys: 2.53 s, total: 53.9 s
         Wall time: 47 s

In [12]: tradingbot.plot_treward(agent)
```
```

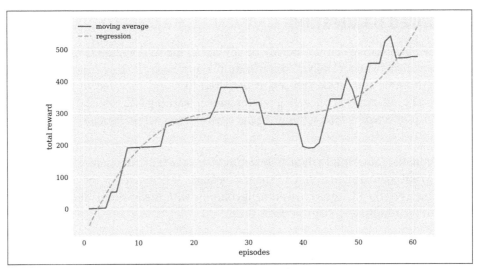

Figure 11-1. Average total reward per training episode

Figure 11-2 compares the gross performance of the trading bot on the training data—exhibiting quite some variance due to alternating between exploitation and exploration—with the one on the validation data set making use of exploitation only:

```
In [13]: tradingbot.plot_performance(agent)
```

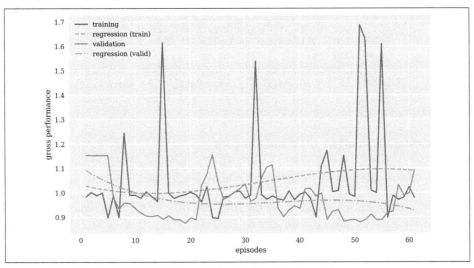

Figure 11-2. Gross performance on training and validation data set

This trained trading bot is used for backtesting in the following sections.

Vectorized Backtesting

Vectorized backtesting cannot directly be applied to the trading bot. Chapter 10 uses dense neural networks (DNNs) to illustrate the approach. In this context, the data with the features and labels sub-sets is prepared first and then fed to the DNN to generate all predictions at once. In a reinforcement learning (RL) context, data is generated and collected by interacting with the environment action by action and step by step.

To this end, the following Python code defines the `backtest` function, which takes as input a `TradingBot` instance and a `Finance` instance. It generates in the original `Data Frame` objects of the `Finance` environment columns with the positions the trading bot takes and the resulting strategy performance:

```
In [14]: def reshape(s):
             return np.reshape(s, [1, learn_env.lags,
                                   learn_env.n_features])   ❶
```

```
In [15]: def backtest(agent, env):
             env.min_accuracy = 0.0
             env.min_performance = 0.0
             done = False
             env.data['p'] = 0   ❷
             state = env.reset()
             while not done:
                 action = np.argmax(
                     agent.model.predict(reshape(state))[0, 0])   ❸
                 position = 1 if action == 1 else -1   ❹
                 env.data.loc[:, 'p'].iloc[env.bar] = position   ❺
                 state, reward, done, info = env.step(action)
             env.data['s'] = env.data['p'] * env.data['r'] * learn_env.leverage   ❻
```

❶ Reshapes a single feature-label combination

❷ Generates a column for the position values

❸ Derives the optimal action (prediction) given the trained DNN

❹ Derives the resulting position (+1 for long/upwards, −1 for short/downwards)…

❺ …and stores in the corresponding column at the appropriate index position

❻ Calculates the strategy log returns given the position values

Equipped with the `backtest` function, vectorized backtesting boils down to a few lines of Python code as in Chapter 10.

Figure 11-3 compares the passive benchmark investment's gross performance with the strategy gross performance:

```
In [16]: env = agent.learn_env  ❶

In [17]: backtest(agent, env)  ❷

In [18]: env.data['p'].iloc[env.lags:].value_counts()  ❸
Out[18]:  1    961
         -1    786
         Name: p, dtype: int64

In [19]: env.data[['r', 's']].iloc[env.lags:].sum().apply(np.exp)  ❹
Out[19]: r    0.7725
         s    1.5155
         dtype: float64

In [20]: env.data[['r', 's']].iloc[env.lags:].sum().apply(np.exp) - 1  ❺
Out[20]: r    -0.2275
         s     0.5155
         dtype: float64

In [21]: env.data[['r', 's']].iloc[env.lags:].cumsum(
                    ).apply(np.exp).plot(figsize=(10, 6));
```

❶ Specifies the relevant environment

❷ Generates the additional data required

❸ Counts the number of long and short positions

❹ Calculates the gross performances for the passive benchmark investment (r) and the strategy (s)...

❺ ...as well as the corresponding net performances

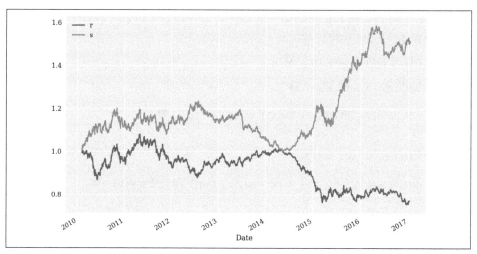

Figure 11-3. Gross performance of the passive benchmark investment and the trading bot (in-sample)

To get a more realistic picture of the performance of the trading bot, the following Python code creates a test environment with data that the trading bot has not yet seen. Figure 11-4 shows how the trading bot fares compared to the passive benchmark investment:

```
In [22]: test_env = finance.Finance(symbol, features=learn_env.features,
                                     window=learn_env.window,
                                     lags=learn_env.lags,
                                     leverage=learn_env.leverage,
                                     min_performance=0.0, min_accuracy=0.0,
                                     start=a + b + c, end=None,
                                     mu=learn_env.mu, std=learn_env.std)

In [23]: env = test_env

In [24]: backtest(agent, env)

In [25]: env.data['p'].iloc[env.lags:].value_counts()
Out[25]: -1    437
          1     56
         Name: p, dtype: int64

In [26]: env.data[['r', 's']].iloc[env.lags:].sum().apply(np.exp)
Out[26]: r    0.9144
         s    1.0992
         dtype: float64

In [27]: env.data[['r', 's']].iloc[env.lags:].sum().apply(np.exp) - 1
Out[27]: r    -0.0856
         s     0.0992
```

```
          dtype: float64

In [28]: env.data[['r', 's']].iloc[env.lags:].cumsum(
                 ).apply(np.exp).plot(figsize=(10, 6));
```

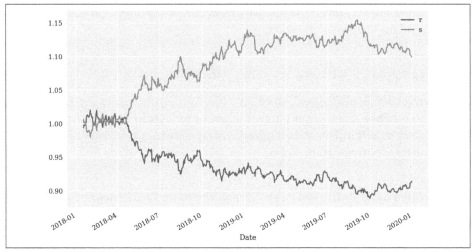

Figure 11-4. Gross performance of the passive benchmark investment and the trading bot (out-of-sample)

The out-of-sample performance without any risk measures implemented seems already promising. However, to be able to properly judge the real performance of a trading strategy, risk measures should be included. This is where event-based backtesting comes into play.

Event-Based Backtesting

Given the results of the previous section, the out-of-sample performance without any risk measures seems already promising. However, to be able to properly analyze risk measures, such as trailing stop loss orders, *event-based backtesting* is required. This section introduces this alternative approach to judging the performance of algorithmic trading strategies.

"Backtesting Base Class" on page 339 presents the BacktestingBase class that can be flexibly used to test different types of directional trading strategies. The code has detailed comments on the important lines. This base class provides the following methods:

get_date_price()
> For a given bar (index value for the DataFrame object containing the financial data), it returns the relevant date and price.

`print_balance()`

For a given bar, it prints the current (cash) balance of the trading bot.

`calculate_net_wealth()`

For a given price, it returns the net wealth composed of the current (cash) balance and the instrument position.

`print_net_wealth()`

For a given bar, it prints the net wealth of the trading bot.

`place_buy_order()`, `place_sell_order()`

For a given bar and a given number of units or a given amount, these methods place buy or sell orders and adjust relevant quantities accordingly (for example, accounting for transaction costs).

`close_out()`

At a given bar, this method closes open positions and calculates and reports performance statistics.

The following Python code illustrates how an instance of the `BacktestingBase` class functions based on some simple steps:

```
In [29]: import backtesting as bt

In [30]: bb = bt.BacktestingBase(env=agent.learn_env, model=agent.model,
                                 amount=10000, ptc=0.0001, ftc=1.0,
                                 verbose=True)  ❶

In [31]: bb.initial_amount  ❷
Out[31]: 10000

In [32]: bar = 100  ❸

In [33]: bb.get_date_price(bar)  ❹
Out[33]: ('2010-06-25', 1.2374)

In [34]: bb.env.get_state(bar)  ❺
Out[34]:              EUR=       r       s       m       v
         Date
         2010-06-22 -0.0242 -0.5622 -0.0916 -0.2022 1.5316
         2010-06-23  0.0176  0.6940 -0.0939 -0.0915 1.5563
         2010-06-24  0.0354  0.3034 -0.0865  0.6391 1.0890

In [35]: bb.place_buy_order(bar, amount=5000)  ❻
         2010-06-25 | buy 4040 units for 1.2374
         2010-06-25 | current balance = 4999.40

In [36]: bb.print_net_wealth(2 * bar)  ❼
         2010-11-16 | net wealth = 10450.17
```

```
In [37]: bb.place_sell_order(2 * bar, units=1000)  ❽
         2010-11-16 | sell 1000 units for 1.3492
         2010-11-16 | current balance = 6347.47

In [38]: bb.close_out(3 * bar)  ❾
         ================================================
         2011-04-11 | *** CLOSING OUT ***
         2011-04-11 | sell 3040 units for 1.4434
         2011-04-11 | current balance = 10733.97
         2011-04-11 | net performance [%] = 7.3397
         2011-04-11 | number of trades [#] = 3
         ================================================
```

❶ Instantiates a BacktestingBase object

❷ Looks up the initial_amount attribute value

❸ Fixes a bar value

❹ Retrieves the date and price values for the bar

❺ Retrieves the state of the Finance environment for the bar

❻ Places a buy order using the amount parameter

❼ Prints the net wealth at a later point (2 * bar)

❽ Places a sell order at that later point using the units parameter

❾ Closes out the remaining long position even later (3 * bar)

Inheriting from the BacktestingBase class, the TBBacktester class implements the event-based backtesting for the trading bot:

```
In [39]: class TBBacktester(bt.BacktestingBase):
             def _reshape(self, state):
                 ''' Helper method to reshape state objects.
                 '''
                 return np.reshape(state, [1, self.env.lags, self.env.n_features])
             def backtest_strategy(self):
                 ''' Event-based backtesting of the trading bot's performance.
                 '''
                 self.units = 0
                 self.position = 0
                 self.trades = 0
                 self.current_balance = self.initial_amount
                 self.net_wealths = list()
                 for bar in range(self.env.lags, len(self.env.data)):
                     date, price = self.get_date_price(bar)
```

```
        if self.trades == 0:
            print(50 * '=')
            print(f'{date} | *** START BACKTEST ***')
            self.print_balance(bar)
            print(50 * '=')
        state = self.env.get_state(bar)  ❶
        action = np.argmax(self.model.predict(
                    self._reshape(state.values))[0, 0])  ❷
        position = 1 if action == 1 else -1  ❸
        if self.position in [0, -1] and position == 1:  ❹
            if self.verbose:
                print(50 * '-')
                print(f'{date} | *** GOING LONG ***')
            if self.position == -1:
                self.place_buy_order(bar - 1, units=-self.units)
            self.place_buy_order(bar - 1,
                                 amount=self.current_balance)
            if self.verbose:
                self.print_net_wealth(bar)
            self.position = 1
        elif self.position in [0, 1] and position == -1:  ❺
            if self.verbose:
                print(50 * '-')
                print(f'{date} | *** GOING SHORT ***')
            if self.position == 1:
                self.place_sell_order(bar - 1, units=self.units)
            self.place_sell_order(bar - 1,
                                  amount=self.current_balance)
            if self.verbose:
                self.print_net_wealth(bar)
            self.position = -1
        self.net_wealths.append((date,
                                 self.calculate_net_wealth(price)))  ❻
    self.net_wealths = pd.DataFrame(self.net_wealths,
                                    columns=['date', 'net_wealth'])  ❻
    self.net_wealths.set_index('date', inplace=True)  ❻
    self.net_wealths.index = pd.DatetimeIndex(
                                self.net_wealths.index)  ❻
    self.close_out(bar)
```

❶ Retrieves the state of the Finance environment

❷ Generates the optimal action (prediction) given the state and the model object

❸ Derives the optimal position (long/short) given the optimal action (prediction)

❹ Enters a *long* position if the conditions are met

❺ Enters a *short* position if the conditions are met

---

❻ Collects the net wealth values over time and transforms them into a `DataFrame` object

The application of the `TBBacktester` class is straightforward, given that the `Finance` and `TradingBot` instances are already available. The following code backtests the trading bot first on the *learning environment* data—without and with transaction costs. Figure 11-5 compares the two cases visually over time:

```
In [40]: env = learn_env

In [41]: tb = TBBacktester(env, agent.model, 10000,
                           0.0, 0, verbose=False)  ❶

In [42]: tb.backtest_strategy()  ❶
         ================================================
         2010-02-05 | *** START BACKTEST ***
         2010-02-05 | current balance = 10000.00
         ================================================

         ================================================
         2017-01-12 | *** CLOSING OUT ***
         2017-01-12 | current balance = 14601.85
         2017-01-12 | net performance [%] = 46.0185
         2017-01-12 | number of trades [#] = 828
         ================================================

In [43]: tb_ = TBBacktester(env, agent.model, 10000,
                            0.00012, 0.0, verbose=False)

In [44]: tb_.backtest_strategy()  ❷
         ================================================
         2010-02-05 | *** START BACKTEST ***
         2010-02-05 | current balance = 10000.00
         ================================================

         ================================================
         2017-01-12 | *** CLOSING OUT ***
         2017-01-12 | current balance = 13222.08
         2017-01-12 | net performance [%] = 32.2208
         2017-01-12 | number of trades [#] = 828
         ================================================

In [45]: ax = tb.net_wealths.plot(figsize=(10, 6))
         tb_.net_wealths.columns = ['net_wealth (after tc)']
         tb_.net_wealths.plot(ax=ax);
```

❶ Event-based backtest in-sample *without* transaction costs

❷ Event-based backtest in-sample *with* transaction costs

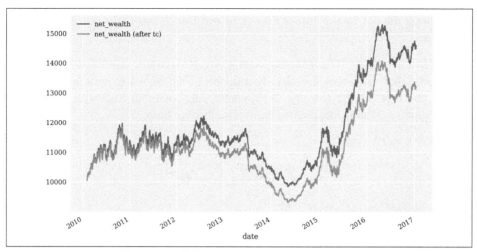

Figure 11-5. Gross performance of the trading bot before and after transaction costs (in-sample)

Figure 11-6 compares the gross performances of the trading bot for the *test environment* data over time—again, before and after transaction costs:

```
In [46]: env = test_env

In [47]: tb = TBBacktester(env, agent.model, 10000,
                           0.0, 0, verbose=False)  ❶

In [48]: tb.backtest_strategy()  ❶
         ==================================================
         2018-01-17 | *** START BACKTEST ***
         2018-01-17 | current balance = 10000.00
         ==================================================
         ==================================================
         2019-12-31 | *** CLOSING OUT ***
         2019-12-31 | current balance = 10936.79
         2019-12-31 | net performance [%] = 9.3679
         2019-12-31 | number of trades [#] = 186
         ==================================================

In [49]: tb_ = TBBacktester(env, agent.model, 10000,
                            0.00012, 0.0, verbose=False)

In [50]: tb_.backtest_strategy()  ❷
         ==================================================
         2018-01-17 | *** START BACKTEST ***
         2018-01-17 | current balance = 10000.00
         ==================================================
         ==================================================
         2019-12-31 | *** CLOSING OUT ***
         2019-12-31 | current balance = 10695.72
```

```
2019-12-31 | net performance [%] = 6.9572
2019-12-31 | number of trades [#] = 186
==================================================
```

```
In [51]: ax = tb.net_wealths.plot(figsize=(10, 6))
         tb_.net_wealths.columns = ['net_wealth (after tc)']
         tb_.net_wealths.plot(ax=ax);
```

❶ Event-based backtest out-of-sample *without* transaction costs

❷ Event-based backtest out-of-sample *with* transaction costs

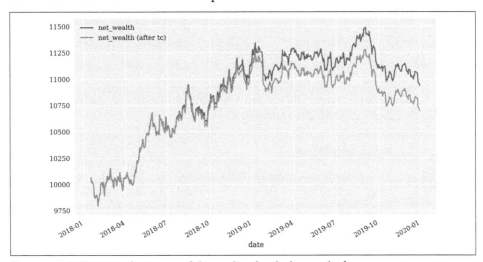

Figure 11-6. Gross performance of the trading bot before and after transaction costs (out-of-sample)

How does the performance before transaction costs from the event-based backtesting compare to the performance from the vectorized backtesting? Figure 11-7 shows the normalized net wealth compared to the gross performance over time. Due to the different technical approaches, the two time series are not exactly the same but are pretty similar. The performance difference can be mainly explained by the fact that the event-based backtesting assumes the same amount for every position taken. Vectorized backtesting takes compound effects into account, leading to a slightly higher reported performance:

```
In [52]: ax = (tb.net_wealths / tb.net_wealths.iloc[0]).plot(figsize=(10, 6))
         tp = env.data[['r', 's']].iloc[env.lags:].cumsum().apply(np.exp)
         (tp / tp.iloc[0]).plot(ax=ax);
```

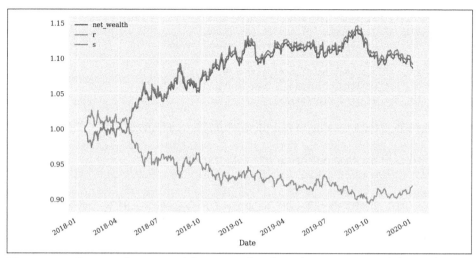

Figure 11-7. Gross performance of the passive benchmark investment and the trading bot (vectorized and event-based backtesting)

Performance Differences

The performance numbers from the vectorized and the event-based backtesting are close but not exactly the same. In the first case, it is assumed that financial instruments are perfectly divisible. Compounding is also done continuously. In the latter case, only full units of the financial instrument are accepted for trading, which is closer to reality. The net wealth calculations are based on price differences. The event-based code as it is used does not, for example, check whether the current balance is large enough to cover a certain trade by cash. This is for sure a simplifying assumption, and buying on margin, for instance, may not always be possible. Code adjustments in this regard are easily added to the `BacktestingBase` class.

Assessing Risk

The implementation of risk measures requires the understanding of the risks involved in trading the chosen financial instrument. Therefore, to properly set parameters for risk measures, such as stop loss orders, an assessment of the risk of the underlying instrument is important. There are many approaches available to measure the risk of a financial instrument. There are, for example, *nondirected risk measures*, such as volatility or average true range (ATR). There are also *directed measures*, such as maximum drawdown or value-at-risk (VaR).

A common practice when setting target levels for stop loss (SL), trailing stop loss (TSL), or take profit orders (TP) is to relate such levels to ATR values.[1] The following Python code calculates the ATR in absolute and relative terms for the financial instrument on which the trading bot is trained and backtested (that is, the EUR/USD exchange rate). The calculations rely on the data from the learning environment and use a typical window length of 14 days (bars). Figure 11-8 shows the calculated values, which vary significantly over time:

```
In [53]: data = pd.DataFrame(learn_env.data[symbol])    ❶

In [54]: data.head()    ❶
Out[54]:                EUR=
         Date
         2010-02-02 1.3961
         2010-02-03 1.3898
         2010-02-04 1.3734
         2010-02-05 1.3662
         2010-02-08 1.3652

In [55]: window = 14    ❷

In [56]: data['min'] = data[symbol].rolling(window).min()    ❸

In [57]: data['max'] = data[symbol].rolling(window).max()    ❹

In [58]: data['mami'] = data['max'] - data['min']    ❺

In [59]: data['mac'] = abs(data['max'] - data[symbol].shift(1))    ❻

In [60]: data['mic'] = abs(data['min'] - data[symbol].shift(1))    ❼

In [61]: data['atr'] = np.maximum(data['mami'], data['mac'])    ❽

In [62]: data['atr'] = np.maximum(data['atr'], data['mic'])    ❾

In [63]: data['atr%'] = data['atr'] / data[symbol]    ❿

In [64]: data[['atr', 'atr%']].plot(subplots=True, figsize=(10, 6));
```

❶ The instrument price column from the original `DataFrame` object

❷ The window length to be used for the calculations

❸ The rolling minimum

---

1 For more details on the ATR measure, see ATR (1) Investopedia (*https://oreil.ly/2sUsg*) or ATR (2) Investopedia (*https://oreil.ly/zwrnO*). The definition used in the Python code differs slightly from the one found in these references.

❹ The rolling maximum

❺ The difference between rolling maximum and minimum

❻ The absolute difference between rolling maximum and previous day's price

❼ The absolute difference between rolling minimum and previous day's price

❽ The maximum of the max-min difference and the max-price difference

❾ The maximum between the previous maximum and the min-price difference
    (= ATR)

❿ The ATR value in percent from the absolute ATR value and the price

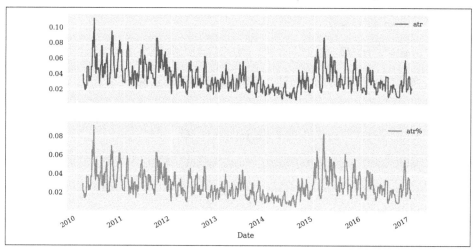

Figure 11-8. Average true range (ATR) in absolute (price) and relative (%) terms

The code that follows displays the final values for ATR in absolute and relative terms.
A typical rule would be to set, for example, the SL level at the entry price minus x
times ATR. Depending on the risk appetite of the trader or investor, x might be
smaller than 1 or larger. This is where human judgment or formal risk policies come
into play. If $x = 1$, then the SL level is set at about 2% below the entry level:

```
In [65]: data[['atr', 'atr%']].tail()
Out[65]:               atr    atr%
         Date
         2017-01-06  0.0218  0.0207
         2017-01-09  0.0218  0.0206
         2017-01-10  0.0218  0.0207
         2017-01-11  0.0199  0.0188
         2017-01-12  0.0206  0.0194
```

However, *leverage* plays an important role in this context. If a leverage of, say, 10 is used, which is actually quite low for foreign exchange trading, then the ATR numbers need to be multiplied by the leverage. As a consequence, for an assumed ATR factor of 1, the same SL level from before now is to be set at about 20% instead of just 2%. Or, when taking the median value of the ATR from the whole data set, it is set to be at about 25%:

```
In [66]: leverage = 10

In [67]: data[['atr', 'atr%']].tail() * leverage
Out[67]:                atr    atr%
         Date
         2017-01-06  0.2180  0.2070
         2017-01-09  0.2180  0.2062
         2017-01-10  0.2180  0.2066
         2017-01-11  0.1990  0.1881
         2017-01-12  0.2060  0.1942

In [68]: data[['atr', 'atr%']].median() * leverage
Out[68]: atr     0.3180
         atr%    0.2481
         dtype: float64
```

The basic idea behind relating SL or TP levels to ATR is that one should avoid setting them either too low or too high. Consider a 10 times leveraged position for which the ATR is 20%. Setting an SL level of only 3% or 5% might reduce the financial risk for the position, but it introduces the risk of a stop out that happens too early and that is due to typical movements in the financial instrument. Such "typical movements" within certain ranges are often called *noise*. The SL order should protect, in general, from unfavorable market movements that are larger than typical price movements (noise).

The same holds true for a take profit level. If it is set too high, say at three times the ATR level, decent profits might not be secured and positions might remain open for too long until they give up previous profits. Even if formal analyses and mathematical formulas can be used in this context, the setting of such target levels involves, as they say, more art than science. In a financial context, there is quite a degree of freedom for setting such target levels, and human judgment can come to the rescue. In other contexts, such as for AVs, this is different, as no human judgment is needed to instruct the AI to avoid any collisions with human beings.

NonNormality and NonLinearity

A *margin stop out* closes a trading position in cases when the margin, or the invested equity, is used up. Assume a leveraged trading position with a margin stop out in place. For a leverage of 10, for example, the margin is 10% equity. An *unfavorable* move of 10% or larger in the traded instrument eats up all the equity and triggers the close out of the position—a loss of 100% of the equity. A *favorable* move of the underlying of, say, 25% leads to a return on equity of 150%. Even if returns of the traded instrument are normally distributed, leverage and margin stop outs lead to nonnormally distributed returns and asymmetric, nonlinear relationships between the traded instrument and the trading position.

Backtesting Risk Measures

Having an idea of the ATR of a financial instrument is often a good start for the implementation of risk measures. To be able to properly backtest the effect of the typical risk management orders, some adjustments to the `BacktestingBase` class are helpful. The following Python code presents a new base class—`BacktestBaseRM`, which inherits from `BacktestingBase`—that helps in tracking the entry price of the previous trade as well as the maximum and minimum prices since that trade. These values are used to calculate the relevant performance measures during the event-based backtesting to which SL, TSL, and TP orders relate:

```
#
# Event-Based Backtesting
# --Base Class (2)
#
# (c) Dr. Yves J. Hilpisch
#
from backtesting import *


class BacktestingBaseRM(BacktestingBase):

    def set_prices(self, price):
        ''' Sets prices for tracking of performance.
            To test for e.g. trailing stop loss hit.
        '''
        self.entry_price = price      ❶
        self.min_price = price        ❷
        self.max_price = price        ❸

    def place_buy_order(self, bar, amount=None, units=None, gprice=None):
        ''' Places a buy order for a given bar and for
            a given amount or number of units.
        '''
        date, price = self.get_date_price(bar)
```

```
        if gprice is not None:
            price = gprice
        if units is None:
            units = int(amount / price)
        self.current_balance -= (1 + self.ptc) * units * price + self.ftc
        self.units += units
        self.trades += 1
        self.set_prices(price)  ❹
        if self.verbose:
            print(f'{date} | buy {units} units for {price:.4f}')
            self.print_balance(bar)

    def place_sell_order(self, bar, amount=None, units=None, gprice=None):
        ''' Places a sell order for a given bar and for
            a given amount or number of units.
        '''
        date, price = self.get_date_price(bar)
        if gprice is not None:
            price = gprice
        if units is None:
            units = int(amount / price)
        self.current_balance += (1 - self.ptc) * units * price - self.ftc
        self.units -= units
        self.trades += 1
        self.set_prices(price)  ❹
        if self.verbose:
            print(f'{date} | sell {units} units for {price:.4f}')
            self.print_balance(bar)
```

❶ Sets the *entry* price for the most recent trade

❷ Sets the initial *minimum* price since the most ecent trade

❸ Sets the initial *maximum* price since the most recent trade

❹ Sets the relevant prices after a trade is executed

Based on this new base class, "Backtesting Class" on page 342 presents a new back-testing class, TBBacktesterRM, that allows the inclusion of SL, TSL, and TP orders. The relevant code parts are discussed in the following sub-sections. The parametriza-tion of the backtesting examples orients itself roughly on an ATR level of about 2%, as calculated in the previous section.

EUT and Risk Measures

EUT, MVP, and the CAPM (see Chapters 3 and 4) assume that financial agents know about the future distribution of the returns of a financial instrument. MPT and the CAPM assume furthermore that returns are normally distributed and that there is, for example, a linear relationship between the market portfolio's returns and the returns of a traded financial instrument. The use of SL, TSL, and TP orders leads—similar and in addition to leverage in combination with margin stop out—to a "guaranteed nonnormal" distribution and to highly asymmetric, nonlinear payoffs of a trading position in relation to the traded instrument.

Stop Loss

The first risk measure is the SL order. It fixes a certain price level or, more often, a fixed percent value that triggers the closing of a position. For example, if the entry price for an unleveraged position is 100 and the SL level is set to 5%, then a long position is closed out at 95 while a short position is closed out at 105.

The following Python code is the relevant part of the `TBBacktesterRM` class that handles an SL order. For the SL order, the class allows one to specify whether the price level for the order is guaranteed or not.[2] Working with guaranteed SL price levels might lead to too-optimistic performance results:

```
# stop loss order
if sl is not None and self.position != 0:     ❶
    rc = (price - self.entry_price) / self.entry_price     ❷
    if self.position == 1 and rc < -self.sl:     ❸
        print(50 * '-')
        if guarantee:
            price = self.entry_price * (1 - self.sl)
            print(f'*** STOP LOSS (LONG  | {-self.sl:.4f}) ***')
        else:
            print(f'*** STOP LOSS (LONG  | {rc:.4f}) ***')
        self.place_sell_order(bar, units=self.units, gprice=price)     ❹
        self.wait = wait     ❺
        self.position = 0     ❻
    elif self.position == -1 and rc > self.sl:     ❼
        print(50 * '-')
        if guarantee:
            price = self.entry_price * (1 + self.sl)
            print(f'*** STOP LOSS (SHORT | -{self.sl:.4f}) ***')
        else:
            print(f'*** STOP LOSS (SHORT | -{rc:.4f}) ***')
```

---

2 A *guaranteed* stop loss order might only be available in certain jurisdictions for certain groups of broker clients, such as retail investors/traders.

```
        self.place_buy_order(bar, units=-self.units, gprice=price)  ➑
        self.wait = wait  ➎
        self.position = 0  ➏
```

➊ Checks whether an SL is defined and whether the position is not neutral

➋ Calculates the performance based on the entry price for the last trade

➌ Checks whether an SL event is given for a *long* position

➍ Closes the *long* position, at either the current price or the guaranteed price level

➎ Sets the number of bars to wait before the next trade happens to `wait`

➏ Sets the position to neutral

➐ Checks whether an SL event is given for a *short* position

➑ Closes the *short* position, at either the current price or the guaranteed price level

The following Python code backtests the trading strategy of the trading bot without and with an SL order. For the given parametrization, the SL order has a negative impact on the strategy performance:

```
In [69]: import tbbacktesterrm as tbbrm

In [70]: env = test_env

In [71]: tb = tbbrm.TBBacktesterRM(env, agent.model, 10000,
                                   0.0, 0, verbose=False)  ➊

In [72]: tb.backtest_strategy(sl=None, tsl=None, tp=None, wait=5)  ➋
         ==================================================
         2018-01-17 | *** START BACKTEST ***
         2018-01-17 | current balance = 10000.00
         ==================================================
         ==================================================
         2019-12-31 | *** CLOSING OUT ***
         2019-12-31 | current balance = 10936.79
         2019-12-31 | net performance [%] = 9.3679
         2019-12-31 | number of trades [#] = 186
         ==================================================

In [73]: tb.backtest_strategy(sl=0.0175, tsl=None, tp=None,
                              wait=5, guarantee=False)  ➌
         ==================================================
         2018-01-17 | *** START BACKTEST ***
         2018-01-17 | current balance = 10000.00
         ==================================================
         --------------------------------------------------
```

```
      *** STOP LOSS (SHORT | -0.0203) ***
      =================================================
      2019-12-31 | *** CLOSING OUT ***
      2019-12-31 | current balance = 10717.32
      2019-12-31 | net performance [%] = 7.1732
      2019-12-31 | number of trades [#] = 188
      =================================================

In [74]: tb.backtest_strategy(sl=0.017, tsl=None, tp=None,
                               wait=5, guarantee=True)  ❹
      =================================================
      2018-01-17 | *** START BACKTEST ***
      2018-01-17 | current balance = 10000.00
      =================================================
      -------------------------------------------------
      *** STOP LOSS (SHORT | -0.0170) ***
      =================================================
      2019-12-31 | *** CLOSING OUT ***
      2019-12-31 | current balance = 10753.52
      2019-12-31 | net performance [%] = 7.5352
      2019-12-31 | number of trades [#] = 188
      =================================================
```

❶ Instantiates the backtesting class for risk management

❷ Backtests the trading bot performance without any risk measure

❸ Backtests the trading bot performance with an SL order (*no* guarantee)

❹ Backtests the trading bot performance with an SL order (*with* guarantee)

Trailing Stop Loss

In contrast to a regular SL order, a TSL order is adjusted whenever a new high is observed after the base order has been placed. Assume the base order for an unleveraged long position has an entry price of 95 and the TSL is set to 5%. If the instrument price reaches 100 and falls back to 95, this implies a TSL event, and the position is closed at the entry price level. If the price reaches 110 and falls back to 104.5, this would imply another TSL event.

The following Python code is the relevant part of the TBBacktesterRM class that handles a TSL order. To handle such an order correctly, the maximum prices (highs) and the minimum prices (lows) need to be tracked. The maximum price is relevant for a long position, whereas the minimum price is relevant for a short position:

```
# trailing stop loss order
if tsl is not None and self.position != 0:
    self.max_price = max(self.max_price, price)  ❶
    self.min_price = min(self.min_price, price)  ❷
```

```
        rc_1 = (price - self.max_price) / self.entry_price    ❸
        rc_2 = (self.min_price - price) / self.entry_price     ❹
        if self.position == 1 and rc_1 < -self.tsl:    ❺
            print(50 * '-')
            print(f'*** TRAILING SL (LONG  | {rc_1:.4f}) ***')
            self.place_sell_order(bar, units=self.units)
            self.wait = wait
            self.position = 0
        elif self.position == -1 and rc_2 < -self.tsl:    ❻
            print(50 * '-')
            print(f'*** TRAILING SL (SHORT | {rc_2:.4f}) ***')
            self.place_buy_order(bar, units=-self.units)
            self.wait = wait
            self.position = 0
```

❶ Updates the *maximum* price if necessary

❷ Updates the *minimum* price if necessary

❸ Calculates the relevant performance for a *long* position

❹ Calculates the relevant performance for a *short* position

❺ Checks whether a TSL event is given for a *long* position

❻ Checks whether a TSL event is given for a *short* position

As the backtesting results that follow show, using a TSL order with the given parametrization reduces the gross performance compared to a strategy without a TSL order in place:

```
In [75]: tb.backtest_strategy(sl=None, tsl=0.015,
                              tp=None, wait=5)    ❶
         ==================================================
         2018-01-17 | *** START BACKTEST ***
         2018-01-17 | current balance = 10000.00
         ==================================================
         --------------------------------------------------
         *** TRAILING SL (SHORT | -0.0152) ***
         --------------------------------------------------
         *** TRAILING SL (SHORT | -0.0169) ***
         --------------------------------------------------
         *** TRAILING SL (SHORT | -0.0164) ***
         --------------------------------------------------
         *** TRAILING SL (SHORT | -0.0191) ***
         --------------------------------------------------
         *** TRAILING SL (SHORT | -0.0166) ***
         --------------------------------------------------
         *** TRAILING SL (SHORT | -0.0194) ***
         --------------------------------------------------
```

```
*** TRAILING SL (SHORT | -0.0172) ***
--------------------------------------------------
*** TRAILING SL (SHORT | -0.0181) ***
--------------------------------------------------
*** TRAILING SL (SHORT | -0.0153) ***
--------------------------------------------------
*** TRAILING SL (SHORT | -0.0160) ***
==================================================
2019-12-31 | *** CLOSING OUT ***
2019-12-31 | current balance = 10577.93
2019-12-31 | net performance [%] = 5.7793
2019-12-31 | number of trades [#] = 201
==================================================
```

❶ Backtests the trading bot performance with a TSL order

Take Profit

Finally, there are TP orders. A TP order closes out a position that has reached a certain profit level. Say an unleveraged long position is opened at a price of 100 and the TP order is set to a level of 5%. If the price reaches 105, the position is closed.

The following code from the TBBacktesterRM class finally shows the part that handles a TP order. The TP implementation is straightforward, given the references of the SL and TSL order codes. For the TP order, there is also the option to backtest with a guaranteed price level as compared to the relevant high/low price levels, which would most probably lead to performance values that are too optimistic:[3]

```
# take profit order
if tp is not None and self.position != 0:
    rc = (price - self.entry_price) / self.entry_price
    if self.position == 1 and rc > self.tp:
        print(50 * '-')
        if guarantee:
            price = self.entry_price * (1 + self.tp)
            print(f'*** TAKE PROFIT (LONG  | {self.tp:.4f}) ***')
        else:
            print(f'*** TAKE PROFIT (LONG  | {rc:.4f}) ***')
        self.place_sell_order(bar, units=self.units, gprice=price)
        self.wait = wait
        self.position = 0
    elif self.position == -1 and rc < -self.tp:
        print(50 * '-')
        if guarantee:
            price = self.entry_price * (1 - self.tp)
            print(f'*** TAKE PROFIT (SHORT | {self.tp:.4f}) ***')
```

---

3 A take profit order has a fixed target price level. Therefore, it is unrealistic to use the high price of a time interval for a long position or the low price of the interval for a short position to calculate the realized profit.

```
        else:
            print(f'*** TAKE PROFIT (SHORT | {-rc:.4f}) ***')
        self.place_buy_order(bar, units=-self.units, gprice=price)
        self.wait = wait
        self.position = 0
```

For the given parametrization, adding a TP order—without guarantee—improves the trading bot performance noticeably compared to the passive benchmark investment. This result might be too optimistic given the considerations from before. Therefore, the TP order with guarantee leads to a more realistic performance value in this case:

```
In [76]: tb.backtest_strategy(sl=None, tsl=None, tp=0.015,
                              wait=5, guarantee=False)   ❶
         ==================================================
         2018-01-17 | *** START BACKTEST ***
         2018-01-17 | current balance = 10000.00
         ==================================================
         --------------------------------------------------
         *** TAKE PROFIT (SHORT | 0.0155) ***
         --------------------------------------------------
         *** TAKE PROFIT (SHORT | 0.0155) ***
         --------------------------------------------------
         *** TAKE PROFIT (SHORT | 0.0204) ***
         --------------------------------------------------
         *** TAKE PROFIT (SHORT | 0.0240) ***
         --------------------------------------------------
         *** TAKE PROFIT (SHORT | 0.0168) ***
         --------------------------------------------------
         *** TAKE PROFIT (SHORT | 0.0156) ***
         --------------------------------------------------
         *** TAKE PROFIT (SHORT | 0.0183) ***
         ==================================================
         2019-12-31 | *** CLOSING OUT ***
         2019-12-31 | current balance = 11210.33
         2019-12-31 | net performance [%] = 12.1033
         2019-12-31 | number of trades [#] = 198
         ==================================================

In [77]: tb.backtest_strategy(sl=None, tsl=None, tp=0.015,
                              wait=5, guarantee=True)   ❷
         ==================================================
         2018-01-17 | *** START BACKTEST ***
         2018-01-17 | current balance = 10000.00
         ==================================================
         --------------------------------------------------
         *** TAKE PROFIT (SHORT | 0.0150) ***
         --------------------------------------------------
         *** TAKE PROFIT (SHORT | 0.0150) ***
         --------------------------------------------------
         *** TAKE PROFIT (SHORT | 0.0150) ***
         --------------------------------------------------
         *** TAKE PROFIT (SHORT | 0.0150) ***
```

```
          -----------------------------------------------
          *** TAKE PROFIT (SHORT | 0.0150) ***
          -----------------------------------------------
          *** TAKE PROFIT (SHORT | 0.0150) ***
          -----------------------------------------------
          *** TAKE PROFIT (SHORT | 0.0150) ***
          ===============================================
          2019-12-31 | *** CLOSING OUT ***
          2019-12-31 | current balance = 10980.86
          2019-12-31 | net performance [%] = 9.8086
          2019-12-31 | number of trades [#] = 198
          ===============================================
```

❶ Backtests the trading bot performance with a TP order (*no* guarantee)

❷ Backtests the trading bot performance with a TP order (*with* guarantee)

Of course, SL/TSL orders can also be combined with TP orders. The backtest results of the Python code that follows are in both cases worse than those for the strategy without the risk measures in place. In managing risk, there is hardly any free lunch:

```
In [78]: tb.backtest_strategy(sl=0.015, tsl=None,
                              tp=0.0185, wait=5)  ❶
          ===============================================
          2018-01-17 | *** START BACKTEST ***
          2018-01-17 | current balance = 10000.00
          ===============================================
          -----------------------------------------------
          *** STOP LOSS (SHORT | -0.0203) ***
          -----------------------------------------------
          *** TAKE PROFIT (SHORT | 0.0202) ***
          -----------------------------------------------
          *** TAKE PROFIT (SHORT | 0.0213) ***
          -----------------------------------------------
          *** TAKE PROFIT (SHORT | 0.0240) ***
          -----------------------------------------------
          *** STOP LOSS (SHORT | -0.0171) ***
          -----------------------------------------------
          *** TAKE PROFIT (SHORT | 0.0188) ***
          -----------------------------------------------
          *** STOP LOSS (SHORT | -0.0153) ***
          -----------------------------------------------
          *** STOP LOSS (SHORT | -0.0154) ***
          ===============================================
          2019-12-31 | *** CLOSING OUT ***
          2019-12-31 | current balance = 10552.00
          2019-12-31 | net performance [%] = 5.5200
          2019-12-31 | number of trades [#] = 201
          ===============================================

In [79]: tb.backtest_strategy(sl=None, tsl=0.02,
                              tp=0.02, wait=5)  ❷
```

```
=======================================================
2018-01-17 | *** START BACKTEST ***
2018-01-17 | current balance = 10000.00
=======================================================
-------------------------------------------------------
*** TRAILING SL (SHORT | -0.0235) ***
-------------------------------------------------------
*** TRAILING SL (SHORT | -0.0202) ***
-------------------------------------------------------
*** TAKE PROFIT (SHORT | 0.0250) ***
-------------------------------------------------------
*** TAKE PROFIT (SHORT | 0.0227) ***
-------------------------------------------------------
*** TAKE PROFIT (SHORT | 0.0240) ***
-------------------------------------------------------
*** TRAILING SL (SHORT | -0.0216) ***
-------------------------------------------------------
*** TAKE PROFIT (SHORT | 0.0241) ***
-------------------------------------------------------
*** TRAILING SL (SHORT | -0.0206) ***
=======================================================
2019-12-31 | *** CLOSING OUT ***
2019-12-31 | current balance = 10346.38
2019-12-31 | net performance [%] = 3.4638
2019-12-31 | number of trades [#] = 198
=======================================================
```

❶ Backtests the trading bot performance with an SL and TP order

❷ Backtests the trading bot performance with a TSL and TP order

Performance Impact

Risk measures have their reasoning and benefits. However, reducing risk may come at the price of lower overall performance. On the other hand, the backtesting example with the TP order shows performance improvements that can be explained by the fact that, given the ATR of a financial instrument, a certain profit level can be considered good enough to realize the profit. Any hope to see even higher profits typically is smashed by the market turning around again.

Conclusions

This chapter has three main topics. It backtests the performance of a trading bot (that is, a trained deep Q-learning agent) out-of-sample in both vectorized and event-based fashion. It also assesses risks in the form of the average true range (ATR) indicator that measures the *typical* variation in the price of the financial instrument of interest. Finally, the chapter discusses and backtests event-based typical risk measures in the form of stop loss (SL), trailing stop loss (TSL), and take profit (TP) orders.

Similar to autonomous vehicles (AVs), trading bots are hardly ever deployed based on the predictions of their AI only. To avoid large downside risks and to improve the (risk-adjusted) performance, risk measures usually come into play. Standard risk measures, as discussed in this chapter, are available on almost every trading platform, as well as for retail traders. The next chapter illustrates this in the context of the Oanda (*http://oanda.com*) trading platform. The event-based backtesting approach provides the algorithmic flexibility to properly backtest the effects of such risk measures. While "reducing risk" may sound appealing, the backtest results indicate that the reduction in risk often comes at a cost: the performance might be lower when compared to the pure strategy without any risk measures. However, when finely tuned, the results also show that TP orders, for example, can also have a positive effect on the performance.

References

Books and papers cited in this chapter:

Agrawal, Ajay, Joshua Gans, and Avi Goldfarb. 2018. *Prediction Machines: The Simple Economics of Artificial Intelligence.* Boston: Harvard Business Review Press.

Hilpisch, Yves. 2020. *Python for Algorithmic Trading: From Idea to Cloud Deployment.* Sebastopol: O'Reilly.

Khonji, Majid, Jorge Dias, and Lakmal Seneviratne. 2019. "Risk-Aware Reasoning for Autonomous Vehicles." arXiv. October 6, 2019. *https://oreil.ly/2Z6WR*.

Python Code

Finance Environment

The following is the Python module with the `Finance` environment class:

```python
#
# Finance Environment
#
# (c) Dr. Yves J. Hilpisch
# Artificial Intelligence in Finance
#
import math
import random
import numpy as np
import pandas as pd


class observation_space:
    def __init__(self, n):
        self.shape = (n,)


class action_space:
    def __init__(self, n):
        self.n = n

    def sample(self):
        return random.randint(0, self.n - 1)


class Finance:
    intraday = False
    if intraday:
        url = 'http://hilpisch.com/aiif_eikon_id_eur_usd.csv'
    else:
        url = 'http://hilpisch.com/aiif_eikon_eod_data.csv'

    def __init__(self, symbol, features, window, lags,
                 leverage=1, min_performance=0.85, min_accuracy=0.5,
                 start=0, end=None, mu=None, std=None):
        self.symbol = symbol
        self.features = features
        self.n_features = len(features)
        self.window = window
        self.lags = lags
        self.leverage = leverage
        self.min_performance = min_performance
        self.min_accuracy = min_accuracy
        self.start = start
        self.end = end
```

```python
        self.mu = mu
        self.std = std
        self.observation_space = observation_space(self.lags)
        self.action_space = action_space(2)
        self._get_data()
        self._prepare_data()

    def _get_data(self):
        self.raw = pd.read_csv(self.url, index_col=0,
                                parse_dates=True).dropna()
        if self.intraday:
            self.raw = self.raw.resample('30min', label='right').last()
            self.raw = pd.DataFrame(self.raw['CLOSE'])
            self.raw.columns = [self.symbol]

    def _prepare_data(self):
        self.data = pd.DataFrame(self.raw[self.symbol])
        self.data = self.data.iloc[self.start:]
        self.data['r'] = np.log(self.data / self.data.shift(1))
        self.data.dropna(inplace=True)
        self.data['s'] = self.data[self.symbol].rolling(self.window).mean()
        self.data['m'] = self.data['r'].rolling(self.window).mean()
        self.data['v'] = self.data['r'].rolling(self.window).std()
        self.data.dropna(inplace=True)
        if self.mu is None:
            self.mu = self.data.mean()
            self.std = self.data.std()
        self.data_ = (self.data - self.mu) / self.std
        self.data['d'] = np.where(self.data['r'] > 0, 1, 0)
        self.data['d'] = self.data['d'].astype(int)
        if self.end is not None:
            self.data = self.data.iloc[:self.end - self.start]
            self.data_ = self.data_.iloc[:self.end - self.start]

    def _get_state(self):
        return self.data_[self.features].iloc[self.bar -
                                        self.lags:self.bar]

    def get_state(self, bar):
        return self.data_[self.features].iloc[bar - self.lags:bar]

    def seed(self, seed):
        random.seed(seed)
        np.random.seed(seed)

    def reset(self):
        self.treward = 0
        self.accuracy = 0
        self.performance = 1
        self.bar = self.lags
        state = self.data_[self.features].iloc[self.bar -
                                        self.lags:self.bar]
```

```
        return state.values

    def step(self, action):
        correct = action == self.data['d'].iloc[self.bar]
        ret = self.data['r'].iloc[self.bar] * self.leverage
        reward_1 = 1 if correct else 0
        reward_2 = abs(ret) if correct else -abs(ret)
        self.treward += reward_1
        self.bar += 1
        self.accuracy = self.treward / (self.bar - self.lags)
        self.performance *= math.exp(reward_2)
        if self.bar >= len(self.data):
            done = True
        elif reward_1 == 1:
            done = False
        elif (self.performance < self.min_performance and
                self.bar > self.lags + 15):
            done = True
        elif (self.accuracy < self.min_accuracy and
                self.bar > self.lags + 15):
            done = True
        else:
            done = False
        state = self._get_state()
        info = {}
        return state.values, reward_1 + reward_2 * 5, done, info
```

Trading Bot

The following is the Python module with the `TradingBot` class, based on a financial Q-learning agent:

```
#
# Financial Q-Learning Agent
#
# (c) Dr. Yves J. Hilpisch
# Artificial Intelligence in Finance
#
import os
import random
import numpy as np
from pylab import plt, mpl
from collections import deque
import tensorflow as tf
from keras.layers import Dense, Dropout
from keras.models import Sequential
from keras.optimizers import Adam, RMSprop

os.environ['PYTHONHASHSEED'] = '0'
plt.style.use('seaborn')
mpl.rcParams['savefig.dpi'] = 300
mpl.rcParams['font.family'] = 'serif'
```

```
def set_seeds(seed=100):
    ''' Function to set seeds for all
        random number generators.
    '''
    random.seed(seed)
    np.random.seed(seed)
    tf.random.set_seed(seed)


class TradingBot:
    def __init__(self, hidden_units, learning_rate, learn_env,
                 valid_env=None, val=True, dropout=False):
        self.learn_env = learn_env
        self.valid_env = valid_env
        self.val = val
        self.epsilon = 1.0
        self.epsilon_min = 0.1
        self.epsilon_decay = 0.99
        self.learning_rate = learning_rate
        self.gamma = 0.5
        self.batch_size = 128
        self.max_treward = 0
        self.averages = list()
        self.trewards = []
        self.performances = list()
        self.aperformances = list()
        self.vperformances = list()
        self.memory = deque(maxlen=2000)
        self.model = self._build_model(hidden_units,
                                       learning_rate, dropout)

    def _build_model(self, hu, lr, dropout):
        ''' Method to create the DNN model.
        '''
        model = Sequential()
        model.add(Dense(hu, input_shape=(
            self.learn_env.lags, self.learn_env.n_features),
            activation='relu'))
        if dropout:
            model.add(Dropout(0.3, seed=100))
        model.add(Dense(hu, activation='relu'))
        if dropout:
            model.add(Dropout(0.3, seed=100))
        model.add(Dense(2, activation='linear'))
        model.compile(
            loss='mse',
            optimizer=RMSprop(lr=lr)
        )
        return model
```

```python
    def act(self, state):
        ''' Method for taking action based on
            a) exploration
            b) exploitation
        '''
        if random.random() <= self.epsilon:
            return self.learn_env.action_space.sample()
        action = self.model.predict(state)[0, 0]
        return np.argmax(action)

    def replay(self):
        ''' Method to retrain the DNN model based on
            batches of memorized experiences.
        '''
        batch = random.sample(self.memory, self.batch_size)
        for state, action, reward, next_state, done in batch:
            if not done:
                reward += self.gamma * np.amax(
                    self.model.predict(next_state)[0, 0])
            target = self.model.predict(state)
            target[0, 0, action] = reward
            self.model.fit(state, target, epochs=1,
                           verbose=False)
        if self.epsilon > self.epsilon_min:
            self.epsilon *= self.epsilon_decay

    def learn(self, episodes):
        ''' Method to train the DQL agent.
        '''
        for e in range(1, episodes + 1):
            state = self.learn_env.reset()
            state = np.reshape(state, [1, self.learn_env.lags,
                                       self.learn_env.n_features])
            for _ in range(10000):
                action = self.act(state)
                next_state, reward, done, info = self.learn_env.step(action)
                next_state = np.reshape(next_state,
                                        [1, self.learn_env.lags,
                                         self.learn_env.n_features])
                self.memory.append([state, action, reward,
                                    next_state, done])
                state = next_state
                if done:
                    treward = _ + 1
                    self.trewards.append(treward)
                    av = sum(self.trewards[-25:]) / 25
                    perf = self.learn_env.performance
                    self.averages.append(av)
                    self.performances.append(perf)
                    self.aperformances.append(
                        sum(self.performances[-25:]) / 25)
                    self.max_treward = max(self.max_treward, treward)
```

```
            templ = 'episode: {:2d}/{} | treward: {:4d} | '
            templ += 'perf: {:5.3f} | av: {:5.1f} | max: {:4d}'
            print(templ.format(e, episodes, treward, perf,
                                av, self.max_treward), end='\r')
                break
        if self.val:
            self.validate(e, episodes)
        if len(self.memory) > self.batch_size:
            self.replay()
    print()

def validate(self, e, episodes):
    ''' Method to validate the performance of the
        DQL agent.
    '''
    state = self.valid_env.reset()
    state = np.reshape(state, [1, self.valid_env.lags,
                              self.valid_env.n_features])
    for _ in range(10000):
        action = np.argmax(self.model.predict(state)[0, 0])
        next_state, reward, done, info = self.valid_env.step(action)
        state = np.reshape(next_state, [1, self.valid_env.lags,
                                       self.valid_env.n_features])
        if done:
            treward = _ + 1
            perf = self.valid_env.performance
            self.vperformances.append(perf)
            if e % int(episodes / 6) == 0:
                templ = 71 * '='
                templ += '\nepisode: {:2d}/{} | VALIDATION | '
                templ += 'treward: {:4d} | perf: {:5.3f} | eps: {:.2f}\n'
                templ += 71 * '='
                print(templ.format(e, episodes, treward,
                                    perf, self.epsilon))
            break


def plot_treward(agent):
    ''' Function to plot the total reward
        per training episode.
    '''
    plt.figure(figsize=(10, 6))
    x = range(1, len(agent.averages) + 1)
    y = np.polyval(np.polyfit(x, agent.averages, deg=3), x)
    plt.plot(x, agent.averages, label='moving average')
    plt.plot(x, y, 'r--', label='regression')
    plt.xlabel('episodes')
    plt.ylabel('total reward')
    plt.legend()


def plot_performance(agent):
```

```
''' Function to plot the financial gross
    performance per training episode.
'''
plt.figure(figsize=(10, 6))
x = range(1, len(agent.performances) + 1)
y = np.polyval(np.polyfit(x, agent.performances, deg=3), x)
plt.plot(x, agent.performances[:], label='training')
plt.plot(x, y, 'r--', label='regression (train)')
if agent.val:
    y_ = np.polyval(np.polyfit(x, agent.vperformances, deg=3), x)
    plt.plot(x, agent.vperformances[:], label='validation')
    plt.plot(x, y_, 'r-.', label='regression (valid)')
plt.xlabel('episodes')
plt.ylabel('gross performance')
plt.legend()
```

Backtesting Base Class

The following is the Python module with the `BacktestingBase` class for event-based backtesting:

```
#
# Event-Based Backtesting
# --Base Class (1)
#
# (c) Dr. Yves J. Hilpisch
# Artificial Intelligence in Finance
#


class BacktestingBase:
    def __init__(self, env, model, amount, ptc, ftc, verbose=False):
        self.env = env                            ❶
        self.model = model                        ❷
        self.initial_amount = amount              ❸
        self.current_balance = amount             ❸
        self.ptc = ptc                            ❹
        self.ftc = ftc                            ❺
        self.verbose = verbose                    ❻
        self.units = 0                            ❼
        self.trades = 0                           ❽

    def get_date_price(self, bar):
        ''' Returns date and price for a given bar.
        '''
        date = str(self.env.data.index[bar])[:10]     ❾
        price = self.env.data[self.env.symbol].iloc[bar]   ❿
        return date, price

    def print_balance(self, bar):
        ''' Prints the current cash balance for a given bar.
        '''
```

```
        date, price = self.get_date_price(bar)
        print(f'{date} | current balance = {self.current_balance:.2f}')   ⑪

    def calculate_net_wealth(self, price):
        return self.current_balance + self.units * price   ⑫

    def print_net_wealth(self, bar):
        ''' Prints the net wealth for a given bar
            (cash + position).
        '''
        date, price = self.get_date_price(bar)
        net_wealth = self.calculate_net_wealth(price)
        print(f'{date} | net wealth = {net_wealth:.2f}')   ⑬

    def place_buy_order(self, bar, amount=None, units=None):
        ''' Places a buy order for a given bar and for
            a given amount or number of units.
        '''
        date, price = self.get_date_price(bar)
        if units is None:
            units = int(amount / price)   ⑭
            # units = amount / price   ⑭
        self.current_balance -= (1 + self.ptc) * \
            units * price + self.ftc   ⑮
        self.units += units   ⑯
        self.trades += 1   ⑰
        if self.verbose:
            print(f'{date} | buy {units} units for {price:.4f}')
            self.print_balance(bar)

    def place_sell_order(self, bar, amount=None, units=None):
        ''' Places a sell order for a given bar and for
            a given amount or number of units.
        '''
        date, price = self.get_date_price(bar)
        if units is None:
            units = int(amount / price)   ⑭
            # units = amount / price   ⑭
        self.current_balance += (1 - self.ptc) * \
            units * price - self.ftc   ⑮
        self.units -= units   ⑯
        self.trades += 1   ⑰
        if self.verbose:
            print(f'{date} | sell {units} units for {price:.4f}')
            self.print_balance(bar)

    def close_out(self, bar):
        ''' Closes out any open position at a given bar.
        '''
        date, price = self.get_date_price(bar)
        print(50 * '=')
        print(f'{date} | *** CLOSING OUT ***')
```

```
        if self.units < 0:
            self.place_buy_order(bar, units=-self.units)    ⓲
        else:
            self.place_sell_order(bar, units=self.units)    ⓳
        if not self.verbose:
            print(f'{date} | current balance = {self.current_balance:.2f}')
        perf = (self.current_balance / self.initial_amount - 1) * 100    ⓴
        print(f'{date} | net performance [%] = {perf:.4f}')
        print(f'{date} | number of trades [#] = {self.trades}')
        print(50 * '=')
```

❶ The relevant Finance environment

❷ The relevant DNN model (from the trading bot)

❸ The initial/current balance

❹ Proportional transaction costs

❺ Fixed transaction costs

❻ Whether the prints are verbose or not

❼ The initial number of units of the financial instrument traded

❽ The initial number of trades implemented

❾ The relevant *date* given a certain bar

❿ The relevant *instrument price* at a certain bar

⓫ The output of the *date* and *current balance* for a certain bar

⓬ The calculation of the *net wealth* from the current balance and the instrument position

⓭ The output of the *date* and the *net wealth* at a certain bar

⓮ The number of units to be traded given the trade amount

⓯ The impact of the trade and the associated costs on the current balance

⓰ The adjustment of the number of units held

⓱ The adjustment of the number of trades implemented

① The closing of a *short* position...

⑲ ...or of a *long* position

⑳ The net performance given the initial amount and the final current balance

Backtesting Class

The following is the Python module with the `TBBacktesterRM` class for event-based backtesting including risk measures (stop loss, trailing stop loss, take profit orders):

```python
#
# Event-Based Backtesting
# --Trading Bot Backtester
# (incl. Risk Management)
#
# (c) Dr. Yves J. Hilpisch
#
import numpy as np
import pandas as pd
import backtestingrm as btr


class TBBacktesterRM(btr.BacktestingBaseRM):
    def _reshape(self, state):
        ''' Helper method to reshape state objects.
        '''
        return np.reshape(state, [1, self.env.lags, self.env.n_features])

    def backtest_strategy(self, sl=None, tsl=None, tp=None,
                          wait=5, guarantee=False):
        ''' Event-based backtesting of the trading bot's performance.
            Incl. stop loss, trailing stop loss and take profit.
        '''
        self.units = 0
        self.position = 0
        self.trades = 0
        self.sl = sl
        self.tsl = tsl
        self.tp = tp
        self.wait = 0
        self.current_balance = self.initial_amount
        self.net_wealths = list()
        for bar in range(self.env.lags, len(self.env.data)):
            self.wait = max(0, self.wait - 1)
            date, price = self.get_date_price(bar)
            if self.trades == 0:
                print(50 * '=')
                print(f'{date} | *** START BACKTEST ***')
                self.print_balance(bar)
                print(50 * '=')
```

```python
        # stop loss order
        if sl is not None and self.position != 0:
            rc = (price - self.entry_price) / self.entry_price
            if self.position == 1 and rc < -self.sl:
                print(50 * '-')
                if guarantee:
                    price = self.entry_price * (1 - self.sl)
                    print(f'*** STOP LOSS (LONG  | {-self.sl:.4f}) ***')
                else:
                    print(f'*** STOP LOSS (LONG  | {rc:.4f}) ***')
                self.place_sell_order(bar, units=self.units, gprice=price)
                self.wait = wait
                self.position = 0
            elif self.position == -1 and rc > self.sl:
                print(50 * '-')
                if guarantee:
                    price = self.entry_price * (1 + self.sl)
                    print(f'*** STOP LOSS (SHORT | -{self.sl:.4f}) ***')
                else:
                    print(f'*** STOP LOSS (SHORT | -{rc:.4f}) ***')
                self.place_buy_order(bar, units=-self.units, gprice=price)
                self.wait = wait
                self.position = 0

        # trailing stop loss order
        if tsl is not None and self.position != 0:
            self.max_price = max(self.max_price, price)
            self.min_price = min(self.min_price, price)
            rc_1 = (price - self.max_price) / self.entry_price
            rc_2 = (self.min_price - price) / self.entry_price
            if self.position == 1 and rc_1 < -self.tsl:
                print(50 * '-')
                print(f'*** TRAILING SL (LONG  | {rc_1:.4f}) ***')
                self.place_sell_order(bar, units=self.units)
                self.wait = wait
                self.position = 0
            elif self.position == -1 and rc_2 < -self.tsl:
                print(50 * '-')
                print(f'*** TRAILING SL (SHORT | {rc_2:.4f}) ***')
                self.place_buy_order(bar, units=-self.units)
                self.wait = wait
                self.position = 0

        # take profit order
        if tp is not None and self.position != 0:
            rc = (price - self.entry_price) / self.entry_price
            if self.position == 1 and rc > self.tp:
                print(50 * '-')
                if guarantee:
                    price = self.entry_price * (1 + self.tp)
                    print(f'*** TAKE PROFIT (LONG  | {self.tp:.4f}) ***')
```

```
            else:
                print(f'*** TAKE PROFIT (LONG  | {rc:.4f}) ***')
            self.place_sell_order(bar, units=self.units, gprice=price)
            self.wait = wait
            self.position = 0
        elif self.position == -1 and rc < -self.tp:
            print(50 * '-')
            if guarantee:
                price = self.entry_price * (1 - self.tp)
                print(f'*** TAKE PROFIT (SHORT | {self.tp:.4f}) ***')
            else:
                print(f'*** TAKE PROFIT (SHORT | {-rc:.4f}) ***')
            self.place_buy_order(bar, units=-self.units, gprice=price)
            self.wait = wait
            self.position = 0

    state = self.env.get_state(bar)
    action = np.argmax(self.model.predict(
        self._reshape(state.values))[0, 0])
    position = 1 if action == 1 else -1
    if self.position in [0, -1] and position == 1 and self.wait == 0:
        if self.verbose:
            print(50 * '-')
            print(f'{date} | *** GOING LONG ***')
        if self.position == -1:
            self.place_buy_order(bar - 1, units=-self.units)
        self.place_buy_order(bar - 1, amount=self.current_balance)
        if self.verbose:
            self.print_net_wealth(bar)
        self.position = 1
    elif self.position in [0, 1] and position == -1 and self.wait == 0:
        if self.verbose:
            print(50 * '-')
            print(f'{date} | *** GOING SHORT ***')
        if self.position == 1:
            self.place_sell_order(bar - 1, units=self.units)
        self.place_sell_order(bar - 1, amount=self.current_balance)
        if self.verbose:
            self.print_net_wealth(bar)
        self.position = -1
    self.net_wealths.append((date, self.calculate_net_wealth(price)))
self.net_wealths = pd.DataFrame(self.net_wealths,
                                columns=['date', 'net_wealth'])
self.net_wealths.set_index('date', inplace=True)
self.net_wealths.index = pd.DatetimeIndex(self.net_wealths.index)
self.close_out(bar)
```

## CHAPTER 12

Execution and Deployment

Considerable progress is needed before autonomous vehicles can operate reliably in mixed urban traffic, heavy rain and snow, unpaved and unmapped roads, and where wireless access is unreliable.

—Todd Litman (2020)

An investment firm that engages in algorithmic trading shall have in place effective systems and risk controls suitable to the business it operates to ensure that its trading systems are resilient and have sufficient capacity, are subject to appropriate trading thresholds and limits and prevent the sending of erroneous orders or the systems otherwise functioning in a way that may create or contribute to a disorderly market.

—MiFID II (Article 17)

Chapter 11 trains a trading bot in the form of a financial Q-learning agent based on historical data. It introduces event-based backtesting as an approach flexible enough to account for typical risk measures, such as trailing stop loss orders or take profit targets. However, all this happens asynchronously in a sandbox environment based on historical data only. As with an autonomous vehicle (AV), there is the problem of deploying the AI in the real world. For an AV this means combining the AI with the car hardware and deploying the AV on test and public streets. For a trading bot this means connecting the trading bot with a trading platform and deploying it such that orders are executed automatically. In other words, the algorithmic side is clear—execution and deployment now need to be added to implement algorithmic trading.

This chapter introduces the Oanda (*http://oanda.com*) trading platform for algorithmic trading. Therefore, the focus is on the v20 API (*https://oreil.ly/TbGKN*) of the platform and not on applications that provide users with an interface for manual trading. To simplify the code, the wrapper package `tpqoa` (*https://oreil.ly/72pWe*) is introduced and used. It relies on the `v20` (*https://oreil.ly/H_pIj*) Python package from Oanda and provides a more Pythonic user interface.

"Oanda Account" on page 346 details the prerequisites to use a *demo account* with Oanda. "Data Retrieval" on page 347 shows how to retrieve historical and real-time (streaming) data from the API. "Order Execution" on page 351 deals with the execution of buy and sell orders, potentially including other orders, such as trailing stop loss orders. "Trading Bot" on page 357 trains a trading bot based on historical intraday data from Oanda and backtests its performance in vectorized fashion. Finally, "Deployment" on page 364 shows how to deploy the trading bot in real-time and an automated fashion.

Oanda Account

The code in this chapter relies on the Python wrapper package `tpqoa` (*https://oreil.ly/72pWe*). This package can be installed via `pip` as follows:

```
pip install --upgrade git+https://github.com/yhilpisch/tpqoa.git
```

To make use of this package, a demo account with Oanda (*http://oanda.com*) is sufficient. Once the account is open, an *access token* is generated on the account page (after login). The access token and the *account id* (also found on the account page) are then stored in a configuration text file as follows:

```
[oanda]
account_id = XYZ-ABC-...
access_token = ZYXCAB...
account_type = practice
```

If the name of the configuration file is *aiif.cfg* and if it is stored in the current working directory, then the `tpqoa` package can be used as follows:

```
import tpqoa
api = tpqoa.tpqoa('aiif.cfg')
```

Risk Disclaimers and Disclosures

Oanda is a platform for *foreign exchange* (FX) and *contracts for difference* (CFD) trading. These instruments involve considerable risks, in particular when traded with leverage. It is strongly recommended that you read all relevant risk disclaimers and disclosures from Oanda on its website (*http://oanda.com*) carefully before moving on (check for the appropriate jurisdiction).

All code and examples presented in this chapter are for technical illustration only and do not constitute any investment advice or similar.

Data Retrieval

As usual, some Python imports and configurations come first:

```
In [1]: import os
        import time
        import numpy as np
        import pandas as pd
        from pprint import pprint
        from pylab import plt, mpl
        plt.style.use('seaborn')
        mpl.rcParams['savefig.dpi'] = 300
        mpl.rcParams['font.family'] = 'serif'
        pd.set_option('mode.chained_assignment', None)
        pd.set_option('display.float_format', '{:.5f}'.format)
        np.set_printoptions(suppress=True, precision=4)
        os.environ['PYTHONHASHSEED'] = '0'
```

Depending on the relevant jurisdiction of the account, Oanda offers a number of tradable FX and CFD instruments. The following Python code retrieves the available instruments for a given account:

```
In [2]: import tpqoa    ❶
```

```
In [3]: api = tpqoa.tpqoa('../aiif.cfg')    ❷
```

```
In [4]: ins = api.get_instruments()    ❸
```

```
In [5]: ins[:5]    ❹
Out[5]: [('AUD/CAD', 'AUD_CAD'),
         ('AUD/CHF', 'AUD_CHF'),
         ('AUD/HKD', 'AUD_HKD'),
         ('AUD/JPY', 'AUD_JPY'),
         ('AUD/NZD', 'AUD_NZD')]
```

❶ Imports the tpqoa package

❷ Instantiates an API object given the account credentials

❸ Retrieves the list of available instruments in the format (display_name, technical_name)

❹ Shows a select few of these instruments

Oanda provides a wealth of historical data via its v20 API. The following examples retrieve historical data for the EUR/USD currency pair—the granularity is set to D (that is, *daily*).

Figure 12-1 plots the closing (ask) prices:

```
In [6]: raw = api.get_history(instrument='EUR_USD',   ❶
                              start='2018-01-01',      ❷
                              end='2020-07-31',        ❸
                              granularity='D',         ❹
                              price='A')               ❺

In [7]: raw.info()
        <class 'pandas.core.frame.DataFrame'>
        DatetimeIndex: 671 entries, 2018-01-01 22:00:00 to 2020-07-30 21:00:00
        Data columns (total 6 columns):
         #   Column    Non-Null Count  Dtype
        ---  ------    --------------  -----
         0   o         671 non-null    float64
         1   h         671 non-null    float64
         2   l         671 non-null    float64
         3   c         671 non-null    float64
         4   volume    671 non-null    int64
         5   complete  671 non-null    bool
        dtypes: bool(1), float64(4), int64(1)
        memory usage: 32.1 KB

In [8]: raw.head()
Out[8]:                          o       h       l       c  volume  complete
        time
        2018-01-01 22:00:00  1.20101 1.20819 1.20051 1.20610   35630      True
        2018-01-02 22:00:00  1.20620 1.20673 1.20018 1.20170   31354      True
        2018-01-03 22:00:00  1.20170 1.20897 1.20049 1.20710   35187      True
        2018-01-04 22:00:00  1.20692 1.20847 1.20215 1.20327   36478      True
        2018-01-07 22:00:00  1.20301 1.20530 1.19564 1.19717   27618      True

In [9]: raw['c'].plot(figsize=(10, 6));
```

❶ Specifies the instrument…

❷ …the starting date…

❸ …the end date…

❹ …the granularity (D = daily)…

❺ …and the type of the price series (A = ask)

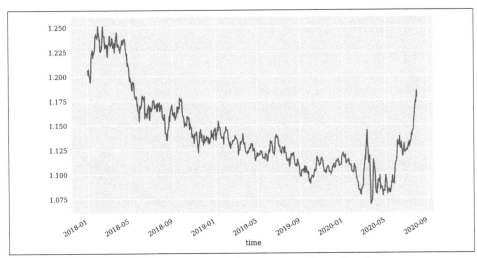

Figure 12-1. Historical daily closing prices for EUR/USD from Oanda

Intraday data is as easily retrieved and used as daily data, as the code that follows shows. Figure 12-2 visualizes minute bar (mid) price data:

```
In [10]: raw = api.get_history(instrument='EUR_USD',
                               start='2020-07-01',
                               end='2020-07-31',
                               granularity='M1',   ❶
                               price='M')          ❷

In [11]: raw.info()
         <class 'pandas.core.frame.DataFrame'>
         DatetimeIndex: 30728 entries, 2020-07-01 00:00:00 to 2020-07-30 23:59:00
         Data columns (total 6 columns):
          #   Column    Non-Null Count  Dtype
         ---  ------    --------------  -----
          0   o         30728 non-null  float64
          1   h         30728 non-null  float64
          2   l         30728 non-null  float64
          3   c         30728 non-null  float64
          4   volume    30728 non-null  int64
          5   complete  30728 non-null  bool
         dtypes: bool(1), float64(4), int64(1)
         memory usage: 1.4 MB

In [12]: raw.tail()
Out[12]:                            o        h        l        c  volume  complete
         time
         2020-07-30 23:55:00  1.18724  1.18739  1.18718  1.18738      57      True
         2020-07-30 23:56:00  1.18736  1.18758  1.18722  1.18757      57      True
         2020-07-30 23:57:00  1.18756  1.18756  1.18734  1.18734      49      True
         2020-07-30 23:58:00  1.18736  1.18737  1.18713  1.18717      36      True
         2020-07-30 23:59:00  1.18718  1.18724  1.18714  1.18722      31      True
```

```
In [13]: raw['c'].plot(figsize=(10, 6));
```

❶ Specifies the granularity (M1 = one minute)...

❷ ...and the type of the price series (M = mid)

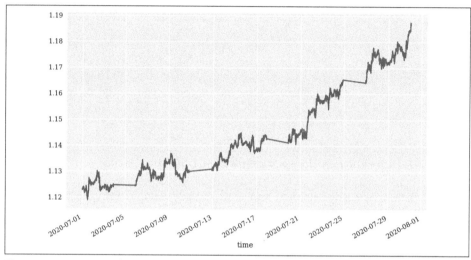

Figure 12-2. Historical one-minute bar closing prices for EUR/USD from Oanda

Whereas historical data is important, for instance, to train and test a trading bot, real-time (streaming) data is required to deploy such a bot for algorithmic trading. tpqoa allows the synchronous streaming of real-time data for all available instruments with a single method call. The method prints by default the time stamp and the bid/ask prices. For algorithmic trading, this default behavior can be adjusted, as "Deployment" on page 364 shows:

```
In [14]: api.stream_data('EUR_USD', stop=10)
         2020-08-13T12:07:09.735715316Z 1.18328 1.18342
         2020-08-13T12:07:16.245253689Z 1.18329 1.18343
         2020-08-13T12:07:16.397803785Z 1.18328 1.18342
         2020-08-13T12:07:17.240232521Z 1.18331 1.18346
         2020-08-13T12:07:17.358476854Z 1.18334 1.18348
         2020-08-13T12:07:17.778061207Z 1.18331 1.18345
         2020-08-13T12:07:18.016544856Z 1.18333 1.18346
         2020-08-13T12:07:18.144762415Z 1.18334 1.18348
         2020-08-13T12:07:18.689365678Z 1.18331 1.18345
         2020-08-13T12:07:19.148039139Z 1.18331 1.18345
```

Order Execution

The AI of an AV needs to be able to control the physical vehicle. To this end it sends different types of signals to the vehicle, for example, to accelerate, break, turn left, or turn right. A trading bot needs to be able to place orders with the trading platform. This section covers different types of orders, such as market orders and stop loss orders.

The most fundamental type of order is a *market order*. This order allows buying or selling a financial instrument at the current market price (that is, the *ask price* when buying and the *bid price* when selling). The following examples are based on an account leverage of 20 and relatively small order sizes. Therefore, liquidity issues, for example, do not play a role. When executing orders via the Oanda v20 API, the API returns a detailed order object. First, a *buy market order* is placed:

```
In [15]: order = api.create_order('EUR_USD', units=25000,
                                  suppress=True, ret=True)    ❶
         pprint(order)    ❶
         {'accountBalance': '98553.3172',
          'accountID': '101-004-13834683-001',
          'batchID': '1625',
          'commission': '0.0',
          'financing': '0.0',
          'fullPrice': {'asks': [{'liquidity': '10000000', 'price': 1.18345}],
                        'bids': [{'liquidity': '10000000', 'price': 1.18331}],
                        'closeoutAsk': 1.18345,
                        'closeoutBid': 1.18331,
                        'type': 'PRICE'},
          'fullVWAP': 1.18345,
          'gainQuoteHomeConversionFactor': '0.840811914585',
          'guaranteedExecutionFee': '0.0',
          'halfSpreadCost': '1.4788',
          'id': '1626',
          'instrument': 'EUR_USD',
          'lossQuoteHomeConversionFactor': '0.849262285586',
          'orderID': '1625',
          'pl': '0.0',
          'price': 1.18345,
          'reason': 'MARKET_ORDER',
          'requestID': '787572415478121S4',
          'time': '2020-08-13T12:07:19.434407966Z',
          'tradeOpened': {'guaranteedExecutionFee': '0.0',
                          'halfSpreadCost': '1.4788',
                          'initialMarginRequired': '832.5',
                          'price': 1.18345,
                          'tradeID': '1626',
                          'units': '25000.0'},
          'type': 'ORDER_FILL',
          'units': '25000.0',
          'userID': 13834683}
```

```
In [16]: def print_details(order):                ❷
             details = (order['time'][:-7], order['instrument'], order['units'],
                        order['price'], order['pl'])
             return details

In [17]: print_details(order)     ❷
Out[17]: ('2020-08-13T12:07:19.434', 'EUR_USD', '25000.0', 1.18345, '0.0')

In [18]: time.sleep(1)
```

❶ Places a *buy market order* and prints the order object details

❷ Selects and shows the `time`, `instrument`, `units`, `price`, and `pl` details of the order

Second, the position is closed via a *sell market order* of the same size. Whereas the first trade has a profit/loss (P&L) of zero by its nature—before accounting for transaction costs—the second trade in general has a nonzero P&L:

```
In [19]: order = api.create_order('EUR_USD', units=-25000,
                                  suppress=True, ret=True)     ❶
         pprint(order)     ❶
         {'accountBalance': '98549.283',
          'accountID': '101-004-13834683-001',
          'batchID': '1627',
          'commission': '0.0',
          'financing': '0.0',
          'fullPrice': {'asks': [{'liquidity': '9975000', 'price': 1.18339}],
                        'bids': [{'liquidity': '10000000', 'price': 1.18326}],
                        'closeoutAsk': 1.18339,
                        'closeoutBid': 1.18326,
                        'type': 'PRICE'},
          'fullVWAP': 1.18326,
          'gainQuoteHomeConversionFactor': '0.840850994445',
          'guaranteedExecutionFee': '0.0',
          'halfSpreadCost': '1.3732',
          'id': '1628',
          'instrument': 'EUR_USD',
          'lossQuoteHomeConversionFactor': '0.849301758209',
          'orderID': '1627',
          'pl': '-4.0342',
          'price': 1.18326,
          'reason': 'MARKET_ORDER',
          'requestID': '78757241552009237',
          'time': '2020-08-13T12:07:20.586564454Z',
          'tradesClosed': [{'financing': '0.0',
                            'guaranteedExecutionFee': '0.0',
                            'halfSpreadCost': '1.3732',
                            'price': 1.18326,
                            'realizedPL': '-4.0342',
                            'tradeID': '1626',
                            'units': '-25000.0'}],
```

```
        'type': 'ORDER_FILL',
        'units': '-25000.0',
        'userID': 13834683}

In [20]: print_details(order) ❷
Out[20]: ('2020-08-13T12:07:20.586', 'EUR_USD', '-25000.0', 1.18326, '-4.0342')

In [21]: time.sleep(1)
```

❶ Places a *sell market order* and prints the order object details

❷ Selects and shows the `time`, `instrument`, `units`, `price`, and `pl` details of the order

Limit Orders

This chapter covers *market orders* as a type of base order only. With a market order, buying or selling a financial instrument happens at the price that is current when the order is placed. By contrast, a *limit order*, as the other main type of base order, allows the placement of an order with a minimum price or a maximum price. Only when the minimum/maximum price is reached is the order executed. Until that point, no transaction takes place.

Next, consider an example for the same combination of trades but this time with a *stop loss* (SL) order. An SL order is treated as a separate (limit) order. The following Python code places the orders and shows the details of the SL order object:

```
In [22]: order = api.create_order('EUR_USD', units=25000,
                              sl_distance=0.005, ❶
                              suppress=True, ret=True)

In [23]: print_details(order)
Out[23]: ('2020-08-13T12:07:21.740', 'EUR_USD', '25000.0', 1.18343, '0.0')

In [24]: sl_order = api.get_transaction(tid=int(order['id']) + 1) ❷

In [25]: sl_order ❷
Out[25]: {'id': '1631',
        'time': '2020-08-13T12:07:21.740825489Z',
        'userID': 13834683,
        'accountID': '101-004-13834683-001',
        'batchID': '1629',
        'requestID': '78757241556206373',
        'type': 'STOP_LOSS_ORDER',
        'tradeID': '1630',
        'price': 1.17843,
        'distance': '0.005',
        'timeInForce': 'GTC',
        'triggerCondition': 'DEFAULT',
        'reason': 'ON_FILL'}
```

```
In [26]: (sl_order['time'], sl_order['type'], order['price'],
          sl_order['price'], sl_order['distance']) ❸
Out[26]: ('2020-08-13T12:07:21.740825489Z',
          'STOP_LOSS_ORDER',
          1.18343,
          1.17843,
          '0.005')

In [27]: time.sleep(1)

In [28]: order = api.create_order('EUR_USD', units=-25000, suppress=True, ret=True)

In [29]: print_details(order)
Out[29]: ('2020-08-13T12:07:23.059', 'EUR_USD', '-25000.0', 1.18329, '-2.9725')
```

❶ The SL distance is defined in currency units.

❷ Selects and shows the SL order object data.

❸ Selects and shows some relevant details of the two order objects.

A *trailing stop loss* (TSL) order is handled in the same way. The only difference is that there is no fixed price attached to a TSL order:

```
In [30]: order = api.create_order('EUR_USD', units=25000,
                                   tsl_distance=0.005, ❶
                                   suppress=True, ret=True)

In [31]: print_details(order)
Out[31]: ('2020-08-13T12:07:23.204', 'EUR_USD', '25000.0', 1.18341, '0.0')

In [32]: tsl_order = api.get_transaction(tid=int(order['id']) + 1) ❷

In [33]: tsl_order ❷
Out[33]: {'id': '1637',
          'time': '2020-08-13T12:07:23.204457044Z',
          'userID': 13834683,
          'accountID': '101-004-13834683-001',
          'batchID': '1635',
          'requestID': '787572415645598562',
          'type': 'TRAILING_STOP_LOSS_ORDER',
          'tradeID': '1636',
          'distance': '0.005',
          'timeInForce': 'GTC',
          'triggerCondition': 'DEFAULT',
          'reason': 'ON_FILL'}

In [34]: (tsl_order['time'][:-7], tsl_order['type'],
          order['price'], tsl_order['distance']) ❸
Out[34]: ('2020-08-13T12:07:23.204', 'TRAILING_STOP_LOSS_ORDER', 1.18341, '0.005')
```

```
In [35]: time.sleep(1)

In [36]: order = api.create_order('EUR_USD', units=-25000,
                                  suppress=True, ret=True)

In [37]: print_details(order)
Out[37]: ('2020-08-13T12:07:24.551', 'EUR_USD', '-25000.0', 1.1833, '-2.3355')

In [38]: time.sleep(1)
```

❶ The TSL distance is defined in currency units.

❷ Selects and shows the TSL order object data.

❸ Selects and shows some relevant details of the two order objects.

Finally, here is a *take profit* (TP) order. This order requires a fixed TP target price. Therefore, the following code uses the execution price from the previous order to define the TP price in relative terms. Beyond this small difference, the handling is again the same as before:

```
In [39]: tp_price = round(order['price'] + 0.01, 4)
         tp_price
Out[39]: 1.1933

In [40]: order = api.create_order('EUR_USD', units=25000,
                                  tp_price=tp_price,   ❶
                                  suppress=True, ret=True)

In [41]: print_details(order)
Out[41]: ('2020-08-13T12:07:25.712', 'EUR_USD', '25000.0', 1.18344, '0.0')

In [42]: tp_order = api.get_transaction(tid=int(order['id']) + 1)   ❷

In [43]: tp_order   ❷
Out[43]: {'id': '1643',
          'time': '2020-08-13T12:07:25.712531725Z',
          'userID': 13834683,
          'accountID': '101-004-13834683-001',
          'batchID': '1641',
          'requestID': '78757241572993078',
          'type': 'TAKE_PROFIT_ORDER',
          'tradeID': '1642',
          'price': 1.1933,
          'timeInForce': 'GTC',
          'triggerCondition': 'DEFAULT',
          'reason': 'ON_FILL'}

In [44]: (tp_order['time'][:-7], tp_order['type'],
          order['price'], tp_order['price'])   ❸
Out[44]: ('2020-08-13T12:07:25.712', 'TAKE_PROFIT_ORDER', 1.18344, 1.1933)
```

```
In [45]: time.sleep(1)

In [46]: order = api.create_order('EUR_USD', units=-25000,
                                  suppress=True, ret=True)

In [47]: print_details(order)
Out[47]: ('2020-08-13T12:07:27.020', 'EUR_USD', '-25000.0', 1.18332, '-2.5478')
```

❶ The TP target price is defined relative to the previous execution price.

❷ Selects and shows the TP order object data.

❸ Selects and shows some relevant details of the two order objects.

The code so far only deals with transaction details of single orders. However, it is also of interest to have an overview of multiple *historical transactions*. To this end, the following method call provides overview data for all the main orders placed in this section, including P&L data:

```
In [48]: api.print_transactions(tid=int(order['id']) - 22)
         1626 | 2020-08-13T12:07:19.434407966Z |    EUR_USD |    25000.0 |     0.0
         1628 | 2020-08-13T12:07:20.586564454Z |    EUR_USD |   -25000.0 |  -4.0342
         1630 | 2020-08-13T12:07:21.740825489Z |    EUR_USD |    25000.0 |     0.0
         1633 | 2020-08-13T12:07:23.059178023Z |    EUR_USD |   -25000.0 |  -2.9725
         1636 | 2020-08-13T12:07:23.204457044Z |    EUR_USD |    25000.0 |     0.0
         1639 | 2020-08-13T12:07:24.551026466Z |    EUR_USD |   -25000.0 |  -2.3355
         1642 | 2020-08-13T12:07:25.712531725Z |    EUR_USD |    25000.0 |     0.0
         1645 | 2020-08-13T12:07:27.020414342Z |    EUR_USD |   -25000.0 |  -2.5478
```

Yet another method call provides a snapshot of the *account details*. The details shown are from an Oanda demo account that has been in use for quite some time for technical testing purposes:

```
In [49]: api.get_account_summary()
Out[49]: {'id': '101-004-13834683-001',
          'alias': 'Primary',
          'currency': 'EUR',
          'balance': '98541.4272',
          'createdByUserID': 13834683,
          'createdTime': '2020-03-19T06:08:14.363139403Z',
          'guaranteedStopLossOrderMode': 'DISABLED',
          'pl': '-1248.5543',
          'resettablePL': '-1248.5543',
          'resettablePLTime': '0',
          'financing': '-210.0185',
          'commission': '0.0',
          'guaranteedExecutionFees': '0.0',
          'marginRate': '0.0333',
          'openTradeCount': 1,
          'openPositionCount': 1,
```

```
'pendingOrderCount': 0,
'hedgingEnabled': False,
'unrealizedPL': '941.9536',
'NAV': '99483.3808',
'marginUsed': '380.83',
'marginAvailable': '99107.2283',
'positionValue': '3808.3',
'marginCloseoutUnrealizedPL': '947.9546',
'marginCloseoutNAV': '99489.3818',
'marginCloseoutMarginUsed': '380.83',
'marginCloseoutPercent': '0.00191',
'marginCloseoutPositionValue': '3808.3',
'withdrawalLimit': '98541.4272',
'marginCallMarginUsed': '380.83',
'marginCallPercent': '0.00383',
'lastTransactionID': '1646'}
```

This concludes the discussion of the basics of executing orders with Oanda. All elements are now together to support the deployment of a trading bot. The remainder of this chapter trains a trading bot on Oanda data and deploys it in automated fashion.

Trading Bot

Chapter 11 shows in detail how to train a deep Q-learning trading bot and how to backtest it in vectorized and event-based fashion. This section now repeats selected core steps in this regard based on historical data from Oanda. "Oanda Environment" on page 369 provides a Python module that contains the environment class `OandaEnv` to work with Oanda data. It can be used in the same way as the `Finance` class from Chapter 11.

The following Python code instantiates the learning environment object. During this step, the major data-related parameters driving the learning, validation, and testing are fixed. The `OandaEnv` class allows the inclusion of leverage, which is typical for FX and CFD trading. Leverage amplifies the realized returns, thereby increasing the profit potential but also the loss risks:

```
In [50]: import oandaenv as oe

In [51]: symbol = 'EUR_USD'

In [52]: date = '2020-08-11'

In [53]: features = [symbol, 'r', 's', 'm', 'v']

In [54]: %%time
         learn_env = oe.OandaEnv(symbol=symbol,
                        start=f'{date} 08:00:00',
                        end=f'{date} 13:00:00',
                        granularity='S30',     ❶
```

```
                price='M',      ❷
                features=features,   ❸
                window=20,      ❹
                lags=3,      ❺
                leverage=20,      ❻
                min_accuracy=0.4,      ❼
                min_performance=0.85      ❽
                )
        CPU times: user 23.1 ms, sys: 2.86 ms, total: 25.9 ms
        Wall time: 26.8 ms

In [55]: np.bincount(learn_env.data['d'])
Out[55]: array([299, 281])

In [56]: learn_env.data.info()
        <class 'pandas.core.frame.DataFrame'>
        DatetimeIndex: 580 entries, 2020-08-11 08:10:00 to 2020-08-11 12:59:30
        Data columns (total 6 columns):
         #   Column   Non-Null Count   Dtype
        ---  ------   --------------   -----
         0   EUR_USD  580 non-null     float64
         1   r        580 non-null     float64
         2   s        580 non-null     float64
         3   m        580 non-null     float64
         4   v        580 non-null     float64
         5   d        580 non-null     int64
        dtypes: float64(5), int64(1)
        memory usage: 31.7 KB
```

❶ Sets the granularity for the data to five seconds

❷ Sets the price type to mid prices

❸ Defines the set of features to be used

❹ Defines the window length for rolling statistics

❺ Specifies the number of lags

❻ Fixes the leverage

❼ Sets the required minimum accuracy

❽ Sets the required minimum performance

In a next step, the validation environment is instantiated, relying on the parameters of the learning environment—apart from the time interval, for obvious reasons.

Figure 12-3 shows the closing prices of EUR/USD as used in the learning, validation, and test environments (from left to right):

```
In [57]: valid_env = oe.OandaEnv(symbol=learn_env.symbol,
                        start=f'{date} 13:00:00',
                        end=f'{date} 14:00:00',
                        granularity=learn_env.granularity,
                        price=learn_env.price,
                        features=learn_env.features,
                        window=learn_env.window,
                        lags=learn_env.lags,
                        leverage=learn_env.leverage,
                        min_accuracy=0,
                        min_performance=0,
                        mu=learn_env.mu,
                        std=learn_env.std
                        )
```

```
In [58]: valid_env.data.info()
         <class 'pandas.core.frame.DataFrame'>
         DatetimeIndex: 100 entries, 2020-08-11 13:10:00 to 2020-08-11 13:59:30
         Data columns (total 6 columns):
          #   Column   Non-Null Count  Dtype
         ---  ------   --------------  -----
          0   EUR_USD  100 non-null    float64
          1   r        100 non-null    float64
          2   s        100 non-null    float64
          3   m        100 non-null    float64
          4   v        100 non-null    float64
          5   d        100 non-null    int64
         dtypes: float64(5), int64(1)
         memory usage: 5.5 KB
```

```
In [59]: test_env = oe.OandaEnv(symbol=learn_env.symbol,
                        start=f'{date} 14:00:00',
                        end=f'{date} 17:00:00',
                        granularity=learn_env.granularity,
                        price=learn_env.price,
                        features=learn_env.features,
                        window=learn_env.window,
                        lags=learn_env.lags,
                        leverage=learn_env.leverage,
                        min_accuracy=0,
                        min_performance=0,
                        mu=learn_env.mu,
                        std=learn_env.std
                        )
```

```
In [60]: test_env.data.info()
         <class 'pandas.core.frame.DataFrame'>
         DatetimeIndex: 340 entries, 2020-08-11 14:10:00 to 2020-08-11 16:59:30
         Data columns (total 6 columns):
```

```
 #   Column  Non-Null Count  Dtype
---  ------  --------------  -----
 0   EUR_USD 340 non-null    float64
 1   r       340 non-null    float64
 2   s       340 non-null    float64
 3   m       340 non-null    float64
 4   v       340 non-null    float64
 5   d       340 non-null    int64
dtypes: float64(5), int64(1)
memory usage: 18.6 KB
```

```
In [61]: ax = learn_env.data[learn_env.symbol].plot(figsize=(10, 6))
         plt.axvline(learn_env.data.index[-1], ls='--')
         valid_env.data[learn_env.symbol].plot(ax=ax, style='-.')
         plt.axvline(valid_env.data.index[-1], ls='--')
         test_env.data[learn_env.symbol].plot(ax=ax, style='-.');
```

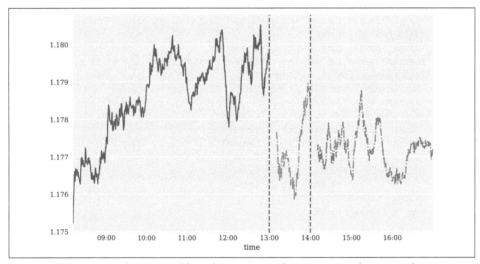

Figure 12-3. Historical 30-second bar closing prices for EUR/USD from Oanda (learning = left, validation = middle, testing = right)

Based on the Oanda environment, the trading bot from Chapter 11 can be trained and validated. The following Python code performs this task and visualizes the performance results (see Figure 12-4):

```
In [62]: import sys
         sys.path.append('../ch11/')   ❶
```

```
In [63]: import tradingbot   ❶
         Using TensorFlow backend.
```

```
In [64]: tradingbot.set_seeds(100)
         agent = tradingbot.TradingBot(24, 0.001, learn_env=learn_env,
                                       valid_env=valid_env)   ❷
```

```
In [65]: episodes = 31

In [66]: %time agent.learn(episodes)  ❷
         ================================================================
         episode:  5/31 | VALIDATION | treward:   97 | perf: 1.004 | eps: 0.96
         ================================================================

         ================================================================
         episode: 10/31 | VALIDATION | treward:   97 | perf: 1.005 | eps: 0.91
         ================================================================

         ================================================================
         episode: 15/31 | VALIDATION | treward:   97 | perf: 0.986 | eps: 0.87
         ================================================================

         ================================================================
         episode: 20/31 | VALIDATION | treward:   97 | perf: 1.012 | eps: 0.83
         ================================================================

         ================================================================
         episode: 25/31 | VALIDATION | treward:   97 | perf: 0.995 | eps: 0.79
         ================================================================

         ================================================================
         episode: 30/31 | VALIDATION | treward:   97 | perf: 0.972 | eps: 0.75
         ================================================================
         episode: 31/31 | treward:   16 | perf: 0.981 | av: 376.0 | max:   577
         CPU times: user 22.1 s, sys: 1.17 s, total: 23.3 s
         Wall time: 20.1 s

In [67]: tradingbot.plot_performance(agent)  ❸
```

❶ Imports the `tradingbot` module from Chapter 11

❷ Trains and validates the trading bot based on Oanda data

❸ Visualizes the performance results

As discussed in the previous two chapters, the training and validation performances are just an indicator of the trading bot performance.

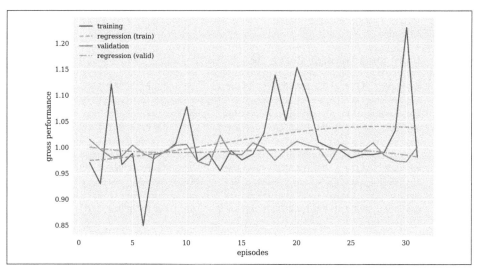

Figure 12-4. Training and validation performance results of the trading bot for Oanda data

The following code implements a vectorized backtest of the trading bot performance for the test environment—again with the same parameters as the learning environment apart from the time interval used. The code makes use of the function `backt est()` as provided in the Python module presented in "Vectorized Backtesting" on page 372. The reported performance numbers include a leverage of 20. This holds true for both the gross performance of the passive benchmark investment and the trading bot over time, as shown in Figure 12-5:

```
In [68]: import backtest as bt

In [69]: env = test_env

In [70]: bt.backtest(agent, env)

In [71]: env.data['p'].iloc[env.lags:].value_counts()    ❶
Out[71]: 1     263
         -1     74
         Name: p, dtype: int64

In [72]: sum(env.data['p'].iloc[env.lags:].diff() != 0)    ❷
Out[72]: 25

In [73]: (env.data[['r', 's']].iloc[env.lags:] * env.leverage).sum(
                 ).apply(np.exp)    ❸
Out[73]: r    0.99966
         s    1.05910
         dtype: float64
```

```
In [74]: (env.data[['r', 's']].iloc[env.lags:] * env.leverage).sum(
             ).apply(np.exp) - 1  ❹
Out[74]: r    -0.00034
         s     0.05910
         dtype: float64

In [75]: (env.data[['r', 's']].iloc[env.lags:] * env.leverage).cumsum(
             ).apply(np.exp).plot(figsize=(10, 6));  ❺
```

❶ Shows the total number of long and short positions

❷ Shows the number of trades required to implement the strategy

❸ Calculates the gross performance including leverage

❹ Calculates the net performance including leverage

❺ Visualizes the gross performance over time including leverage

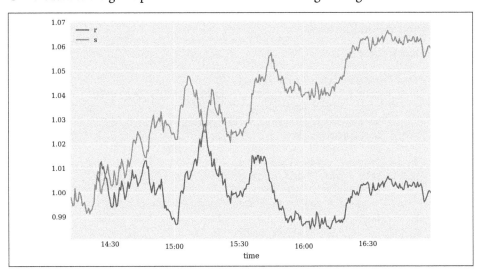

Figure 12-5. Gross performance of the passive benchmark investment and the trading bot over time (including leverage)

Simplified Backtesting

The training and backtesting of the trading bot in this section happen under assumptions that are not realistic. The trading strategy based on the 30-second bars might lead to a large number of trades over a short period of time. Assuming typical transaction costs (bid-ask spreads), such a strategy often is not economically viable. Longer bars or a strategy with fewer trades would be more realistic. However, to allow for a "quick" deployment demo in the next section, the training and backtest are implemented intentionally on the relatively short 30-second bars.

Deployment

This section combines the major elements of the previous sections to deploy the trained trading bot in automated fashion. This is comparable to the point in time at which an AV is prepared to be deployed on the streets. The class OandaTradingBot presented in the following code inherits from the tpqoa class and adds some helper functions and the trading logic:

```
In [76]: import tpqoa

In [77]: class OandaTradingBot(tpqoa.tpqoa):
             def __init__(self, config_file, agent, granularity, units,
                          verbose=True):
                 super(OandaTradingBot, self).__init__(config_file)
                 self.agent = agent
                 self.symbol = self.agent.learn_env.symbol
                 self.env = agent.learn_env
                 self.window = self.env.window
                 if granularity is None:
                     self.granularity = agent.learn_env.granularity
                 else:
                     self.granularity = granularity
                 self.units = units
                 self.trades = 0
                 self.position = 0
                 self.tick_data = pd.DataFrame()
                 self.min_length = (self.agent.learn_env.window +
                                    self.agent.learn_env.lags)
                 self.pl = list()
                 self.verbose = verbose
             def _prepare_data(self):
                 self.data['r'] = np.log(self.data / self.data.shift(1))
                 self.data.dropna(inplace=True)
                 self.data['s'] = self.data[self.symbol].rolling(
                                                     self.window).mean()
                 self.data['m'] = self.data['r'].rolling(self.window).mean()
                 self.data['v'] = self.data['r'].rolling(self.window).std()
                 self.data.dropna(inplace=True)
```

```
        # self.data_ = (self.data - self.env.mu) / self.env.std  ❶
        self.data_ = (self.data - self.data.mean()) / self.data.std()  ❶
    def _resample_data(self):
        self.data = self.tick_data.resample(self.granularity,
                        label='right').last().ffill().iloc[:-1]  ❷
        self.data = pd.DataFrame(self.data['mid'])  ❷
        self.data.columns = [self.symbol,]  ❷
        self.data.index = self.data.index.tz_localize(None)  ❷
    def _get_state(self):
        state = self.data_[self.env.features].iloc[-self.env.lags:]  ❸
        return np.reshape(state.values, [1, self.env.lags,
                                    self.env.n_features])  ❸
    def report_trade(self, time, side, order):
        self.trades += 1
        pl = float(order['pl'])  ❹
        self.pl.append(pl)  ❹
        cpl = sum(self.pl)  ❺
        print('\n' + 75 * '=')
        print(f'{time} | *** GOING {side} ({self.trades}) ***')
        print(f'{time} | PROFIT/LOSS={pl:.2f} | CUMULATIVE={cpl:.2f}')
        print(75 * '=')
        if self.verbose:
            pprint(order)
            print(75 * '=')
    def on_success(self, time, bid, ask):
        df = pd.DataFrame({'ask': ask, 'bid': bid,
                           'mid': (bid + ask) / 2},
                          index=[pd.Timestamp(time)])
        self.tick_data = self.tick_data.append(df)  ❷
        self._resample_data()  ❷
        if len(self.data) > self.min_length:
            self.min_length += 1
            self._prepare_data()
            state = self._get_state()  ❻
            prediction = np.argmax(
                self.agent.model.predict(state)[0, 0])  ❻
            position = 1 if prediction == 1 else -1  ❻
            if self.position in [0, -1] and position == 1:  ❼
                order = self.create_order(self.symbol,
                        units=(1 - self.position) * self.units,
                            suppress=True, ret=True)
                self.report_trade(time, 'LONG', order)
                self.position = 1
            elif self.position in [0, 1] and position == -1:  ❽
                order = self.create_order(self.symbol,
                        units=-(1 + self.position) * self.units,
                            suppress=True, ret=True)
                self.report_trade(time, 'SHORT', order)
                self.position = -1
```

❶ For demonstration, the normalization is done with the real-time data statistics.[1]

❷ Collects the tick data and resamples it to the required granularity.

❸ Returns the current state of the financial market.

❹ Collects the P&L figures for every trade.

❺ Calculates the cumulative P&L for all trades.

❻ Predicts the market direction and derives the signal (position).

❼ Checks whether the conditions for a *long position* (buy order) are met.

❽ Checks whether the conditions for a *short position* (sell order) are met.

The application of this class is straightforward. First, an object is instantiated, providing as the major input the trained trading bot `agent` from the previous section. Second, the streaming for the instrument to be traded needs to be started. Whenever new tick data arrives, the `.on_success()` method is called, which contains the main logic for both the processing of the tick data and the placement of trades. To speed things up a bit, the deployment example relies, as did the backtesting before, on 30-second bars. In a production context, when managing real money, a longer time interval might be the better choice—if only to reduce the number of trades and therewith the transaction costs:

```
In [78]: otb = OandaTradingBot('../aiif.cfg', agent, '30s',
                               25000, verbose=False)  ❶

In [79]: otb.tick_data.info()
         <class 'pandas.core.frame.DataFrame'>
         Index: 0 entries
         Empty DataFrame
In [80]: otb.stream_data(agent.learn_env.symbol, stop=1000)  ❷

         =======================================================================
         2020-08-13T12:19:32.320291893Z | *** GOING SHORT (1) ***
         2020-08-13T12:19:32.320291893Z | PROFIT/LOSS=0.00 | CUMULATIVE=0.00
         =======================================================================


         =======================================================================
         2020-08-13T12:20:00.083985447Z | *** GOING LONG (2) ***
         2020-08-13T12:20:00.083985447Z | PROFIT/LOSS=-6.80 | CUMULATIVE=-6.80
```

---

[1] This little trick leads more quickly to trades in this particular context given the data used. For real deployment, the statistics from the learning environment data are to be used for the normalization.

```
        ===========================================================================
        ===========================================================================
        2020-08-13T12:25:00.099901587Z | *** GOING SHORT (3) ***
        2020-08-13T12:25:00.099901587Z | PROFIT/LOSS=-7.86 | CUMULATIVE=-14.66
        ===========================================================================

In [81]: print('\n' + 75 * '=')
         print('*** CLOSING OUT ***')
         order = otb.create_order(otb.symbol,
                       units=-otb.position * otb.units,
                       suppress=True, ret=True)   ❸
         otb.report_trade(otb.time, 'NEUTRAL', order)   ❸
         if otb.verbose:
             pprint(order)
         print(75 * '=')


         ===========================================================================
         *** CLOSING OUT ***

         ===========================================================================
         2020-08-13T12:25:16.870357562Z | *** GOING NEUTRAL (4) ***
         2020-08-13T12:25:16.870357562Z | PROFIT/LOSS=-3.19 | CUMULATIVE=-17.84
         ===========================================================================
         ===========================================================================
```

❶ Instantiates the `OandaTradingBot` object

❷ Starts the streaming of the real-time data and the trading

❸ Closes the final position after a certain number of ticks retrieved

During the deployment, P&L figures are collected in the `pl` attribute, which is a `list` object. Once the trading has stopped, the P&L figures can be analyzed:

```
In [82]: pl = np.array(otb.pl)   ❶

In [83]: pl   ❶
Out[83]: array([ 0.    , -6.7959, -7.8594, -3.1862])

In [84]: pl.cumsum()   ❷
Out[84]: array([ 0.    ,  -6.7959, -14.6553, -17.8415])
```

❶ P&L figures for all trades

❷ Cumulative P&L figures

The simple deployment example illustrates that one can trade algorithmically and in automated fashion with a deep Q-learning trading bot in less than 100 lines of Python code. The major prerequisite is the trained trading bot (i.e., an instance of the tradingbot class). Many important aspects are intentionally left out here. For example, in a production environment, one would probably like to persist the data. One would also like to persist the order objects. Measures to make sure that the socket connection is still alive are also important (for example, by monitoring a heartbeat). Overall, security, reliability, logging, and monitoring are not really addressed. Some more details in this regard are provided in Hilpisch (2020).

The Python script in "Oanda Trading Bot" on page 373 presents a standalone executable version of the OandaTradingBot class. This represents a major step toward a more robust deployment option as compared to an interactive context such as Jupyter Notebook or Jupyter Lab. The script also includes functionality to add SL, TSL, or TP orders for the execution. The script expects a pickled version of the agent object in the current working directory. The following Python code pickles the object for later usage by the script and saves the Keras model object separately:

```
In [85]: import pickle

In [86]: agent.model.save('tradingbot')

In [87]: agent.model = None

In [88]: pickle.dump(agent, open('trading.bot', 'wb'))
```

Conclusions

This chapter discusses central aspects of the execution of an algorithmic trading strategy and the deployment of a trading bot. The Oanda trading platform provides directly or indirectly with its v20 API all necessary capabilities to do the following:

- Retrieve historical data
- Train and backtest a trading bot (deep Q-learning agent)
- Stream real-time data
- Place market (and limit) orders
- Make use of SL, TSL, and TP orders
- Deploy a trading bot in an automated manner

The prerequisites to implement all these steps are a demo account with Oanda, standard hardware and software (open source only), and a stable internet connection. In other words, the barriers of entry to algorithmic trading for the purposes of exploiting economic inefficiencies are pretty low. This is in stark contrast, for example, to the training, design, and construction of AVs for deployment on public streets—the budgets of companies in the AV space run into the billions of dollars. In other words, the finance domain has distinctive advantages compared to other industries and domains with regard to the real-world deployment of AI agents, such as trading bots, as focused on in this and the previous chapter.

References

Books and papers cited in this chapter:

Hilpisch, Yves. 2020. *Python for Algorithmic Trading: From Idea to Cloud Deployment.* Sebastopol: O'Reilly.

Litman, Todd. 2020. "Autonomous Vehicle Implementation Predictions." *Victoria Transport Policy Institute. https://oreil.ly/ds7YM.*

Python Code

This section contains code used and referenced in the main body of the chapter.

Oanda Environment

The following is the Python module with the OandaEnv class to train a trading bot based on historical Oanda data:

```
#
# Finance Environment
#
# (c) Dr. Yves J. Hilpisch
# Artificial Intelligence in Finance
#
#
import math
import tpqoa
import random
import numpy as np
import pandas as pd


class observation_space:
    def __init__(self, n):
        self.shape = (n,)


class action_space:
    def __init__(self, n):
        self.n = n

    def sample(self):
        return random.randint(0, self.n - 1)
```

```
class OandaEnv:
    def __init__(self, symbol, start, end, granularity, price,
                 features, window, lags, leverage=1,
                 min_accuracy=0.5, min_performance=0.85,
                 mu=None, std=None):
        self.symbol = symbol
        self.start = start
        self.end = end
        self.granularity = granularity
        self.price = price
        self.api = tpqoa.tpqoa('../aiif.cfg')
        self.features = features
        self.n_features = len(features)
        self.window = window
        self.lags = lags
        self.leverage = leverage
        self.min_accuracy = min_accuracy
        self.min_performance = min_performance
        self.mu = mu
        self.std = std
        self.observation_space = observation_space(self.lags)
        self.action_space = action_space(2)
        self._get_data()
        self._prepare_data()

    def _get_data(self):
        ''' Method to retrieve data from Oanda.
        '''
        self.fn = f'../../source/oanda/'                                ❶
        self.fn += f'oanda_{self.symbol}_{self.start}_{self.end}_'      ❷
        self.fn += f'{self.granularity}_{self.price}.csv'              ❷
        self.fn = self.fn.replace(' ', '_').replace('-', '_').replace(':', '_')
        try:
            self.raw = pd.read_csv(self.fn, index_col=0, parse_dates=True)   ❸
        except:
            self.raw = self.api.get_history(self.symbol, self.start,
                                            self.end, self.granularity,
                                            self.price)                 ❹
            self.raw.to_csv(self.fn)                                    ❺
        self.data = pd.DataFrame(self.raw['c'])                         ❻
        self.data.columns = [self.symbol]                              ❼

    def _prepare_data(self):
        ''' Method to prepare additional time series data
            (such as features data).
        '''
        self.data['r'] = np.log(self.data / self.data.shift(1))
        self.data.dropna(inplace=True)
        self.data['s'] = self.data[self.symbol].rolling(self.window).mean()
        self.data['m'] = self.data['r'].rolling(self.window).mean()
        self.data['v'] = self.data['r'].rolling(self.window).std()
        self.data.dropna(inplace=True)
```

```
        if self.mu is None:
            self.mu = self.data.mean()
            self.std = self.data.std()
        self.data_ = (self.data - self.mu) / self.std
        self.data['d'] = np.where(self.data['r'] > 0, 1, 0)
        self.data['d'] = self.data['d'].astype(int)

    def _get_state(self):
        ''' Privat method that returns the state of the environment.
        '''
        return self.data_[self.features].iloc[self.bar -
                                 self.lags:self.bar].values

    def get_state(self, bar):
        ''' Method that returns the state of the environment.
        '''
        return self.data_[self.features].iloc[bar - self.lags:bar].values

    def reset(self):
        ''' Method to reset the environment.
        '''
        self.treward = 0
        self.accuracy = 0
        self.performance = 1
        self.bar = self.lags
        state = self._get_state()
        return state

    def step(self, action):
        ''' Method to step the environment forwards.
        '''
        correct = action == self.data['d'].iloc[self.bar]
        ret = self.data['r'].iloc[self.bar] * self.leverage
        reward_1 = 1 if correct else 0                          ❽
        reward_2 = abs(ret) if correct else -abs(ret)          ❾
        reward = reward_1 + reward_2 * self.leverage           ❿
        self.treward += reward_1
        self.bar += 1
        self.accuracy = self.treward / (self.bar - self.lags)
        self.performance *= math.exp(reward_2)
        if self.bar >= len(self.data):
            done = True
        elif reward_1 == 1:
            done = False
        elif (self.accuracy < self.min_accuracy and
                self.bar > self.lags + 15):
            done = True
        elif (self.performance < self.min_performance and
                self.bar > self.lags + 15):
            done = True
        else:
            done = False
```

```
        state = self._get_state()
        info = {}
        return state, reward, done, info
```

❶ Defines the path for the data file

❷ Defines the filename of the data file

❸ Reads the data if a corresponding data file exists

❹ Retrieves the data for the API if no such file exists

❺ Writes the data as a CSV file to disk

❻ Selects the column with the closing prices

❼ Renames the column to the instrument name (symbol)

❽ Reward for correct prediction

❾ Reward for the realized performance (return)

❿ Combined reward for prediction and performance

Vectorized Backtesting

The following is the Python module with the helper function `backtest` to generate the data to do a vectorized backtest for a deep Q-learning trading bot. The code is also used in Chapter 11:

```
#
# Vectorized Backtesting of
# Trading Bot (Financial Q-Learning Agent)
#
# (c) Dr. Yves J. Hilpisch
# Artificial Intelligence in Finance
#
import numpy as np
import pandas as pd
pd.set_option('mode.chained_assignment', None)

def reshape(s, env):
    return np.reshape(s, [1, env.lags, env.n_features])

def backtest(agent, env):
    done = False
    env.data['p'] = 0
    state = env.reset()
```

```
    while not done:
        action = np.argmax(
            agent.model.predict(reshape(state, env))[0, 0])
        position = 1 if action == 1 else -1
        env.data.loc[:, 'p'].iloc[env.bar] = position
        state, reward, done, info = env.step(action)
    env.data['s'] = env.data['p'] * env.data['r']
```

Oanda Trading Bot

The following is the Python script with the OandaTradingBot class and code to deploy the class:

```
#
# Oanda Trading Bot
# and Deployment Code
#
# (c) Dr. Yves J. Hilpisch
# Artificial Intelligence in Finance
#
import sys
import tpqoa
import keras
import pickle
import numpy as np
import pandas as pd

sys.path.append('../ch11/')


class OandaTradingBot(tpqoa.tpqoa):
    def __init__(self, config_file, agent, granularity, units,
                 sl_distance=None, tsl_distance=None, tp_price=None,
                 verbose=True):
        super(OandaTradingBot, self).__init__(config_file)
        self.agent = agent
        self.symbol = self.agent.learn_env.symbol
        self.env = agent.learn_env
        self.window = self.env.window
        if granularity is None:
            self.granularity = agent.learn_env.granularity
        else:
            self.granularity = granularity
        self.units = units
        self.sl_distance = sl_distance
        self.tsl_distance = tsl_distance
        self.tp_price = tp_price
        self.trades = 0
        self.position = 0
        self.tick_data = pd.DataFrame()
        self.min_length = (self.agent.learn_env.window +
                           self.agent.learn_env.lags)
```

```
        self.pl = list()
        self.verbose = verbose
    def _prepare_data(self):
        ''' Prepares the (lagged) features data.
        '''
        self.data['r'] = np.log(self.data / self.data.shift(1))
        self.data.dropna(inplace=True)
        self.data['s'] = self.data[self.symbol].rolling(self.window).mean()
        self.data['m'] = self.data['r'].rolling(self.window).mean()
        self.data['v'] = self.data['r'].rolling(self.window).std()
        self.data.dropna(inplace=True)
        self.data_ = (self.data - self.env.mu) / self.env.std
    def _resample_data(self):
        ''' Resamples the data to the trading bar length.
        '''
        self.data = self.tick_data.resample(self.granularity,
                              label='right').last().ffill().iloc[:-1]
        self.data = pd.DataFrame(self.data['mid'])
        self.data.columns = [self.symbol,]
        self.data.index = self.data.index.tz_localize(None)
    def _get_state(self):
        ''' Returns the (current) state of the financial market.
        '''
        state = self.data_[self.env.features].iloc[-self.env.lags:]
        return np.reshape(state.values, [1, self.env.lags, self.env.n_features])
    def report_trade(self, time, side, order):
        ''' Reports trades and order details.
        '''
        self.trades += 1
        pl = float(order['pl'])
        self.pl.append(pl)
        cpl = sum(self.pl)
        print('\n' + 71 * '=')
        print(f'{time} | *** GOING {side} ({self.trades}) ***')
        print(f'{time} | PROFIT/LOSS={pl:.2f} | CUMULATIVE={cpl:.2f}')
        print(71 * '=')
        if self.verbose:
            pprint(order)
            print(71 * '=')
    def on_success(self, time, bid, ask):
        ''' Contains the main trading logic.
        '''
        df = pd.DataFrame({'ask': ask, 'bid': bid, 'mid': (bid + ask) / 2},
                       index=[pd.Timestamp(time)])
        self.tick_data = self.tick_data.append(df)
        self._resample_data()
        if len(self.data) > self.min_length:
            self.min_length += 1
            self._prepare_data()
            state = self._get_state()
            prediction = np.argmax(self.agent.model.predict(state)[0, 0])
            position = 1 if prediction == 1 else -1
```

```
            if self.position in [0, -1] and position == 1:
                order = self.create_order(self.symbol,
                        units=(1 - self.position) * self.units,
                        sl_distance=self.sl_distance,
                        tsl_distance=self.tsl_distance,
                        tp_price=self.tp_price,
                        suppress=True, ret=True)
                self.report_trade(time, 'LONG', order)
                self.position = 1
            elif self.position in [0, 1] and position == -1:
                order = self.create_order(self.symbol,
                        units=-(1 + self.position) * self.units,
                        sl_distance=self.sl_distance,
                        tsl_distance=self.tsl_distance,
                        tp_price=self.tp_price,
                        suppress=True, ret=True)
                self.report_trade(time, 'SHORT', order)
                self.position = -1


if __name__ == '__main__':
    model = keras.models.load_model('tradingbot')
    agent = pickle.load(open('trading.bot', 'rb'))
    agent.model = model
    otb = OandaTradingBot('../aiif.cfg', agent, '5s',
                        25000, verbose=False)
    otb.stream_data(agent.learn_env.symbol, stop=1000)
    print('\n' + 71 * '=')
    print('*** CLOSING OUT ***')
    order = otb.create_order(otb.symbol,
                    units=-otb.position * otb.units,
                    suppress=True, ret=True)
    otb.report_trade(otb.time, 'NEUTRAL', order)
    if otb.verbose:
        pprint(order)
    print(71 * '=')
```

## PART V

Outlook

This part of the book serves as an epilogue. It provides an outlook on the consequences that the widespread adoption of AI in finance could have. It is concerned primarily, as is the rest of the book, with the trading domain to keep the discussion focused. This final part consists of two chapters:

- Chapter 13 discusses aspects of AI-driven competition in the financial industry, such as new requirements for finance education or competitive scenarios that might arise.
- Chapter 14 considers the prospect of a financial singularity and the emergence of an artificial financial intelligence—a trading bot consistently generating profits through algorithmic trading well beyond known human or institutional capabilities.

This part is largely speculative, argues on a high level, and neglects many relevant and interesting details. It can serve, however, as a starting point for a more in-depth discussion and analysis of the important topics addressed in it.

## CHAPTER 13

AI-Based Competition

One high-stakes and extremely competitive environment in which AI systems operate today is the global financial market.

—Nick Bostrom (2014)

Financial services companies are becoming hooked on artificial intelligence, using it to automate menial tasks, analyze data, improve customer service and comply with regulations.

—Nick Huber (2020)

This chapter addresses topics related to competition in the financial industry based on the systematic and strategic application of AI. "AI and Finance" on page 380 serves as a review and summary of the importance that AI might have for the future of finance. "Lack of Standardization" on page 382 argues that AI in finance is still at a nascent stage, making the implementation in many instances anything but straight-forward. This, on the other hand, leaves the competitive landscape wide open for financial players to secure competitive advantages through AI. The rise of AI in finance requires a rethinking and redesign of finance education and training. Today's requirements cannot be met anymore by traditional finance curricula. "Fight for Resources" on page 385 discusses how financial institutions will fight for necessary resources to apply AI at a large scale in finance. As in many other areas, AI experts are often the bottleneck for which financial companies compete with technology companies, startups, and companies from other industries.

"Market Impact" on page 386 explains how AI is both a major cause of and the only solution for the age of *microscopic alpha*—alpha that is, like gold nowadays, still to be found but only at small scales and in many cases to be mined only with industrial effort. "Competitive Scenarios" on page 387 discusses reasons for and against future scenarios for the financial industry characterized by a monopoly, oligopoly, or perfect competition. Finally, "Risks, Regulation, and Oversight" on page 388 has a brief look at risks arising from AI in finance in general and major problems regulators and industry watchdogs are faced with.

AI and Finance

This book primarily focuses on the use of AI in finance as applied to the prediction of financial time series. The goal is to discover *statistical inefficiencies*, situations in which the AI algorithm outperforms a baseline algorithm in predicting future market movements. Such statistical inefficiencies are the basis for *economic inefficiencies*. An economic inefficiency requires that there be a trading strategy that can exploit the statistical inefficiency in such a way that above-market returns are realized. In other words, there is a strategy—composed of the prediction algorithm and an execution algorithm—that generates *alpha*.

There are, of course, many other areas in which AI algorithms can be applied to finance. Examples include the following:

Credit scoring
> AI algorithms can be used to derive credit scores for potential debtors, thereby supporting credit decisions or even fully automating them. For example, Golbayani et al. (2020) apply a neural network–based approach to corporate credit ratings, whereas Babaev et al. (2019) use RNNs in the context of retail loan applications.

Fraud detection
> AI algorithms can identify unusual patterns (for example, in transactions related to credit cards), thereby preventing fraud from remaining undetected or even from happening. Yousefi et al. (2019) provide a survey of the literature on the topic.

Trade execution
> AI algorithms can learn how to best execute trades related to large blocks of shares, for example, thereby minimizing market impact and transaction costs. The paper by Ning et al. (2020) applies a double deep Q-learning algorithm to learn optimal trade execution policies.

Derivatives hedging
> AI algorithms can be trained to optimally execute hedge transactions for single derivative instruments or portfolios composed of such instruments. The approach is often called *deep hedging*. Buehler et al. (2019) apply a reinforcement learning approach to implement deep hedging.

Portfolio management

AI algorithms can be used to compose and rebalance portfolios of financial instruments, say, in the context of long-term retirement savings plans. The recent book by López de Prado (2020) covers this topic in detail.

Customer service

AI algorithms can be used to process natural language, such as in the context of customer inquiries. Chat bots have therefore—like in many other industries—become quite popular in finance. The paper by Yu et al. (2020) discusses a financial chat bot based on the popular *bidirectional encoder representations from transformers* (BERT) model, which has its origin within Google.

All these application areas of AI in finance and others not listed here benefit from the programmatic availability of large amounts of relevant data. Why can we expect machine, deep, and reinforcement learning algorithms to perform better than traditional methods from financial econometrics, such as OLS regression? There are a number of reasons:

Big data

While traditional statistical methods can often cope with larger data sets, they at the same time do not benefit too much performance-wise from increasing data volumes. On the other hand, neural network–based approaches often benefit tremendously when trained on larger data sets with regard to the relevant performance metrics.

Instability

Financial markets, in contrast to the physical world, do not follow constant laws. They are rather changing over time, sometimes in rapid fashion. AI algorithms can take this more easily into account by incrementally updating neural networks through online training, for example.

Nonlinearity

OLS regression, for example, assumes an inherent linear relationship between the features and the labels data. AI algorithms, such as neural networks, can in general more easily cope with nonlinear relationships.

Nonnormality

In financial econometrics, the assumption of normally distributed variables is ubiquitous. AI algorithms in general do not rely that much on such constraining assumptions.

High dimensionality

Traditional methods from financial econometrics have proven useful for problems characterized by low dimensionality. Many problems in finance are cast into a context with a pretty low number of features (independent variables), such as one (CAPM) or maybe a few more. More advanced AI algorithms can easily deal with problems characterized by high dimensionality, taking into account even several hundred different features if required.

Classification problems

The toolbox of traditional econometrics is mainly based on approaches for estimation (regression) problems. These problems for sure form an important category in finance. However, classification problems are probably equally important. The toolbox of machine and deep learning provides a large menu of options for attacking classification problems.

Unstructured data

Traditional methods from financial econometrics can basically only deal with structured, numerical data. Machine and deep learning algorithms are able to also efficiently handle unstructured, text-based data. They can also handle both structured and unstructured data efficiently at the same time.

Although the application of AI is in many parts of finance still at a nascent stage, some areas of application have proven to benefit tremendously from the paradigm shift to AI-first finance. It is therefore relatively safe to predict that machine, deep, and reinforcement learning algorithms will significantly reshape the way finance is approached and conducted in practice. Furthermore, AI has become the number one instrument in the pursuit of competitive advantages.

Lack of Standardization

Traditional, normative finance (see Chapter 3) has reached a high degree of standardization. There are a number of textbooks available on different formal levels that basically teach and explain the very same theories and models. Two examples in this context are Copeland et al. (2005) and Jones (2012). The theories and models in turn rely in general on research papers published over the previous decades.

When Black and Scholes (1973) and Merton (1973) published their theories and models to price European option contracts with a closed-form analytical formula, the financial industry immediately accepted the formula and the ideas behind it as a benchmark. Almost 50 years later, with many improved theories and models suggested in between, the Black-Scholes-Merton model and formula are still considered to be *a* benchmark, if not *the* benchmark, in option pricing.

On the other hand, AI-first finance lacks a noticeable degree of standardization. There are numerous research papers published essentially on a daily basis (for example, on *http://arxiv.org*). Among other reasons, this is due to the fact that traditional publication venues with peer review are in general too slow to keep up with the fast pace in the field of AI. Researchers are keen to share their work with the public as fast as possible, often to not be outpaced by competing teams. A peer review process, which also has its merits in terms of quality assurance, might take months, during which the research would not be published. In that sense, researchers more and more trust in the community to take care of the review while also ensuring early credit for their discoveries.

Whereas it was not unusual decades ago that a new finance working paper circulated for years among experts before being peer reviewed and finally published, today's research environment is characterized by much faster turnaround times and the willingness of researchers to put out work early that might not have been thoroughly reviewed and tested by others. As a consequence, there are hardly any standards or benchmark implementations available for the multitude of AI algorithms that are being applied to financial problems.

These fast research publication cycles are in large part driven by the easy applicability of AI algorithms to financial data. Students, researchers, and practitioners hardly need more than a typical consumer notebook to apply the latest breakthroughs in AI to the financial domain. This is an advantage when compared to the constraints of econometric research some decades ago (in the form of limited data availability and limited compute power, for example). But it also often leads to the idea of "throwing as much spaghetti as possible at the wall" in the hope that some might stick.

To some extent, the eagerness and urgency are also caused by investors, pushing investment managers to come up with new investment approaches at a faster pace. This often requires the dismissal of traditional research approaches in finance in favor of more practical approaches. As López de Prado (2018) puts it:

> Problem: Mathematical proofs can take years, decades, and centuries. No investor will wait that long.
>
> Solution: Use experimental math. Solve hard, intractable problems, not by proof but by experiment.

Overall, the lack of standardization provides ample opportunity for single financial players to exploit the advantages of AI-first finance in a competitive context. At the time of this writing in mid-2020, it feels like the race to leverage AI to revolutionize how finance is approached is moving at full speed. The remainder of this chapter addresses important aspects of AI-based competition beyond those of this and the previous section.

Education and Training

Entering the field of finance and the financial industry happens quite often via a formal education in the field. Typical degrees have names such as the following:

- Master of Finance
- Master of Quantitative Finance

- Master of Computational Finance
- Master of Financial Engineering
- Master of Quantitative Enterprise Risk Management

Essentially, all such degrees today require the students to master at least one programming language, often Python, to address the data processing requirements of data-driven finance. In this regard, universities address the demand for these skills from the industry. Murray (2019) points out:

> The workforce will have to adapt as companies use artificial intelligence for more tasks.
>
> [T]here are opportunities for Master's in Finance (MiF) graduates. The blend of technological and financial knowledge is a sweet spot.
>
> Perhaps the highest demand comes from quantitative investors that use AI to trawl markets and colossal data sets to identify potential trades.

It is not only universities that adjust their curricula in finance-related degrees to include programming, data science, and AI. The companies themselves also invest heavily in training programs for new and existing staff to be ready for data-driven and AI-first finance. Noonan (2018) describes the large-scale training efforts of JPMorgan Chase, one of the largest banks in the world, as follows:

> JPMorgan Chase is putting hundreds of new investment bankers and asset managers through mandatory coding lessons, in a sign of Wall Street's heightened need for technology skills.
>
> With technology, from artificial intelligence trading to online lending platforms, shaping the future of banking, financial services groups are developing software to help them boost efficiency, create innovative products and fend off the threat from start-ups and tech giants.
>
> The coding training for this year's juniors was based on Python programming, which will help them to analyze very large data sets and interpret unstructured data such as free language text. Next year, the asset management division will expand the mandatory tech training to include data science concepts, machine learning and cloud computing.

In summary, more and more roles in the financial industry will require staff skilled in programming, basic and advanced data science concepts, machine learning, and other technical aspects, such as cloud computing. Universities and financial institutions on both the buy and sell sides react to this trend by adjusting their curricula and by investing heavily in training their workforces, respectively. In both cases, it is a matter of competing effectively—or even of staying relevant and being able to survive—in a financial landscape changed for good by the increasing importance of AI.

Fight for Resources

In the quest to make use of AI in a scalable, significant way in finance, players in the financial markets compete for the best resources. Four major resources are of paramount importance: human resources, algorithms, data, and hardware.

Probably the most important and, at the same time, scarcest resource is experts in AI in general and AI for finance in particular. In this regard, financial institutions compete with technology companies, financial technology (fintech) startups, and other groups for the best talent. Although banks are generally prepared to pay relatively high salaries to such experts, cultural aspects of technology companies and, for example, the promise of stock options in startups might make it difficult for them to attract top talent. Often, financial institutions resort to nurturing talent internally.

Many algorithms and models in machine and deep learning can be considered standard algorithms that are well researched, tested, and documented. In many instances, however, it is not clear from the outset how to apply them best in a financial context. This is where financial institutions invest heavily in research efforts. For many of the larger buy-side institutions, such as systematic hedge funds, investment and trading strategy research is at the very core of their business models. However, as Chapter 12 shows, deployment and production are of equal importance. Both strategy research and deployment are, of course, highly technical disciplines in this context.

Algorithms without data are often worthless. Similarly, algorithms with "standard" data from typical data sources, such as exchanges or data service providers like Refinitiv or Bloomberg, might only be of limited value. This is due to the fact that such data is intensively analyzed by many, if not all, relevant players in the market, making it hard or even impossible to identify alpha-generating opportunities or similar competitive advantage. As a consequence, large buy-side institutions invest particularly heavily in getting access to *alternative data* (see "Data Availability" on page 104).

How important alternative data is considered to be nowadays is reflected in investments that buy-side players and other investors make in companies active in the field. For example, in 2018 a group of investment companies invested $95 million in the data group Enigma. Fortado (2018) describes the deal and its rationale as follows:

> Hedge funds, banks and venture capital firms are piling into investments in data companies in the hope of cashing in on a business they are using a lot more themselves.
>
> In recent years, there has been a proliferation of start-ups that trawl through reams of data and sell it to investment groups searching for an edge.
>
> The latest to attract investor interest is Enigma, a New York-based start-up that received funding from sources including quant giant Two Sigma, activist hedge fund Third Point and venture capital firms NEA and Glynn Capital in a $95m capital raising announced on Tuesday.

The fourth resource that financial institutions are competing for is the best hardware options to process big financial data, implement the algorithms based on traditional and alternative data sets, and thereby apply AI efficiently to finance. Recent years have seen tremendous innovation in hardware dedicated to making machine and deep learning efforts faster, more energy-efficient, and more cost-effective. While traditional processors, such as CPUs, play a minor role in the field, specialized hardware such as GPUs by Nvidia (*https://nvidia.com*) or newer options such as TPUs by Google (*https://oreil.ly/3HHUy*) and IPUs by startup Graphcore (*https://www.graphcore.ai*) have taken over in AI. The interest of financial institutions in new, specialized hardware is, for example, reflected in the research efforts of Citadel, one of the largest hedge funds and market makers, into IPUs. Its effort are documented in the comprehensive research report Jia et al. (2019), which illustrates the potential benefits of specialized hardware compared to alternative options.

In the race to dominance in AI-first finance, financial institutions invest billions per year in talent, research, data, and hardware. Whereas large institutions seem well positioned to keep up with the pace in the field, smaller or medium-sized players will find it hard to comprehensively shift to an AI-first approach to their business.

Market Impact

The increasing and now widespread usage of data science, machine learning, and deep learning algorithms in the financial industry without a doubt has an impact on financial markets, investment, and trading opportunities. As the many examples in this book illustrate, ML and DL methods are able to discover statistical inefficiencies and even economic inefficiencies that are not discoverable by traditional econometric methods, such as multivariate OLS regression. It is therefore to be assumed that new and better analysis methods make it harder to discover alpha-generating opportunities and strategies.

Comparing the current situation in financial markets with the one in gold mining, Lopéz de Prado (2018) describes the situation as follows:

> If a decade ago it was relatively common for an individual to discover macroscopic alpha (i.e., using simple mathematical tools like econometrics), currently the chances of that happening are quickly converging to zero. Individuals searching nowadays for macroscopic alpha, regardless of their experience or knowledge, are fighting overwhelming odds. The only true alpha left is microscopic, and finding it requires capital-intensive industrial methods. Just like with gold, microscopic alpha does not mean smaller overall profits. Microscopic alpha today is much more abundant than macroscopic alpha has ever been in history. There is a lot of money to be made, but you will need to use heavy ML tools.

Against this background, financial institutions almost seem to be required to embrace AI-first finance to not be left behind and eventually maybe even go out of business. This holds true not only in investing and trading, but in other areas as well. While banks historically have nurtured long-term relationships with commercial and retail debtors and organically built their ability to make sound credit decisions, AI today levels the playing field and renders long-term relationships almost worthless. Therefore, new entrants in the field, such as fintech startups, relying on AI can often quickly grab market share from incumbents in a controlled, viable fashion. On the other hand, these developments incentivize incumbents to acquire and merge younger, innovative fintech startups to stay competitive.

Competitive Scenarios

Looking forward, say, three to five years, how might the competitive landscape driven by AI-first finance look? Three scenarios are come to mind:

Monopoly

One financial institution reaches a dominant position through major, unmatched breakthroughs in applying AI to, say, algorithmic trading. This is, for example, the situation in internet searches, where Google has a global market share of about 90%.

Oligopoly

A smaller number of financial institutions are able to leverage AI-first finance to achieve leading positions. An oligopoly is, for example, also present in the hedge fund industry, in which a small number of large players dominate the field in terms of assets under management.

Perfect competition

All players in the financial markets benefit from advances in AI-first finance in similar fashion. No single player or group of players enjoys any competitive advantages compared to others. Technologically speaking, this is comparable to the situation in computer chess nowadays. A number of chess programs, running on standard hardware such as smartphones, are significantly better at playing chess than the current world champion (Magnus Carlsen at the time of this writing).

It is hard to forecast which scenario is more likely. One can find arguments and describe possible paths for all three of them. For example, an argument for a monopoly might be that a major breakthrough in algorithmic trading, for example, might lead to a fast, significant outperformance that helps accumulate more capital through reinvestments, as well as through new inflows. This in turn increases the available technology and research budget to protect the competitive advantage and attracts talent that would be otherwise hard to win over. This whole cycle is self-reinforcing, and the example of Google in search—in connection with the core online advertising business—is a good one in this context.

Similarly, there are good reasons to anticipate an oligopoly. Currently, it is safe to assume that any large player in the trading business invests heavily in research and technology, with AI-related initiatives making up a significant part of the budget. As in other fields, say, recommender engines—think Amazon for books, Netflix for films, and Spotify for music—multiple companies might be able to reach similar breakthroughs at the same time. It is conceivable that the current leading systemic traders will be able to use AI-first finance to cement their leading positions.

Finally, many technologies have become ubiquitous over the years. Strong chess programs are only one example. Others might be maps and navigation systems or speech-based personal assistants. In a perfect competition scenario, a pretty large number of financial players would compete for minuscule alpha-creating opportunities or even might be unable to generate returns distinguishable from plain market returns.

At the same time, there are arguments against the three scenarios. The current landscape has many players with equal means and incentives to leverage AI in finance. This makes it unlikely that only a single player will stand out and grab market share in investment management that is comparable to Google in search. At the same time, the number of small, medium-sized, and large players doing research in the field and the low barriers of entry in algorithmic trading make it unlikely that a select few can secure defendable competitive advantages. An argument against perfect competition is that, in the foreseeable future, algorithmic trading at a large scale requires a huge amount of capital and other resources. With regard to chess, DeepMind has shown with AlphaZero that there is always room for innovation and significant improvements, even if a field almost seems settled once and for all.

Risks, Regulation, and Oversight

A simple Google search reveals that there is an active discourse going on about the risks of AI and its regulation in general, as well as in the financial services industry.[1] This section cannot address all relevant aspects in this context, but it can address at least a few important ones.

The following are some of the risks that the application of AI in finance introduces:

Privacy
> Finance is a sensitive area with tight privacy laws. The use of AI at a large scale requires the use of—at least partly—private data from customers. This increases the risk that private data will be leaked or used in inappropriate ways. Such a risk

---

1 For a brief overview of these topics, see these articles by McKinsey: Confronting the risks of artificial intelligence (*https://bit.ly/aiif_mck_01*) and Derisking machine learning and artificial intelligence (*https://bit.ly/aiif_mck_02*).

obviously does not arise when publicly available data sources, such as for financial time series data, are used.

Bias

AI algorithms can easily learn biases that are inherent in data related, for example, to retail or corporate customers. Algorithms can only be as good and as objective in, say, judging the creditworthiness of a potential debtor as the data allows.[2] Again, the problem of learning biases is not really a problem when working with market data, for instance.

Inexplicability

In many areas, it is important that decisions can be explained, sometimes in detail and in hindsight. This might be required by law or by investors wanting to understand why particular investment decisions have been taken. Take the example of investment and trading decisions. If an AI, based on a large neural network, decides *algorithmically* when and what to trade, it might be pretty difficult and often impossible to explain in detail why the AI has traded the way it has. Researchers work actively and intensively on "explainable AI," (*https://oreil.ly/P3YFQ*) but there are obvious limits in this regard.

Herding

Since the stock market crash of 1987, it is clear what kind of risk herding in financial trading represents. In 1987, positive feedback trading in the context of large-scale synthetic replication programs for put options—in combination with stop loss orders—triggered the downward spiral. A similar herding effect could be observed in the 2008 hedge fund meltdown, which for the first time revealed the extent to which different hedge funds implement similar kinds of strategies. With regard to the flash crash in 2010, for which algorithmic trading was blamed by some, the evidence seems unclear. However, the more widespread use of AI in trading might pose a similar risk when more and more institutions apply similar approaches that have proven fruitful. Other areas are also prone to such an effect. Credit decision agents might learn the same biases based on different data sets and might make it impossible for certain groups or individuals to get credit at all.

Vanishing alpha

As has been argued before, the more widespread use of AI in finance at ever larger scales might make alpha in the markets disappear. Techniques must get better, and data may become "more alternative" to secure any competitive advantage. Chapter 14 takes a closer look at this in the context of a potential *financial singularity*.

---

2 For more on the problem of bias through AI and solutions to it, see Klein (2020).

Beyond the typical risks of AI, AI introduces new risks specific to the financial domain. At the same time, it is difficult for lawmakers and regulators to keep up with the developments in the field and to comprehensively assess individual and systemic risks arising from AI-first finance. There are several reasons for this:

Know-how

Lawmakers and regulators need to acquire, like the financial players themselves, new know-how related to AI in finance. In this respect, they compete with the big financial institutions and technology companies that are known to pay salaries well above the possibilities of lawmakers and regulators.

Insufficient data

In many application areas, there is simply little or even no data available that watchdogs can use to judge the real impact of AI. In some instances, it might not even be known whether AI plays a role or not. And even if it is known and data might be available, it might be hard to separate the impact of AI from the impact of other relevant factors.

Little transparency

While almost all financial institutions try to make use of AI to secure or gain competitive advantages, it is hardly ever transparent what a single institution does in this regard and how exactly it is implemented and used. Many treat their effort in this context as intellectual property and their own "secret sauce."

Model validation

Model validation is a central risk management and regulatory tool in many financial areas. Take the simple example of the pricing of a European option based on the Black-Scholes-Merton (1973) option pricing model. The prices that a specific implementation of the model generates can be validated, for example, by the use of the Cox et al. (1979) binomial option pricing model—and vice versa. This is often quite different with AI algorithms. There is hardly ever a model that, based on a parsimonious set of parameters, can validate the outputs of a complex AI algorithm. Reproducibility might be, however, an attainable goal (that is, the option to have third parties verify the outputs based on an exact replication of all steps involved). But this in turn would require the third party, say, a regulator or an auditor, to have access to the same data, an infrastructure as powerful as the one used by the financial institution, and so on. For larger AI efforts, this seems simply unrealistic.

Hard to regulate

Back to the option pricing example, a regulator can specify that both the Black-Scholes-Merton (1973) and the Cox et al. (1979) option pricing models are acceptable for the pricing of European options. Even when lawmakers and regulators specify that both support vector machine (SVM) algorithms and neural networks are "acceptable algorithms," this leaves open how these algorithms are trained, used, and so on. It is difficult to be more specific in this context. For example, should a regulator limit the number of hidden layers and/or hidden units in a neural network? What about the software packages to be used? The list of hard questions seems endless. Therefore, only general rules will be formulated.

Technology companies and financial institutions alike usually prefer a more lax approach to AI regulation—for often obvious reasons. In Bradshaw (2019), Google CEO Sundar Pichai speaks of "smart" regulation and asks for an approach that differentiates between different industries:

> Google's chief executive has warned politicians against knee-jerk regulation of artificial intelligence, arguing that existing rules may be sufficient to govern the new technology.
>
> Sundar Pichai said that AI required "smart regulation" that balanced innovation with protecting citizens...."It is such a broad cross-cutting technology, so it's important to look at [regulation] more in certain vertical situations," Mr Pichai said.

On the other hand, there are popular proponents of a more stringent regulation of AI, such as Elon Musk in Matyus (2020):

> "Mark my words," Musk warned. "A.I. is far more dangerous than nukes. So why do we have no regulatory oversight?"

The risks from AI in finance are manifold, as are the problems faced by lawmakers and regulators. Nevertheless, it is safe to predict that tighter regulation and oversight addressing AI in finance specifically is certainly to come in many jurisdictions.

Conclusions

This chapter addresses aspects of using AI to compete in the financial industry. The benefits are clear in many application areas. However, so far hardly any standards have been established, and the field seems still wide open for players to strive for competitive advantages. Because new technologies and approaches from data science, machine learning, deep learning, and more generally AI infiltrate almost any financial discipline, education and training in finance must take this into account. Many master's programs have already adjusted their curricula, while big financial institutions invest heavily in training incoming and existing staff in the required skills. Beyond human resources, financial institutions also compete for other resources in the field, such as alternative data. In the financial markets, AI-powered investment and trading make it harder to identify sustainable alpha opportunities. On the other hand, with traditional econometric methods it might be impossible today to identify and mine microscopic alpha.

It is difficult to predict a competitive end scenario for the financial industry at a point when AI has taken over. Scenarios ranging from a monopoly to an oligopoly to perfect competition seem still reasonable. Chapter 14 revisits this topic. AI-first finance confronts researchers, practitioners, and regulators with new risks and new challenges in addressing these risks appropriately. One such risk, playing a prominent role in many discussions, is the black box characteristic of many AI algorithms. Such a risk usually can only be mitigated to some extent with today's state-of-the-art explainable AI.

References

Books, papers, and articles cited in this chapter:

Babaev, Dmitrii et al. 2019. "E.T.-RNN: Applying Deep Learning to Credit Loan Applications." *https://oreil.ly/ZK5G8*.

Black, Fischer, and Myron Scholes. 1973. "The Pricing of Options and Corporate Liabilities." *Journal of Political Economy* 81 (3): 638–659.

Bradshaw, Tim. 2019. "Google chief Sundar Pichai warns against rushing into AI regulation." *Financial Times*, September 20, 2019.

Bostrom, Nick. 2014. *Superintelligence: Paths, Dangers, Strategies.* Oxford: Oxford University Press.

Buehler, Hans et al. 2019. "Deep Hedging: Hedging Derivatives Under Generic Market Frictions Using Reinforcement Learning." Finance Institute Research Paper No. 19-80. *https://oreil.ly/_oDaO*.

Copeland, Thomas, Fred Weston, and Kuldeep Shastri. 2005. *Financial Theory and Corporate Policy.* 4th ed. Boston: Pearson.

Cox, John, Stephen Ross, and Mark Rubinstein. 1979. "Option Pricing: A Simplified Approach." *Journal of Financial Economics* 7, (3): 229–263.

Fortado, Lindsay. 2018. "Data specialist Enigma reels in investment group cash." *Financial Times*, September 18, 2018.

Golbayani, Parisa, Dan Wang, and Ionut Florescu. 2020. "Application of Deep Neural Networks to Assess Corporate Credit Rating." *https://oreil.ly/U3eXF*.

Huber, Nick. 2020. "AI 'Only Scratching the Surface' of Potential in Financial Services." *Financial Times*, July 1, 2020.

Jia, Zhe et al. 2019. "Dissecting the Graphcore IPU Architecture via Microbenchmarking." *https://oreil.ly/3ZgTO*.

Jones, Charles P. 2012. *Investments: Analysis and Management.* 12th ed. Hoboken: John Wiley & Sons.

Klein, Aaron. 2020. "Reducing Bias in AI-based Financial Services." The Brookings Institution Report, July 10, 2020, *https://bit.ly/aiif_bias*.

López de Prado, Marcos. 2018. *Advances in Financial Machine Learning*. Hoboken: Wiley Finance.

———. 2020. *Machine Learning for Asset Managers*. Cambridge: Cambridge University Press.

Matyus, Allison. 2020. "Elon Musk Warns that All A.I. Must Be Regulated, Even at Tesla." *Digital Trends*, February 18, 2020. *https://oreil.ly/JmAKZ*.

Merton, Robert C. 1973. "Theory of Rational Option Pricing." *Bell Journal of Economics and Management Science* 4 (Spring): 141–183.

Murray, Seb. 2019. "Graduates with Tech and Finance Skills in High Demand." *Financial Times*, June 17, 2019.

Ning, Brian, Franco Ho Ting Lin, and Sebastian Jaimungal. 2020. "Double Deep Q-Learning for Optimal Execution." *https://oreil.ly/BSBNV*.

Noonan, Laura. 2018. "JPMorgan's requirement for new staff: coding lessons." *Financial Times*, October 8, 2018.

Yousefi, Niloofar, Marie Alaghband, and Ivan Garibay. 2019. "A Comprehensive Survey on Machine Learning Techniques and User Authentication Approaches for Credit Card Fraud Detection." *https://oreil.ly/fFjAJ*.

Yu, Shi, Yuxin Chen, and Hussain Zaidi. 2020. "AVA: A Financial Service Chatbot based on Deep Bidirectional Transformers." *https://oreil.ly/2NVNH*.

## CHAPTER 14

Financial Singularity

We find ourselves in a thicket of strategic complexity, surrounded by a dense mist of uncertainty.

—Nick Bostrom (2014)

"Most trading and investment roles will disappear and over time, probably most roles that require human services will be automated," says Mr Skinner. "What you will end up with is banks that are run primarily by managers and machines. The managers decide what the machines need to do, and the machines do the job."

—Nick Huber (2020)

Can AI-based competition in the financial industry lead to a financial singularity? This is the main question that this final chapter discusses. It starts with "Notions and Definitions" on page 396, which defines expressions such as *financial singularity* and *artificial financial intelligence* (AFI). "What Is at Stake?" on page 396 illustrates what, in terms of potential wealth accumulation, is at stake in the race for an AFI. "Paths to Financial Singularity" on page 400 considers, against the background of Chapter 2, paths that might lead to an AFI. "Orthogonal Skills and Resources" on page 401 argues that there are a number of resources that are instrumental and orthogonal to the goal of creating an AFI. Anybody involved in the race for an AFI will compete for these resources. Finally, "Star Trek or Star Wars" on page 403 considers whether an AFI, as discussed in this chapter, will benefit only a few people or humanity as a whole.

Notions and Definitions

The expression *financial singularity* dates back at least to the 2015 blog post by Shiller. In this post, Shiller writes:

> Will alpha eventually go to zero for every imaginable investment strategy? More fundamentally, is the day approaching when, thanks to so many smart people and smarter computers, financial markets really do become perfect, and we can just sit back, relax, and assume that all assets are priced correctly?

> This imagined state of affairs might be called the financial singularity, analogous to the hypothetical future technological singularity, when computers replace human intelligence. The financial singularity implies that all investment decisions would be better left to a computer program, because the experts with their algorithms have figured out what drives market outcomes and reduced it to a seamless system.

A bit more generally, one could define the *financial singularity* as the point in time from which computers and algorithms begin to take over control of finance and the whole financial industry, including banks, asset managers, exchanges, and so on, with humans taking a back seat as managers, supervisors, and controllers, if anything.

On the other hand, one could define the financial singularity—in the spirit of this book's focus—as the point in time from which *a trading bot exists that shows a consistent capability to predict movements in financial markets at superhuman and super-institutional levels, as well as with unprecedented accuracy*. In that sense, such a trading bot would be characterized as an artificial narrow intelligence (ANI) instead of an artificial general intelligence (AGI) or superintelligence (see Chapter 2).

It can be assumed that it is much easier to build such an AFI in the form of a trading bot than an AGI or even a superintelligence. This holds true for AlphaZero in the same way, as it is easier to build an AI agent that is superior to any human being or any other agent in playing the game of Go. Therefore, even if it is not yet clear whether there will ever be an AI agent that qualifies as an AGI or superintelligence, it is in any case much more likely that a trading bot will emerge that qualifies as an ANI or AFI.

In what follows, the focus lies on a trading bot that qualifies as an AFI to keep the discussion as specific as possible and embedded in the context of this book.

What Is at Stake?

The pursuit of an AFI might be challenging and exciting in and of itself. However, as is usual in finance, not too many initiatives are driven by altruistic motives; rather, most are driven by the financial incentives (that is, hard cash). But what exactly is at stake in the race to build an AFI? This cannot be answered with certainty or generality, but some simple calculations can shed light on the question.

To understand how valuable it is to have an AFI as compared to inferior trading strategies, consider the following benchmarks:

Bull strategy
A trading strategy that goes long only on a financial instrument in the expectation of rising prices.

Random strategy
A trading strategy that chooses a long or short position randomly for a given financial instrument.

Bear strategy
A trading strategy that goes short only on a financial instrument in the expectation of falling prices.

These benchmark strategies shall be compared to AFIs with the following success characteristics:

X% top
The AFI gets the top X% up and down movements correct, with the remaining market movements being predicted randomly.

X% AFI
The AFI gets X% of all randomly chosen market movements correct, with the remaining market movements being predicted randomly.

The following Python code imports the known time series data set with EOD data for a number of financial instruments. The examples to follow rely on five years' worth of EOD data for a single financial instrument:

```
In [1]: import random
        import numpy as np
        import pandas as pd
        from pylab import plt, mpl
        plt.style.use('seaborn')
        mpl.rcParams['savefig.dpi'] = 300
        mpl.rcParams['font.family'] = 'serif'

In [2]: url = 'https://hilpisch.com/aiif_eikon_eod_data.csv'

In [3]: raw = pd.read_csv(url, index_col=0, parse_dates=True)

In [4]: symbol = 'EUR='

In [5]: raw['bull'] = np.log(raw[symbol] / raw[symbol].shift(1))    ❶

In [6]: data = pd.DataFrame(raw['bull']).loc['2015-01-01':]    ❶

In [7]: data.dropna(inplace=True)
```

```
In [8]: data.info()
        <class 'pandas.core.frame.DataFrame'>
        DatetimeIndex: 1305 entries, 2015-01-01 to 2020-01-01
        Data columns (total 1 columns):
         #   Column  Non-Null Count  Dtype
        ---  ------  --------------  -----
         0   bull    1305 non-null   float64
        dtypes: float64(1)
        memory usage: 20.4 KB
```

❶ The *bull* benchmark returns (long only)

With the bull strategy being already defined by the log returns of the base financial instrument, the following Python code specifies the other two benchmark strategies and derives the performances for the AFI strategies. In this context, a number of AFI strategies are considered to illustrate the impact of improvements in the accuracy of the AFI's predictions:

```
In [9]: np.random.seed(100)

In [10]: data['random'] = np.random.choice([-1, 1], len(data)) * data['bull']   ❶

In [11]: data['bear'] = -data['bull']   ❷

In [12]: def top(t):
             top = pd.DataFrame(data['bull'])
             top.columns = ['top']
             top = top.sort_values('top')
             n = int(len(data) * t)
             top['top'].iloc[:n] = abs(top['top'].iloc[:n])
             top['top'].iloc[n:] = abs(top['top'].iloc[n:])
             top['top'].iloc[n:-n] = np.random.choice([-1, 1],
                     len(top['top'].iloc[n:-n])) * top['top'].iloc[n:-n]
             data[f'{int(t * 100)}_top'] = top.sort_index()

In [13]: for t in [0.1, 0.15]:
             top(t)   ❸

In [14]: def afi(ratio):
             correct = np.random.binomial(1, ratio, len(data))
             random = np.random.choice([-1, 1], len(data))
             strat = np.where(correct, abs(data['bull']), random * data['bull'])
             data[f'{int(ratio * 100)}_afi'] = strat

In [15]: for ratio in [0.51, 0.6, 0.75, 0.9]:
             afi(ratio)   ❹
```

❶ The *random* benchmark returns

❷ The *bear* benchmark returns (short only)

❸ The *X% top* strategy returns

❹ The *X% AFI* strategy returns

Using the standard vectorized backtesting approach, as introduced in Chapter 10 (neglecting transaction costs), it becomes clear what significant increases in the prediction accuracy imply in financial terms. Consider the "90% AFI," which is not perfect in its predictions but rather lacks any edge in 10% of all cases. The assumed 90% accuracy leads to a gross performance that over five years returns almost 100 times the invested capital (before transaction costs). With 75% accuracy, the AFI would still return almost 50 times the invested capital (see Figure 14-1). This excludes leverage, which can easily be added in an almost risk-less fashion in the presence of such prediction accuracies:

```
In [16]: data.head()
Out[16]:                    bull    random      bear   10_top    15_top    51_afi  \
         Date
         2015-01-01  0.000413 -0.000413 -0.000413  0.000413 -0.000413  0.000413
         2015-01-02 -0.008464  0.008464  0.008464  0.008464  0.008464  0.008464
         2015-01-05 -0.005767 -0.005767  0.005767 -0.005767  0.005767 -0.005767
         2015-01-06 -0.003611 -0.003611  0.003611 -0.003611  0.003611  0.003611
         2015-01-07 -0.004299 -0.004299  0.004299  0.004299  0.004299  0.004299

                       60_afi    75_afi    90_afi
         Date
         2015-01-01  0.000413  0.000413  0.000413
         2015-01-02  0.008464  0.008464  0.008464
         2015-01-05  0.005767 -0.005767  0.005767
         2015-01-06  0.003611  0.003611  0.003611
         2015-01-07  0.004299  0.004299  0.004299

In [17]: data.sum().apply(np.exp)
Out[17]: bull        0.926676
         random      1.097137
         bear        1.079126
         10_top      9.815383
         15_top     21.275448
         51_afi     12.272497
         60_afi     22.103642
         75_afi     49.227314
         90_afi     98.176658
         dtype: float64

In [18]: data.cumsum().apply(np.exp).plot(figsize=(10, 6));
```

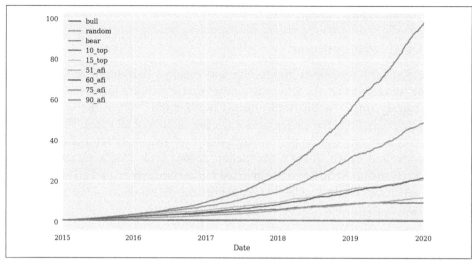

Figure 14-1. Gross performance of benchmark and theoretical AFI strategies over time

The analyses show that quite a lot is at stake, although several simplifying assumptions are of course made. Time plays an important role in this context. Reimplementing the same analyses over a 10-year period makes the numbers even more impressive—almost unimaginable in a trading context. As the following output illustrates for "90% AFI," the gross return would be more than 16,000 times the invested capital (before transaction costs). The effect of compounding and reinvesting is tremendous:

```
bull         0.782657
random       0.800253
bear         1.277698
10_top     165.066583
15_top    1026.275100
51_afi     206.639897
60_afi     691.751006
75_afi    2947.811043
90_afi   16581.526533
dtype: float64
```

Paths to Financial Singularity

The emergence of an AFI would be a rather specific event in a rather specified environment. It is, for example, not necessary to emulate the brain of a human being since AGI or superintelligence is not the major goal. Given that there is no human being who seems to be consistently superior in trading in the financial markets compared to everybody else, it might even be a dead end street, trying to emulate a human brain to arrive at an AFI. There is also no need to worry about embodiment. An AFI can live as software only on an appropriate infrastructure connecting to the required data and trading APIs.

On the other hand, AI seems to be a promising path to an AFI because of the very nature of the problem: take as input large amounts of financial and other data and generate predictions about the future direction of a price movement. This is exactly what the algorithms presented and applied in this book are all about—in particular those that fall in the supervised and reinforcement learning categories.

Another option might be a hybrid of human and machine intelligence. Whereas machines have supported human traders for decades, in many instances the roles have changed. Humans support the machines in trading by providing the ideal environment and up-to-date data, intervening only in extreme situations, and so forth. In many cases, the machines are already completely autonomous in their algorithmic trading decisions. Or as Jim Simons—founder of Renaissance Technologies, one of the most successful and secretive systematic trading hedge funds—puts it: "The only rule is we never override the computer."

While it is quite unclear which paths might lead to superintelligence, from today's perspective, it seems most likely that AI might pave the way to the financial singularity and an AFI.

Orthogonal Skills and Resources

Chapter 13 discusses the competition for resources in the context of AI-based competition in the financial industry. The four major resources in this context are human resources (experts), algorithms, and software, financial and alternative data, and high-performance hardware. We can add a fifth resource in this context in the form of the capital needed to acquire the other resources.

According to the orthogonality hypothesis, it is sensible and even imperative to acquire such orthogonal skills and resources, which are instrumental no matter how exactly an AFI will be achieved. Financial institutions taking part in the race to build an AFI will try to acquire as many high-quality resources as they can afford and justify to position themselves as advantageously as possible for the point in time at which *the*, or at least *one*, path to an AFI becomes clear.

In a world driven by AI-first finance, such behavior and positioning might make the difference between thriving, merely surviving, or leaving the market. It cannot be excluded that progress could be made much faster than expected. When Nick Bostrom in 2014 predicted that it might take 10 years until an AI could beat the world champion in the game of Go, basically nobody expected that it would happen only two years later. The major driver has been breakthroughs in the application of reinforcement learning to such games, from which other applications still benefit today. Such unforeseen breakthroughs cannot be excluded in finance either.

Scenarios Before and After

It is safe to assume that every major financial institution around the world and many other nonfinancial entities currently do research and have practical experience with AI applied to finance. However, not all players in the financial industry are positioned equally well to arrive at a trading AFI first. Some, like banks, are rather restricted by regulatory requirements. Others simply follow different business models, such as exchanges. Others, like certain assets managers, focus on providing low-cost, commoditized investment products, such as ETFs, that mimic the performance of broader market indices. In other words, generating alpha is not the major goal for every financial institution.

From an outside perspective, larger hedge funds therefore seem best positioned to make the most out of AI-first finance and AI-powered algorithmic trading. In general, they already have a lot of the required resources important in this field: talented and well-educated people, experience with trading algorithms, and almost limitless access to traditional and alternative data sources, as well as a scalable, professional trading infrastructure. If something is missing, large technology budgets ensure quick and targeted investments.

It is not clear whether there will be one AFI first with others coming later or if several AFIs may emerge at the same time. If several AFIs are present, one could speak of a multipolar or oligopolistic scenario. The AFIs would probably mostly compete against each other, with "non-AFI" players being sidelined. The sponsors of the single projects would strive to gain advantages, however small, because this might allow one AFI to take over completely and finally become a singleton or monopoly.

It is also conceivable that a "winner take all" scenario might prevail from the start. In such a scenario, a single AFI emerges and is able to quickly reach a level of dominance in financial trading that cannot be matched by any other competitor. This could be for several reasons. One reason might be that the first AFI generates returns so impressive that the assets under management swell at a tremendous pace, leading to ever higher budgets that in turn allows it to acquire ever more relevant resources. Another reason might be that the first AFI quickly reaches a size at which its actions can have a market impact—with the ability to manipulate market prices, for instance —such that it becomes the major, or even the only, driving force in financial markets.

Regulation could in theory prevent an AFI from becoming too big or gaining too much market power. The major questions would be if such laws are enforceable in practice and how exactly they would need to be designed to have their desired effects.

Star Trek or Star Wars

The financial industry, for many people, represents the purest form of capitalism: the industry in which greed drives everything. It has been and is for sure a highly competitive industry, no arguing about that. Trading and investment management in particular are often symbolized by billionaire managers and owners who are willing to bet big and go head-to-head with their rivals in order to land the next mega deal or trade. The advent of AI provides ambitious managers with a rich tool set to push the competition to the next level, as discussed in Chapter 13.

However, the question is whether AI-first finance, potentially culminating in an AFI, will lead to financial utopia or dystopia. The systematic, infallible accumulation of wealth could theoretically serve only a few people, or it could potentially serve humanity. Unfortunately, it is to be assumed that only the sponsors of the project leading to an AFI will directly benefit from the type of AFI imagined in this chapter. This is because such an AFI would only generate profits by trading in the financial markets and not by inventing new products, solving important problems, or growing businesses and industries. In other words, an AFI that merely trades in the financial markets to generate profits is taking part in a zero-sum game and does not directly increase the distributable wealth.

One could argue that, for example, pension funds investing in a fund managed by the AFI would also benefit from its exceptional returns. But this would again only benefit a certain group and not humanity as a whole. It would also be in question whether the sponsors of a successful AFI project would be willing to open up to outside investors. A good example in this regard is the Medallion fund, managed by Renaissance Technologies and one of the best-performing investment vehicles in history. Renaissance closed Medallion, which is essentially run exclusively by machines, to outside investors in 1993. Its stellar performance for sure would have attracted large amounts of additional assets. However, specific considerations, such as the capacity of certain strategies, play a role in this context, and similar considerations might also apply to an AFI.

Therefore, whereas one could expect a superintelligence to help overcome fundamental problems faced by humanity as a whole—serious diseases, environmental problems, unknown threats from outer space, and so forth—an AFI more probably leads to more inequality and fiercer competition in the markets. Instead of a *Star Trek*-like world, characterized by equality and inexhaustible resources, it cannot be excluded that an AFI might rather lead to a *Star Wars*-like world, characterized by intensive trade wars and fights over available resources. At the time of this writing, global trade wars, such as the one between the US and China, seem more intense than ever, and technology and AI are important battlegrounds.

Conclusions

This chapter takes a high-level perspective and discusses the concepts of financial singularity and artificial financial intelligence. AFI is an ANI that would lack many of the capabilities and characteristics of a superintelligence. An AFI could rather be compared to AlphaZero, which is an ANI for playing board games such as chess or Go. An AFI would excel at the game of trading financial instruments. Of course, in financial trading, a lot more is at stake compared to playing board games.

Similar to AlphaZero, AI is more likely to pave the way to an AFI as compared to alternative paths, such as the emulation of the human brain. Even if the path is not yet fully visible, and although one cannot know for sure how far single projects have progressed already, there are a number of instrumental resources that are important no matter which path will prevail: experts, algorithms, data, hardware, and capital. Large and successful hedge funds seem best positioned to win the race for an AFI.

Even if it might prove impossible to create an AFI as sketched in this chapter, the systematic introduction of AI to finance will certainly spur innovation and in many cases intensify competition in the industry. Rather than being a fad, AI is a trend that finally will lead to a paradigm shift in the industry.

References

Books and papers cited in this chapter:

Bostrom, Nick. 2014. *Superintelligence: Paths, Dangers, Strategies*. Oxford: Oxford University Press

Huber, Nick. 2020. "AI 'Only Scratching the Surface' of Potential in Financial Services." *Financial Times*, July 1, 2020.

Shiller, Robert. 2015. "The Mirage of the Financial Singularity." *Yale Insights* (blog). *https://oreil.ly/cnWBh*.

## PART VI

Appendixes

This part serves as an appendix and presents additional material to support the contents, code, and examples presented in the other parts of this book. This part consists of three appendixes:

- Appendix A covers fundamental notions related to neural networks, such as tensor operations.
- Appendix B presents classes implementing simple and shallow neural networks from scratch.
- Appendix C illustrates the application of convolutional neural networks with the `Keras` package.

APPENDIX A

Interactive Neural Networks

This appendix explores fundamental notions of neural networks with basic Python code—on the basis of both simple and shallow neural networks. The goal is to provide a good grasp and intuition for important concepts that often disappear behind high-level, abstract APIs when working with standard machine and deep learning packages.

The appendix has the following sections:

- "Tensors and Tensor Operations" on page 407 covers the basics of *tensors* and the operations implemented on them.

- "Simple Neural Networks" on page 409 discusses *simple neural networks*, or neural networks that only have an input and an output layer.

- "Shallow Neural Networks" on page 417 focuses on *shallow neural networks*, or neural networks with one hidden layer.

Tensors and Tensor Operations

In addition to implementing several imports and configurations, the following Python code shows the four types of tensors relevant for the purposes of this appendix: scalar, vector, matrix, and cube tensors. Tensors are generally represented as potentially multidimensional `ndarray` objects in Python. For more details and examples, see Chollet (2017, ch. 2):

```
In [1]: import math
        import numpy as np
        import pandas as pd
        from pylab import plt, mpl
        np.random.seed(1)
```

```
plt.style.use('seaborn')
mpl.rcParams['savefig.dpi'] = 300
mpl.rcParams['font.family'] = 'serif'
np.set_printoptions(suppress=True)

In [2]: t0 = np.array(10)      ❶
        t0  ❶
Out[2]: array(10)

In [3]: t1 = np.array((2, 1))    ❷
        t1  ❷
Out[3]: array([2, 1])

In [4]: t2 = np.arange(10).reshape(5, 2)    ❸
        t2  ❸
Out[4]: array([[0, 1],
               [2, 3],
               [4, 5],
               [6, 7],
               [8, 9]])

In [5]: t3 = np.arange(16).reshape(2, 4, 2)    ❹
        t3  ❹
Out[5]: array([[[ 0,  1],
               [ 2,  3],
               [ 4,  5],
               [ 6,  7]],

              [[ 8,  9],
               [10, 11],
               [12, 13],
               [14, 15]]])
```

❶ Scalar tensor

❷ Vector tensor

❸ Matrix tensor

❹ Cube tensor

In a neural network context, several mathematical operations on tensors are of importance, such as element-wise operations or the dot product:

```
In [6]: t2 + 1   ❶
Out[6]: array([[ 1,  2],
               [ 3,  4],
               [ 5,  6],
               [ 7,  8],
               [ 9, 10]])
```

```
In [7]: t2 + t2  ❷
Out[7]: array([[ 0,  2],
               [ 4,  6],
               [ 8, 10],
               [12, 14],
               [16, 18]])

In [8]: t1
Out[8]: array([2, 1])

In [9]: t2
Out[9]: array([[0, 1],
               [2, 3],
               [4, 5],
               [6, 7],
               [8, 9]])

In [10]: np.dot(t2, t1)  ❸
Out[10]: array([ 1,  7, 13, 19, 25])

In [11]: t2[:, 0] * 2 + t2[:, 1] * 1  ❹
Out[11]: array([ 1,  7, 13, 19, 25])

In [12]: np.dot(t1, t2.T)  ❸
Out[12]: array([ 1,  7, 13, 19, 25])
```

❶ Broadcasting operation

❷ Element-wise operation

❸ Dot product with NumPy function

❹ Dot product in explicit notation

Simple Neural Networks

Equipped with the basics of tensors, consider simple neural networks, which only have an input layer and an output layer.

Estimation

The first problem is an *estimation problem* for which the labels are real-valued:

```
In [13]: features = 3  ❶

In [14]: samples = 5  ❷

In [15]: l0 = np.random.random((samples, features))  ❸
         l0  ❸
Out[15]: array([[0.417022  , 0.72032449, 0.00011437],
```

```
                [0.30233257, 0.14675589, 0.09233859],
                [0.18626021, 0.34556073, 0.39676747],
                [0.53881673, 0.41919451, 0.6852195 ],
                [0.20445225, 0.87811744, 0.02738759]])

In [16]: w = np.random.random((features, 1))   ❹
         w   ❹
Out[16]: array([[0.67046751],
                [0.4173048 ],
                [0.55868983]])

In [17]: l2 = np.dot(l0, w)   ❺
         l2   ❺
Out[17]: array([[0.58025848],
                [0.31553474],
                [0.49075552],
                [0.91901616],
                [0.51882238]])

In [18]: y = l0[:, 0] * 0.5 + l0[:, 1]   ❻
         y = y.reshape(-1, 1)   ❻
         y   ❻
Out[18]: array([[0.9288355 ],
                [0.29792218],
                [0.43869083],
                [0.68860288],
                [0.98034356]])
```

❶ Number of features

❷ Number of samples

❸ Random input layer

❹ Random weights

❺ Output layer via dot product

❻ Labels to be learned

The following Python code goes step by step through a learning episode, from the calculation of the errors to the calculation of the mean-squared error (MSE) after the weights have been updated:

```
In [19]: e = l2 - y   ❶
         e   ❶
Out[19]: array([[-0.34857702],
                [ 0.01761256],
                [ 0.05206469],
                [ 0.23041328],
```

```
                [-0.46152118]])

In [20]: mse = (e ** 2).mean()  ❷
         mse  ❷
Out[20]: 0.07812379019517127

In [21]: d = e * 1  ❸
         d  ❸
Out[21]: array([[-0.34857702],
                [ 0.01761256],
                [ 0.05206469],
                [ 0.23041328],
                [-0.46152118]])

In [22]: a = 0.01  ❹

In [23]: u = a * np.dot(l0.T, d)  ❺
         u  ❺
Out[23]: array([[-0.0010055 ],
                [-0.00539194],
                [ 0.00167488]])

In [24]: w  ❻
Out[24]: array([[0.67046751],
                [0.4173048 ],
                [0.55868983]])

In [25]: w -= u  ❻

In [26]: w  ❻
Out[26]: array([[0.67147301],
                [0.42269674],
                [0.55701495]])

In [27]: l2 = np.dot(l0, w)  ❼

In [28]: e = l2 - y  ❽

In [29]: mse = (e ** 2).mean()  ❾
         mse  ❾
Out[29]: 0.07681782193617318
```

❶   Errors in estimation

❷   MSE value given the estimation

❸ Backward propagation (here d = e)[1]

❹ The learning rate

❺ The update values

❻ Weights before and after update

❼ New output layer (estimation) after update

❽ New error values after update

❾ New MSE values after update

To improve the estimation, the same procedure needs to be repeated in general a larger number of times. In the following code, the learning rate is increased and the procedure is executed a few hundred times. The final MSE value is quite low and the estimation quite good:

```
In [30]: a = 0.025  ❶
```

```
In [31]: w = np.random.random((features, 1))  ❷
         w  ❷
Out[31]: array([[0.14038694],
                [0.19810149],
                [0.80074457]])
```

```
In [32]: steps = 800  ❸
```

```
In [33]: for s in range(1, steps + 1):
             l2 = np.dot(l0, w)
             e = l2 - y
             u = a * np.dot(l0.T, e)
             w -= u
             mse = (e ** 2).mean()
             if s % 50 == 0:
                 print(f'step={s:3d} | mse={mse:.5f}')
         step= 50 | mse=0.03064
         step=100 | mse=0.01002
         step=150 | mse=0.00390
         step=200 | mse=0.00195
         step=250 | mse=0.00124
         step=300 | mse=0.00092
         step=350 | mse=0.00074
         step=400 | mse=0.00060
```

---

1 Since there is no hidden layer, backward propagation does take place with a factor of 1 as the value of the derivative. Output and input layers are directly connected.

```
step=450 | mse=0.00050
step=500 | mse=0.00041
step=550 | mse=0.00035
step=600 | mse=0.00029
step=650 | mse=0.00024
step=700 | mse=0.00020
step=750 | mse=0.00017
step=800 | mse=0.00014
```

```
In [34]: l2 - y  ❹
Out[34]: array([[-0.01240168],
                [-0.01606065],
                [ 0.01274072],
                [-0.00087794],
                [ 0.01072845]])
```

```
In [35]: w  ❺
Out[35]: array([[0.41907514],
                [1.02965827],
                [0.04421136]])
```

❶   Adjusted learning rate

❷   Initial random weights

❸   Number of learning steps

❹   Residual errors of the estimation

❺   Final weights of the network

Classification

The second problem is a *classification problem* for which the labels are binary and integer-valued. To improve the performance of the learning algorithm, a *sigmoid function* is used for activation (of the output layer). Figure A-1 shows the sigmoid function with its first derivative and compares it to a simple step function:

```
In [36]: def sigmoid(x, deriv=False):
             if deriv:
                 return sigmoid(x) * (1 - sigmoid(x))
             return 1 / (1 + np.exp(-x))
```

```
In [37]: x = np.linspace(-10, 10, 100)
```

```
In [38]: plt.figure(figsize=(10, 6))
         plt.plot(x, np.where(x > 0, 1, 0), 'y--', label='step function')
         plt.plot(x, sigmoid(x), 'r', label='sigmoid')
         plt.plot(x, sigmoid(x, True), '--', label='derivative')
         plt.legend();
```

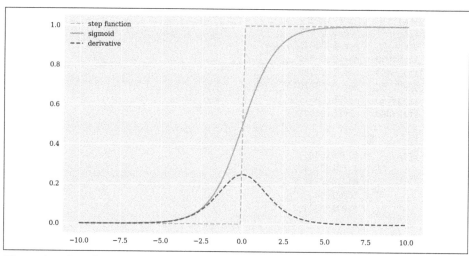

Figure A-1. Step function, sigmoid function, and its first derivative

To keep things simple, the classification problem is based on random binary features and binary labels data. Apart from the different features and labels data, only the activation for the output layer is different from the estimation problem. The learning algorithm for the updating of the neural networks' weights is basically the same:

```
In [39]: features = 4
         samples = 5

In [40]: l0 = np.random.randint(0, 2, (samples, features))  ❶
         l0 ❶
Out[40]: array([[1, 1, 1, 1],
                [0, 1, 1, 0],
                [0, 1, 0, 0],
                [1, 1, 1, 0],
                [1, 0, 0, 1]])

In [41]: w = np.random.random((features, 1))
         w
Out[41]: array([[0.42110763],
                [0.95788953],
                [0.53316528],
                [0.69187711]])

In [42]: l2 = sigmoid(np.dot(l0, w))  ❷
         l2
Out[42]: array([[0.93112111],
                [0.81623654],
                [0.72269905],
                [0.87126189],
                [0.75268514]])
```

```
In [43]: l2.round()
Out[43]: array([[1.],
               [1.],
               [1.],
               [1.],
               [1.]])

In [44]: y = np.random.randint(0, 2, samples)   ❸
         y = y.reshape(-1, 1)   ❸
         y   ❸
Out[44]: array([[1],
               [1],
               [0],
               [0],
               [0]])

In [45]: e = l2 - y
         e
Out[45]: array([[-0.06887889],
               [-0.18376346],
               [ 0.72269905],
               [ 0.87126189],
               [ 0.75268514]])

In [46]: mse = (e ** 2).mean()
         mse
Out[46]: 0.37728788783411127

In [47]: a = 0.02

In [48]: d = e * sigmoid(l2, True)   ❹
         d
Out[48]: array([[-0.01396723],
               [-0.03906484],
               [ 0.15899479],
               [ 0.18119776],
               [ 0.16384833]])

In [49]: u = a * np.dot(l0.T, d)
         u
Out[49]: array([[0.00662158],
               [0.00574321],
               [0.00256331],
               [0.00299762]])

In [50]: w
Out[50]: array([[0.42110763],
               [0.95788953],
               [0.53316528],
               [0.69187711]])

In [51]: w -= u
```

```
In [52]: w
Out[52]: array([[0.41448605],
                [0.95214632],
                [0.53060197],
                [0.68887949]])
```

❶ Input layer with binary features

❷ Sigmoid activated output layer

❸ Binary labels data

❹ Backward propagation via the first derivative

As before, a loop with a larger number of iterations for the learning step is required to get to accurate classification results. Depending on the random numbers drawn, an accuracy of 100% is possible, as in the following example:

```
In [53]: steps = 3001

In [54]: a = 0.025

In [55]: w = np.random.random((features, 1))
         w
Out[55]: array([[0.41253884],
                [0.03417131],
                [0.62402999],
                [0.66063573]])

In [56]: for s in range(1, steps + 1):
             l2 = sigmoid(np.dot(l0, w))
             e = l2 - y
             d = e * sigmoid(l2, True)
             u = a * np.dot(l0.T, d)
             w -= u
             mse = (e ** 2).mean()
             if s % 200 == 0:
                 print(f'step={s:4d} | mse={mse:.4f}')
         step= 200 | mse=0.1899
         step= 400 | mse=0.1572
         step= 600 | mse=0.1349
         step= 800 | mse=0.1173
         step=1000 | mse=0.1029
         step=1200 | mse=0.0908
         step=1400 | mse=0.0806
         step=1600 | mse=0.0720
         step=1800 | mse=0.0646
         step=2000 | mse=0.0583
         step=2200 | mse=0.0529
         step=2400 | mse=0.0482
```

```
         step=2600 | mse=0.0441
         step=2800 | mse=0.0405
         step=3000 | mse=0.0373

In [57]: l2
Out[57]: array([[0.71220474],
                [0.92308745],
                [0.16614971],
                [0.20193503],
                [0.17094583]])

In [58]: l2.round() == y
Out[58]: array([[ True],
                [ True],
                [ True],
                [ True],
                [ True]])

In [59]: w
Out[59]: array([[-3.86002022],
                [-1.61346536],
                [ 4.09895004],
                [ 2.28088807]])
```

Shallow Neural Networks

The neural network of the previous section consists only of an input layer and an output layer. In other words, input and output layers are directly connected. A *shallow neural network* has one hidden layer that is between the input and output layer. Given this structure, two sets of weights are required to connect the total of three layers in the neural network. This section analyzes shallow neural networks for estimation and classification.

Estimation

As in the previous section, let's take the estimation problem first. The following Python code builds the neural network with the three layers and the two sets of weights. This first sequence of steps is usually called *forward propagation*. The input layer matrix in this context is in general of full rank, indicating that a perfect estimation result is possible:

```
In [60]: features = 5
         samples = 5

In [61]: l0 = np.random.random((samples, features))    ❶
         l0    ❶
Out[61]: array([[0.29849529, 0.44613451, 0.22212455, 0.07336417, 0.46923853],
                [0.09617226, 0.90337017, 0.11949047, 0.52479938, 0.083623  ],
                [0.91686133, 0.91044838, 0.29893011, 0.58438912, 0.56591203],
```

```
                     [0.61393832, 0.95653566, 0.26097898, 0.23101542, 0.53344849],
                     [0.94993814, 0.49305959, 0.54060051, 0.7654851 , 0.04534573]])

In [62]: np.linalg.matrix_rank(l0)   ❷
Out[62]: 5

In [63]: units = 3   ❸

In [64]: w0 = np.random.random((features, units))   ❹
         w0   ❹
Out[64]: array([[0.13996612, 0.79240359, 0.02980136],
                [0.88312548, 0.54078819, 0.44798018],
                [0.89213587, 0.37758434, 0.53842469],
                [0.65229888, 0.36126102, 0.57100856],
                [0.63783648, 0.12631489, 0.69020459]])

In [65]: l1 = np.dot(l0, w0)   ❺
         l1   ❺
Out[65]: array([[0.98109007, 0.64743919, 0.69411448],
                [1.31351565, 0.81000928, 0.82927653],
                [1.94121167, 1.61435539, 1.32042417],
                [1.65444429, 1.25315104, 1.08742312],
                [1.57892999, 1.50576525, 1.00865941]])

In [66]: w1 = np.random.random((units, 1))   ❻
         w1   ❻
Out[66]: array([[0.6477494 ],
                [0.35393909],
                [0.76323305]])

In [67]: l2 = np.dot(l1, w1)   ❼
         l2   ❼
Out[67]: array([[1.39442565],
                [1.77045418],
                [2.83659354],
                [2.3451617 ],
                [2.32554234]])

In [68]: y = np.random.random((samples, 1))   ❽
         y   ❽
Out[68]: array([[0.35653172],
                [0.75278835],
                [0.88134183],
                [0.01166919],
                [0.49810907]])
```

❶   The random input layer

❷   The rank of the input layer matrix

❸   The number of hidden units

---

❹ The first set of random weights, given the `features` and `units` parameters

❺ The hidden layer, given the input layer and the weights

❻ The second set of random weights

❼ The output layer, given the hidden layer and the weights

❽ The random labels data

The second sequence of steps is usually called *backward propagation*—with respect to the estimation errors. The two sets of weights are updated, starting at the output layer and updating the set of weights w1 between the hidden layer and the output layer. Afterwards, taking the updated weights w1 into account, the set of weights w0 between the input layer and the hidden layer is updated:

```
In [69]: e2 = l2 - y  ❶
         e2  ❶
Out[69]: array([[1.03789393],
                [1.01766583],
                [1.95525171],
                [2.33349251],
                [1.82743327]])

In [70]: mse = (e2 ** 2).mean()
         mse
Out[70]: 2.9441152813655007

In [71]: d2 = e2 * 1  ❶
         d2  ❶
Out[71]: array([[1.03789393],
                [1.01766583],
                [1.95525171],
                [2.33349251],
                [1.82743327]])

In [72]: a = 0.05

In [73]: u2 = a * np.dot(l1.T, d2)  ❶
         u2  ❶
Out[73]: array([[0.64482837],
                [0.51643336],
                [0.42634283]])

In [74]: w1  ❶
Out[74]: array([[0.6477494 ],
                [0.35393909],
                [0.76323305]])

In [75]: w1 -= u2  ❶
```

```
In [76]: w1  ❶
Out[76]: array([[ 0.00292103],
                [-0.16249427],
                [ 0.33689022]])

In [77]: e1 = np.dot(d2, w1.T)  ❷

In [78]: d1 = e1 * 1  ❷

In [79]: u1 = a * np.dot(l0.T, d1)  ❷

In [80]: w0 -= u1  ❷

In [81]: w0  ❷
Out[81]: array([[ 0.13918198,  0.8360247 , -0.06063583],
                [ 0.88220599,  0.59193836,  0.34193342],
                [ 0.89176585,  0.39816855,  0.49574861],
                [ 0.65175984,  0.39124762,  0.50883904],
                [ 0.63739741,  0.15074009,  0.63956519]])
```

❶ Update procedure for the set of weights w1

❷ Update procedure for the set of weights w0

The following Python code implements the learning (that is, the updating of the network weights) as a for loop with a larger number of iterations. By increasing the number of iterations, the estimation results can be made arbitrarily precise:

```
In [82]: a = 0.015
         steps = 5000

In [83]: for s in range(1, steps + 1):
             l1 = np.dot(l0, w0)
             l2 = np.dot(l1, w1)
             e2 = l2 - y
             u2 = a * np.dot(l1.T, e2)
             w1 -= u2
             e1 = np.dot(e2, w1.T)
             u1 = a * np.dot(l0.T, e1)
             w0 -= u1
             mse = (e2 ** 2).mean()
             if s % 750 == 0:
                 print(f'step={s:5d} | mse={mse:.6f}')
         step=  750 | mse=0.039263
         step= 1500 | mse=0.009867
         step= 2250 | mse=0.000666
         step= 3000 | mse=0.000027
         step= 3750 | mse=0.000001
         step= 4500 | mse=0.000000

In [84]: l2
```

```
Out[84]: array([[0.35634333],
               [0.75275415],
               [0.88135507],
               [0.01179945],
               [0.49809208]])

In [85]: y
Out[85]: array([[0.35653172],
               [0.75278835],
               [0.88134183],
               [0.01166919],
               [0.49810907]])

In [86]: (l2 - y)
Out[86]: array([[-0.00018839],
               [-0.00003421],
               [ 0.00001324],
               [ 0.00013025],
               [-0.00001699]])
```

Classification

Next is the classification problem. The implementation in this context is pretty close to the estimation problem. However, the sigmoid function is used again for activation. The following Python code generates the random sample data first:

```
In [87]: features = 5
         samples = 10
         units = 10

In [88]: np.random.seed(200)
         l0 = np.random.randint(0, 2, (samples, features))    ❶
         w0 = np.random.random((features, units))
         w1 = np.random.random((units, 1))
         y = np.random.randint(0, 2, (samples, 1))    ❷

In [89]: l0    ❶
Out[89]: array([[0, 1, 0, 0, 0],
               [1, 0, 1, 1, 0],
               [1, 1, 1, 1, 0],
               [0, 0, 1, 1, 1],
               [1, 1, 1, 1, 0],
               [1, 1, 0, 1, 0],
               [0, 1, 0, 1, 0],
               [0, 1, 0, 0, 1],
               [0, 1, 1, 1, 1],
               [0, 0, 1, 0, 0]])

In [90]: y    ❷
Out[90]: array([[1],
               [0],
               [1],
```

```
                        [0],
                        [1],
                        [0],
                        [0],
                        [0],
                        [1],
                        [1]])
```

❶ Binary features data (input layer)

❷ Binary labels data

The implementation of the learning algorithm again makes use of a for loop to repeat the weights-updating step as often as necessary. Depending on the random numbers generated for the features and labels data, an accuracy of 100% can be achieved after enough learning steps:

```
In [91]: a = 0.1
         steps = 20000

In [92]: for s in range(1, steps + 1):
             l1 = sigmoid(np.dot(l0, w0))  ❶
             l2 = sigmoid(np.dot(l1, w1))  ❶
             e2 = l2 - y  ❷
             d2 = e2 * sigmoid(l2, True)  ❷
             u2 = a * np.dot(l1.T, d2)  ❷
             w1 -= u2  ❷
             e1 = np.dot(d2, w1.T)  ❷
             d1 = e1 * sigmoid(l1, True)  ❷
             u1 = a * np.dot(l0.T, d1)  ❷
             w0 -= u1  ❷
             mse = (e2 ** 2).mean()
             if s % 2000 == 0:
                 print(f'step={s:5d} | mse={mse:.5f}')
         step= 2000 | mse=0.00933
         step= 4000 | mse=0.02399
         step= 6000 | mse=0.05134
         step= 8000 | mse=0.00064
         step=10000 | mse=0.00013
         step=12000 | mse=0.00009
         step=14000 | mse=0.00007
         step=16000 | mse=0.00007
         step=18000 | mse=0.00012
         step=20000 | mse=0.00015

In [93]: acc = l2.round() == y  ❸
         acc  ❸
Out[93]: array([[ True],
                [ True],
                [ True],
                [ True],
```

```
             [ True],
             [ True],
             [ True],
             [ True],
             [ True],
             [ True]])

In [94]: sum(acc) / len(acc)   ❸
Out[94]: array([1.])
```

❶ Forward propagation

❷ Backward propagation

❸ Accuracy of the classification

References

Books cited in this appendix:

Chollet, Francois. 2017. *Deep Learning with Python*. Shelter Island: Manning.

Neural Network Classes

Building on the foundations from Appendix A, this appendix provides simple, class-based implementations of neural networks that mimic the APIs of packages such as scikit-learn. The implementation is based on pure, simple Python code and is for illustration and instruction. The classes presented in this appendix cannot replace robust, efficient, and scalable implementations found in the standard Python packages, such as scikit-learn or TensorFlow in combination with Keras.

The appendix comprises the following sections:

- "Activation Functions" on page 425 introduces a Python function with different activation functions.
- "Simple Neural Networks" on page 426 presents a Python class for *simple neural networks*.
- "Shallow Neural Networks" on page 431 presents a Python class for *shallow neural networks*.
- "Predicting Market Direction" on page 435 applies the class for shallow neural networks to financial data.

The implementations and examples in this appendix are simple and straightforward. The Python classes are not well suited to attack larger estimation or classification problems. The idea is rather to show easy-to-understand Python implementations from scratch.

Activation Functions

Appendix A uses two activation functions implicitly or explicitly: linear function and sigmoid function. The Python function activation adds the relu (rectified linear unit) and `softplus` functions to the set of options. For all these activation functions, the first derivative is also defined:

```python
In [1]: import math
        import numpy as np
        import pandas as pd
        from pylab import plt, mpl
        plt.style.use('seaborn')
        mpl.rcParams['savefig.dpi'] = 300
        mpl.rcParams['font.family'] = 'serif'
        np.set_printoptions(suppress=True)

In [2]: def activation(x, act='linear', deriv=False):
            if act == 'sigmoid':
                if deriv:
                    out = activation(x, 'sigmoid', False)
                    return out * (1 - out)
                return 1 / (1 + np.exp(-x))
            elif act == 'relu':
                if deriv:
                    return np.where(x > 0, 1, 0)
                return np.maximum(x, 0)
            elif act == 'softplus':
                if deriv:
                    return activation(x, act='sigmoid')
                return np.log(1 + np.exp(x))
            elif act == 'linear':
                if deriv:
                    return 1
                return x
            else:
                raise ValueError('Activation function not known.')

In [3]: x = np.linspace(-1, 1, 20)

In [4]: activation(x, 'sigmoid')
Out[4]: array([0.26894142, 0.29013328, 0.31228169, 0.33532221, 0.35917484,
               0.38374461, 0.40892261, 0.43458759, 0.46060812, 0.48684514,
               0.51315486, 0.53939188, 0.56541241, 0.59107739, 0.61625539,
               0.64082516, 0.66467779, 0.68771831, 0.70986672, 0.73105858])

In [5]: activation(x, 'sigmoid', True)
Out[5]: array([0.19661193, 0.20595596, 0.21476184, 0.22288122, 0.23016827,
               0.23648468, 0.24170491, 0.24572122, 0.24844828, 0.24982695,
               0.24982695, 0.24844828, 0.24572122, 0.24170491, 0.23648468,
               0.23016827, 0.22288122, 0.21476184, 0.20595596, 0.19661193])
```

Simple Neural Networks

This section presents a class for *simple neural networks* that has an API similar to those of models from standard Python packages for machine or deep learning (in particular, `scikit-learn` and `Keras`). Consider the class `sinn` as presented in the following Python code. It implements a simple neural network and defines the two main methods `.fit()` and `.predict()`. The `.metrics()` method calculates typical performance metrics: the mean-squared error (MSE) for estimation and the accuracy for classification. The class also implements two methods for the forward and backward propagation steps:

```
In [6]: class sinn:
            def __init__(self, act='linear', lr=0.01, steps=100,
                         verbose=False, psteps=200):
                self.act = act
                self.lr = lr
                self.steps = steps
                self.verbose = verbose
                self.psteps = psteps
            def forward(self):
                ''' Forward propagation.
                '''
                self.l2 = activation(np.dot(self.l0, self.w), self.act)
            def backward(self):
                ''' Backward propagation.
                '''
                self.e = self.l2 - self.y
                d = self.e * activation(self.l2, self.act, True)
                u = self.lr * np.dot(self.l0.T, d)
                self.w -= u
            def metrics(self, s):
                ''' Performance metrics.
                '''
                mse = (self.e ** 2).mean()
                acc = float(sum(self.l2.round() == self.y) / len(self.y))
                self.res = self.res.append(
                    pd.DataFrame({'mse': mse, 'acc': acc}, index=[s,])
                )
                if s % self.psteps == 0 and self.verbose:
                    print(f'step={s:5d} | mse={mse:.6f}')
                    print(f'              | acc={acc:.6f}')
            def fit(self, l0, y, steps=None, seed=None):
                ''' Fitting step.
                '''
                self.l0 = l0
                self.y = y
                if steps is None:
                    steps = self.steps
                self.res = pd.DataFrame()
                samples, features = l0.shape
                if seed is not None:
                    np.random.seed(seed)
                self.w = np.random.random((features, 1))
                for s in range(1, steps + 1):
                    self.forward()
```

```
            self.backward()
            self.metrics(s)
    def predict(self, X):
        ''' Prediction step.
        '''
        return activation(np.dot(X, self.w), self.act)
```

Estimation

First is an estimation problem that can be solved by the use of regression techniques:

```
In [7]: features = 5
        samples = 5

In [8]: np.random.seed(10)
        l0 = np.random.standard_normal((samples, features))
        l0
Out[8]: array([[ 1.3315865 ,  0.71527897, -1.54540029, -0.00838385,  0.62133597],
               [-0.72008556,  0.26551159,  0.10854853,  0.00429143, -0.17460021],
               [ 0.43302619,  1.20303737, -0.96506567,  1.02827408,  0.22863013],
               [ 0.44513761, -1.13660221,  0.13513688,  1.484537  , -1.07980489],
               [-1.97772828, -1.7433723 ,  0.26607016,  2.38496733,  1.12369125]])

In [9]: np.linalg.matrix_rank(l0)
Out[9]: 5

In [10]: y = np.random.random((samples, 1))
         y
Out[10]: array([[0.8052232 ],
                [0.52164715],
                [0.90864888],
                [0.31923609],
                [0.09045935]])

In [11]: reg = np.linalg.lstsq(l0, y, rcond=-1)[0]   ❶

In [12]: reg   ❶
Out[12]: array([[-0.74919308],
                [ 0.00146473],
                [-1.49864704],
                [-0.02498757],
                [-0.82793882]])

In [13]: np.allclose(np.dot(l0, reg), y)   ❶
Out[13]: True
```

❶ Exact solution by regression

Applying the sinn class to the estimation problem requires quite some effort in the form of repeated learning steps. However, by increasing the number of steps, one can make the estimate arbitrarily precise:

```
In [14]: model = sinn(lr=0.015, act='linear', steps=6000,
                      verbose=True, psteps=1000)

In [15]: %time model.fit(l0, y, seed=100)
         step= 1000 | mse=0.008086
                    | acc=0.000000
         step= 2000 | mse=0.000545
                    | acc=0.000000
         step= 3000 | mse=0.000037
                    | acc=0.000000
         step= 4000 | mse=0.000002
                    | acc=0.000000
         step= 5000 | mse=0.000000
                    | acc=0.000000
         step= 6000 | mse=0.000000
                    | acc=0.000000
         CPU times: user 5.23 s, sys: 29.7 ms, total: 5.26 s
         Wall time: 5.26 s

In [16]: model.predict(l0)
Out[16]: array([[0.80512489],
                [0.52144986],
                [0.90872498],
                [0.31919803],
                [0.09045743]])

In [17]: model.predict(l0) - y   ❶
Out[17]: array([[-0.0000983 ],
                [-0.00019729],
                [ 0.0000761 ],
                [-0.00003806],
                [-0.00000191]])
```

❶ Residual errors of the neural network estimation

Classification

Second is a classification problem that can also be attacked with the sinn class. Here, standard regression techniques are in general of no use. For the particular set of random features and labels, the sinn model reaches an accuracy of 100%. Again, quite some effort is required in the form of repeated learning steps. Figure B-1 shows how the prediction accuracy changes with the number of learning steps:

```
In [18]: features = 5
         samples = 10

In [19]: np.random.seed(3)
```

```
         l0 = np.random.randint(0, 2, (samples, features))
         l0
Out[19]: array([[0, 0, 1, 1, 0],
                [0, 0, 1, 1, 1],
                [0, 1, 1, 1, 0],
                [1, 1, 0, 0, 0],
                [0, 1, 1, 0, 0],
                [0, 1, 0, 0, 0],
                [0, 1, 0, 1, 1],
                [0, 1, 0, 0, 1],
                [1, 0, 0, 1, 0],
                [1, 0, 1, 1, 1]])


In [20]: np.linalg.matrix_rank(l0)
Out[20]: 5


In [21]: y = np.random.randint(0, 2, (samples, 1))
         y
Out[21]: array([[1],
                [0],
                [1],
                [0],
                [0],
                [1],
                [1],
                [1],
                [0],
                [0]])


In [22]: model = sinn(lr=0.01, act='sigmoid')   ❶


In [23]: %time model.fit(l0, y, 4000)
         CPU times: user 3.57 s, sys: 9.6 ms, total: 3.58 s
         Wall time: 3.59 s


In [24]: model.l2
Out[24]: array([[0.51118415],
                [0.34390898],
                [0.84733758],
                [0.07601979],
                [0.40505454],
                [0.84145926],
                [0.95592461],
                [0.72680243],
                [0.11219587],
                [0.00806003]])


In [25]: model.predict(l0).round() == y   ❷
Out[25]: array([[ True],
                [ True],
                [ True],
                [ True],
```

```
                [ True],
                [ True],
                [ True],
                [ True],
                [ True],
                [ True]])

In [26]: ax = model.res['acc'].plot(figsize=(10, 6),
                   title='Prediction Accuracy | Classification')
         ax.set(xlabel='steps', ylabel='accuracy');
```

❶ The sigmoid function is used for activation

❷ Perfect accuracy on this particular data set

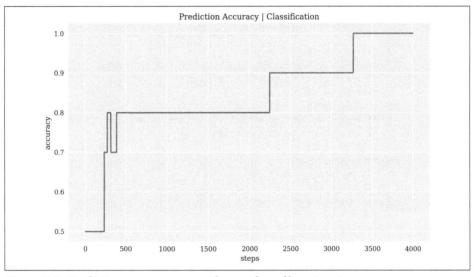

Figure B-1. Prediction accuracy versus the number of learning steps

Shallow Neural Networks

This section applies the class shnn, which implements *shallow neural networks* with one hidden layer, to estimation and classification problems. The class structure is along the lines of the sinn class from the previous section:

```
In [27]: class shnn:
             def __init__(self, units=12, act='linear', lr=0.01, steps=100,
                          verbose=False, psteps=200, seed=None):
                 self.units = units
                 self.act = act
                 self.lr = lr
                 self.steps = steps
                 self.verbose = verbose
```

```
        self.psteps = psteps
        self.seed = seed
    def initialize(self):
        ''' Initializes the random weights.
        '''
        if self.seed is not None:
            np.random.seed(self.seed)
        samples, features = self.l0.shape
        self.w0 = np.random.random((features, self.units))
        self.w1 = np.random.random((self.units, 1))
    def forward(self):
        ''' Forward propagation.
        '''
        self.l1 = activation(np.dot(self.l0, self.w0), self.act)
        self.l2 = activation(np.dot(self.l1, self.w1), self.act)
    def backward(self):
        ''' Backward propagation.
        '''
        self.e = self.l2 - self.y
        d2 = self.e * activation(self.l2, self.act, True)
        u2 = self.lr * np.dot(self.l1.T, d2)
        self.w1 -= u2
        e1 = np.dot(d2, self.w1.T)
        d1 = e1 * activation(self.l1, self.act, True)
        u1 = self.lr * np.dot(self.l0.T, d1)
        self.w0 -= u1
    def metrics(self, s):
        ''' Performance metrics.
        '''
        mse = (self.e ** 2).mean()
        acc = float(sum(self.l2.round() == self.y) / len(self.y))
        self.res = self.res.append(
            pd.DataFrame({'mse': mse, 'acc': acc}, index=[s,])
        )
        if s % self.psteps == 0 and self.verbose:
                print(f'step={s:5d} | mse={mse:.5f}')
                print(f'          | acc={acc:.5f}')
    def fit(self, l0, y, steps=None):
        ''' Fitting step.
        '''
        self.l0 = l0
        self.y = y
        if steps is None:
            steps = self.steps
        self.res = pd.DataFrame()
        self.initialize()
        self.forward()
        for s in range(1, steps + 1):
            self.backward()
            self.forward()
            self.metrics(s)
    def predict(self, X):
```

```
    ''' Prediction step.
    '''
    l1 = activation(np.dot(X, self.w0), self.act)
    l2 = activation(np.dot(l1, self.w1), self.act)
    return l2
```

Estimation

Again, the estimation problem comes first. For 5 features and 10 samples, a perfect regression solution is unlikely to exist. As a result, the MSE value of the regression is relatively high:

```
In [28]: features = 5
         samples = 10

In [29]: l0 = np.random.standard_normal((samples, features))

In [30]: np.linalg.matrix_rank(l0)
Out[30]: 5

In [31]: y = np.random.random((samples, 1))

In [32]: reg = np.linalg.lstsq(l0, y, rcond=-1)[0]

In [33]: (np.dot(l0, reg)  - y)
Out[33]: array([[-0.10226341],
                [-0.42357164],
                [-0.25150491],
                [-0.30984143],
                [-0.85213261],
                [-0.13791373],
                [-0.52336502],
                [-0.50304204],
                [-0.7728686 ],
                [-0.3716898 ]])

In [34]: ((np.dot(l0, reg)  - y) ** 2).mean()
Out[34]: 0.23567187607888118
```

However, the shallow neural network estimate based on the shnn class is quite good and shows a relatively low MSE value compared to the regression value:

```
In [35]: model = shnn(lr=0.01, units=16, act='softplus',
                 verbose=True, psteps=2000, seed=100)

In [36]: %time model.fit(l0, y, 8000)
         step= 2000 | mse=0.00205
                    | acc=0.00000
         step= 4000 | mse=0.00098
                    | acc=0.00000
         step= 6000 | mse=0.00043
                    | acc=0.00000
```

```
      step= 8000 | mse=0.00022
                 | acc=0.00000
      CPU times: user 8.15 s, sys: 69.2 ms, total: 8.22 s
      Wall time: 8.3 s

In [37]: model.l2 - y
Out[37]: array([[-0.00390976],
                [-0.00522077],
                [ 0.02053932],
                [-0.0042113 ],
                [-0.0006624 ],
                [-0.01001395],
                [ 0.01783203],
                [-0.01498316],
                [-0.0177866 ],
                [ 0.02782519]])
```

Classification

The classification example takes the estimation numbers and applies rounding to them. The shallow neural network converges quickly to predict the labels with 100% accuracy (see Figure B-2):

```
In [38]: model = shnn(lr=0.025, act='sigmoid', steps=200,
                      verbose=True, psteps=50, seed=100)

In [39]: l0.round()
Out[39]: array([[ 0., -1., -2.,  1., -0.],
                [-1., -2., -0., -0., -2.],
                [ 0.,  1., -1., -1., -1.],
                [-0.,  0., -1., -0., -1.],
                [ 1., -1.,  1.,  1., -1.],
                [ 1., -1.,  1., -2.,  1.],
                [-1., -0.,  1., -1.,  1.],
                [ 1.,  2., -1., -0., -0.],
                [-1.,  0.,  0.,  0.,  2.],
                [ 0.,  0., -0.,  1.,  1.]])

In [40]: np.linalg.matrix_rank(l0)
Out[40]: 5

In [41]: y.round()
Out[41]: array([[0.],
                [1.],
                [1.],
                [1.],
                [1.],
                [1.],
                [0.],
                [1.],
                [0.],
                [0.]])
```

```
In [42]: model.fit(l0.round(), y.round())
         step=   50 | mse=0.26774
                  | acc=0.60000
         step=  100 | mse=0.22556
                  | acc=0.60000
         step=  150 | mse=0.19939
                  | acc=0.70000
         step=  200 | mse=0.16924
                  | acc=1.00000
```

```
In [43]: ax = model.res.plot(figsize=(10, 6), secondary_y='mse')
         ax.get_legend().set_bbox_to_anchor((0.2, 0.5));
```

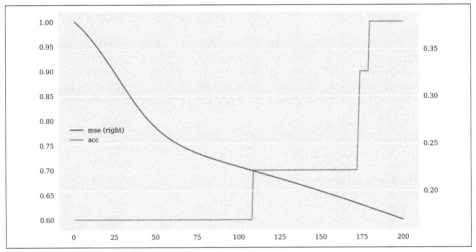

Figure B-2. Performance metrics for the shallow neural network (classification)

Predicting Market Direction

This section applies the shnn class to predict the future direction of the EUR/USD exchange rate. The analysis is in-sample only to illustrate the application of shnn to real-world data. See Chapter 10 for the implementation of a more realistic setup for the vectorized backtesting of such prediction-based strategies.

The following Python code imports the financial data—10 years' worth of EOD data—and creates lagged, normalized log returns used as the features. The labels data is the direction of the price series as a binary data set:

```
In [44]: url = 'http://hilpisch.com/aiif_eikon_eod_data.csv'
```

```
In [45]: raw = pd.read_csv(url, index_col=0, parse_dates=True).dropna()
```

```
In [46]: sym = 'EUR='
```

```
In [47]: data = pd.DataFrame(raw[sym])

In [48]: lags = 5
         cols = []
         data['r'] = np.log(data / data.shift(1))
         data['d'] = np.where(data['r'] > 0, 1, 0)  ❶
         for lag in range(1, lags + 1):
             col = f'lag_{lag}'
             data[col] = data['r'].shift(lag)  ❷
             cols.append(col)
         data.dropna(inplace=True)
         data[cols] = (data[cols] - data[cols].mean()) / data[cols].std()  ❸

In [49]: data.head()
Out[49]:                 EUR=       r  d     lag_1      lag_2      lag_3     lag_4  \
         Date
         2010-01-12  1.4494 -0.001310  0  1.256582   1.177935  -1.142025  0.560551
         2010-01-13  1.4510  0.001103  1 -0.214533   1.255944   1.178974 -1.142118
         2010-01-14  1.4502 -0.000551  0  0.213539  -0.214803   1.256989  1.178748
         2010-01-15  1.4382 -0.008309  0 -0.079986   0.213163  -0.213853  1.256758
         2010-01-19  1.4298 -0.005858  0 -1.456028  -0.080289   0.214140 -0.214000

                        lag_5
         Date
         2010-01-12 -0.511372
         2010-01-13  0.560740
         2010-01-14 -1.141841
         2010-01-15  1.178904
         2010-01-19  1.256910
```

❶ Market direction as the labels data

❷ Lagged log returns as the features data

❸ Gaussian normalization of the features data

With the data preprocessing accomplished, the application of the shallow neural network class shnn for a supervised classification is straightforward. Figure B-3 shows that the prediction-based strategy in-sample significantly outperforms the passive benchmark investment:

```
In [50]: model = shnn(lr=0.0001, act='sigmoid', steps=10000,
                      verbose=True, psteps=2000, seed=100)

In [51]: y = data['d'].values.reshape(-1, 1)

In [52]: %time model.fit(data[cols].values, y)
         step= 2000 | mse=0.24964
                    | acc=0.51594
         step= 4000 | mse=0.24951
                    | acc=0.52390
```

```
          step= 6000 | mse=0.24945
                     | acc=0.52231
          step= 8000 | mse=0.24940
                     | acc=0.52510
          step=10000 | mse=0.24936
                     | acc=0.52430
          CPU times: user 9min 1s, sys: 40.9 s, total: 9min 42s
          Wall time: 1min 21s

In [53]: data['p'] = np.where(model.predict(data[cols]) > 0.5, 1, -1)  ❶

In [54]: data['p'].value_counts()  ❶
Out[54]:  1    1257
         -1    1253
         Name: p, dtype: int64

In [55]: data['s'] = data['p'] * data['r']  ❷

In [56]: data[['r', 's']].sum().apply(np.exp)  ❸
Out[56]: r    0.772411
         s    1.885677
         dtype: float64

In [57]: data[['r', 's']].cumsum().apply(np.exp).plot(figsize=(10, 6));  ❹
```

❶ Derives the position values from the prediction values

❷ Calculates the strategy returns from the position values and the log returns

❸ Calculates the gross performance of the strategy and the benchmark investment

❹ Shows the gross performance of the strategy and the benchmark investment over time

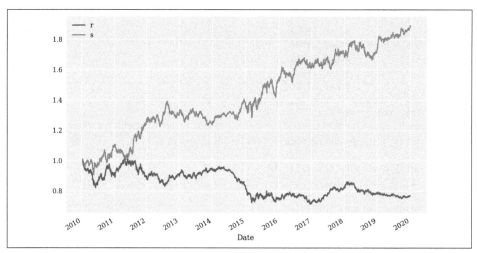

Figure B-3. Gross performance of prediction-based strategy compared to passive bench-mark investment (in-sample)

Convolutional Neural Networks

Part III focuses on dense neural networks (DNNs) and recurrent neural networks (RNNs) as two standard types of neural networks. The charm of DNNs lies in the fact that they are good universal approximators. The examples in the book for reinforcement learning, for instance, make use of DNNs to approximate the optimal action policy. On the other hand, RNNs are specifically designed to handle sequential data, such as time series data. This is helpful when trying, for example, to predict future values of financial time series.

However, *convolutional neural networks* (CNNs) are another standard type of neural network that is widely used in practice. They have been particularly successful, among other domains, in computer vision. CNNs were able to set new benchmarks in a number of standard tests and challenges, such as the ImageNet Challenge; for more on this, see *The Economist* (2016) or Gerrish (2018). Computer vision in turn is important in such domains as autonomous vehicles or security and surveillance.

This brief appendix illustrates the application of a CNN to the prediction of financial time series data. For details on CNNs, see Chollet (2017, ch. 5) and Goodfellow et al. (2016, ch. 9).

Features and Labels Data

The following Python code first takes care of the required imports and customizations. It then imports the data set that contains end-of-day (EOD) data for a number of financial instruments. This data set is used throughout the book for different examples:

```
In [1]: import os
        import math
        import numpy as np
        import pandas as pd
```

```
            from pylab import plt, mpl
            plt.style.use('seaborn')
            mpl.rcParams['savefig.dpi'] = 300
            mpl.rcParams['font.family'] = 'serif'
            os.environ['PYTHONHASHSEED'] = '0'

In [2]: url = 'http://hilpisch.com/aiif_eikon_eod_data.csv'   ❶

In [3]: symbol = 'EUR='   ❶

In [4]: data = pd.DataFrame(pd.read_csv(url, index_col=0,
                                  parse_dates=True).dropna()[symbol])   ❶

In [5]: data.info()   ❶
        <class 'pandas.core.frame.DataFrame'>
        DatetimeIndex: 2516 entries, 2010-01-04 to 2019-12-31
        Data columns (total 1 columns):
         #   Column  Non-Null Count  Dtype
        ---  ------  --------------  -----
         0   EUR=    2516 non-null   float64
        dtypes: float64(1)
        memory usage: 39.3 KB
```

❶ Retrieves and selects the financial time series data

The next step is to generate the features data, lag the data, split it into training and test data sets, and finally normalize it based on the statistics of the training data set:

```
In [6]: lags = 5

In [7]: features = [symbol, 'r', 'd', 'sma', 'min', 'max', 'mom', 'vol']

In [8]: def add_lags(data, symbol, lags, window=20, features=features):
            cols = []
            df = data.copy()
            df.dropna(inplace=True)
            df['r'] = np.log(df / df.shift(1))
            df['sma'] = df[symbol].rolling(window).mean()   ❶
            df['min'] = df[symbol].rolling(window).min()    ❷
            df['max'] = df[symbol].rolling(window).max()    ❸
            df['mom'] = df['r'].rolling(window).mean()      ❹
            df['vol'] = df['r'].rolling(window).std()       ❺
            df.dropna(inplace=True)
            df['d'] = np.where(df['r'] > 0, 1, 0)
            for f in features:
                for lag in range(1, lags + 1):
                    col = f'{f}_lag_{lag}'
                    df[col] = df[f].shift(lag)
                    cols.append(col)
            df.dropna(inplace=True)
            return df, cols
```

```
In [9]: data, cols = add_lags(data, symbol, lags, window=20, features=features)

In [10]: split = int(len(data) * 0.8)

In [11]: train = data.iloc[:split].copy()    ❻

In [12]: mu, std = train[cols].mean(), train[cols].std()    ❻

In [13]: train[cols] = (train[cols] - mu) / std    ❻

In [14]: test = data.iloc[split:].copy()    ❼

In [15]: test[cols] = (test[cols] - mu) / std    ❼
```

❶ Simple moving average feature

❷ Rolling minimum value feature

❸ Rolling maximum value feature

❹ Time series momentum feature

❺ Rolling volatility feature

❻ Gaussian normalization of training data set

❼ Gaussian normalization of test data set

Training the Model

The implementation of CNNs is similar to that of DNNs. First, the Python code that follows takes care of the imports from Keras and the definition of the function to set all relevant seed values of the random number generators:

```
In [16]: import random
         import tensorflow as tf
         from keras.models import Sequential
         from keras.layers import Dense, Conv1D, Flatten
         Using TensorFlow backend.

In [17]: def set_seeds(seed=100):
             random.seed(seed)
             np.random.seed(seed)
             tf.random.set_seed(seed)
```

The following Python code implements and trains a simple CNN. At the core of the model is a *one-dimensional convolutional layer* that is suited for time series data (see Keras convolutional layers (*https://oreil.ly/AXQ33*) for details):

```
In [18]: set_seeds()
         model = Sequential()
         model.add(Conv1D(filters=96, kernel_size=5, activation='relu',
                          input_shape=(len(cols), 1)))
         model.add(Flatten())
         model.add(Dense(10, activation='relu'))
         model.add(Dense(1, activation='sigmoid'))

         model.compile(optimizer='adam',
                       loss='binary_crossentropy',
                       metrics=['accuracy'])
```

```
In [19]: model.summary()
         Model: "sequential_1"
```

Layer (type)	Output Shape	Param #
conv1d_1 (Conv1D)	(None, 36, 96)	576
flatten_1 (Flatten)	(None, 3456)	0
dense_1 (Dense)	(None, 10)	34570
dense_2 (Dense)	(None, 1)	11

```
         Total params: 35,157
         Trainable params: 35,157
         Non-trainable params: 0
```

```
In [20]: %%time
         h = model.fit(np.atleast_3d(train[cols]), train['d'],
                 epochs=60, batch_size=48, verbose=False,
                 validation_split=0.15, shuffle=False)
         CPU times: user 10.1 s, sys: 1.87 s, total: 12 s
         Wall time: 4.78 s
```

```
Out[20]: <keras.callbacks.callbacks.History at 0x7ffe3f32b110>
```

Figure C-1 presents the performance metrics for the training and validation data sets over the different training epochs:

```
In [21]: res = pd.DataFrame(h.history)
```

```
In [22]: res.tail(3)
Out[22]:    val_loss  val_accuracy      loss  accuracy
         57  0.699932      0.508361  0.635633  0.597165
         58  0.719671      0.501672  0.634539  0.598937
```

```
       59  0.729954        0.505017  0.634403  0.601890
```

```
In [23]: res.plot(figsize=(10, 6));
```

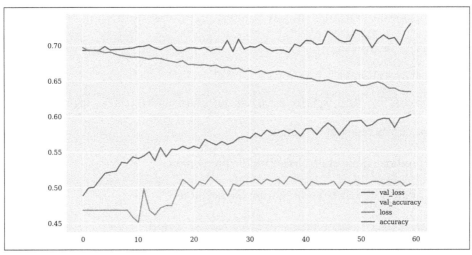

Figure C-1. Performance metrics for the training and validation of the CNN

Testing the Model

Finally, the Python code that follows applies the trained model to the test data set. The CNN model outperforms the passive benchmark investment significantly. However, taking into account transaction costs in the form of typical (retail) bid-ask spreads, it eats up larger parts of the outperformance. Figure C-2 visualizes the performances over time:

```
In [24]: model.evaluate(np.atleast_3d(test[cols]), test['d'])  ❶
         499/499 [==============================] - 0s 25us/step

Out[24]: [0.7364848222665653, 0.5210421085357666]

In [25]: test['p'] = np.where(model.predict(np.atleast_3d(test[cols])) > 0.5, 1, 0)

In [26]: test['p'] = np.where(test['p'] > 0, 1, -1)  ❷

In [27]: test['p'].value_counts()  ❷
Out[27]: -1    478
          1     21
         Name: p, dtype: int64

In [28]: (test['p'].diff() != 0).sum()  ❸
Out[28]: 41

In [29]: test['s'] = test['p'] * test['r']  ❹
```

```
In [30]: ptc = 0.00012 / test[symbol]   ❺

In [31]: test['s_'] = np.where(test['p'] != 0, test['s'] - ptc, test['s'])   ❻

In [32]: test[['r', 's', 's_']].sum().apply(np.exp)
Out[32]: r      0.931992
         s      1.086525
         s_     1.031307
         dtype: float64

In [33]: test[['r', 's', 's_']].cumsum().apply(np.exp).plot(figsize=(10, 6));
```

❶ The accuracy ratio out-of-sample

❷ The positions (long/short) based on the predictions

❸ The number of trades resulting from the positions

❹ Proportional transaction costs for given bid-ask spread

❺ The strategy performance *before* transaction costs

❻ The strategy performance *after* transaction costs

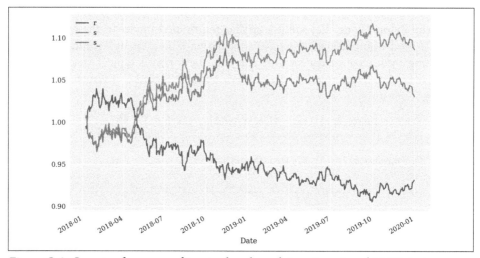

Figure C-2. Gross performance of passive benchmark investment and CNN strategy (before/after transaction costs)

Resources

Books and papers cited in this appendix:

Chollet, François. 2017. *Deep Learning with Python*. Shelter Island: Manning.

Economist, The. 2016. "From Not Working to Neural Networking." *The Economist* Special Report, June 23, 2016. *https://oreil.ly/6VvlS*.

Gerrish, Sean. 2018. *How Smart Machines Think*. Cambridge: MIT Press.

Goodfellow, Ian, Yoshua Bengio, and Aaron Courville. 2016. *Deep Learning*. Cambridge: MIT Press. *http://deeplearningbook.org*.

Index

A

absolute risk aversion (see ARA)
accuracy ratio, 162
action space, CartPole environment, 253
action-value policy, in QL, 260
activation functions, neural networks, 20, 425
AFI (artificial financial intelligence), 396-403
agent, in RL, 250
agents, 250
    (see also algorithmic trading)
    DQLAgent, 260-270
    FQLAgent, 271-276, 304-307, 335
    Monte Carlo simulation, 255-257
    preferences in normative finance, 67
    QL agent, 33, 260-270, 357-363, 372
AGI (artificial general intelligence), 45
Agrawal, Ajay, 303
AI (artificial intelligence), 1
    (see also AI-first finance)
    AI-based competition in finance, 379-391
    algorithms, 3-9
    forms of intelligence, 44
    importance of data, 22-29
    importance of hardware for progress in, 42-44
    machine learning (see ML)
    neural networks in, 9-22
    risks, regulation, and oversight issues, 388-391
    SI and, 49-50
    success stories, 32-42
AI-first finance, 185-205
    efficient markets hypothesis, 186-191
    financial singularity, 395-403
    intraday market prediction, 204-205
    market prediction with more features, 199-203
    returns data as basis for market prediction, 192-198, 240-242
    utopian versus dystopian outcomes, 54-56, 403
ALE (Arcade Learning Environment), 33, 38
algorithmic trading
    data retrieval, 347-350
    deployment, 364-368
    event-based backtesting, 357-364, 369-372
    execution, 345-364
    lack of research standardization, 382-383
    Oanda environment, 345-346, 356-364, 369-373
    risk management (see risk management)
    strategies, 280
    vectorized backtesting (see vectorized backtesting)
algorithms, generally, 3-9, 385
Allais paradox, 119-120, 121
alpha (above-market returns), 281, 379
AlphaGo algorithm, 38-40, 42-44
AlphaGo Zero (AlphaZero), 39-40, 41-42, 44, 46
alternative data sources, 113-117, 385
ambiguity in decision making, 118, 120-121
ANI (artificial narrow intelligence), 45, 49, 396
approximation task (see estimation task)
APT (arbitrage pricing theory), 90-95
    basic assumption of, 100
    in data-driven finance, 134-143
    risk measures and, 64-66, 90-95, 324

(see also classification task; estimation task)
big data, 28, 122, 381
in finance and use of AI, 381
larger data, 26-28
for neural networks, 22-29
resources for finance industry, 385
small data set, 23-26
training algorithms, 172, 174-176, 178-182
volume and variety in prediction, 28
Data, News, Analytics platform (see DNA)
data-driven finance, 99-155
data availability, 104-117
debunking central assumptions, 143-155
financial econometrics and regression, 100-104
normative theories and, 117-143
scientific method, 100
Deep Blue, 41
deep hedging, 380
deep learning (see DL)
deep RNNs, 245
DeepMind, 32-40, 42-44
dense neural networks (see DNNs)
dependent values, 10
deployment of trained trading bot, 364-368
derivatives hedging, applying AI to, 380
dimensionality reduction, CartPole environment, 255
direct reward, in QL, 260
directed risk measures, financial instruments, 318
direction as binary feature, 200
discounted value, in QL, 260
distributed learning, bagging as, 227
DL (deep learning), 9
(see also Keras deep learning package)
convolutional neural networks, 33, 439-444
dense neural networks (see DNNs)
finding resources for, 385
predictive performance based on returns data, 192
recurrent neural networks (see RNNs)
DNA (Data, News, Analytics) platform, 112-113
DNNs (dense neural networks), 211-228
bagging method to avoid overfitting, 225-227
baseline prediction, 214-218
data for example, 212-213

dropout, 220-222, 224
estimation task, 14-19
market efficiency, 195, 197, 200-205
normalization, 193, 218-220
optimizers, 227-228
regularization, 222-225
small data set, 25
vectorized backtesting, 289-301, 308-311
DQLAgent, in RL, 260-270
dropout, managing
DNNs, 220-222, 224
RNNs, 245

E

econometrics, 101
economic inefficiencies, 192
(see also algorithmic trading)
efficient frontier, 81
efficient market hypothesis (see EMH)
efficient versus inefficient portfolio, MVP theory, 81
Eikon Data API, 105-108, 110, 212
Ellsberg paradox, 120-121
EMH (efficient market hypothesis), 186-191
environment, in RL, 250
EOD (end-of-day) versus intraday data, 110, 203
episode, in RL, 251
estimation task, 8
evaluation of algorithm, 172-177
machine learning example, 165-171
neural networks applied to, 14-19, 167-171, 243-244, 409-413, 417-420
OLS regression, 165-167
European call option, 64
EUT (expected utility theory), 66-71
basic assumption of, 100
in data-driven finance, 118-122
versus MVP and CAPM, 72, 87
risk measures and, 118, 324
event-based backtesting, 311-318
Oanda environment, 357-364, 369-372
transaction costs, 315-318
excess return of portfolio, MVP theory, 74
execution of trading algorithms
account details, 356
applying AI to, 380
historical transactions, 356
order execution, 351-357

RNNs (see RNNs)
Sequential model, 197, 200, 222, 227
KerasClassifier class, 225
KMeans algorithm, 5-6
know-how risk of AI in finance, 390

L
labels data type, 4
learning, 4-8, 162
    (see also ML)
leverage, ATR risk measurement in backtesting,
    321
limit order, 353
linear activation function, 20, 425
linear algebra, 43
linear regression, in neural networks example,
    11, 14
linear relationship assumption, 153-155
LSTM (long-short term memory) layer, 238,
    244

M
machine intelligence (see AI)
machine learning (see ML)
margin stop out, 322
market orders
    backtesting risk measures, 319, 321, 324-331
    execution of, 312, 351-357
market portfolios (see portfolios)
market prediction
    with CNNs, 439-444
    DNN with FX data, 211-228
    expected returns (see expected returns)
    intraday market prediction, 204-205
    with more features, 199-203
    with neural networks, 175-177, 194-205,
        435-437
    with OLS regression, 177, 193, 196, 198
    returns data as basis for, 192-198, 240-242
    with RNNs, 240-242
    with trading bots (see algorithmic trading)
market risk, 85
Markov property of random walks, 187
maximum Sharpe ratio portfolio, 79
mean squared error (see MSE)
mean-variance portfolio (MVP) theory (see
    MVP)
.metrics() method, 427
microscopic alpha, 379

minimum volatility portfolio, 79
ML (machine learning), 9, 161-182
    bias and variance, 178-180
    capacity of model or algorithm, 169-171,
        182
    cross-validation, 180-182
    deep learning, 9
    evaluation of estimation algorithm, 172-177
    finding resources for, 385
    MSE of model or algorithm, 165-168
    sample data set, 162-164
    SL, 4, 122
MLP (multi-layer perceptron) (see DNNs)
MLPClassifier model, scikit-learn, 25, 200
MLPRegressor class, scikit-learn, 14, 195, 197
model validation risk of AI in finance, 390
momentum feature, 199, 243
monopoly, AI-first finance landscape as, 387
Monte Carlo simulations, 39, 77-78, 255-257
Morgenstern, Oskar, 66-69
motivation selection methods, SI control, 53
MSE (mean squared error), 11, 162, 165-168,
    174-177
multipolar outcome of technological singular-
    ity, 55
multivariate linear OLS regression, 92
Musk, Elon, 48, 391
MVP (mean-variance portfolio) theory, 72-82
    basic assumption of, 100
    versus CAPM, 83
    in data-driven finance, 123-130
    versus EUT, 72
    quadratic utility function in, 87
    risk measures and, 72-82

N
natural language processing (see NLP)
ndarray objects, tensors represented as, 407
neural networks
    activation functions, 20, 425
    in Atari story, 33-38
    CartPole game, 34-38, 257-260
    class-based implementations, 425-437
    in classification task, 20-22, 214, 244
    CNNs, 33, 439-444
    cross-validation, 181
    deep learning, 9
    dense neural networks (see DNNs)
    in estimation task, 14-19, 167-171, 243-244

unstructured data
    AI's ability to adjust to, 382
    historical, 110-111
    streaming, 112-113
unsupervised learning (see UL)
uploading (see WBE)
utility functions, normative finance, 68
utopian versus dystopian perspectives on AI,
    54-56, 403

V

validation data set, training algorithm, 172,
    174-176, 178-182
vanishing alpha risk of AI in finance, 389
VaR (value-at-risk) risk measure, 318
vectorized backtesting, 281-301
    DNNs, 289-301, 308-311
    Oanda environment, 361-364, 372
    SMA-based, 282-288
    transaction costs, 288, 298-301, 318

versions of life, Tegmark's, 47
volatility
    ATR risk measure, 318-321
    expected volatility in MVP theory, 124-129
    minimum volatility portfolio, 79
    rolling volatility feature, 199, 243
von Neumann, John, 66-69

W

WBE (whole brain emulation), 48
weak form market efficiency, 186, 192, 198, 205
weights in neural network, 14, 222, 225

X

X% AFI success characteristic, 399

Z

z-score normalization, 193

About the Author

Dr. Yves J. Hilpisch is founder and managing partner of The Python Quants (*http://tpq.io*), a group focusing on the use of open source technologies for financial data science, artificial intelligence, algorithmic trading, and computational finance. He is also founder and CEO of The AI Machine (*http://aimachine.io*), a company focused on AI-powered algorithmic trading via a proprietary strategy execution platform.

In addition to this book, he is the author of the following books:

- *Python for Algorithmic Trading* (*http://books.tpq.io*) (O'Reilly, 2020)
- *Python for Finance* (*http://py4fi.tpq.io*) (2nd ed., O'Reilly, 2018)
- *Derivatives Analytics with Python* (*http://dawp.tpq.io*) (Wiley, 2015)
- *Listed Volatility and Variance Derivatives* (*http://lvvd.tpq.io*) (Wiley, 2017)

Yves is an adjunct professor of computational finance and lectures on algorithmic trading at the CQF Program (*http://cqf.com*). He is also the director of the first online training programs leading to university certificates in Python for Algorithmic Trading (*http://certificate.tpq.io*) and Python for Computational Finance (*http://compfinance.tpq.io*).

Yves wrote the financial analytics library DX Analytics (*http://dx-analytics.com*) and organizes meetups, conferences, and bootcamps about Python for quantitative finance and algorithmic trading in London, Frankfurt, Berlin, Paris, and New York. He has given keynote speeches at technology conferences in the United States, Europe, and Asia.

Colophon

The animal on the cover of *Artificial Intelligence in Finance* is a bank vole (*myodes glareolus*). These voles can be found in forests, banks, and swamps throughout Europe and Central Asia, with notable populations in Finland and the United Kingdom.

Bank voles are small, only 10-11 cm in length and 17-20 g on average, and have small eyes and ears. Their fur is thick and typically brown or gray, and covers their whole body. Bank voles have short tails and small brains relative to their body size. Pups are born blind and helpless in litters of four to eight, after which they mature rather quickly, with females reaching maturity in two to three weeks and males maturing at six to eight weeks. The average lifespan for a bank vole mirrors this quick maturation, with most individuals living one half to two years.

These small rodents are primarily active during twilight, though they can be diurnal or nocturnal as well. They have an omnivorous diet consisting mostly of plant matter, and what they eat changes with the seasons. Socially, female bank voles are dominant over males, the latter dispersing once reaching maturity, while female bank voles will typically stay closer to where they were born.

Given their relatively healthy population numbers and wide distributions, the bank vole's current conservation status is that of "Least Concern." Many of the animals on O'Reilly covers are endangered; all of them are important to the world.

The cover illustration is by Karen Montgomery, based on a black and white engraving from *British Quadrupeds*. The cover fonts are Gilroy Semibold and Guardian Sans. The text font is Adobe Minion Pro; the heading font is Adobe Myriad Condensed; and the code font is Dalton Maag's Ubuntu Mono.

Milton Keynes UK
Ingram Content Group UK Ltd.
UKHW011314231024
450044UK00003B/5